FIRST NATIONS EDUCATION POLICY IN CANADA: PROGRESS OR GRIDLOCK?

How can First Nations schools in Canada offer quality education that is authentically and deeply Aboriginal yet meets the curriculum content requirements and standards of the provincial and territorial systems? In this ambitious work, Jerry Paquette and Gérald Fallon address this question through an in-depth critical analysis of the major policy issues affecting First Nations education, with particular focus on developments that have occurred since the mid-1980s.

Building on previous work on the subject, Paquette and Fallon challenge the fundamental assumptions about Aboriginal education that have led to a balkanized and ineffective educational system that fails to meet the needs of its students. In response to this 'gridlock,' the authors have formulated a conceptual framework that re-envisions the social, political, and educational goals of a self-governing First Nations educational system. Based on the underlying principles and vision within this framework, the authors present a series of recommendations for future policy changes. Offering much-need fresh perspective on a wide spectrum of issues, *First Nations Education Policy in Canada* lays the groundwork for a new conception not only of Aboriginal education but also of the future of Aboriginal self-determination.

JERRY PAQUETTE is a professor in the Faculty of Education at the University of Western Ontario.

GÉRALD FALLON is an assistant professor in the Department of Educational Studies at the University of British Columbia and an adjunct professor at the Universities of Saskatchewan and Western Ontario.

JERRY PAQUETTE AND GÉRALD FALLON

First Nations Education Policy in Canada

Progress or Gridlock?

UNIVERSITY OF TORONTO PRESS
Toronto Buffalo London

© University of Toronto Press Incorporated 2010
Toronto Buffalo London
www.utppublishing.com
Printed in Canada

ISBN 978-1-4426-4153-2 (cloth)
ISBN 978-1-4426-1072-9 (paper)

Printed on acid-free, 100% post-consumer recycled paper with vegetable-based inks.

Library and Archives Canada Cataloguing in Publication

Paquette, Jerry, 1946–
First Nations education policy in Canada : progress or gridlock? / Jerry Paquette and Gérald Fallon.

Includes bibliographical references and index.
ISBN 978-1-4426-4153-2 (bound).
ISBN 978-1-4426-1072-9 (pbk).

1. Native peoples – Education – Canada.   2. Education and state – Canada.
I. Fallon, Gérald   II. Title.

E96.2.P366 2010   371.829'97071   C2010-903923-8

University of Toronto Press acknowledges the financial assistance to its publishing program of the Canada Council for the Arts and the Ontario Arts Council.

 Canada Council   Conseil des Arts
for the Arts   du Canada

 ONTARIO ARTS COUNCIL
CONSEIL DES ARTS DE L'ONTARIO

University of Toronto Press acknowledges the financial support for its publishing activities of the Government of Canada through the Canada Book Fund.

Contents

Tables and Figures

Preface

In contrast to the rich complexity of provincial legislation framing public education across Canada, the legislative and policy bases for First Nations education in Canada is starkly threadbare. The *Indian Act*[1] lays out the basic legislative mandate for federal responsibility in providing elementary and secondary education to status Indian children living in a First Nations community. Sections 114 through 120 of the *Indian Act* delineate the specific powers of the minister of Indian Affairs in this regard. Essentially the minister is empowered to enter into agreements with provinces, territories, schools, school boards, or private schools for the provision of such education and can also provide education directly in a First Nations community. Subject to certain conditions, the minister can enforce the attendance of First Nations persons between seven and sixteen years of age (and, under certain circumstances, up to eighteen years of age) living in a First Nations community. Finally, in the case of schools run under the control of the minister, the minister is required to ensure that Protestant Indians have access to instruction by Protestant teachers and Catholic Indians have access to instruction by Catholic teachers. No specific statutory mandate exists in regard to post-secondary education for status Indian students.

In the space available in this book, we seek to analyse, as critically and comprehensively as possible, policy affecting First Nations education in Canada since 1986, the date of publication of a short predecessor piece (Paquette 1986). Despite its brevity and unpretentious scope, this earlier publication went through three printings and attracted considerable attention at the time, accomplishing three things. First, it described various arrangements under which Aboriginal and especially First Nations education was occurring during that period. Second, it described and critiqued in clearer terms than others had done up to that point the crucial 'parity paradox' at the heart of Aboriginal education, namely, that such education ought to provide a range of knowledge and competencies comparable to those provided in provincial and territorial schools; yet, to justify its existence as a separate and distinct educational process with its own particular mission, Aboriginal education needed to provide a sound grounding in relevant Aboriginal culture and language. Paquette's reasoning on this seminal issue of purpose and parity was highly embryonic in its day. We believe the current work moves far beyond the sense of worried perplexity reflected in his 1986 monograph and towards an enthusiastic embrace of the possibilities that such a dual mission might offer. Furthermore, in the present work we offer what we think is a robust and sophisticated conceptual framework for critically analysing past and current policy directions while providing a workable policy path towards self-governance in Aboriginal education. Thirdly, the 1986 work insisted on the importance of self-taxation as a necessary centrepiece of educational self-governance and offered a number of models of equalization to prevent egregious inequities as a result of at least partial reliance on self-taxation. This insistence proved most unwelcome in a great many quarters – although a number of First Nations in British Columbia have entered into self-government agreements which do provide for local taxation. In the current work we have vastly expanded our analysis of resource issues as well as those relating to ethics, transparency, and responsibility-accountability. We have not, moreover, limited our discussion solely to questions of self-governance in education but have expanded it to address more fundamental and generic questions of *whose* self-governance and *for whose common good* in education and beyond.

Given our intention to provide a sequel to the 1986 publication, albeit a sequel much more substantial and broadly grounded than its predecessor, there have been two guiding questions for this work: What of substance, if anything, has changed in the policy environment within which First Nations students have been and are being educated in Canada over the last two decades, and in particular in recent years? and What needs to change in the future? That said, the policy framing First Nations education over the last two decades did not emerge from a vacuum but from a rich, although troubled, and much contested history. We do not wish to allocate an undue amount of space to a history that has been and is being told from various perspectives by those far more skilled in historical analysis than we are. Yet we cannot plunge into a presentation and analysis of recent policy on First Nations education in Canada without some attention to relevant aspects of its history. To do so would be to engage in an arrogant and unhelpfully ahistoric account of First Nations education policy in our time, something we have no intention of doing.

Equally, we cannot fail to engage broadly and deeply with fundamental questions of social and educational purpose and paradigm, first generally, and then specifically within the evolving theoretical and practical context of First Nations aspirations for self-government. Moreover, that engagement cannot be either cursory or superficial without vitiating any claim on our part to making a useful contribution to the current literature on First Nations education. On the other hand, from the beginning, we have been intensely conscious that we are not writing a socio-political analysis or some sort of pedagogical-political manifesto.

One of the great challenges in preparing this work, then, has been balance. In particular, we have faced the challenge of providing enough theoretical context to support and illuminate the positions to which we have been led on key educational policy issues within the First Nations context without losing our way in broader social and political theory considerations. Part of the difficulty here, frankly, is that the broader literatures on social and political theory underpinning, directly and indirectly, First Nations self-government are evolving in ways that we find both intellectually compelling and morally engaging. Major threads in those literatures, moreover, are of crucial importance in framing a coherent and intellectually robust view of the recent past and possible future of First Nations education in Canada.

Yet our task here is not to synthesize those broader literatures but rather to provide a theoretically insightful and practically useful critique of recent and evolving Aboriginal and especially First Nations educational policy. Making sure the critique is situated clearly and consistently within these broader literatures is no mean task, as it turns out.

We argue in our concluding chapter that we have reached something of a 'critical juncture' (Koenig 1986) in the evolution of Aboriginal and, particularly, First Nations education. Rightly or wrongly, we are convinced that we are at a fork in the road of policy surrounding that education. It can go in one of two directions: towards assumption by First Nations people of authentic responsibility for the education of their young or towards oblivion as a discredited option in the annals of the history of public education in Canada. For reasons we describe at some length in the final two chapters of this work we do not believe that anything like the status quo in Aboriginal and especially in First Nations education is sustainable over the long or even over the medium term.

We have not, then, set ourselves the task of rewriting the history of First Nations education. Nonetheless, we concluded early in the planning of this text that we would need, at least minimally, to situate our analysis within some broad-brush-stroke account of what we consider fundamental and formative from a policy perspective in the history of First Nations education in Canada. That is the first contextualizing task to which we turn in this account of recent and potential future First Nations education policy.

Chapter 1 presents as brief a history of Aboriginal and First Nations education in Canada as we could manage that is consistent with our purpose of providing necessary context for our analysis and critique of Aboriginal education policy since the mid-1980s. It concludes with what we believe to be convincing evidence of pervasive and ongoing 'structural failure' followed by a short *avant gout* of some of the fundamental changes we believe are urgently needed to save Aboriginal and especially First Nations education from collapse, if not 'implosion,' in the not-so-distant future.

Chapter 2 delineates the conceptual framework within which we frame our analysis and understanding of Aboriginal education and its past, current, and potential future policy context, our basic critique of that education and context, and outlines broad recommendations for future change. No doubt many readers will find this framework both difficult and unlikely. Nonetheless, we believe that it provides the kind of framework on which one needs to 'stand' if the goal is to create a deep and useful understanding of Aboriginal education in Canada, which could give Aboriginal and non-Aboriginal communities the potential to reach out to each other and create new and authentic self-determining Aboriginal governance structures and patterns of institutional behaviour in education.

We begin with the powerfully integrative paradigmatic analysis of Bertrand and Valois (1980), an analysis regrettably not well known outside of Quebec. Bertrand and Valois began with the proposition that there exist only a limited number of socio-political 'paradigms,' four in fact, within which societies orient themselves and shape their actions and destinies. Furthermore, Bertrand and Valois posit and support convincingly the proposition that each of these four socio-political paradigms is associated with one or at the most two educational paradigms that reflect a sense of purpose, direction, and social destiny encapsulated within the overall socio-political paradigm within which it is situated. We use the Bertrand-Valois paradigmatic scheme to frame the overall historical, existing, and potential future orientations and purposes of Aboriginal education, and we believe that it serves us well towards that end. We are convinced, moreover, that readers who 'stay with' our synthesis and application of the Bertrand-Valois model will agree.

The next level is a conceptual framework we borrow from Timothy Schouls' (2003) insightful analysis of three different approaches to pluralism and his application of that analysis to Aboriginal and especially First Nations affairs in Canada. We believe that the Schouls' framework for understanding pluralism adds substantial power to our analysis of evolving Aboriginal and First Nations educational policy and governance. While we agree that each of the three types of pluralism that Schouls identifies has relevance to Aboriginal education as well as to any meaningful understanding of it in context, we also believe that he is incontestably correct that only 'relational pluralism' offers a broadly secure, coherent, and plausible grounding for Aboriginal self-determination as a whole and, for Aboriginal education within it, a grounding capable of giving birth to and sustaining an underlying policy dynamism that alone can nurture an ongoing cycle of sociocultural self-renewal, healing, and transformation.

Finally, we borrow extensively from Dale Turner's (2006) brilliantly insightful analysis of the potential place of Aboriginal and especially First Nations self-determination within the liberal *ethos* that frames mainstream Canadian policy and politics. We do so because we believe that Turner offers a more balanced and plausible vision of what self-determination might look like within what he describes as 'Kymlicka's constraint,' the inescapable reality that, to be taken seriously, what he aptly labels 'word warriors' must be able to engage mainstream power-brokers on their own intellectual, philosophical, and political 'turf.' We find within Turner's analysis exactly the raw materials that we need to construct a plausible vision of what Aboriginal education can and should become, a vision which, in our view, finally resolves the 'parity paradox' of an education that is at once authentically and deeply Aboriginal but at the same time comparable in content, quality, and standards to provincial and territorial education. The work of Schouls on the one hand, and of Bertrand and Valois on the other, allows us to position that vision within the larger questions of social and political place and purpose, and to 'complete the circle' of Aboriginal education within the renewed relationships of fruitful interdependence between Aboriginal peoples and settler governments.

The conceptual framework we present in chapter 2 is central to understanding the kind of shift needed – a profound transformation of the thoughts, perceptions, and values that have formed the particular vision of reality used to frame past and current policies in Aboriginal education. Such a conceptual framework is required to undertake a deep re-examination of the main premises and values underlying current policy that, as we argue later, have long outlived any usefulness and have created the pervasive fragmentation and diseconomies of scale in Aboriginal education. Furthermore, our conceptual framework guides our discussion about the need for transforming relationships between Aboriginal and non-Aboriginal peoples and about forms of governance organization that should go far beyond the current superficial measures of administrative and political readjustment being considered by today's policy-makers. Our conceptual framework provides a solid ground for advocating a *functionally aggregated*, authentic self-determining Aboriginal education system – a governance structure that would balance two opposing tendencies: an integrative tendency for individual Aboriginal communities to work together as part of a larger whole, and a self-assertive tendency for Aboriginal communities to preserve their individual specificity and autonomy. Our conceptual framework, our 'place to stand,' provides a space to discuss the possibility of an Aboriginal self-determining governance structure of education in which there is a balance between integration and self-assertion – a balance that is not static but consists of a dynamic interplay between two complementary tendencies. This would result in a functionally aggregated Aboriginal self-governance structure that would provide predictable structure and order yet be flexible and open to change, including transformative changes where needed.

Chapter 3 zeroes in on the particular policy context of Aboriginal and especially First Nations education. It starts by reviewing competing discourses on such education and the evolving policy context within which First Nations education occurs. Next, it looks at the particular problematic of policy 'receivership' as it impinges on education. Logically, it then picks up the unhappy policy history of supposed 'devolution' of control over First Nations education to First Nations people. In that context, we frame our first partial critique of the abject failure of that process and of the debacle that it has led to within the mythology of Indian control of Indian education as a synonym for local, that is a community-level, control.

Within our exploration of the 'devolution debacle,' we set forth our preliminary arguments and position on the promise and problems of aggregation for service delivery in Aboriginal education. We then provide as terse and painless a summary as possible of key issues in contemporary education finance and discuss the relevance of these issues for Aboriginal and especially for First Nations education. We conclude chapter 3 with some general propositions on what a better approach to financing Aboriginal education might look like and why.

Chapter 4 reviews post-secondary issues in Aboriginal education. It begins with an examination of both provincial efforts in the area and, more substantively in most cases, institutional efforts. Next, we review post-secondary funding issues and, as in the case of elementary/secondary education, we do so within the context of the broader literature on post-secondary funding and its characteristic underpinning assumptions and issues.

We then review the treaty-right rationale for educational support on the one hand, and the inherent-right rationale on the other, and critique the relative prospects for claims rooted in each of these two types of rights for post-secondary support as against elementary-secondary support. We address questions about the adequacy of current INAC funding both for post-secondary programs and institutions, and critique the Royal Commission on Aboriginal Peoples' (RCAP) approach to post-secondary education and funding. Finally, we conclude chapter 4 with our reflections on situating the funding of Aboriginal post-secondary education within relational-pluralist assumptions.

In chapter 5 we dissect as carefully as possible in this context the crossed lines of governance in First Nations education and contrast them with the relatively coherent lines of 'voice,' 'authority,' and 'power' in provincial education. We then turn our attention to ways in which First Nations have sought in recent years to establish some degree of self-determination and, within it, some degree of control over the education of their youth. In the same vein, we analyse the content of all education and self-government agreements currently in effect between First Nations and the Government of Canada. Not surprisingly, these topics lead to a conclusion focused on 'pervasive policy gridlock points' in Aboriginal but especially in First Nations education across Canada.

All of this brings us quite inescapably to the problem of 'what to do about this.' In chapter 6, then, we look at challenges and options for breaking the current gridlock while emphasizing that the central aspect of the solution we propose is not merely the transfer of administrative control, but rather the institutionalization of functionally aggregated self-governance structures in First Nations education. We begin here with our own ideas on the synergy of self-determination and First Nations education – ideas which are, at least in some respects, considerably at variance from those of the Royal Commission on Aboriginal Peoples. We examine the dimensions of the demographic challenge within which Aboriginal education finds itself. We then suggest key ingredients for uncrossing currently scrambled lines of accountability in Aboriginal and particularly in First Nations education and for creating meaningful Aboriginal 'jurisdiction' in education – that is, transparency, ethics, accountability, and adequate and appropriate resources. As we do so we pay particular attention to the way in which current INAC meta-policy on educational programming prevents bicultural and/or bilingual programming in First Nations schools. Having done all this, we are at last in a position to 'unpack' the details surrounding our central concerns with control, aggregation, and own-source resources.

We next review special education within the First Nations context and turn our attention to twelve mould-breaking Aboriginal schools, schools that for one reason or another and by diverse means and in diverse circumstances have managed to be recognized as providing education of unusually high quality to the Aboriginal students who study in them. In our view, there are two things here that are of particular note: first, nothing like a one-size-fits-all approach either to education or to administration emerges from these case studies; second, if there is a 'common denominator' among the schools, it surely must be the focus on respect, integrity, and the value of education.

Chapter 7 examines what we consider essential for revitalizing, renewing, and improving Aboriginal education: values, principles, and ethics, which are discussed within the context of a sociocultural paradigm characterized by the sustainability of Aboriginal school systems and non-hierarchical complementarily of individuals and communities as ways of being, governing, and relating in Aboriginal societies! We start with a general overview of the nature and importance of ethics. Given the inherently 'cross-cultural' nature of Aboriginal education within the broader context of mainstream Canadian education and the increasingly obvious failure of the Western moral-philosophy project of specifying a universally acceptable and accepted 'objective' set of moral virtues and vices, we have turned to Joseph Margolis'(2004) idea of a *faute de mieux*, second-best morality as the most plausible moral-philosophy grounding for our observations, critiques, and recommendations in the area of ethics and values. As well, we situate our analysis within a substantial body of literature focused on organizational dysfunction and dishonesty, particularly on the recent activities and concerns within business ethics literature. We thus canvass issues such as greed, arrogance, egocentrism, political economy, goal displacement, empire building, and just plain bureaucratic bloat as major components of organizational dysfunction and inefficiency. A long and detailed section is devoted to the First Nations University of Canada and, in particular, to the 2005 'take over' of that institution by the Federation of Saskatchewan Indian Nations. We devote considerable attention to that incident because, in our view, it is a bellwether of central and pervasive problems of purpose, ethics, and governance in Aboriginal and especially in First Nations education.

We recognize that the history and situation of Aboriginal and First Nations peoples in Canada are radically different from those of African Americans. Nonetheless, we believe that the critique that Shelby Steele (2006) provides of the subversion of the civil rights movement in the United States by a view of social justice that seeks little more than to re-establish 'white' hegemony over Black Americans through a process of 'disassociation from racism' has deep and powerful resonances with the current situation of Aboriginal and First Nations peoples in Canada today. In our view, not only is Steele's critique directly relevant to the whole issue of self-determination in Aboriginal affairs but it also has stunning resonances with the current and enduring gridlock in First Nations educational policy in Canada! The issue is nothing less than having to decide between empowerment and responsibility on the one hand, and perpetual 'fiduciary' victimhood and tutelage on the other.

In the conclusion to chapter 7, we marshal our observations and critique with regard to ethical governance and leadership into what we believe is a persuasive argument in favour of an ethos of servant leadership. We also close another important 'circle' in our argumentation by spelling out the implications of 'Kymlicka's constraint' for a strong code of enforceable and enforced ethics in Aboriginal and especially in First Nations education.

With all this in place, we then turn in chapter 8 to the second set of essential elements for effective, efficient, and appropriate Aboriginal education: a coherent and sufficiently powerful vision and purpose. Here we bring together what we believe to be a plausible vision of a better future, nothing less than a functional national integration – a *beau risque* for all those involved, to be sure, but probably the last best chance for turning a pervasively dysfunctional 'non-system' into an instrument that can create an 'education plus,' 'word warrior' education. Stepping outside the current 'box' of gridlock and dysfunction can only happen when and if Aboriginal peoples accept responsibility, including financial responsibility, for the education of their children. We recognize, of course, that most Aboriginal communities, including most First Nations communities, do not currently have the fiscal capacity to do so, at least not to any substantial extent. Nonetheless, the goal must be responsibility, and responsibility necessarily includes providing resources to the best extent of one's ability. We unpack these arguments and their implications in the course of a final plea for an ethical, transparent *functional integration* of First Nations education on a Canada-wide basis.

Lastly, we argue that responsibility includes stewardship for *results*, and we present a results-based-management model that we believe to be appropriate, workable, and necessary if First Nations education is to be transformed into the 'education plus,' 'word warrior' vision that it can and ought to embody. We explain why, in our view, the status quo is immoral and furthermore simply untenable. It is fundamentally immoral because, with few exceptions, it squanders resources and, worse still, it squanders the lives of students who are the victims of its 'self-serve' logic. It is untenable because it is highly unlikely that Canadian taxpayers will choose to continue to pay for it over the medium term, much less the longer one.

Acknowledgments

We wish to gratefully acknowledge the help of several persons without whose help this work in its present form would have been impossible. First we wish to acknowledge the patience and forbearance of our spouses in the face of the long, often seemingly interminable hours of work on our part invested in this manuscript. We are thankful as well to William J. Smith for reviewing and providing the tough and useful feedback of a critical friend on certain portions of this work at various stages of its development.

We wish to thank the 'interviewee' who consented to be interviewed with respect to the First Nations University of Canada takeover episode and its context. The knowledge and insight of that person contributed greatly to our understanding of the larger problematic that we examine in the book. Our thanks, as well, to Allen Pearson, then dean of the Faculty of Education at the University of Western Ontario for making possible travel to undertake this key interview.

We especially wish to thank Julia O'Sullivan, Dean of the Faculty of Education at the University of Western Ontario, for her encouragement of and strong support for this work. Without her support, this book might never have seen the light of day. Dean O'Sullivan facilitated travel to a key collaborative work session of the authors at the University of Saskatchewan in 2008. Above all, we are indebted to Dean O'Sullivan for ensuring financial support from the Faculty of Education at Western necessary to making the publication of this book possible, and, of course, to the Faculty of Education for in fact providing that support.

We are also grateful to the Faculty of Education at the University of Saskatchewan for underwriting the cost of Dr Paquette's lodging in Saskatoon during the 2008 collaborative work session.

Finally, we are grateful to Virgil Duff, Executive Editor at the University of Toronto Press. His patient guidance and gentle support for this book through what proved to be a long and challenging process helped keep us going through some very difficult moments.

FIRST NATIONS EDUCATION POLICY IN CANADA:
PROGRESS OR GRIDLOCK?

1 Prologue: Historic Context

The treatment of children in indian [*sic*] residential schools is a sad chapter in our history.

Two primary objectives of the residential schools system were to remove and isolate children from the influence of their homes, families, traditions and cultures, and to assimilate them into the dominant culture. These objectives were based on the assumption aboriginal cultures and spiritual beliefs were inferior and unequal. Indeed, some sought, as it was infamously said, 'to kill the Indian in the child.' Today, we recognize that this policy of assimilation was wrong, has caused great harm, and has no place in our country.

...

The government now recognizes that the consequences of the Indian residential schools policy were profoundly negative and that this policy has had a lasting and damaging impact on aboriginal culture, heritage and language.

...

The government recognizes that the absence of an apology has been an impediment to healing and reconciliation. Therefore, on behalf of the government of Canada and all Canadians, I stand before you, in this chamber so central to our life as a country, to apologize to aboriginal peoples for Canada's role in the Indian residential schools system.

Stephen Harper, June 11, 2008

Our purpose here is not to provide a comprehensive review and critique of the history of residential education as it pertains to Aboriginal youth in Canada (this category includes any form of education designed to isolate Aboriginal children from their parents and kinship group). Others far more capable of completing that task have provided abundant thought- and conscience-provoking scholarship on the matter, and they will continue to do so. Nonetheless, we do not engage in ahistorical policy analysis, either generally or in respect to educational policy affecting Aboriginal youth. Thus, because of our sense of the extraordinary pertinence of past residential education to any meaningful discussion of recent, current, and future policy on Aboriginal education in Canada, we wish to pick up several threads from that history that we regard as particularly trenchant and salient for our purposes. We do so with humility and respect, first for those who suffered and continue to suffer, in many cases dreadfully, from the impact of the residential schools, and second for scholars who specialize in this domain, and on whose shoulders we stand almost completely in our treatment of the residential school history.[1]

In some ways, the post-contact history of the education of First Nations children by the settler nations has varied widely over time and space. For instance, only the French resorted to sending a small number of First Nations children back to their home country for education, and then only in the earliest days of New France's settlement. A few residential schools offered more than cultural repression and denigration, abuse, and child-labour exploitation. In some cases, staff members befriended and supported students (Miller 1996, 428). Overall, the Oblates of Mary Immaculate and the Jesuits preferred to try to work in and with Native languages (more on that subject below) as did the Anglican Christian Missionary Society (Miller 1996, 415).

On the whole, however, any review of efforts to 'educate' First Nations children tends to highlight the remarkable constancy in purpose, paradigm, method, and key underlying assumptions in the schooling offered to and frequently imposed on First Nations children by those who colonized the land mass which now constitutes Canada. 'For the past 300 years, Aboriginal (Indian) education was characterized by non-Aboriginal people using non-Aboriginal methods to administer the education of Aboriginal peoples' (Cardinal 1999, 1). The purpose of education was the repression of ancestral cultures and languages, and their replacement with mainstream settler cultures and languages. The paradigm was essentially one of positivist industrialism, that is, Aboriginal students should be inducted, forcibly if necessary, into 'superior' Euro-Canadian ways of being, thinking, and acting. However, this education would only provide Aboriginal students with the means to enter into the lowest level of the new Euro-Canadian economy. Towards this end all methods were considered acceptable, including horrific abuse and torture perpetrated by many of those who worked in the residential schools. The key underlying assumption is perhaps best captured in Egerton Ryerson's crisp summary of his view of the ideal 'education' for Indians, 'a plain English education adapted to the working farmer and mechanic' (also cited in Milloy 1999, 16; Tschanz 1980, 6). Indians were regarded at best as intellectually inferior[2] and thus needed to be inducted into the knowledge base and lifestyle appropriate to the 'working farmer' or 'mechanic,' an essentially racist perspective (see, for instance, Paquette 1989b). Those who designed residential school education did so with virtually unquestioning acceptance that its rightful mission was to 're-educate' young Aboriginal students by completely replacing their ancestral cultures and languages through a process of repression, exclusion, and especially intellectual marginalization of First Nations ways of being, thinking, and acting. The goal was to create schools that would 'encapsulate hierarchically' First Nations persons on the lowest rung of Canadian society by training them not to think or reach beyond the script of the lowest position in the social system. Within this logic, they needed to be – and rightfully ought to be – 'encapsulated' on the lowest level of Canadian society because of their presumed intellectual inferiority. Given this perception of Aboriginal students and their capacity, the governments and churches involved in attempts to 'educate' them felt justified in investing only the most meagre resources to that end, another subject to which we will return.

In many ways, the attempts of the Récollets and Jesuits in New France to find some means of 'educating' and 'francizing' Aboriginal youth foreshadowed the challenges, methods, and essential failures of subsequent attempts to impose residential school 'total institution' approaches on the cultural and religious 're-education' of Aboriginal children. From the earliest consideration of the problems with imposing European education on Aboriginal children by the Récollets in the 1620s, it was widely believed among the settlers that continued contact between Aboriginal children and their parents and people was a virtually insurmountable obstacle to even the most rudimentary form of European-style education. The greatest impediment resulting from this contact was the inability of the would-be educators to impose European values and ways of being on Aboriginal students by using punitive discipline. The bottom line was that neither parents nor children would support any form of corporal punishment. Educators at the time believed the sole remedy to this obstacle was separation of the child from parents and family, and the more absolute this was, the better.

Subsequent attempts during the 1630s on the part of the Jesuits to establish a *séminaire*, essentially a residential school, were not much more successful. Even Huron children transported hundreds of kilometres from their families managed to escape and return home, and support for the school from neighbouring Montagnais and Algonquin parents was minimal once the heavy proselytizing and discipline agendas of the school and the irrelevance of the education it offered to Aboriginal lifestyles became evident (Beaulieu 1990, 143–5). Overall, the residential experiment in New France was a failure that, in the judgment of the Jesuits themselves, bore 'no notable fruit' (Miller 1996, 47).

At Confederation, the government of Canada found itself charged with responsibility for 'Indians, and Lands reserved for the Indians' under section 91 of the *Constitution Act, 1867*. In 1868, the government brought in legislation authorizing allocations from the 'Indian Fund' to establish and maintain schools attended by Indians. Thus, with assumption of the funding of some fifty-seven schools, all classified as 'industrial schools,' (except for Mount Elgin and Mohawk, which were residential schools) the government of Canada embarked on its earliest efforts to 'educate' Aboriginal peoples. By 1879 the government was sponsoring two more residential schools, Shingwauk and Wikwemikong. 'Thereafter the numbers mushroomed. By 1923 there were seventy-one schools, sixteen of them industrial schools and fifty-five boarding schools with 5,347 in residence' (Milloy 1999, 52).

Shingwauk House, and the vision of Augustine Shingwauk who requested its establishment at Garden River, serves as touchstone for Miller's (1996) detailed history and most fundamental criticism of the system. In his introduction, Miller cites Shingwauk's plea for establishment of a school:

> I wondered often in my mind – and my people wondered too – why the Christian religion should have halted so long at Garden River, just at the entrance to the Great lake of the Chippeways [Superior]; and how it was that forty winters had passed away, and yet religion still slept, and the poor Indians of the Great Chippeway Lake pleaded in vain for teachers to be sent to them. I said that we Indians know our Great Mother, the Queen of the English nation, is strong; but my people are weak. Why do you not help us? It is not good. I told the Blackcoats I hoped that before I died I

should see a big teaching wigwam built at Garden River, where children from the Great Chippeway Lake would be received and clothed, and fed, and taught how to read and how to write; and also how to farm and build houses, and make clothing; so that by and by they might go back and teach their own people. (5–6)

To paraphrase, Shingwauk pleads, 'Come teach us how to adapt to and prosper in your new way of life and its economic order!' Such proactive efforts to attract schools, moreover, were not unusual. While it can hardly be said that First Nations groups sought the establishment of 'residential schools,' they often did plead, and plead repeatedly, for schooling to help them adapt to the new social and economic order (Miller 1996, 409).

From its origins, although the industrial residential school system (which was actually more of a network) was funded by the Government of Canada, it grew mainly under the guidance of the churches, especially the Church of England and the Roman Catholic Church. To a lesser extent, other churches managed some residential schools as well. From the beginning, the federal government struggled to find an approach to funding that would impose austerity on those who operated the schools who, for the most part, were church leaders. Milloy cites Vankughnet, deputy superintendent general from 1874 to 1893, writing to Prime Minister Macdonald to say that industrial and boarding schools were the best way 'of advancing the Indians in civilization' and therefore 'every encouragement should be given to persons undertaking the establishment of such institutions' (Milloy 1999, 61). Under Vankughnet, funding for boarding schools was set on a per capita amount while the government underwrote the full cost of construction and management of the industrial schools (62). Costs burgeoned, and the government's determination to impose fiscal austerity redoubled. Per capita funding was deliberately set substantially below actual cost to force churches to practice more 'economical management' (63). From its inception and throughout its existence, residential education of First Nations children existed under a regime of debilitating fiscal restraint (66–7).

While inadequate funding can hardly explain all of the failures and horrors of residential schools throughout their history, it goes a long way to explaining the persistence and severity of many. Completely inadequate and inappropriate physical accommodation, including cramped quarters, non-existent ventilation, lack of attention to rampant tuberculosis infection, inadequate and poor-quality nutrition; the list of non-teaching-related failures in the system is long and grave. No one knows how many children died directly or indirectly as a result of the poor-quality facilities in which they were housed and schooled, but what evidence exists suggests that a very high proportion of the 'inmates' in such institutions died of causes related to inadequate provision of the basic *physical* necessities. In 1907 Dr P.H. Bryce, then medical inspector to the Department of the Interior and Indian Affairs, published the results of a survey to which only fifteen schools responded. Nonetheless, of 1,537 students accounted for in this survey, 24 per cent had died, all described as having succumbed to 'consumption.' Bryce estimated that by accounting for those who died *shortly after* time spent in a residential school, the mortality rate could be as high as 42 per cent (Milloy 1999, 91). Aboriginal parents were justified in fearing to send their children to schools that were basically death camps for a large percentage of them.

Not surprisingly, given its minimalist, 'hierarchical encapsulation' agenda, the education offered in residential schools was generally grossly inadequate instruction by incompetent and unqualified teachers – another chronic symptom, at least in part, of inadequate funding. Incompetent and unqualified teachers, after all, at least had the virtue of coming cheap. The churches tolerated disreputable teaching, as Miller points out, for two basic reasons. First, trapped between what Ottawa was willing to pay and the real cost of competent, qualified, adequate teachers, they had two choices: to get out of the residential school business altogether, or hire whoever would work for them. Second, the evangelization motive remained at the centre of their sense of purpose in the matter. 'And for both government and church, a major reason for their inconstant dedication to the pursuit of learning was their commitment to the assimilative program that had always underlain their understanding of the purpose of residential schools' (Miller 1996, 419).

What kind of instructional program was employed in residential schools? No single answer to this question can be given over time and differing locations. Some schools, and the one located near Spanish, Ontario, is a particularly noteworthy example, offered high-quality instruction in the traditional 'forms' of knowledge and within the existing Ontario curriculum and its assumptions (there was no place at all, of course, for Aboriginal knowledge, culture, or language). The Spanish school did so, however, at the cost of extreme stress to both Jesuit and Daughters-of-Mary staff and, of course, to the students who lived, learned, and worked there, always under the never-ending pall of inadequate resources and a pervasive need for student labour to help make ends meet. Shanahan (2004) summarizes his interview results regarding the Spanish experience for students this way:

> In interviewing graduates of Spanish for this book, there were many who had ambivalent attitudes towards their time there. They also still felt anger when they thought of the better food enjoyed by the Jesuits, the endless rules and regulations, the incredible loneliness and the long hours of work involved in making the farm and garden fruitful. They remember the complete lack of privacy: their letters opened and read before being mailed home; the shame they were made to feel about being who they were: native children with a different culture, language and way of looking at the world.
>
> They still feel deprived of years that could have been spent with their families, learning their traditional wisdom and growing in understanding of who they were as native people. For them, Spanish was many things. It was a place where they were confined for years, being alienated from their families and communities, no longer even considered Indian by some. It was a place where they learned to read and write and received an education for which they are grateful and from which they have gained a great deal of benefit. For some, the cost was too high. For others, these were the best years of their lives. (257)

Indeed, for profound ambivalence about the Spanish residential school, one can do little better than turn to its most famous graduate (Johnston 1988). And Spanish is generally conceded to have been one of the very best of the residential schools.

Over time, a general evolution in the 'program' offered in residential schools does seem discernable. In the immediate post-Confederation period the emphasis was on basic agricultural, manual, and 'industrial' skills. By 1890, when residential schools began to outnumber industrial schools, the content of residential school programs, at least on paper, paralleled provincial curricula in their emphasis on 'English, "general knowledge," writing, arithmetic, geography, history, ethics, reading, recitation, vocal music, callisthenics, and religious instruction.' By the 1920s, the Department of Indian Affairs reported that 'Indian schools follow the provincial curricula,' but with 'special emphasis ... on language, reading, domestic science, manual training and agriculture' (Miller 1996, 155). In the twentieth century these emphases were divided, with some schools trying to move to closer conformity with provincial curricula while others focused mainly on vocational training. However, the distinguishing feature of the instructional program in all Indian schools was their 'half-day system,' a practice copied from Egerton Ryerson's prescription for pre-Confederation schools in the Canadian West. Thus, well into the 1950s, students spent half of each day in the classroom (the father-in-law of one author recalls that, at his residential school, the 'half day' of instruction tended to be very short indeed!) and half in manual labour (Miller 1996, 153–5).

Finally, no account of residential schools, however brief, would be complete without acknowledging the physical, sexual, psychological, and spiritual abuse that so many First Nations students suffered in these total institutions. Penury did not *cause* abuse by itself, but, as Miller (1996) points out, it certainly contributed to it.

> A special place in perdition must be reserved those who abused residential students sexually. If there are explanations for poor food, heavy workloads, and harsh discipline, there can be no justification of the subjection of young boys and girls to the sexual appetites of male staff members. The failure of church organizations to take action to weed out sexual exploiters, and to prevent the entry of others, leaves the missionaries open to severe censure. Too often missionary efforts at prevention and correction of deviants on their staffs were limited to moving them out of a posting when their actions made their proclivities notorious. No matter how severe the labour shortage might have been at various times, there can be no justification for restricting preventive action to maintenance of a 'black list,' or moving a malefactor from a school to a parish to get him away from the scene of the crime. More complex is the issue of student sexual abuse at the hands of other residential schools students. Again the evidence is overwhelming that a great deal of the sexual exploitation and violence perpetrated on male, and in rare instances on female, students was the work of older students. School staff *should* have known and taken action to thwart such exploitation. In some instances they did punish wrongdoers, though such retributive effort was rare, perhaps deterred by fear of negative publicity. However, even the rare examples of action against student sexual abusers stand out eloquently in condemnatory contrast to the silence and inaction of missionary bodies when it came to dealing with their own. (423–4)

Chrisjohn provides a sombre inventory of the diverse types of physical, sexual, and psychological abuse to which residential schoolchildren were subjected. Even so, his list excludes corporal discipline practices in general use during the later nineteenth and first two-thirds of the twentieth century. It is difficult to imagine how individuals acting in the place of parents could subject those under their care to multiple forms of sexual abuse, and to such extreme forms of physical abuse, including sticking needles in tongues and other parts of the anatomy, and beating children to the point of inflicting fractured skulls, broken arms, legs, and the like (Chrisjohn, Young, and Maraun 1997, 47–51). Knockwood recounts a beating so severe that she suspects the victim – who simply 'disappeared' afterwards – likely died as a result (Knockwood and Thomas 1992, 107–8). Humiliation, isolation, head-shaving, a bread and water diet, along with whippings and beatings for use of a First Nations language all figured among disciplinary 'tools' used in residential schools (Haig-Brown 1988, 76–7, 93; Stephens 2004, 82). Indeed, some students learned to endure certain punishments, such as vicious whippings for use of their language, without flinching, just to anger their persecutors (92).

Psychological and spiritual trauma from such actions spans generations. The children and the children of children of residential school victims continue to pay a heavy price for what happened in those institutions. These victims lost all sense of belonging to their family and kinship group, all sense of what a loving, caring parent–child relationship is; they were taught to be ashamed of their culture and language, and equally damaging, that their language and culture could never form any part of a meaningful vision of 'the educated person.' They require deep healing if they are to avoid revisiting the sins of the residential schools on their own families. It can be hoped that one day, the vision statement of the Aboriginal Healing Foundation (2005) will be realized, and this scourge will finally be exorcised from the heritage of residential school survivors:

> Our vision is one where those affected by the legacy of Physical Abuse and Sexual Abuse experienced in Residential School have addressed the effects of unresolved trauma in meaningful terms, have broken the cycle of abuse, and have enhanced their capacity as individuals, families, communities and nations to sustain their well being and that of future generations. (n.p.)

We shall argue later that the way in which governance and leadership

have developed in residential schools encouraged a perverse and destructive vision: leadership was the exercise of absolute power with
impunity. That vision of leadership continues to exact a heavy toll on
Aboriginal education to this day (see discussion in chapter 7, 'The First
Nations University of Canada').

As is the case with any repressive regime, resistance grew, and its
forms multiplied. Various types of complaint against residential school
practices to which parents objected emerged over time. Oral complaints
to school officials were supplemented by complaints to Indian Affairs
officials, then by letters and petitions. Perhaps the most pervasive –
and powerful – form of parental resistance was the simple refusal to
send their children to a residential school. This action had various levels of success, since the effectiveness of measures to enforce attendance
ranged from non-existent to virtual kidnapping, depending on time
and place (Miller 1996, 344–55).

Students voted 'no' to residential schools in many ways, perhaps
most frequently with their feet. Students who ran away were a chronic
and widespread problem. They were generally punished severely, and
occasionally the truancy itself led to tragic consequences. In various
ways, and despite severely punitive consequences, students subverted
the rules, regulations, and discipline to which they were subjected. Student gestures of resistance ranged from name-calling to the refusal to
participate in activities or study, from the theft of everything from food
and communion wine, and covert amorous rendezvous, all the way to
urinating in milk destined for sisters and the school priest (Miller 1996,
360–2). Sometimes simple stoic endurance of punishment provided a
particularly eloquent form of resistance (Haig-Brown 1988, 92).

Language, talisman of culture that it is, was always a major focal
point of punishment and resistance. Some of the most inhuman tortures
to which residential school students were subjected were the result of
students simply speaking their own languages. In some respects, this
visceral response on the part of residential school administrators and
teachers is comprehensible. Beyond the linguistic replacement agenda of the residential schools, access to a language your teachers and
principal don't understand, after all, constitutes a means of potentially
subversive clandestine communication, a seditious form of power. One
of us remembers visiting the class of a talented, competent, confident
teacher in a First Nations school where he served as principal over a
generation ago. Students were busy completing an assignment, working in their own language. Despite his exceptional experience, confi-

dence, and aplomb, the teacher approached the author (who was fluent in the language) after class and asked timorously whether the students had been 'talking about him.' If such a teacher in a modern community school could have these fears, imagine the paranoid reaction which the instructors in the residential school system would have had if students were permitted to converse in their own language, especially if these teachers were aware of their own personal incompetence and ineptness!

After all, First Nations languages were not, as the same author once heard them disparagingly described, the 'simple languages of simple people.' They often present formidable linguistic complexity, which makes Native-like fluency almost inaccessible even to the most intelligent, well-trained, and determined adult learners. The author in question is particularly struck by a passage from the *Jesuit Relations* in which Lejeune (who was fluent in several European languages) itemizes some of what he found to be the most perplexing aspects of Algonquin languages. Lejeune's long litany of the grammatical mysteries of Algonquin languages (Beaulieu 1990, 63–4) has many strong resonances for the author, who learned Northern Ojibwe as an adult. Taken together, languages far too difficult and too different from Indo-European languages for non-Native educators to learn, along with the 'secret code' character of a foreign language to a linguistic outsider combined to give a visceral immediacy to residential school personnel's need to suppress Native languages, an urgency that the most evangelical commitment to assimilation could never have given alone. This unhappy combination likely added much of the neurotic and frequently psychotic obsession teachers had with rooting out every trace of First Nations languages from the minds and hearts of the students in their charge. How humiliating it would have been for residential school teachers and administrators to be confronted with the linguistic reality that the languages they were exterminating were so devilishly difficult to learn in part *because they were more precise than English,* or even than the traditional 'language of diplomacy,' French, so esteemed in pre-nineteenth-century Europe for its precision!

In terms of long-term impact, surely the most effective resistance to residential schools is also the supreme irony of the residential school legacy – some of those individuals who were the products of residential school education ultimately found the strength to challenge both it and the colonial system on which it was predicated, people such as Harold Cardinal and Verna Kirkness. Despite everything and against all odds, the residential schools succeeded, not in what their architects hoped, but instead in sowing the seeds of their own destruction. They further succeeded in facilitating relentless challenges to the values that drove and justified them, well enough for the government of Canada to finally be paying damage settlements to victims of residential school torment and humiliation through the residential schools resolution program (Indian and Northern Affairs Canada 2006).

With singular consistency, Native groups wanted education to cope with the new settler economic 'game.' What they got was child labour, exploitation, separation from families and culture, loneliness, and abuse, along with attempts to Christianize them on the one hand, and to demonize their cultural and religious beliefs and customs – including their languages – on the other. As Miller (1996) states, 'Residential schools failed in many ways, but above all, they failed to educate – the very reason for which Aboriginal leaders who asked for them wanted them in the first place. For the most part at least, residential schools failed *as schools*' (emphasis added). They remain, he continues, 'a glaring example of structural failure so far as their pedagogical role was concerned':

> While Native submissions [to the Special Joint Committee of the 1940s] frequently mentioned inadequate care, overwork, and excessive religious proselytization, their greatest stress was on the failure of residential schools as schools. Given the long-standing commitment of many of the Aboriginal peoples who came into contact with Euro-Canadians to pursue a strategy of adjustment through education, this reaction is to be expected. Peter Jones, Mistawasis, Kate Dudoward, or any of the large number of others had sought schools to prepare their children, and eventually their entire community, for life in a world dominated by the strange newcomers. Instruction was the Native peoples' primary objective; residential schooling was their greatest disappointment. (418)

Table 1.1 provides a schematic overview of milestones along this sad journey of progressive 'pathologization' in Aboriginal education. On the heels of the failure of the Récollets' patently unsuccessful experiment with exporting Aboriginal students to France, a practice very briefly imitated by the Jesuits before being abandoned forever, the Jesuits opted for creation of a 'seminary,' the first real experiment with residential school education for Aboriginal students in what was to become Canada. Despite their best efforts to impose Christianity and

Table 1.1
Pathologization of First Nations education over time

Historical milestones	Purposes	Outcomes
1620 – Récollets' unsuccessful educational experiment with imposing European-style education on Aboriginal youth initially by sending them to France.	Cultural and religious re-education by imposing European values and ways of being, acting, and thinking on Aboriginal children.	Failure due to the irrelevance to Aboriginal lifestyle and strong Aboriginal aversion to corporal punishment.
1630 – Creation of 'seminaries' (first residential school experiment in Canada)	Attempt to create bilingual partisans of French culture and ways of life.	
1868 – Involvement of the federal government and the religious service providers.

Establishment of the industrial residential school system under a 'regime of debilitating fiscal restraints and inadequate instruction' (Milloy 1999, 66–7).

1920–1950 – Creation of an instructional program for First Nations that nominally paralleled provincial curricula but was delivered through a 'half-day system' (in theory, a half-day of instruction and half-day of manual labour). | Pursuit of an assimilative program of evangelization and integration of Aboriginal communities into the lowest level of non-Aboriginal way of life and its economic order ('hierarchical encapsulation').

Ruling out of order everything Aboriginal in the implicit vision of the 'educated person' embodied in the residential schools. | Marginalization of First Nations languages and cultures.

Subordination and dependence of First Nations.

Loss of self-respect, belonging, and kinships as the result of various forms of sexual, psychological, and physical abuses.

First Nations branded as human failures forced to rely on state welfare in the narrow sense of the word – regarded as irresponsible fiduciary wards incapable of exercising meaningful human agency.

Leadership is defined as the exercise of absolute power with impunity and was taught to successive generations of students. |

European-style education – and discipline – this experiment failed due to its irrelevance to Aboriginal lifestyle and to strong Aboriginal aversion and resistance to the corporal punishment of children.

With Confederation came the unhappy marriage of sectarian Christian proselytization and federal determination to provide the least education possible to Aboriginal students and, above all, to do so with minimal cost to the Canadian state, a marriage which gave birth to the misery that became the residential school network across Canada. The principal outcomes of that 'experiment' were marginalization of First Nations language and cultures, subordination and dependence of First Nations peoples, loss of respect for self and others, destruction of all sense of belonging and kinship, and a collective loss of responsibility as autonomous human agents in all domains of life, including parenthood – indeed, systematic undermining of the very idea that Aboriginal persons could be autonomous human agents. In the same vein, the image of the 'educated person,' such as it was, fostered by the residential schools, had no room for anything rooted in Aboriginal knowledge or culture. Within the value system that created and sustained residential schools, 'Indian' was virtually a synonym for 'ignorant.'

Even with nominal adherence to provincial curricula in the 1920s, 'half-day' residential schools continued to provide what was, even by the standards of the time, a notably inferior education. Finally, and of ominous significance for the future of Aboriginal education and governance in general, the residential schools imbued their students with a vision of leadership as the exercise of absolute power without responsibility and with total impunity.

Moving beyond 'Structural Failure': Seeking Legal Remedies or Looking Forward

In reaction to the partial collapse of Aboriginal life-organization into an imposed and artificial homogeneity in the wake of the residential school legacy in general and the band council system in particular, a consistent theme in policy on Aboriginal, and especially First Nations education, since at least the time of *Indian Control of Indian Education* (National Indian Brotherhood 1972/1984), has been the importance of Aboriginal people [re]assuming control of the education of their children – and of their playing a key role as educators in that process. To move beyond the 'structural failure' embodied in the residential school system, Aboriginal education must come to mean, in every sense, 'education by Aboriginal people,' not education of Aboriginal students *by* others. Although some progress in that direction has no doubt been made over the last two decades, some authors still argue, rightly in our view, that in spite of an increased control of Aboriginal education by Aboriginal communities, method, content, and teachers remain predominantly non-Aboriginal (Hampton 1993, cited in Cardinal 1999, 10).

In the end, to put 'structural failure' securely in the past, First Nations education will need to move beyond resistance to domination, marginalization, and assimilation by mainstream culture. As a senior First Nations educational administrator once put it to one of us, 'We're all victims, but one has to move beyond being victims.' Aboriginal education must move beyond responding to victimization to establish and nurture an identity and purpose of its own. Surely if the history of 'structural failure' of colonial education for assimilation has taught us anything, it is that that legacy of educational failure will endure as long as the central philosophical assumptions (or underlying sociocultural and educational paradigm) of Aboriginal education remain entrenched in mainstream cultural tradition.

We are tempted here to speak of an emerging educational vision among Aboriginal communities, a vision that enhances what it means to be First Nations, an education that builds on and strengthens what makes Aboriginal peoples unique. Various bodies, from the Hawthorn Committee (see Canada Indian Affairs Branch, and Hawthorn 1967, 5) to the Royal Commission on Aboriginal Peoples (1996a) that have evaluated Aboriginal education and its policy context have certainly recommended such reinforcement of uniqueness as a starting point. Still, it would probably be presumptuous to express 'triumph' and assert the pervasive emergence of such a vision, although some authors insist that is the case (Friesen and Friesen 2002, 93, 94, 109, and especially 137). More pertinently, an 'isolationist' Aboriginal education anchored exclusively in cultural difference and its preservation runs a strong risk of being ignored in the larger 'marketplace of ideas' (Turner 2006, 113). With a small territorial base, and with Aboriginal languages and knowledge threatened by imminent extinction, Aboriginal peoples will need to make their voices heard in that larger market of ideas. They will be able to do so only if the education *they* provide to their young equips them with the ability to engage in the discourse of state power from within – but to do so with a firm understanding and sense of pride in the identities *they choose to construct* as Aboriginal peoples.

Finally, it seems to us that if there were ever fertile ground for successful 'educational malpractice' litigation (i.e., litigation based upon failure to fulfil a legally binding duty of care to a required standard), it would surely be the residential school legacy. Mackay and Dickinson (1998) review succinctly the onerous burden of proof that a plaintiff who succeeds in such litigation would have to surmount to become the first to succeed at trial with an educational malpractice case. Despite a potentially expansive list of grounds for an educational malpractice finding (see Foster 1985, 171–2), damages ('injury') and causality are notoriously difficult to establish in such cases, so much so that in *Hoffman v. Board of Education of City of New York*[3] the court went so far as to say that 'as a matter of policy, educational malpractice claims should not be entertained' (MacKay and Dickinson 1998, 106). Nonetheless, in *Gould v. Regina (East) School Division No. 77*,[4] while rejecting the malpractice claim, the court noted that '[o]nly if the conduct is sufficiently egregious and offensive to community standards of acceptable fair play should the courts even consider entertaining any type of claim in the nature of educational malpractice' (par. 47). MacKay and Dickinson (1998) therefore reason that 'it seems open to would-be plaintiffs to argue in future cases that their facts fall within the exception established in *Gould* and it will be up to future courts to determine, in concrete terms, exactly what Matheson J had in mind' (110).

Thus, beyond the physical, sexual, and emotional abuse issues, residential school operators and the Canadian government could conceivably, under the *Gould* criterion, be liable for educational malpractice. After all, if pressed to design a system more 'egregiously' abhorrent and 'offensive to community standards' (conceivably, even community standards of the past), one would be hard pressed to come up with anything closer to the mark than the residential school system taken as a whole. Moreover, given the essentially educational nature of the residential school failure, '[i]nstruction was the Native peoples' primary objective; residential schooling was their greatest disappointment' (Miller 1996, 418), a certain poetic justice would complement legal justice in a first-ever finding of educational malpractice against the proprietors and federal funder of the residential school system.

However intellectually interesting the possible success of educational malpractice litigation might be, these questions are unlikely to ever find an answer in Canadian courts. Although the Indian Residential Schools Resolution Settlement Agreement (Government of Canada, 2006) recognizes the possibility that some potential beneficiaries may choose to litigate outside of the agreement, it provides only a 'common experience payment' of $10,000 for the first year as a student in an Indi-an residential school, and $3,000 for each subsequent year of enrolment. In addition, it establishes an 'Independent Assessment Process' to ad-judicate damage claims related to sexual or serious physical abuse. The only other recourse available to residential school victims is to litigate outside of the purview of the agreement.[5] In short, the agreement com-pletely sidesteps the educational malpractice/failure issue. Given the nature and shape of the agreement, it seems unlikely, although not en-tirely impossible, that the central issue of liability for failure to provide a minimally acceptable quality of education in the residential schools will ever be tested in court.

2 Framing First Nations Education within Self-Government and Self-Determination

Any potentially coherent and useful critical analysis of Aboriginal education must occur within a cogent conceptual framework that situates Aboriginal education within larger self-governance discourses. It must, in short, address foundational issues of purpose and paradigm in Aboriginal governance and education, and do so in a way that deals overtly with self-government issues, claims, and counterclaims. Only such grounding can provide a conceptual 'place to stand' for useful and coherent critical analysis of Aboriginal education generally, and of First Nations education in particular.

We needed a conceptual framework with which to examine critically both past and current educational policies shaping Aboriginal education. To do so would allow us to envision new and original institutional structures and ways of acting and levels and, at the same time, allow us to consider policy knowledge and actions whose relevance for Aboriginal education remain unexplored. In the end, we needed a 'place to stand' that would support a series of broad shifts to change the way Aboriginal education is conceptualized and tied to action. For example, shifts from

- administrative simplicity to sociocultural and educational complexity
- singularity to heterogeneity and hybridity
- linearity to non-linearity
- fragmentation and diseconomies of scale to connection, collaboration, and congruence
- static boundary formation to flexible functional boundaries
- the short-term and the ephemeral to the long-term and concrete, and

- analysis and imposition to synthesis and dialogue between Aboriginal and non-Aboriginal communities

Our conceptual framework offers meaning for policy research, education, and problem-solving in an Aboriginal context. It draws on both Aboriginal and non-Aboriginal knowledge. It fosters wisdom and ethical accountability. It encourages more complex and robust understanding of Aboriginal education and longer-lasting influence. *We see our 'place to stand' as a discursive site where the central tenets of self-determining Aboriginal education system can be enacted by Aboriginal and non-Aboriginal communities.* Furthermore, we think that our conceptual framework could, potentially, be used as a platform for Aboriginal and non-Aboriginal communities to move from simply establishing new relationships towards creating transformative mutual understandings – to begin to address the urgent demands for responsible action. We strongly believe that a need exists for such a 'place to stand,' a shared multiple-perspectives framework of contemporary issues in Aboriginal education. Only within such a framework can robust and appropriate discussion lead towards resolution of issues of formidable scale and scope in Aboriginal education.

A 'Place to Stand'

The most practical thing in the world is a good theory.
                                                    – Hermann von Helmholtz

Charting a clear position on possible generic relationships among broad political goals, social policy, and educational policy is a necessary first step in constructing a coherent conceptual 'place to stand' in order to assess the recent history and possible futures of First Nations education in Canada. To build this foundational level of our conceptual framework, we begin our analysis with the broadly integrative work by Bertrand and Valois (1980), although it has been necessarily updated in light of more recent policy critique, in particular that associated with post-modernism and post-industrialism.

After establishing a coherent position on the broader issues of generic socio-political options and their relationship to foundational educational policy choices, we turn to current discourse and debate on Aboriginal self-government, a discussion which is framed in a literature that we find to be quite extraordinary in its intellectual ferment.

Figure 2.1 General conceptual framework

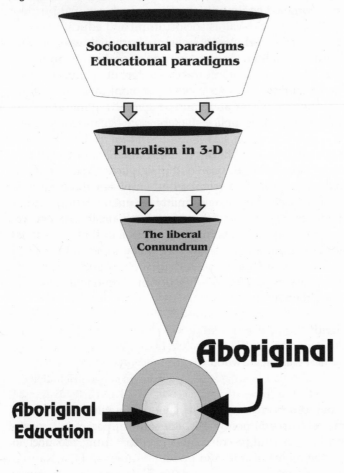

Together, these provide a conceptual 'foundation' for our analysis. With clear ideas about both foundational issues of social and educational purpose and issues related to First Nations self-government and self-determination, we engage with the pivotal questions we seek to address, namely, What of substance, if anything, has changed in the policy environment within which First Nations students are educated in Canada over the last two decades and, in particular, in recent years? and What needs to change in the future and how?

Figure 2.1 shows schematically the overall framework we have used for our analysis. First, we deal with current sociocultural and political paradigms that frame competing conceptions of educational purpose. One of the generic Bertrand-Valois sociocultural and educational purpose paradigms reflects very closely holistic Aboriginal ways of being in the universe and of understanding one's relationship to nature. The Bertrand-Valois framework has informed much of our thinking in this respect, but we recognize that other views of social purpose, particularly those informed by postmodern perspectives, have influenced the thinking of the public and of policy-makers since Bertrand and Valois (1980).

From this 'paradigm' level, following Schouls (2003), we weigh critically conflicting ideas of identity and the significance of alternative views of pluralism for both Aboriginal self-government and Aboriginal education; we then apply these to Aboriginal education. Using Schouls' analysis of the trade-offs among different conceptualizations of pluralism for Native peoples, we draw on Turner (2006) to 'flesh out,' to the greatest extent possible, first, the history of liberal theory and, second, the implications of that history for Aboriginal self-determination. We then apply the analysis of the larger context of Aboriginal self-determination to the problem of reinventing Aboriginal education so that it satisfactorily resolves the 'parity paradox' (the challenge of balancing the need for distinctively Aboriginal process and content with the need to master knowledge and skills characteristic of mainstream Canadian education), which was highlighted two decades ago in *Aboriginal Self-Government and Education in Canada* (Paquette 1986).

This is by no means a straightforward conceptual and critical agenda, but we are convinced that the rich interplay of ideas within and among each of these levels provides a conceptually solid and practically useful place to stand in analysing the recent history and future prospects of Aboriginal education in Canada.

A Word on Scope and Choosing

Our principal, although not exclusive focus will be on First Nations education; that is, on status Indian groups who identify with a First Nations collectivity in which they hold membership, whether or not they actually reside on the land base of that group.

We cannot provide broad coverage of all pertinent topics for all Aboriginal groups. However, as Schouls' work in particular reminds us, neither can we ignore Aboriginal groups with divergent interests and values. Take urban Aboriginals, for example. Just as we could not make this group a major focus of our work, neither could we dare to ignore individuals who compose more than half the Aboriginal population in Canada. By the same token, we cannot ignore Aboriginal women, Métis, non-status Indians, and First Nations youth, nor bypass issues that are pertinent to some groups and not to others, and so forth. Choosing what to emphasize and to what degree involved making difficult choices. We know some readers will take issue with those choices, but we also trust that we have struck a reasonable balance in the choices we have made.

Towards a Conceptual Framework for Analysing Aboriginal Education

The question we seek to address in this section is *not* what paradigmatic assumptions currently *do* form the basis of all, most, or some Aboriginal education. Instead, we seek to answer the normative question: What kind of values, assumptions, and concepts *should*, in general, form the basis for Aboriginal education?

Aboriginal education, *like all education*, occurs within what Bertrand and Valois (1980) call a sociocultural paradigm and a related educational paradigm.

Paradigm Base: Purpose, Paradigm, and Policy

Bertrand and Valois (1980) propose, and in our view, support convincingly the hypothesis that 'the choice of an educational paradigm is based upon the choice of a sociocultural paradigm' (7).[1] In brief, we choose what we teach and how based upon what we believe about the sociocultural and political nature of society. This position is very close to the pivotal claim advanced by Paquette (1991) over a decade and a half ago: 'Schooling and social purpose interact with each other in a complex and endless cycle of purpose, meaning, interpretation and action, a sort of hermeneutic cycle of social policy' (173).

More precisely, Bertrand and Valois (1980) offer the following definition of a sociocultural paradigm: 'The action exercised by a society, as a result of its activity, on its social and cultural practices, by the combination of five elements: a concept of knowledge, a concept of relations among persons, society, and nature, a set of values, a way of doing things, and an overarching sense of significance' (69).

An 'educational paradigm,' according to Bertrand and Valois (1980), consists of two parts: (1) a group of general orientations, of norms and rules that define educational reflection and action, and (2) praxis implications for 'how to proceed.' It is thus, in a certain way, 'exemplary' (95).

They identify four archetypal sociocultural paradigms:

1 the industrial paradigm
2 the paradigm of societies centred on the person
3 the paradigm of 'worker societies,' and
4 the paradigm of 'new democratic communities' (122–3)

Each sociocultural paradigm fosters – and justifies normatively – at least one of five relatively distinct educational paradigms situated within one of the four sociocultural paradigms. The five educational paradigms that Bernard and Valois see as aligning themselves with these sociocultural paradigms are:

- the *rational paradigm* centred on transmission of forms of knowledge and dominant values
- the *technological paradigm* centred on the efficiency of educational communication
- the *existential paradigm* centred on development of the person
- the *institutional-pedagogy paradigm* centred on abolition of relationships between those who dominate and those they dominate, and
- the *inventive paradigm* centred on construction of communities and persons (150)[2]

Their analysis is extremely detailed and borrows eclectically from a broad swath of classic socio-political and sociocultural thought, and it spans several fundamentally different approaches to ontology and epistemology. From this framework, they have created a relatively simple 'synopsis' of educational paradigms and their relationship to sociocultural paradigms, as illustrated in table 2.1. It is, in effect, a 'working hypothesis' of the key relationships as they understand them.

THE INDUSTRIAL PARADIGM
The industrial paradigm, according to Bertrand and Valois, is characterized by positivistic assumptions about knowledge and the relationships among persons, society, and nature. Observer and 'subject' are

Table 2.1 Synopsis of sociocultural and educational paradigms

	EDUCATIONAL PARADIGM	
SOCIOCULTURAL PARADIGM	NORMATIVE DIMENSION	EXEMPLARY (Practice/Praxis) DIMENSION
Industrial society paradigm	Rational paradigm Technological paradigm	Mechanistic approach Techno-systemic approach
Paradigm of societies centred on the person (existential)	Humanist paradigm	Organic approach
Paradigm of new democratic societies (symbiosynergetic)	Inventive paradigm	Approach based on social pedagogy of progressive self-development

Source: Bertrand and Valois (1980), 127, table 3.3.
Note: We have omitted discussion of Bertrand and Valois' 'workers' (dialectic) paradigm' because it is both irrelevant and largely anachronistic.

separate; the classic scientific method is the gold standard for knowledge creation; and knowledge is generally taken as consisting of quantitative measures of 'objective variables.' The individual person is subordinate to society as a whole; indeed, he/she is significant only as a 'cog' in the larger economy of his/her society. Salvation (meaning) is achieved through hard work, self-discipline, and conformity to society and, in particular, to its 'economic projects.' Competition and market values are the sole way forward for society as for the individual. When the 'invisible hand' of the marketplace is left to do its work, the results are liberty, absence of coercion, choice, and meritocracy, which are sufficient and desirable enough social ends. This description is remarkably convergent with Bowers' analysis, over a generation later, of the fundamental characteristics of Western industrial societies based on 'pre-ecological' ways of thinking (Bowers 2006, 2–3, 32).

Capitalist accumulation, industrialization, and competition are the basic ways of doing things (at once both the socio-political and economic *modus operandi*, if you will) in a society dominated by the industrial paradigm. Although such accumulation benefits some more than others, a 'trickle down' effect (Bertrand and Valois never use the term but it seems apt here) ensures a decent standard of living to most in a society grounded in such a paradigm. Utilitarianism is the gold standard of socio-economic theory. Science and its technology handmaiden are the only way forward within the industrial paradigm. Scientific rationality, in short, leads to and assures economic and technological development.

Little needs to be changed to adjust this paradigm to the realities and *dominant* values of 'post-industrialized' societies of today, which are ensconced in an ever more tightly woven global economy. Competition, accumulation, and utilitarianism are the 'way we do things around here' – except that 'here' is now a global community interlocked with a global economy. True, other values and other ways of doing and understanding things bubble up to and around the surface in our globalized, 'postmodern' world, but these tend to be much more sporadic, localized, and transitory.

Post-industrial societies redefine the social domain in terms of the economic – arguably to a greater extent than ever occurred under classic 'modernity' – both are now governed by the rational choices of entrepreneurial individuals who see everything they do in terms of maximizing their human and material capital. The role of the state is thus recast, as are the actions of entrepreneurs. In the discourse of post-industrialism, society becomes synonymous with market, democracy, and individual choice; indeed, these are equated with being a consumer, and individual gain and advantage prevail over the common good. Basically, post-industrial societies apply economic rationality to most spheres of human interactions.[3]

Educational Paradigms Rooted in the Industrial Sociocultural Paradigm. Bertrand and Valois claim that two reasonably distinct educational paradigms have emerged from the assumptions and beliefs that characterize the industrial sociocultural paradigm: a 'rational paradigm' and a 'technological paradigm.'

The Rational Paradigm. The rational paradigm, according to Bertrand and Valois, simply entails the transmission of knowledge, of credible ways of thinking, and of accepted cognitive structures. Teachers teach established 'canons' of knowledge; learners learn them. The positivistically conceived 'truths' to be transmitted are unique in their domain, yet they are predictable, replicable, and law-like, and take normal science as their model of what is worth knowing and how it can be known. The cultural 'function' of education is largely to 'initiate the individual to the idea of progress and consumption, and to foster a vision of creativity as synonymous with economic, scientific, and technological progress.' Consistent with this view of purpose and paradigm, education should present human relations in terms of economic relations and foster the image of the desirable individual as one who is 'opportunist, materialist, and conformist' (Bertrand and Valois 1980, table 4.2, 173) – not far indeed from some contemporary constructions of 'entrepreneurial education' (see, for example, Smyth, 1999).

Politically, education within the rational paradigm, should 'contribute to maintaining an oligarchic social structure, acceptance that an [elite] minority make decisions on behalf of the majority; in short, education should reflect and legitimate a hierarchical decision-making structure' (Bertrand and Valois 1980, table 4.2, 173).

In terms of the socio-economic order, such education should 'relativise the importance of the student as a person whilst maximising her importance as a future worker.' It should 'promote intellectual aptitudes, contribute to reproducing the [existing] social divisions in work, and promote the legitimacy of the established order and its values' (ibid.). The overarching function of education thus conceived is, not surprisingly, its contribution to maintaining the status quo of industrial and post-industrial society as a whole.

The Technological Paradigm. Also rooted in the industrial sociocultural paradigm, the technological paradigm of education seeks to transform education into a science. Its central goals are to produce the technological person, to organize efficiently the communication of knowledge, and to choose modes and strategies appropriate to such communication (Bertrand and Valois 1980, 199). In short, *to promote rational learning and knowing – and to do so with the tools and perspectives of applied science.*

Within the technological paradigm, teachers teach established canons of knowledge but every effort is made to bring the entire education enterprise into a process of ongoing systemic technical improvement and perfection.[4] Indeed, such continuous, science-and-technology-driven improvement is the hallmark of this educational paradigm according to Bertrand and Valois (1980). The central cultural function of education within this paradigm is 'to transmit technological development and utilisation of technologies *as* [the most important] *image of creativity*' (199; emphasis added). Consistent with its overarching technological focus, the political function of education within this paradigm focuses on 'atomising and "deideologizing" social debates, problems, and questions; [as in the case of the rational paradigm, therefore, it also focuses] on perpetuating an oligarchic concept of democracy; [and on] promoting 'the expert' as the foundation of all models of decision-making and problem solution' (199). For Bertrand and Valois the socio-economic role of this educational paradigm is 'to reflect an apparent neutrality by abstaining from all normative critique; to promote method and efficiency, control and the economy; and to transmit a "mecanomorphic" image of the person' (199).

Finally, as in the case of the rational paradigm, the overarching function of the technological paradigm is the preservation of the status quo in society.

THE EXISTENTIAL PARADIGM

Bertrand and Valois' (1980) existential paradigm (a paradigm centred on the person) is radically different from just about every criterion that applies to the industrial/post-industrial paradigm. Knowledge within this view of sociocultural reality is a 'holistic process of the human organism.'[5] Knowledge, on this view, is a matter of interaction, not subject–object separation as in the industrial paradigm; knowledge is subjective and truth is existential. Human awareness is practically without limits and humans can even attain a 'cosmic conscience.'[6] Knowledge is produced by suppressing 'reductionisms,' by the quest to understand relations, and by the 'systematization' of subjective experience. Science is *not* neutral.[7] All experiences – intuitive, mystic, religious, and psychic – can be meaningfully integrated (225).

With regard to relations among persons, society, and nature, the existential paradigm, according to Bertrand and Valois, offers an essentially teleological concept of life and evolution. The world is a system of relationships between *means* and *ends*. The ultimate purpose of society is neither scientific nor economic; rather, the purpose is to facilitate the full development of all of a person's potential so that he/she becomes a 'fully functioning' person. Society and groups within it are but means to that end. Such an end may require *some* domination of the person over his/her biophysical, social, and cultural milieu. Individuals need to be open to their experiences, to live existentially, to be active rather than reactive.

The values of interest in this view of society are those arising from personal experience of 'the hierarchy of the levels of consciousness,' the meaning of life, conscious participation in personal growth, equal rights for each person, and maximum freedom for each person to the extent compatible with similar freedom for all.

The existential paradigm, in short, fosters and creates an environment that is *centred on the person* in order to assure a full life. Production of goods and services and profit should be oriented towards full personal development. Each individual should decide how best to pursue such development while taking into account that others are pursuing their own visions of desirable personal development.

The overall significance of this paradigm, Bertrand and Valois argue, is the centring of society on the person as the end of society and of existence, on affirmation of the 'extra-rational,' and on the possibility of attaining consciousness of the reality of a world beyond the phenomenological world (225).[8]

The Humanist Paradigm. Bertrand and Valois (1980) see education occurring within an existential sociocultural paradigm as characteristically 'humanist.' In their view, the general function of education in a humanist view is to develop the child and to fashion students into persons who are comfortable with themselves and who 'function'[9] fully. The epistemological function of such education is to promote a concept of knowledge that is built on subjectivity and transformed into a quality of being. In this view, knowing is not aimed at accumulation but at *being*, at the organic integration of one's various achievements.

The cultural function of humanist education, for Bertrand and Valois, is to promote subjective creativity as the model of creativity. It is meant to promote self-expression, communication, joy, and love. It is meant 'to propose a "new" image of the person within which the person is internally free to move in any direction' and to choose freely how to be a 'changing process' in order that he/she can live fully and experience the present moment as a creative person, confident in his/her being, and possessing a sense of liberty (245).

Politically such education criticizes the manner in which a so-called democratic society treats individuals, and it aims to restore power to the individual. From a socio-economic perspective, humanist education encourages (at least partially) the dominant social order to centre itself on the person. Thus humanist education critiques authoritarian structures.

Bertrand and Valois' (1980) view of the overarching function of humanist education leads them into one of the most ambivalent conclusions in their entire paradigmatic taxonomy. They contend that humanism in education does not necessarily lead towards one, or even two, overall functions. Depending on the context (how existentially focused a society is at the moment one is considering it, for instance), humanistic education might lead in one of three global directions: maintenance of the status quo, maintenance of the existing order coupled with efforts to reshape it into a more 'human' character, or creation of a new society that is centred on the person (where a society, for instance, is currently largely focused on economic efficiency). Thus, unlike the educational paradigms associated with the industrial sociocultural paradigm, humanistic education adjusts its principal 'function' to its context (245).

In terms of what Bertrand and Valois (1980) call the 'exemplary dimension,' humanistic education focuses mainly on support and providing incentives for the self-directing learner who is the ultimate 'active agent' in the educational process (252). In this view, the didactic sage-on-the-stage teacher is replaced by a supportive guide who responds to the child's learning preferences and priorities. The exemplary dimension of humanist education is, in a word, 'child-centred.'

THE NEW DEMOCRATIC SOCIETY PARADIGM[10]

Within Bertrand and Valois' new democratic society or 'symbiosynergetic' paradigm, the focus on a symbiotic mode of knowing leads to a view that is centred on unity between 'subject' and 'object.' Indeed, those words cease to have much meaning as the distinction dissolves in the overarching unity and identity of forces between the two. The symbiosynergetic perspective recognizes the metaphoric character of all explanation[11] and 'the different non-contradictory levels of perception and explanation of physical, biological, and spiritual reality.' It views reality as unitary, as part of a new and all-embracing 'totalism' and 'imminentism,' in its search for a global science of life.

With respect to relationships among persons, society, and nature, the symbiosynergetic paradigm takes the person as a 'holon,' a *blending of an individual's identity with its intimate connections to others*. Opposition among persons, society, and nature becomes minimized in a comprehensive ecosystem. *Community replaces society as society is transformed into community*. Persons and their society-community become one. Ironically, claim Bertrand and Valois, this paradigm leads to communities of unique and liberated persons but this paradox is only possible where altruism and charity shape human and community development. Since all are part of a greater 'one,' a symbiosynergy develops among persons and between persons and their biophysical milieu.

The way of doing things within this paradigm becomes, in short, a 'symbiosynergy of heterogeneity.' While many writers, especially recent proponents of a relational approach to pluralism in society (more on this later) have vaunted the potential benefits to society of such symbiosynergy, the concept is difficult to capture in a succinct expression – a difficulty to which Bertrand and Valois' rather prolix and academic expression bears witness. We are reminded of a simpler and more accessible formulation set forth many years ago in an article published in a United Church publication (for which we have long since lost the reference). In that article the author(s) spoke of a 'cohesive diversity.'[12] Accumulation of difference within an overarching and vital unity is the order of the day. All contribute in different and complementary ways to 'community and cosmic projects.' With regard to the technical and practical aspects of existence, this paradigm promotes counter-technology and soft technology, including self-production of physical elements necessary to life (in our own time this would seem to translate into discourses about renewable resources and sustainable development).

The global sense framed by the symbiosynergetic paradigm is, as this label suggests, 'the symbiosynergy of persons and communities'; in other words, of the 'total person,' because persons, as holons, can be whole only when fully united with a society that has been transformed into a meta-community (Bertrand and Valois 1980, 277).

Symbiosynergetic assumptions resonate with Bowers' (2006) critique of the malaise of contemporary industrial monoculture and its values. It resonates as well with Aboriginal traditions of seeking sustainable unity with nature and finding guidance towards that end from a dream or vision quest to link to a guiding spirit (Denis 1997, 133–4). Gone are views of nature as an object or resource to be exploited with scientific efficiency by human 'captains of the universe' who represent the apex of evolution and are thus entitled to exploit the spoils of their superiority ruthlessly and scientifically. Instead, the wholeness of the human spirit is directly dependent on symbiotic integration with nature, including all forms of life, both animal and human. Gone are ideas of linear scientific progress towards ever greater 'enclosure of the commons' in the interest of multinational corporate profit. In their place is a quest for wholeness through the individual's oneness with nature, the universe, and other living beings in all their symbiotic diversity.

The Inventive Paradigm. Bertrand and Valois (1980) map out what they call the inventive paradigm on the principles, values, and beliefs of the symbiosynergetic sociocultural paradigm. The general function of the inventive paradigm, as they see it, is to develop the capacity for 'social invention' and for 'creation of new social institutions' among 'persons [and] communities' (295). Education situated within the inventive paradigm seeks 'to discover the significance and implications of intentions or projects' and to invent future situations and intervention modes capable of bringing about such new social institutions (in short, new democratic societies).

Bertrand and Valois go on to say that epistemologically such education promotes a symbiotic mode of knowing that takes as its starting point the essential union of observer and observed seen as having an 'identity of force' (and thus dissolving the subject–object distinction). Such education facilitates meaningful listening and develops 'a critical consciousness of the situation of the person in the universe.' It valorizes knowledge that enables individuals to situate themselves and to become their own beings, but to do so in the realization that individuals cannot define themselves 'except by reference to the whole' (Bertrand and Valois 1980, table 6.2, 295).

Culturally, the inventive paradigm promotes, as its model of creativity, the symbiosynergy of heterogeneity or cohesive diversity, which embraces differences within the essential union of the person and the totality of the universe. (We cannot resist observing how close this is to traditional Aboriginal views of the place of the person in the universe!) Education within the inventive paradigm, Bertrand and Valois insist, fosters the image of the person as part of a greater whole, as a holon, unique but inextricably united to others in an overarching and all-encompassing *us*.

Politically, such education promotes decision-making based on non-hierarchical mutualism. Again, we see an overlap here with the practice of consensus-based political decision-making within traditional Aboriginal communities and societies.

Bertrand and Valois (1980) see the socio-economic role of the inventive paradigm as encouraging persons to engage fully with each of the sociocultural contexts within which they work and to promote conditions that will encourage others to engage as well. Education constituted within inventive principles should 'resituate personal development within community development and community development within personal development'(table 6.2, 295). In short, the inventive paradigm should promote universal but diversified participation in the symbiosynergy of the world as a whole.

The overarching function of such education for Bertrand and Valois (1980) is to contribute to the symbiosynergy of heterogeneity and to the universal recognition of the 'complementarity of differences' within a fundamental and vital union of persons with each other and with the entire universe. In this way the inventive paradigm contributes to the creation of new democratic communities and to the disappearance of industrial societies (295).

The application of these principles in education will create 'constituents' out of students. (In the political sense – a revealing concept of students – and once again one not far removed from traditional First Nations teaching–learning relationships). As constituents, students will take charge of their development and learn what they need to learn in order to live, think, speak, share, and act together in such a way as to re-situate these fundamental human acts in the daily context of their lives. Control over the educational context belongs to the constituents – not to members of an educational hierarchy. Learning occurs as constituents reflect on the experience of their lives. As in the humanist paradigm, teachers work with constituents and thus reconstitute a more vibrant educational communication network as they do so. The community defines the school, sets its educational character and establishes its social context. Bertrand and Valois (1980) believe that all aspects of a school and school system should contribute to education for a more just, dynamic, and egalitarian society (303).

BERTRAND AND VALOIS IN TELEGRAPHIC COMPRESSION:
TOWARDS A PLACE TO STAND

We embarked on this brief overview of Bertrand and Valois' paradigmatic conceptual framework because it contributes an important piece of the conceptual ground on which we wish to stand in this study. Table 2.2 summarizes this framework and suggests how it can relate to positioning Aboriginal education within the most generic of socio-political and educational paradigms.

The constraint on Aboriginal education both to be distinctively Aboriginal in content, form, and process and to emulate provincial educational programs and standards (what Paquette [1986] tried to capture in the term 'parity paradox') has not gone away. One of our major theoretical purposes in the following section is to deepen and thicken the theoretical foundations of that concept and its place in Aboriginal education. Picking up and developing the parity paradox theoretically, and then moving beyond it, requires that we borrow from at least two of

Table 2.2
Framing versions of First Nation self-government and education within different paradigm theory bases

The Industrial and Post-Industrial Paradigm	The Existentialist Paradigm	The Symbiosynergic Paradigm
*Paradigm Base**		
Sociocultural paradigm characterized by positivist and economic efficiency assumptions about knowledge and the nature of society.	Sociocultural paradigm characterized by a person-centred way of understanding and organizing society.	Sociocultural paradigm characterized by sustainability of life systems and non-hierarchical complementarity of individuals and communities as ways of being and relating in a society.
Corresponding educational paradigms characterized by a conception of education as an efficient transmission of predetermined knowledge designed to promote positivistically rational learning and knowing and maintain and legitimate an oligarchic socio-economic structure.	Corresponding educational paradigm is characterized a conception of education based on the empowerment of a creative, confident, and free individual who shapes his/her learning process.	Corresponding educational paradigm characterized by a conception of education based on a symbiotic mode of knowing in which the learners develop their capacity to create new alternatives by producing knowledge that promotes new ways of being and acting. These in turn support a vision of society based on non-hierarchical and democratic decision-making and a complementarity of differences.

As is the case with education in any other community or society, Aboriginal education occurs within a sociocultural and a related educational paradigm. Which one(s) would be the most appropriate (and why?) to frame educational policies, programs, self-determination arrangements, and all-encompassing purposes of Aboriginal education in the future?

* The concept of paradigm refers to the action exercised by a community or society on its social and cultural practices by the combination of five elements: a concept of knowledge, a concept of relations among persons, society, and nature, a set of values, a way of doing things, and an overreaching sense of significance (Bertrand and Valois 1980). Each sociocultural paradigm frames a specific conception of education (educational paradigm) which defines the norms and rules that determine educational reflection and action on the one hand, and praxis that promotes particular modalities regarding teaching methodologies on the other.

Bertrand and Valois' sociocultural paradigms and their attendant educational paradigms.

Few real-world schools and school systems operate *entirely* within the assumptions and values of only one of each type of paradigm. Nonetheless, we believe that the principal stakeholders have an overall orientation in favour of a particular sociocultural paradigm and a single educational paradigm[13] and that, as Bertrand and Valois hypothesize and seek to demonstrate, the latter flows from the former.

Like education in general, most Aboriginal education occurs mainly within one sociocultural paradigm and one related educational paradigm. Furthermore, we believe that today the purposes and processes of education are tightly aligned with the assumptions, needs, values, and ways of doing things characteristic of the industrial paradigm and therefore with rational and technical approaches to structuring and delivering education. For example, the pervasive reliance on high-stakes testing and successive waves of performance- or results-based educational policy reform across North America and beyond (see Hirschland and Steinmo 2003). Obviously Aboriginal education, which has long been required to conform to provincial curricula in Canada, cannot but be deeply influenced by this strong tilt towards rational-technological approaches to teaching and learning in provincial curricula and policy.

Given that Aboriginal education is to a great extent aligned with provincial values, priorities, and curricula, we now turn to what we see as being the basic conceptual framework questions. *What sociocultural paradigm should provide the epistemological grounding (way of knowing), view of relations among persons, society, and nature, source of values, ways of doing things, and global sense of social purpose for Aboriginal education and why? What other paradigm or paradigms might provide useful and morally legitimate contributions to each of these, to what degree, and why?*

We then must ask the next logical question: What educational paradigm should be the source of the general, epistemological, cultural, political, and economic function[14] of Aboriginal education and why? In addition, which other educational paradigm or paradigms might provide useful and morally legitimate contributions to each of these, to what degree, and why?

Figure 2.2 schematically represents our global response to these questions. First, we take it as self evident that, to be at all coherent with Aboriginal peoples' sense of having intimate relationships with one another, to the earth, and to the universe, Aboriginal education must be situated fundamentally within the symbiosynergetic sociocultural

Figure 2.2 Situating Aboriginal education within principal paradigms

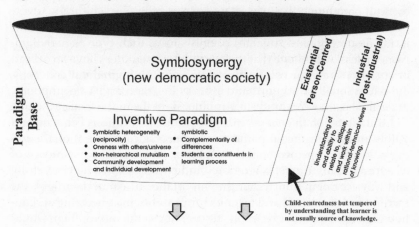

Child-centredness but tempered
by understanding that learner is
not usually source of knowledge.

paradigm and its assumptions of universal interdependence, unity, and symbiosis. Only in this way can education align itself with pervasive Aboriginal assumptions about the deep and enduring relationships among persons, society, and the universe. To represent this fundamental requirement, we have shown the symbiosynergetic paradigm as occupying most of the available space in the sociocultural-paradigm 'layer.'

However, we are painfully aware that much, if not most, education proffered to Aboriginal students is likely grounded mainly in the industrial paradigm and its foundational assumptions. Still, to critique policy framing Aboriginal education, we must have conceptual and normative ground on which to stand and it is that groundwork, and not any claim about what currently exists in Aboriginal education, on which we focus in this section.

We also believe that the person-centredness of the existential paradigm has something to contribute to a framework of overarching sociocultural assumptions for Aboriginal education given the widely documented singular importance attached to persons, to the word of persons, and to children in particular in Aboriginal cultures. The concept of a person as a holon, moreover, seems to us to resonate with Aboriginal teaching that reflects a unitary and integrated, rather than scientifically atomized, view of human nature. Nonetheless, we believe that the overlap of existential assumptions and values within a plausible overall framework for Aboriginal education are, at best, partial and tenuous. Too much that was shared across otherwise culturally divergent Aboriginal groups (consensual decision-making, centrality of the group as people, and so forth) suggests to us that, even though Aboriginal people apparently tolerated with resignation serious violations of social norms and values by individuals, Aboriginal cultures were not based on what we normally think of as existentialist assumptions, in particular, on existentialism's apotheosis of the individual as the sole rightful arbiter of his/her own destiny. Still, the emphasis Bertrand and Valois attribute to this paradigm on a teleological concept of life and evolution, and on meaningful integration of subjective experience of all sorts (intuitive, mystic, religious, and psychic), resonate powerfully with the Aboriginal focus on the importance of connecting with the spirit world in various ways, for example through a vision quest. Cautious borrowing from existential assumptions and values, then, would seem to be useful in framing Aboriginal educational policy and programs and the understandings that underpin them.[15]

Whether they wish it were so or not, Aboriginal people live within a society that takes the industrial paradigm assumptions to be given and immutable, to be the sole cornerstone, in fact, on which scientific, technological, and social progress are possible. Despite growing concern with catastrophic and irreversible damage to the ecosystem on which humanity and all its animal and plant partners in our fragile ecosphere depend, we continue to do exactly what Bertrand and Valois warned of a generation ago, namely, look to technology to solve the problems technology has created. Nonetheless, education that fails to acquaint Aboriginal students with this paradigm and its assumptions and that fails to equip them to be able to work within this paradigm – as well as to challenge its basic assumptions – will do nothing but further entrench the inability of Aboriginal youth to learn within mainstream Canadian post-secondary institutions and to succeed in mainstream Canadian businesses and institutions.

Given our belief that the symbiosynergetic paradigm should provide the principal sociocultural values and form within which Aboriginal education should be framed, we conclude that Aboriginal education should occur within the assumptions of the inventive paradigm, that is, within a commitment to symbiotic heterogeneity and reciprocity (and hence to the importance of relationships and continually maintaining and renewing them). Students, in such a view, are constituents in the learning process that itself is based on the relationship between learner and teacher. This is different in an important way from students determining unilaterally what they will learn and when as in the progressivist assumptions of extreme child-centredness within the existential paradigm. Children in most Aboriginal cultures were taught traditionally by the three Ls: looking, learning, and listening (Miller 1996, 16). While those with teaching authority in a child's life (not necessarily parents) tended to allow, to the extent possible, the learner to choose the timing and tried to seize the teachable moment to impart knowledge, skills, and principles when it arrived, the curriculum was not, for the most part, the child's choice. Rather, it was strongly shaped by the wisdom and experience of the collective regarding what was important and worth knowing.

Social Theory Base: Pluralism in Three Dimensions

Good fences make good neighbors.

Robert Frost, 'Mending Wall'

The next layer of our conceptual framework derives mainly from Schouls' (2003) characterization of the three faces of pluralism, and mainly from its relational face (37).

Pluralism as a sociological principle and political value has long been recognized as having particular relevance to Canada. By 1970, Barbara Ward had already labelled Canada 'the first international nation.' Until recently, pluralism was largely viewed as being composed of two dimensions, one cultural and one structural (see, for instance, Churchill 1986). Cultural pluralism denoted cultural diversity, planned or fortuitous, within a region or country – and political and popular acceptance of such diversity – while structural pluralism designated different political institutions coupled potentially with different legal frameworks or even legal statuses for identifiable groups within a nation-state. Cultural pluralism was widely seen as an attractive alternative to the imposition of a single dominant culture on minorities, although nowhere, even in avowedly multicultural Canada it seems in retrospect, was there great enthusiasm and deep support for *encouraging and sustaining* cultural differences. Some countries, of course – the Netherlands offers a classic case in point – have found that the only way to forge workable political cohesion at the national level is to embrace structural pluralism, that is, different institutions for different cultural groups composing the nation-state. In general, however, nation-states committed to liberal democratic principles have been loath to accord special institutions, much less distinctive legal status, to ethnocultural minority groups, although the situation of Aboriginal peoples in Canada and elsewhere has frequently been viewed as warranting special institutions, and even legal status, for them. The arguments for such special accommodations for Aboriginal peoples, of course, have been controversial and often politically difficult to sustain.

As in so many other areas of life and conceptual theory, the relatively pristine simplicity of cultural versus structural pluralism has vanished in the wake of subsequent analysis and critique. Pluralism is no longer understood as a largely homogeneous value and political alternative to monoculture, universal institutions and laws and rules of universal application. The challenge, moreover, of reconciling small-l liberal principles with the reality of ethnocultural diversity has attracted increasingly thoughtful analysis in recent years. Furthermore, the general failure of Western 'liberal' democracies to accommodate ethnocultural minorities harmoniously continues to manifest itself in disturbing ways. Although the 1965 Watts Riots in Los Angeles seem a world removed in time, place, and culture from the 2005 riots in Paris, on closer inspection the two are remarkably similar in their reflection of persistent, deeply entrenched rejection by mainstream 'host' societies of ethnocultural differences and their exclusion of those perceived as culturally (and racially) different. Two classic 'solutions' have been advanced to such persistent conflict: assimilation and cultural pluralism, mostly in the sense of 'toleration' (frequently aligned with a different approach to pluralism; see our discussion below) as opposed to 'appreciation' (aligned more directly with an identification approach to cultural diversity; again, see below).

By appreciation we mean the capacity of a host society to create policies and institutions that cultivate qualities that make it possible for members of different ethnolinguistic and cultural groups to flourish in every relevant sense, and ultimately to choose, to the greatest possible extent, their own ways of being, acting, and communicating within a pluralistic nation-state. Toleration offers at best a limited scope of policy response (essentially the implementation of some degree of structural pluralism). It offers a way of reaching agreement on policies and institutions (on structures and mechanisms for self-governed Aboriginal education, for instance) without requiring Aboriginal and non-Aboriginal communities to agree on *shared* substantive ends these policies and institutions will serve (i.e., on a shared conception of what it means to flourish both as human beings and as members of cultural reference groups that could shape the collective lives of Aboriginal as well as non-Aboriginal groups).

So far, policies regulating Aboriginal education have focused on establishing a kind of structural pluralism designed mainly to secure a normative integration of Aboriginal communities into mainstream Canadian society. The purpose of these policies has never really been satisfactorily defined from an Aboriginal perspective. Today, this kind of structural pluralism has become increasingly problematic as Aboriginal groups garner enough power to resist repression and 'encapsulation.'

By themselves, in any case, neither assimilation nor cultural pluralism seems to have worked very well as a 'solution' to frictions between mainstream society and minority groups or, for that matter, as a way of resolving frictions among minority groups themselves. Surely, neither has well served Aboriginal peoples in Canada.

Schouls (2003) offers, in our view, a particularly helpful application of recent developments in pluralist theory to the situation of Aboriginal groups in Canada. He also provides a vital key for linking overarching sociocultural and educational paradigms to the dilemma of reconciling liberal democratic principles with Canada's Aboriginal peoples' claims to unextinguished inherent rights to sovereignty and self-determination. Indeed, taken in tandem with Turner's (2006) stunningly insightful critique of liberalism in light of Aboriginal claims to be self-governing nations on the one hand, and with Bertrand and Valois' idea of educational paradigms grounded in sociocultural paradigms on the other, Schouls' work offers the second of three essential elements of a defensible and conceptually rigorous place to stand in our critical review of recent Aboriginal education policy in Canada.

We begin by noting that Schouls takes issue with the pervasive opinion – pervasive at least among those favourable to Aboriginal self-government and self-determination claims, which was the conclusion offered by the Royal Commission on Aboriginal Peoples (RCAP) in its voluminous report – that what matters in Aboriginal self-government is ratification, legal entrenchment, and respect by 'settler' governments of unextinguished and unextinguishable nationhood and cultural identities of Aboriginal peoples in Canada. At first blush, this position on Schouls' part strikes readers familiar with recent Aboriginal inherent rights discourses as unusual and provocative, especially given that Schouls writes essentially in support of Aboriginal self-government or of Aboriginal rights to *self-determination* (unlike Flanagan [2000], for example).

He begins by challenging 'difference based' assumptions about the nature and source of ethnocultural identity. Citing such prestigious authors as Will Kymlicka, Patrick Maclem, Charles Taylor, and James Tully, Schouls (2003, 4–8) outlines what he calls the 'difference approach' to identity (ethnic, cultural, social, and political). In essence that approach takes cultural difference as *the source of personal identity*. According to the cultural difference approach, Schouls argues, 'culture not only *provides* individuals with identity but also divides them from one another at the deepest level of human existence' (5; emphasis added). So central is culture to identity in this view that nations are really cultural communities whose members consider themselves as 'entitled to some form of territorial sovereignty and state power' (6). Within this identity perspective, nations and nationhood come to be seen 'as central to their [individual] identities' (7).

The *identification* approach to cultural identity, according to Schouls (2003), works in precisely the opposite direction to that of the difference perspective. Within the identification approach, cultural identity is malleable and 'can be shaped to meet different kinds of political objectives' (9). Furthermore, following the identification approach, ethnicity is a means of classifying first people and then the groups *with which they 'identify,'* because in this perspective identity is based largely – or at least significantly – on *voluntary personal identification*, not on cultural difference. Generally, the criteria for recognition as a bona fide member of an ethnic group are the following:

- a collective proper name
- a myth of common ancestry
- shared historical memories
- one or more differentiating elements of common culture
- an association with a specific 'homeland,' and
- a sense of solidarity for significant sectors of the group's population (Schouls 2003, 9)

The key point here, however, is that group members *identify themselves* with the group. Thus the *source* of identity in this case is ultimately members' 'sense of solidarity' with the group – not cultural difference per se. Ethnic identity in this view is tied 'to a sense of intergenerational continuity forged around subjective criteria of shared destiny established by those both inside and outside the group' (ibid., 10). Identity is constructed by individuals, not simply inherited. Furthermore, identity becomes important to group members precisely when and because it is perceived to be threatened by non-members, typically by a mainstream 'host' society. Consequently ethnic identity is 'typically used as a tool in political struggles to capture resources (whether political, economic, cultural, or other ...) from outside the group' and to counter oppression from rival groups competing for the same resources (13–14).

Schouls (2003) captures the fundamental opposition between the difference and identification approaches to ethnocultural identity:

> The difference approach starts from the premise that the basis of human identity is in human difference, while the identification approach suggests that the basis of community identity is fluid, negotiated, and subject to change. The difference approach advances the idea that community attributes are the source of identity, while the identification approach counters with the idea that attributes are merely expressions of identity. (15)

Schouls points out the centrality of pluralism to the reality of most modern democracies. Indeed, he claims that the central political problem confronting liberal democracies is how to 'provide spaces' for 'deep diversity' (17). He next describes three 'faces,' or perhaps dimensions, because at one point he suggests that all three can coexist, at least to some extent, within contemporary concepts of pluralism: the communitarian view, the individualist view, and the relational view (37).

Communitarian pluralists like Charles Taylor, Will Kymlicka, and James Tully, Schouls notes, argue that excessive individualism, particularly as manifested in recent (neo)liberal political theory, renders minority-culture groups vulnerable to majority decisions that do not take into account minority interests (21), what has been traditionally referred to as 'tyranny of the majority.' According to Schouls (2003), standard liberal political conventions ('ways of acting' in Bertrand and Valois' sense) such as 'individual rights, universal citizenship, and majority rule in fact discriminate against minority cultural groups' (20). In individualist liberal democracies with no provisions to assure group rights, demographic weight prevails – always. Schouls maintains, moreover, that 'the corrosive cultural effects of un-nuanced [purely individualist] liberalism on minority communities only makes sense when lined up against the difference approach to individual and community identity'

(23). Majorities impose their hegemonic culture on minorities and thus undermine minority cultures by decimating the communities that are the *source* of their cultural identity. In Kymlicka's (1989) words:

> This conception of equality [one in which all personal differences must be chosen] gives no recognition to individuals' cultural membership, and if it operates in a culturally plural country, then it tends to produce a single culture for the whole of the political community, and the undesired assimilation of distinct minority cultural communities. The continued existence of such communities may require restrictions on choice and differentials in opportunity. If liberal equality requires equal citizenship rights, and equal access to a common 'field of opportunity,' then some minority cultures are endangered. And this, I believe, does not respond to our intuitions about the importance of our *cultural membership*. (152; emphasis added to highlight that in this view it is cultural membership, not identity, which is of first importance)

The communitarian version of pluralism fosters a view of justice 'in which ethnic groups are allowed free cultural development on the premise that not doing so will hinder the self-development of their members' (Schouls 2003, 23). Aboriginal communities are taken by some champions of communitarian and pluralist principles, notably Kymlicka, Taylor, and Tully, as being particularly worthy of and in need of protection from suffocation under the majority culture's domination given their extreme vulnerability to imposed assimilation and their historical and legal claims on settler governments.

Individualist pluralism, on the other hand, takes as its starting point 'that individual rights together with provisions for non-discrimination must come before collective cultural goals' (Schouls 2003, 24). This insistence on the primacy of individual rights is, in fact, identical to that of contemporary liberalism, or at least to that of the most radically individualist version of it. The diametrical opposition to communitarian pluralism couldn't be more obvious. Schouls (2003) summarizes that polar opposition:

> Liberal democracy's most basic commitment is to the freedom and equality of individual citizens. Thus, when the quest for community identity is construed in terms of a desire by that community to enhance or cultivate distinct cultural traditions, any ensuing conflict between individuals and their communities is inevitably interpreted in dichotomous terms. The na-

ture of the conflict is posed in the following way. Individual rights are said to have empowered the individual against the state. But if communities are then empowered against the state as part of a commitment to uphold their distinct cultural characteristics, what guarantee is there that individuals will not be totally engulfed by the cultural demands of their communities. (24–5)

Schouls, like Turner whose work we discuss below, cites Flanagan (2000) as exemplifying in a harshly articulate way a hard-line application of individualist principles to the situation of Aboriginal peoples in Canada. Rather than according any 'special' recognition of Aboriginal peoples in response to the obvious fact that they occupied North America before European settlers, the federal and provincial governments should ensure that Aboriginal *persons*, no less than all other citizens, are integrated into the fabric of the liberal democratic Canadian society and state – and into the market economy (Schouls 2003, 25). Flanagan bases this prescription for Aboriginal peoples on three key liberal assumptions: the primacy of individual autonomy in a liberal democracy, the *instrumental* role of groups (one should be able to affiliate with and disaffiliate from groups according to the perceived advantages they offer *to the individual*), and the priority of individual choice (ibid.). Individual rights simply trump group rights, always.

The third face of pluralism for Schouls (2003) is 'relational pluralism.' With regard to group diversity those who subscribe to a relational view of pluralism believe that what matters is 'not cultural difference *per se* but the sorts of relations that establish identity and, more pertinently, who actually wields power in defining those relations' (30). Groups matter here, as in communitarian pluralism, but group rights do not automatically trump individual rights. Nor do groups and group culture form or create individual identity in any complete or fixed sense. Diversity exists, moreover, and should be respected, *within as well as among communities*.

Individuals matter here as well, but both *individual identity and social structures are developmental*, and the right of both to evolve should not be impeded by legal and political arrangements which (a) assume that all community members have personal identities more or less completely defined by an unchanging community culture and (b) which impose on community members an equally immutable political status, structure, and relationship with society as a whole and with other groups within it. *Individuals give communities form* in all their attributes including culture and that form changes, and moreover *should* be free to change and adapt over time (Schouls 2003, 31–2). This definition of relational pluralism displays the dynamics of self-organization of a social entity that exhibits most of the phenomena characteristic of almost any sustainable human, social, or environmental organization – self-renewal, adaptation, and evolution.

Furthermore, group identity flows *from relationships* with society as a whole and with other groups in it, not from immutable cultural traditions or political structures inherited from the past. Social groups need power, and thus access to resources, to *shape* individual members, but they should not have power to conscript them into a particular culture and life form. Equally, however, all group members need power to shape their social group which, if it is a living social entity, is always in varying degrees of constant change (Schouls 2003, 33). Although Schouls does not suggest it, the terminology adopted long ago by Merton (1976) may be useful here. Members of *social reference groups*, as Merton characterized them, 'refer' to groups, and to the relationships of 'their' group(s) with society as a whole and with other groups, as each member constructs his/her personal identity. Conversely, the group is dependent on the insights and activity (political and otherwise) of members to adapt and recraft its own identity and renew its relationships over time. In short, relational pluralists support balanced, reciprocal power between social reference groups and their members.

All of this leads to two 'normative principles' of relational pluralism that flow from respect for human subjectivity. First, members should be equal to one another in shaping and reshaping their sociocultural group. They should have political equality within their group. Second, the group itself should be free from domination by society as a whole (Schouls 2003, 33). Only with such freedom, in fact, can members of the group shape and reshape the group over time, a process which, relational pluralists argue, is the very meaning of self-determination.

How can groups and their members live and work according to these two normative principles? They can do so only if society as a whole accords them a 'protected public space,' that is, if 'they have the political authority to construct boundaries around their members,' boundaries that provide space so that members 'can develop and then express their identities according to their own priorities' (ibid., 34) as opposed to the priorities of society as a whole or of other groups. More generally, from a relational pluralist perspective:

Groups must not be denied the capacity to develop, on their own terms, according to the lives that group members choose to lead. The standard of justice in this scheme remains purely relational. One judges the justice of a political system by the degree of independence and self-direction permitted to social groups of all kinds as they take up their relations with one another. (Schouls 2003, 35)

In this view, social reference groups should be free to declare who and what they are and to do so free from interference from power and priorities without and factions within. Group differences are a function of *relations*, not of cultural, political, or social difference. Groups are threatened when they and their members lose their capacity to continue to identify and act together as a group and 'to define their own identities in their relations with other groups "in positively supportive ways"' (Schouls 2003, 37).

Schouls (2003) argues persuasively that a relational pluralist approach to Aboriginal and especially First Nations claims to the right to determine their own future[16] will ensure meaningful self-determination well into the future in a way that neither a communitarian nor an individualist approach can. The communitarian approach tends to reify (84) and hence 'fossilize' (our term, not his) both Aboriginal cultures and structures of self-government. Schouls is strongly critical of RCAP for its endorsement of culture as *the* source of Aboriginal identity. To base the claim of Aboriginal groups to a right to self-determination on cultural difference, he argues, is a slippery and dangerous path for two reasons. First, from such a communitarian, cultural difference perspective, First Nations that are more fully acculturated into Canadian society as a whole and hence less 'distinctive' would have a correspondingly reduced claim to self-determination. After all, if cultural difference is *the source* of identity, First Nations groups that are less 'different' have less identity to protect and hence a reduced moral claim to effective 'boundaries' around their right to decide their future (70). Furthermore, no group, especially in the globalized, technologically integrated world of the twenty-first century, can return to its historical culture and governance form. In a very real sense, 'you can't go home again' (Wolfe 1941) whether you are Aboriginal or not. Hence, the RCAP prescription for cultural 'revitalization' in the sense of *restoration* is doomed to failure (Schouls 2003, 70–1). '[A]boriginal communities are by nature fluid, changeable, riven by internal pluralities' (ibid., 79).

Second, and even more fundamentally, tying self-government which

Schouls interprets as most meaningful when taken in the sense of political boundaries that allow self-determination to one particular historical instance of a culture and to one particular form of governance freezes in time either the status quo or a restored vision of a historical golden age, and thus paralyses the very self-determination one seeks to assure. This kind of 'preservationist' approach entrenches unchangeable structures and procedures embedded in an unchangeable cultural norm, all in the name of assuring group power *to determine what should change*, surely a near perfect recipe for gridlock and frustration. The way forward, according to Schouls (2003), in terms of Aboriginal self-determination is neither the 'cultural nation' (82) nor any form of one-size-fits all governance structure.

Moreover, communitarian approaches would entrench a 'we-versus-them' dynamic that would poison the well of creative interdependence between Aboriginal groups and Canadian society at large. Just as surely as individual approaches pre-empt evolving group relationships by declaring them out of bounds on a traditional Rawlsian liberal view of justice as grounded exclusively in individual rights (Rawls 1971), so do communitarian approaches deny and suppress 'this [developmental] dimension of flux and process, of ambiguity and complexity, normally associated with *relationship building*' (Schouls 2003, 48; emphasis added).

In sum:

> An effective foundation for Aboriginal self-government should thus have the following characteristics. First, the dominant Canadian governments must relinquish their hegemony over Aboriginal governments by ceding to them power of increased autonomy so that they can control their processes of collective self-definition. Solutions here must seek to empower Aboriginal communities as a whole, not just the individual members of Aboriginal communities. Second, an Aboriginal way of life pursued by a First Nation is simply what Aboriginal persons in the nation define it to be; there are no cultural or political criteria outside their choices that can be imposed on Aboriginal persons on the purported ground that those expressions more authentically represent Aboriginal identity. Third, in return for increased autonomy, Aboriginal governments must provide assurances that the victimization and oppression experienced by their internal minorities will be addressed. Aboriginal individuals in all their diversity must be given freedom to develop and contribute to community life without undue interference from their governing structures. (Schouls 2003, 173)

This view of Aboriginal self-government could, of course, lead to varying degrees of compartmentalization of Canadian society by creating different self-defining spheres of life, that is, clusters of practices, policies, or institutions organized according to particular values, norms, and understanding of human good. However, along the boundaries of these spheres, Aboriginal and non-Aboriginal communities might encounter conflicting expectations. Furthermore, problems might arise in determining where the boundaries are or where they should be drawn and how, to achieve justice and equity between and among the spheres. Moon (1993), in referring to Walzer's work (1983), argues that

> justice in a society marked by a pluralism of spheres requires that the proper boundaries be maintained. The goods[17] of each sphere must be distributed in accordance with their social meanings, and no one should be able to convert a superior position in one sphere into privileges in another. Illicit conversions, such as using wealth to acquire political power, violate the integrity, the social meaning of the good in questions, and constitute a form of tyranny. (17)

To avoid injustice, inequality, conflicts of interest, or relegating everything solely to the law of domination by the strongest, members of both Aboriginal and non-Aboriginal spheres of life must have a shared framework of principles and rules, ethical as well as legal, to which they can appeal in cases of conflict. Such principles and rules constitute a necessary breach in the boundaries around each community. While conflict over any area of dispute may involve varying degrees of opposition of interests up to and including complete opposition, agreed-upon ethical and legal principles and rules shared by both communities can transform internal or intercommunity conflict into opportunities for willing cooperation and interdependence.

Schouls devotes a whole chapter to the pervasive disempowerment of First Nations women and youth under current (band council) governance arrangements and argues that the Canadian *Charter of Rights and Freedoms* can, despite its controversial applicability to Aboriginal peoples among First Nations leaders, contribute to assuring that all Aboriginal group members have voice and influence in determining the future of their groups and communities. In effect, Schouls thus seems to argue that *Charter* application to First Nations governments is a necessary breach in the boundaries around these governments if they are to form a mutually interdependent part of the greater Canadian polity and its essential values. Schouls (2003) weighs in, albeit with many nuances and caveats, on the side of the argument that, 'if Aboriginal self-governing communities are to retain their ties to Canada, they must accept certain commitments to shared citizenship, among them the Charter. The cost of Canadian citizenship to Aboriginal peoples, in other words, is the requirement that Aboriginal governments forgo those practices that violate basic Charter rights' (100–1).

Finally, we take from Schouls' (2003) analysis, particularly in regard to the difficulty of reconciling the entire *gestalt* of liberal-democratic values with a right of Aboriginal peoples to boundaries around their power to determine their own way of life, boundaries that are, in his view the sole 'antidote to colonialism' (131), a lesson that will be of particular importance to our own conclusions regarding the future of Aboriginal education in Canada. Schouls is no starry-eyed idealist. He bluntly acknowledges that 'there is no escape from the realities of social power. Aboriginal individuals are just as capable as anyone else of using power in ways that others might consider as self-serving' (163).

Although Schouls offers this observation in the context of highlighting the need to ensure that all members of Aboriginal communities have voice and 'equal' capacity to exercise influence and power (we resist here, albeit with difficulty, the temptation to pursue a major digression on conceptual issues surrounding 'equality'), the point is, it seems to us, a much broader one. The cost of Canadian citizenship to Aboriginal peoples is more than just complementarity of Aboriginal self-government practices with *Charter* principles. Another very real cost is pursuit of a mutually agreed-upon code of ethics which would be acceptable to Canadian society in general. We recognize the often stunning lack of ethics shown by settler governments with respect to Aboriginal peoples and their historic territorial, governance, and identity rights (to say nothing of royalties on natural resources). Nonetheless, given profound disagreement in contemporary Canadian society about the justification for a significant departure from individualist liberal democratic principles in the case of Aboriginal communities, it would be ill advised for Aboriginal governments or their agencies to stray far outside what is considered ethical by most Canadians. This requirement to conform closely to broadly shared views in Canadian society of ethical corporate, institutional, and individual action is, we believe, of great importance for the future of Aboriginal education. We

Figure 2.3 Identification and the three dimensions of pluralism

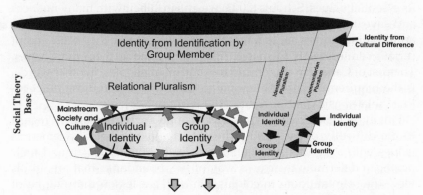

will return to this question in the following section when we discuss what Turner calls 'Kymlicka's constraint' and again at greater length in chapter 7.[18]

Figure 2.3 depicts our application of Schouls' theory and principles to a conceptual framework for Aboriginal education policy. Policy – and program – for Aboriginal education should be crafted *principally*, although not exclusively, from the inventive paradigm within the assumptions and values of the symbiosynergetic sociocultural paradigm.

As figure 2.3 shows, we concur with Schouls (2003) that it is both more useful to the cause of meaningful Aboriginal self-determination, on the one hand, and more congruent with how group members think of and act upon their group and individual identities, on the other, to consider personal identity as something an individual fashions from his/her various memberships and allegiances. Central to this relational pluralist perspective is the claim that identities are not static and frozen in time but are malleable and developmental and evolve over time in the lives of individuals and in the collective existence of the group.

None of this should be seen to detract from the importance of cultural difference in *shaping* (not determining, however, in some positivistically fatalistic and universal way) individual identity. Schouls (2003), after all, begins by suggesting that 'the bases for any group identity include a myth of common ancestry and one or more differentiating elements of common culture.[19] The view of identity, then, that should inform both education policy and educational programming for Aboriginal students, in our view, must be grounded in the key assumptions of relational pluralism as Schouls identifies them.

We have attempted to convey the main features of this perspective on individual and group identity in the relational pluralism section of the lower stratum of figure 2.3. First, individual and group identities are interactive and evolve over time. They evolve, moreover, based on interactions with each other and with society at large (large interaction arrows in fig. 2.3) and on interaction with other groups within society (small black curved interaction arrows in fig. 2.3). Attempts to 'freeze' such evolution on the part of either individuals or the group fail to recognize the foundational liberty imperative of liberal democracy as well as the key assumption in both relational pluralism and the symbiosynergetic paradigm that relations are in constant need of renewal. They also fail to recognize that such renewal expresses itself in ongoing learning, development, self-transformation and self-transcendence, and evolution.

What might the values, assumptions, and perspective of identification pluralism usefully contribute to a conceptual framework for Aboriginal education (and self-determination)? The idea that individuals choose to continue, deepen, distance themselves from, or even sever completely their relationship to groups with which they are affiliated helps in at least two ways. First, this idea reinforces the voluntaristic dimension of relational pluralism. People can and do choose to modify their relationship to groups, including the ethnocultural group(s) into which they are born. That said, the pure neoliberal proposition embedded in unqualified identification pluralism that group membership is like clothes in a wardrobe, to be worn, preserved, or discarded at will, obviously needs to be rejected here. Second, the identification pluralist perspective reminds those who craft policy affecting Aboriginal governance and education that group identity is only meaningful when individuals continue to identify with the group, surely a salutary warning for all concerned.

Cultures can and do profoundly mark and shape individual identity over an entire lifetime. The importance of that culture-on-individual influence should never be forgotten, and, although we believe that relational pluralism provides a complete and balanced conceptual account of individual and group identity formation and development, we welcome, albeit cautiously, communitarian insistence on the importance of group influence on member identity.

Political Rights Theory: Liberal Democratic Theory's Failure in Responding to Aboriginal Self-Determination

The final layer of our conceptual framework is based on Turner's understanding of what should be considered as a viable political theory in the context of achieving Aboriginal self-governance, especially in education.

Turner (2006) (a Temagi Anishnawbe scholar) delineates three different Canadian approaches to the question of Aboriginal rights to self-government, self-determination, cultural preservation, and ancestral territory. All are rooted in liberalism and liberal values. One, Kymlicka's approach, we have already discussed in the context of our summary of Schouls' analysis. We also touched on another of these approaches in our review of Schouls' work, that of complete assimilation and extinction of all special relationships with the state. Following meticulous deconstruction and critique of his three archetypal Canadian liberal approaches to Aboriginal, and in particular, First Nations, rights, Turner sets forth his view of the challenges that await what he calls Aboriginal 'word warriors' (essentially 'border people' between Aboriginal and mainstream cultures but in a very special sense).[20] He also emphasizes the importance of Aboriginal intellectuals generally while calling attention to related challenges that await Aboriginal people who have a deep and special knowledge of Aboriginal philosophies. This latter line of argument on Turner's part is essential in reconceptualizing the future of Aboriginal, and especially First Nations, education and contains within it a powerful raison d'être for truly transcultural excellence. Indeed, Turner's arguments in this respect have converted us from regarding the 'parity paradox' as a very difficult constraint within which with to work, if not an albatross around the neck of First Nations education, to seeing it as an approach that can breathe life, meaning, hope, and intellectual effervescence into such education.

In our post-Turner thinking, we have come to regard a 'fringe dweller' approach to Aboriginal education as the only approach worth pursuing – but also almost certainly the most difficult to implement! A fringe dweller in this sense is an Aboriginal person who, while deeply immersed in mainstream culture and its philosophical and institutional understandings, never loses his/her deep Indigeneity as he/she chooses and understands it. Turner, in our view, gives new and more profound meaning than was available in the past both to the idea of what it might mean for Aboriginal peoples to walk proudly between two worlds and to the highest purposes for doing so. In particular, walking proudly between an Aboriginal culture and mainstream Canadian culture does not mean that Aboriginal persons should either shed the Aboriginal identity they choose to live or that they should be 'bicultural,' in the sense of being cultural chameleons who change cultures depending on the context. We also believe that, in order to achieve mutual understanding and authentic dialogue, an urgent need exists for non-Aboriginal fringe dwellers, that is, mainstream persons who have a deep philosophical and institutional understanding of mainstream Canadian society but *who also succeed in achieving authentic communion with Aboriginal ways of knowing and understanding.*

Turner characterizes the 'no-compromise,' completely assimilationist perspective on dealing with Aboriginal rights claims[21] as 'White Paper liberalism,' which refers to the 1969 federal White Paper on Indian affairs (Chrétien 1969). The White Paper advocated complete assimilation into the political fabric of Canadian society as a whole as the only escape possible for First Nations people (the term was not in use at the time) from the debilitating colonial legacy embodied in the *Indian Act.* Only with the *Indian Act* and its underlying assumptions of differential legal 'status' relegated to the past could Canadian society freely and openly welcome 'Indians' into mainstream Canadian social, economic, and political life.

Turner (2006) summarizes his view of the central problem with the White Paper and the individual-rights-only version of liberalism it embodies: 'The White Paper defends a narrow understanding of equality, one which holds that because rights adhere only to individuals, any special form of recognition that accords rights to groups – rights that would exist over and above what everyone else receives – must be inherently unfair, and therefore wrong' (31). This is precisely the view embedded in what Schouls characterizes as 'individualist pluralism.' It rejects the view that Aboriginal rights were something that should exist if and to an extent that denial of these rights would result in an absolute reduction of First Nations' capability for self-determination and self-transformation over time. Not surprisingly, Turner pounces on the individual who represents the same particularly egregious contemporary example of this uncompromisingly assimilationist stance, Tom Flanagan, spokesperson par excellence for what Turner calls 'white orthodoxy' in the matter (turning the tables on those who, like Flanagan, believe that a pernicious 'Aboriginal orthodoxy' has usurped centre stage in Aboriginal policy). Turner quotes at length Flanagan's (2000) criteria for a bona fide 'civilization': intensive agriculture, urbanization, division of labour, intellectual advances, advanced technology, formalized, hierarchical government aka, a state (cited in Turner 2006, 33). Flanagan, as Turner wryly notes, has drawn his list of attributes of 'superior' cultures from European cultures (although one might dispute advanced technology if 'advanced' signifies long-term ecological sustainability) and has excluded Aboriginal cultures[22] from consideration as 'civilizations' in any meaningful sense. Having done so, Flanagan has only a short step to take to reject all Aboriginal rights claims. According to Turner, Flanagan does this 'by claiming that because civil society has only one way of understanding the meaning of nationhood, "the European concept of nation does not properly describe Aboriginal tribal community ... There can only be one political community at the highest level – one nation – in Canada"' (cited in Turner 2006, 36).

The White Paper proposed abolition of all special relationships between the Crown and First Nations people as the sole route forward towards 'full, free and non-discriminatory participation of Indian people in Canadian society' (cited inTurner 2006, appendix, 124). Harold Cardinal (1969) captured well the anger and indignation of status Indians across Canada to this proposed unilateral disengagement of the Canadian state from its historic, albeit incontestably colonial, relationship with and responsibility to First Nations people. A scathing and now classic critique of the White Paper and its political agenda, Cardinal's *The Unjust Society* countered the ironic claim of the government that implementation of the White Paper would be an important step towards making Canada a just society. In a rare paroxysm of unanimity, First Nations across Canada worked quickly to pull together the first nation-wide Aboriginal political organization, the National Indian Brotherhood (NIB), whose first significant act was to publish a rebuttal to the White Paper and its underlying liberal individualist assumptions in its position paper 'Indian Control of Indian Education' (NIB 1972/1984).

In the course of his critique of White Paper policy, Turner (2006) points out that, according to the Supreme Court of Canada's own criteria for testing whether the 'rule of law' is being respected in any given situation, the claim of the Canadian state to sovereignty over the Canadian land mass is, at the very least, debatable (33). He cites John Borrows (2002, 113) who points out that the Supreme Court has decided that 'the rule of law consists of two inter-related legal principles: it precludes arbitrary state power and requires the maintenance of a positive legal order,' both principles which were arguably seriously violated by Canada's 'unilateral' assertion of sovereignty.

The second generic liberal approach to Aboriginal rights claims, according to Turner, is what he calls the 'citizen plus' view after the well-known and considerably maligned expression Alan Cairns (2000) used to label his approach to dealing with Aboriginal rights. Cairns believes his approach offers 'a workable middle ground between the unjust assimilation policies of the White Paper and the "unreasonable" claims of indigenous nationalists who demand political independence' (cited in Turner 2006, 6). In a chapter whimsically entitled 'Cairns' Canada: Citizens Nonplussed,' Turner first outlines the distinctive features of the Cairns brand of liberalism and its proposed 'accommodation' of Aboriginal rights and then explains why it is unacceptable from an Aboriginal perspective.

Turner (2006) begins his look at Cairns' approach to Aboriginal rights by claiming that it is really no more than 'a reworking of the main ideas from the Hawthorn Report in the context of the post-section-35(1) era of Aboriginal rights' (39).[23] Cairns poses a fundamentally individualist-communitarian dilemma by asking if the goal in sight is a single society with one basic model of belonging or a dualist model involving a side-by-side parallelism, in effect a coexistence of at least technically coeval nations and of two separate political adhesions, or whether the objective is some intermediate position. Cairns, Turner (2006) says, offers two possible models, one is White Paper assimilation, pure and simple, and the second is '(supposedly) assimilation's ideological opposite – the parallelism model, which emphasizes separateness and difference instead of sameness and equality' (40). Despite a good explication of the history of colonial oppression and injustice of Aboriginal people by the Canadian state, Cairns' 'solution,' Turner points out, adds only one thing that is new and interesting to the fundamentals of the White Paper 'solution' to Aboriginal rights claims, the potential for recognition *by Canada* of rights *bestowed on* Aboriginal people by the Canadian state. While it leaves room for special 'rights,' Turner finds Cairns' 'citizen plus' solution unacceptable to Aboriginal peoples and their nations for three reasons:

1. The sovereignty of the Canadian state is absolute and not up for negotiation in the Aboriginal–Canadian state relationship. Cairns does not seriously consider that Aboriginal peoples may have claims

against the state which predate the formation of the Canadian state …

2. Because the sovereignty of the Canadian state is absolute, Aboriginal peoples are first and foremost citizens of the Canadian state. Cairns admits that Aboriginal peoples may belong to an Aboriginal 'nation,' and that this may entail the recognition of special rights; realistically, though, Canadian citizenship is the most important form of membership in the political relationship.

3. Because Aboriginal peoples are full citizens of the Canadian state, the special rights they possess are bestowed on them by the state, and the meaning of those special rights is articulated in the discourse of individual rights. (42–3)

Turner offers several telling stories and metaphors drawn from the Iroquoian Great Law of Peace to illuminate the fatal fallacy in Cairns 'parallelism' logic. One particularly striking anecdote involves the significance of the wampum belt used by Iroquoians to symbolize a treaty relationship. Cairns brings a characteristically Euro-Canadian interpretation to the 'two parallel rows' of the *Guswentha* or two-row wampum. The two rows, in his view, stress the 'permanence of difference' – parallel paths that never converge, an interpretation that could hardly be further from their intended significance. He concludes that the two-row wampum ignores interdependence among parties to a treaty and therefore reflects only the 'separateness' part of who they are.

Turner points out, however, that the two rows are 'separated' by three rows that symbolize peace, respect, and friendship. Furthermore, the view of political relationships that gave meaning and form to the two-row wampum was the antithesis of eternal separateness and difference. Turner cites Chief Michael Mitchell's explanation of the *Guswentha*. The wampum signified a *relationship* and all relationships were viewed as being in need of continual renewal – renewal, moreover, in a context of mutual respect and unflinching respect for the sacredness of the words that formalized the shared understandings of the relationship. Finally, Chief Mitchell characterized the two parallel rows as symbolizing 'two paths of vessels, traveling down the same rivers together. One a birch bark canoe, will be for the Indian people, their laws, their customs and their ways. The other, a ship, will be for the white people and their laws, their customs and their ways. We shall each travel together, side by side, but in our own boat. Neither of us will try to steer the other's vessel' (cited in Turner 2006, 48).

Here, the powerful metaphor of an artefact symbolizing relationships built on mutual peace, respect, friendship, and *non-interference* in each other's ways of existence becomes the antithesis of colonial exploitation and of the exercise of hegemonic power by one party to a relationship over the other. The resonances with Schouls' focus on the centrality of evolving, developmental *relationships* with effective *boundaries* that protect the legitimate interests of each party to a relationship could hardly be stronger or more striking. Nor could the conceptual and value-orientation distance from Cairns' 'citizen plus' arrangement be much greater.

The last generic liberal theory approach to Aboriginal rights claims Turner discusses is Will Kymlicka's minority rights view of Aboriginal rights claims, which we have already touched on in our summary of Schouls. Turner, however, adds considerably to Schouls' critique of the Kymlicka position and does so in ways that are useful for our purposes. In particular, he discusses at length the unavoidable and crucially important contextual reality faced by Aboriginal rights claims, namely, that they will be judged and arbitrated at least in part and often in whole by non-Aboriginals, a reality he calls 'Kymlicka's constraint' and which he presents in the guise of a 'profound reality check for Aboriginal peoples' (Turner 2006, 58).

Turner quotes at some length from Kymlicka's *Liberalism, Community and Culture* (1989) about that 'reality check' and the importance of finding conceptual and value space within liberalism itself for a theory of Aboriginal rights. We believe that quotation to be worth repeating here.

> For better or worse, it is predominantly non-Aboriginal judges and politicians who have the ultimate power to protect and enforce Aboriginal rights, and so it is important to find a justification of them that such people can recognize and understand. Aboriginal people have their own understanding of self-government drawn from their own experience, and that is important. But it is also important, politically, to know how non-Aboriginal Canadians – Supreme Court Justices, for example – will understand Aboriginal rights and relate them to their own experiences and traditions. (Kymlicka 1989, 154, cited in Turner 2006, 58)

But how can essentially individualist liberalism accommodate any version of group rights? Liberal societal policies, Turner reminds us, are shaped by three imperatives:

[F]irst, the government must treat people as equals; second, the government must treat all individuals with equal concern and respect; and third, the government must provide all individuals with the appropriate liberties and resources they need to examine and act on their beliefs. These criteria constitute a liberal [Rawlsian] conception of justice. So for Kymlicka [as for Rawls], it is vital for an individual to choose what is best for the good life and to be free to act on these choices: 'For meaningful individual choice to be possible, individuals need not only access to information, the capacity to reflectively evaluate it, and freedom of expression and association. They also need access to a societal culture. Group-differentiated measures that secure and promote this access may, therefore, have a legitimate role to play in a liberal theory of justice.' (Turner 2006, 61–2)

Thus Kymlicka finds moral and theoretical space for group rights within liberalism. Of course he cannot allow all group-right claims to have equal moral or policy weight. Prior occupancy, Kymlicka argues, must count for something. Aboriginal peoples have legitimate *governance* rights, one of three types of group rights, stronger in his scheme than either of the other two, namely, ethnic and special representation rights. They have them because they were one of the three national minorities ('founding peoples' in another usage) that were incorporated into the original Canadian state. As one of these three national minorities, Aboriginal peoples have, for Kymlicka, governance rights because they share with the other two national minorities a particular status as the initial 'legitimate entities' that formed the multinational state of Canada.

Kymlicka writes, 'Aboriginal cultures, as national minorities, can exercise their rights of governance only to the extent that they do not offset the balance of fairness in relation to the remaining cultures in Canada' (cited in Turner 2006, 66). At the end of the day, then, Kymlicka offers only a highly contingent and contextually dependent right to governance and arguably nothing at all resembling a recognizable defence of Aboriginal sovereignty or 'inherent right' – precisely what Schouls claims is the inevitable result of governance and rights claims built on cultural difference (Turner 2006, 66–7).

Although Kymlicka's minority rights approach comes closer to the mark in terms of satisfying Aboriginal governance and self-determination rights claims, it fails on two essential counts. Like Cairns' proposal, it largely assumes that the Canadian state and Aboriginal peoples – whose unequal bargaining power as has been recognized repeatedly since at least the time of the Penner Report (Canada, House of Commons and Penner 1983) – can simply 'put aside the past' and ahistorically chart a future that ignores the colonial legacy. Second, nothing in the Kymlicka 'solution' requires the participation of Aboriginal peoples in *defining* the meaning and terms of the minority governance rights to which they are entitled. To paraphrase a well-known French maxim, Aboriginal groups can 'propose,' but the Canadian state will 'dispose' when it comes to deciding which rights claims should be honoured, how, under what conditions, how long, and so forth.

The task of defining what section 35(1) entrenches has fallen to two groups, the courts and those involved in land settlement and treaty negotiation activities. That fact alone speaks volumes about the importance of Aboriginal peoples recognizing 'Kymlicka's constraint' and of addressing the question to which Turner turns his attention in what we, as members of the education community, find the most compelling part of his analysis, namely, what can be done to change the *attitudes* of those with power in deciding the fate of Aboriginal rights claims.

Turner insists that all three liberal approaches – 'White Paper liberalism,' Cairns' citizen plus liberalism, and Kymlicka's minority rights view of Aboriginal rights – are not, as he aptly characterizes them in the context of his work, 'peace pipes.' They are not, in his view, for four reasons:

1. They do not adequately address the legacy of colonialism.
2. They do not respect the sui generis nature of indigenous rights as a class of political rights that flow out of indigenous nationhood and that are not bestowed by the Canadian state.
3. They do not question the legitimacy of the Canadian state's unilateral claim of sovereignty over Aboriginal lands and peoples.
4. Most importantly, they do not recognize that a meaningful theory of Aboriginal rights in Canada is impossible without Aboriginal participation. (Turner 2006, 7)

It is obvious from this indictment of the three mainline liberal approaches to Aboriginal rights claims that Turner views recognition of Indigenous nationhood and sovereignty as a *sine qua non* of any real 'peace pipe' resolution to such claims.

He goes further yet, so far as to laud the overtly separatist call of Aboriginal writers like Taiaiake Alfred who believe that 'indigenous peoples possess the unilateral ability to withdraw from the colonial relationship' by simply turning their back on the colonizers and their institutions, most notably INAC in Canada, as a 'courageous stance.' This is part of a tradition that includes Vine Deloria, a 'venerated Lakota thinker' who is also 'strongly critical of mainstream intellectual culture' (Turner 2006, 107).

Turner (2006) is realist enough, however, to acknowledge that in the end, 'the state's legal and political processes are, in many ways, "the only game in town"' (111). Therefore, Aboriginal peoples must engage the dominant culture in a 'dialogical' process (108), in short, enter into a meaningful, evolutionary, developmental *relationship* with settler governments and the people they represent.

If Aboriginal peoples want to claim that they possess different world views, and furthermore, if they want to assert that these differences ought to matter politically in the Aboriginal–Canadian state legal and political relationship, *then* they must engage the Canadian state's legal and political discourses in more effective ways. We need to find ways to shape the legal and political relationship so that it respects indigenous world views while generating a useful 'theory' of Aboriginal rights (99; emphasis in original). The resonances of this prescription with what Schouls calls 'relational pluralism' is more than striking.

For such relation-building to occur, Turner (2006) claims repeatedly, nothing will suffice other than to change the *attitudes* of the newcomers, especially those with political, policy, and judicial power. In particular, no amount of demonstrating the equality or even the superiority of Aboriginal legal or governance practices will have much impact (111). But how can Aboriginal peoples hope to influence those attitudes where they count? How, practically speaking, might they 'engage the Canadian state's legal and political discourses in more effective ways' (5)?

The sole hope for progress in meeting this Kymlicka constraint challenge, in Turner's view, is to nurture what he calls 'word warriors.' Distancing himself from Aboriginal writers who believe that all Aboriginal intellectuals need to do is assert and live the power of Aboriginal ways of knowing, Turner (2006) insists that 'instead of carving out their own communities and asserting their intellectual sovereignty within them, Aboriginal intellectuals must develop a community of practitioners *within* the existing dominant legal and political intellectual communities, while remaining an essential part of a thriving indigenous intellectual community' (90; emphasis in original).

Of course Turner (2006) acknowledges that the real problem is '*how* to establish a thriving Aboriginal intellectual community. This will be especially difficult in more conservative fields such as law, philosophy, economics, and political science' (91; emphasis in original). Turner's challenge is, of course, formidable – and very much long term – as he notes in regard to Bruce Trigger's call for a professional collegiality that would displace the current distinction between historians and anthropologists on the one hand and Native people on the other. Turner surveys the obstacles astutely. 'For most Aboriginal students,' he notes,

> the university remains a hostile environment. Most of the course content encountered by Aboriginal students at universities focuses on Aboriginal peoples as objects of study. Many Aboriginal university students still experience residential-school attitudes, and therefore do not finish their degrees. Trigger's collegial community would consist of well-educated, publishing PhD's; unfortunately, most Aboriginal students do not graduate from high school. (Turner 2006, 91)

However difficult to nurture, the need for such deep Aboriginal presence in the intellectual community of society as a whole

> is a sad, brutal consequence of the Aboriginal–European newcomer relationship. For far too long, Aboriginal peoples have had to use European discourses of rights to explain their place in the political relationship. To renew the relationship by returning Aboriginal voices to their rightful places will take some time. Following Neurath, we will have to rebuild our ship while we are still at sea – one plank at a time. For word warriors to fulfill their responsibilities effectively, they will have to know their way around European intellectual traditions *and* [emphasis in original] know how these traditions have affected Aboriginal intellectual landscapes. Finally, their intellectual labour will have to be useful. That is, the intellectual community will have to be part of a larger and more effective indigenous political machinery, one that is able to assert and protect rights we believe we possess. (Turner 2006, 91–2)

In one sense, Turner (2006), following James Tully, views word warriors as 'mediators,' 'an indigenous person who engages the imposed legal and political discourses of the state guided by the belief that the knowledge and skills to be gained by engaging in such discourses are necessary for the survival of all indigenous peoples' (92), and exilic intellectual but still closely connected to his/her community and its intellectual tradition. The difficulty of the task of such word warriors is comparable to that of a much extended, lifelong in fact, vision quest –

only with much of the quest taking place on European intellectual and philosophical terrain.[24]

Turner warns, however, that it is not enough for word warriors to weave themselves deeply into the fabric of the European intellectual tradition and its 'forms of knowledge' (see, for example, Hirst 1974; Hirst and Peters 1970). They must 'make the indigenous voice the centre of ... [their] intellectual life' (Turner 2006, 105). To speak critically for themselves, however, Aboriginal intellectuals require a rigorous *critical* intellectual environment (105). Turner insists that 'a healthy indigenous intellectual culture must *include* the discourses that have evolved out of the so-called traditional disciplines, many of which have arisen as responses to the oppressive nature of Eurocentric academic disciplines' (106). Word warriors must be steeped in those disciplines so they can engage their discourses. Thus Turner calls for

> greater [Aboriginal] intellectual participation in mainstream academia, although this is not the whole answer to the difficult question of how to generate a rigorous indigenous intellectual culture. If we take seriously the idea that protecting indigenous nationhood is a priority for an indigenous intellectual culture, we need to be able to speak and write convincingly in indigenous terms *and* be able to change how these arguments are used in the institutions of the state. Indigenous intellectuals must be both philosophical *and* political. (106; emphasis in original)

For Turner (2006) the ideas generated by rigorous Aboriginal intellectual activity 'mean little,' however, 'if these ideas do not lead to transformations in indigenous nations. Those nations require intellectual leaders and political leaders to work together' (106).

What, then, in the last analysis, should Aboriginal intellectuals *do*, in Turner's view?

> First, they must engage colonialism in its physical and intellectual contexts and in the process strive to overcome the colonial mindset in both indigenous and non-indigenous communities. Second, they must protect and defend our 'indigeneity'; that is, they must work to ensure that indigenous ways of knowing the world are not devalued, marginalized, or ridiculed in the marketplace of ideas. Third and finally, an indigenous intellectual community must assert and defend the integrity of indigenous political rights in the legal and political discourses of the state. (Turner 2006, 113)

Figure 2.4 A historically respectful, relational liberal social theory

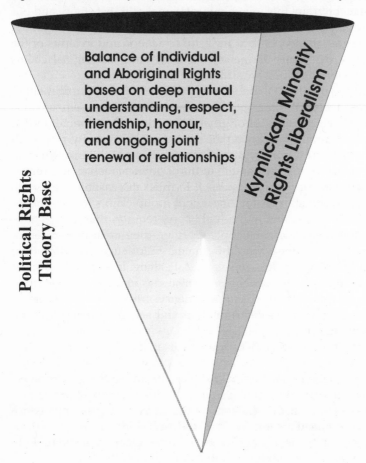

Especially, of course, Aboriginal intellectuals must lead potential future Aboriginal scholars along the intellectual path. 'By showing our young minds that they can participate as intellectual equals in the world without giving up who they are as indigenous peoples, we will empower ourselves to someday return our ways of knowing the world to their rightful place in the landscape of human ideas' (Turner 2006, 117).

Figure 2.4 reflects our position on a viable political rights theory as a basis for working towards Aboriginal self-determination and, with it, Indian control of education (see NIB 1972/1984). Like Turner, we do not presume to know the details of how such a theory would work out over time. We can only say that, given our relational pluralist stance and our pragmatism, we reject any one-size-fits-all solutions to questions about Aboriginal governance, both in terms of education and in terms of the broader self-governance framework within which Aboriginal claims for control over education are situated.

Figure 2.4 shows, on the one hand, that we don't believe that either what Turner labels 'White Paper liberalism' or the Cairns 'citizen plus' approach to dealing with Aboriginal rights claims has much to offer. On the other hand, we believe that the Kymlicka minority rights adaptation of the classic individualist liberal theory, while insufficient, provides at least a starting point in terms of political reasoning situated within the liberal approach to justice. Kymlicka's reasoning, after all, provides two critical bases for Aboriginal group claims to governance rights. First, it argues that individual liberty requires that groups have adequate resources and capacity to carry on their collective existence and activities (otherwise would-be members of such groups cannot choose to belong to them), and second, it recognizes that Aboriginal peoples, as one of the 'national minorities' (founding peoples) that merged with two others to create the Canadian state, have a stronger claim to the right of self-determination and self-governance than do non-national minorities.

Turner criticizes the Kymlicka adaptation of liberal theory for its ahistorical assumption that we can leave the colonial legacy out of renewing relationships between Aboriginal peoples and the settler governments and for the absence of any requirement that Aboriginal peoples participate in defining the meaning and terms of the minority governance rights to which they are entitled. We, too, find it insufficient as a theoretical basis within the precepts of liberal democracy for responding to Aboriginal self-determination in education and in other areas.

In sum, details both of overall self-government and self-determination arrangements, including those affecting education, should be context-specific and should be worked out case by case in the course of renewing relationships between Aboriginal peoples and settler governments. To say this, of course, in no way precludes functional integration at the regional and Canada-wide levels. Those involved in such renewal need to be sensitive, however, to both context and history. All we can really do is provide a general description of what we consider to be the essential values for such renewal. Foremost among these values is mutual respect – and such respect must recognize the current power imbalance between the Canadian state and Aboriginal peoples. It must recognize also the significance of that imbalance in creating reasonable and useful 'boundaries' to protect Aboriginal communities and peoples from interference in their internal affairs by the federal and provincial governments.

Other necessary principles include mutual understanding, friendship, honour, and commitment to ongoing renewal, but renewal that respects the past in an honourable way. The kind of understanding needed here can only be built through the efforts of word warriors, in Turner's sense, on the Aboriginal side and through integrity, openness, and good faith on the settler governments' side. Such relationship renewal, moreover, needs to succeed in creating appropriate 'boundaries' within which Aboriginal communities and groups can exercise governance over education and other social policy domains.

Overall, then, the conceptual framework with which we propose to take measure of how policy has affected Aboriginal education over the last generation will have the general form shown in figure 2.5. At the broadest theoretical level, the top layer in our figure, provides a framework which takes the values, assumptions, and way of doing things that Bertrand and Valois (1980) assign to the symbiosynergetic paradigm as the dominant, although not the only, aspect of the sociocultural context of education – as of self-determination more generally. Consistent with this adherence to a symbiosynergetic orientation, we believe that Aboriginal education is best understood from within the inventive-paradigm and its ideas of the nature and process of education. At the same time we recognize that some reliance on person-centred assumptions and processes will be necessary and appropriate. We acknowledge that Aboriginal students need to be able to work in and contribute to mainstream Canadian society and its economy while providing significant input into how to transform that paradigm into one focused on sustainable relationships among individuals, communities, and environments.

We take relational pluralism as the socio-political theory nucleus around which issues of identity and the place of culture within it should be understood. The focus should be ongoing renewal of malleable relationships that balance individual and group identities in such a way that individuals are free to construct unique personal identities with adequate 'boundaries' in place to protect the integrity of *evolving* Aboriginal cultures. Culture should influence how group members identify but, conversely group members, *all* group members – including wom-

Figure 2.5 Overall conceptual framework

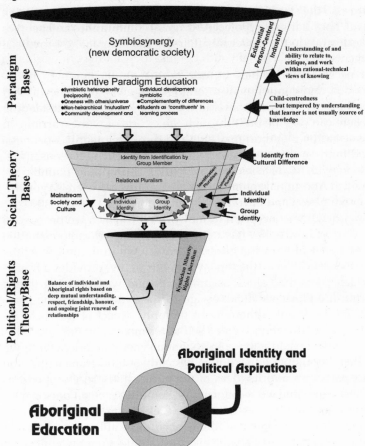

en, youth, and urban-dwelling members of First Nations communities and not just a community or regional elite – should be empowered to participate in shaping the evolving identity of their community and culture.

Finally, binding but flexible agreements can renew relationships between Aboriginal groups and the Canadian and provincial governments. These can be achieved through the efforts of word warriors (as well as number warriors, science warriors, and so on), and through committed Aboriginal leaders who work with both Aboriginal intellectuals, and with influential persons of good faith within mainstream political and legal systems. In such a political rights theory context, we believe that self-determination in education and other social policy and cultural domains can lead to high-quality Aboriginal education that prepares Aboriginal youth not just to 'walk in both worlds' (a now hackneyed, tattered, and unhelpful term in our view) but also to contribute in exciting, innovative, and philosophically and politically important ways to the course of history by helping to make society ecologically and socially sustainable.

This conceptual framework provides us with a standard of sorts against which to assess past and proposed Aboriginal education policy. How and to what degree does policy reflect these perspectives and support and put into practice these principles? How and to what degree does it move Aboriginal peoples, the Government of Canada, and provincial governments towards renewed relationships of mutual respect and creative interdependence, towards boundaries around education and other social programs and activities of a cultural nature that are both 'closed' and 'open' in appropriate ways?

From Concept to Vision and Practice

However practical a good theory may be, it does not necessarily entail a clear vision of where one hopes to go. Having such a vision, moreover, is one thing, but realizing it is distinctly another. We believe that the conceptual framework we have outlined in this chapter represents a solid place to stand for the future of Aboriginal and First Nations education in Canada. The very nature of that framework should signal clearly that we do not believe that there is one, uniform, 'best practice' solution for creating and maintaining educational policy and practice for Aboriginal education. Rather, Aboriginal people themselves, in choosing, crafting, and recrafting their collective and individual identities should shape educational programs and services appropriate to their identity visions.

They should also have the policy and resources to do so. Given the imperative of 'Kymlicka's constraint,' however, Aboriginal education leaders will need to convince not only themselves of the value and worth of the identities and educational vision they seek to build but also those with power over resources and opinions in mainstream Canada of their worth.

Finally, the most brilliant vision and excellent practice can, in a particular context, go badly awry. Circumstances can change over time and what works admirably at one moment in time can be patently dysfunctional in another. Educational policy is fraught with uncertainty, more art than science. Public policy – and especially educational policy, given education's notoriously 'inexact technology' – never offers straightforward cause-and-effect relationships. The history of educational policy is littered with failed attempts to apply 'production function' logic and methods to it. Despite all this, no one involved in education in our accountability-driven times can be indifferent to outcomes and results. In both the public mind and in legislative logic, the 'bottom line' in education, as in any public policy arena, lies in policy outcomes and results. We need to attend carefully, then, to the vision we propose for Aboriginal education in the wake of our analysis. We need to weigh carefully the 'results' implied in such a vision and to search carefully and critically for plausible ways to tighten the linkage within that vision among policy, practice, and results. This we shall do at length in our final chapter.

3 Policy Context: Competing Discourses and Evolution of the Policy Context of First Nations Education

The preceding chapter reveals that a host of discourses have evolved around the question of Aboriginal peoples and their place in Canadian Confederation. As we have shown, these discourses range from the unabashed assimilationism of 'White Paper liberalism' at one extreme to a balance of individual and collective identity choice through relational pluralist assumptions at the other.

Aboriginal and First Nations education has been and continues to be torn by competing discourses surrounding Aboriginal identity (both individual and collective), sovereignty, nationhood, and place within Canada. Our principal focus here is the evolving policy context of First Nations education in terms of rights, control, and funding.

A People in Receivership – of Treaties, Reserves, Colonization, and 'Devolution'

Conceptually, the term 'receivership' is a close opposite to empowerment, autonomy, and self-determination. Bankruptcy receivers, after all, step in to administer the assets, liabilities, and obligations of individuals and corporate entities (public as well as private) recognized by the law as no longer able to look after 'their own *affairs*.'

Colonizers implemented receivership policies for Indigenous peoples from the very beginning of European colonization. This colonizer-imposed receivership pre-structured First Nations political and social life in ways that marginalized First Nations visions of the human good, ended nearly all autonomous agency on their part, and silenced their voices into the bargain. Furthermore, as Battiste (1998) notes, receivership policies were based on the following notion of being 'socially just':

Each really believes that their [sic] unequal relationship is part of the natural order of things or desired by some higher power. The dominator does not feel that he is exercising unjust power, and the dominated do not feel the need to withdraw from his tutelage. The dominator will even believe, in all good faith, that he is looking out for the good of the dominated, while the latter will insist that they want an authority more enlightened than their own to determine their fate. (79)

The semantics here are striking. Aboriginal peoples were deemed incapable of continuing to manage their own 'affairs' and thus in need of some form of protection, just as a corporation can need protection from creditors in order to restructure – or even to simply dissolve under orderly bankruptcy procedures. Thus, the fathers of Confederation included 'Indians, and Lands reserved for the Indians' as an area of federal responsibility in the *British North America Act* (BNA),[1] and appointed the federal government as the guardian responsible for their survival and welfare in what was a receivership type of relationship. This receivership logic, deemed essential to orderly development and settlement of Canada, framed the whole treaty and reserve system as we know it, along with the residential school system, with its cultural and linguistic extinction and replacement agendas as an integral component. That logic was bankrupt morally, spiritually, and ethically, especially in terms of fundamental justice. It is hardly surprising that the 'school system' created from it was a massive 'structural failure,' and not simply because of chronic and severe underfunding.

By the 1960s, the failure of that school system, if not of the receivership logic that underpinned and justified it, was evident to all informed observers. The Hawthorn report[2] summarized and critiqued the existing First Nations receivership package, and laid out a 'new and improved' version endorsed by the Department of Indian Affairs and Northern Development (DIAND, later renamed Indian and Northern Affairs Canada, INAC) at the time. After Confederation, the government and its Indian agents had concluded that minimal literacy and numeracy was about all Aboriginals needed to survive 'on reserve' which, in any case, was about the only place they could.[3]

Times had changed, however, and lives of quiet desperation in seclusion on reserves no longer sufficed for all, or even most Indians. Quite the contrary, the inability to find or create any 'economic base' on most reserves led to a 'new ideology,' being proposed by the government: assimilation (although the Hawthorn Committee and its participants preferred to speak in terms of 'integration'). This would be a cultural and identity 'final solution' to the 'Indian problem.'

> The new ideology favours progressive integration of the Indians within the entire Canadian family from sea to sea. Since the various Indian groups across Canada occupy widely differing economic and social positions, the time required for the process of acculturation and integration will vary considerably from one group to the next. The ultimate aim is as follows: that the Indians be considered on the same footing as the other citizens of the country and that they enjoy the same services and the same standard of living. With this aim in view, the governments will encourage greater participation by the Indians in the management of their own affairs until they are able to assume full responsibility for them. School integration, which allows Indian children to attend the same schools as non-Indians is being encouraged as the principal means of achieving complete social integration. The new policy tends then to encourage as much as possible the attendance at joint schools by Indian children. Curricula are also being planned on an integrationist basis. (Hawthorn, Tremblay, and Bownick 1967, 41)

The Hawthorn definition of integration reflects an essentialist view of culture, that it is 'fixed,' and needs to be preserved at least in part, but that it is only one priority on the Aboriginal education list: 'By integration of the Indians, we mean their full participation in the economic and social life of Canada, together with the *retention* of some of their cultural *characteristics* such as pride of origin, knowledge of their history, passing on of their traditions and preservation of their language' (ibid., 28; emphasis added). 'Integration,' meaning 'full participation in the economic and social life of Canada,' was the order of the day. However, such integration was conceivable to the Hawthorn Committee only within mainstream concepts of person and society, rights and fairness, and principles of justice, along with the values that underpin them. Integration actually meant hierarchical pluralism, in which a pluralistic model of social, governmental, economic, and cultural organization systematically reduced First Nations communities to dysfunctional dependency. Nonetheless, the Hawthorn Committee did question at least once whether the DIAND position on integration was actually a thinly disguised effort at assimilation.

This philosophy, however, displays several flaws or omissions and ambiguities. The government's policy on the preservation of the Indian languages and cultural traditions, for example, is not clear. As a general rule, they are not assigned much importance. This makes it difficult to distinguish between a policy of integration and a policy of assimilation, which allows the loss of the basic cultural values of the integrated ethnic group. (ibid., 41)

With regard to Indian education, the new order would be composed of two parts: schooling with non-Native children in provincial or territorial schools, and a more community-based style of local education for those parents who chose to continue to live on reserves beyond convenient busing distance from provincial schools.

Through such 'integrated' education, Canadian Indians were to be adapted to modern industrial life and the industrial paradigm that framed it (Bertrand and Valois 1980). 'The Indian Affairs Branch intends to educate the Indian child in the same class-room as the White child. To achieve this end, it will provide whatever is needed for Indian children to attend preferably public schools. However, it will retain different types of schools so that isolated Indian children will also receive an adequate education' (Reorganization Plans – Saskatchewan Regional Office cited in Hawthorn, Tremblay, and Bownick 1967, 79). At last, Indians would 'benefit from the same educational services as other citizens' (65). However, in this way *Aboriginal capacity for self-direction could only really be constituted, or even understood, by non-Aboriginal identities and self representations*. In this version of 'the white man's burden,' or as we shall characterize it following Steele (2006) 'white guilt,' *responsibility* for Aboriginal development could only lie with non-Aboriginals!

The strengthening of institutions beyond the control of Aboriginal communities was viewed as central in the development gospel of Aboriginal education. Such external control, however, was devoid of Aboriginal cultural, economic, social, and political context. It ignored other systemic and societal limitations on the capacity of Aboriginal communities to respond effectively and efficiently to the many challenges they were facing at that time. This focus on external control deprived First Nations of what was required for a healthy and sustainable Aboriginal education system that would enable their communities to improve their collective well-being. Such a limited vision of Aboriginal participation in education arrested capacity development and the growth of expertise within Aboriginal communities, *as well as aggregates of communities*. Aboriginal peoples were denied the opportunity to participate in their own development on their own terms. Exclusive reliance on non-Aboriginal expertise minimized Aboriginal ownership of development processes and rendered any useful changes that did occur unsustainable.

This 'repackaged' version of receivership as Indian education policy, and Indian policy in general, would lead to 'Indian people sharing the rights and responsibilities of citizenship and participating on the basis of equality and opportunity through the full spectrum of Canadian life' (The Administration of Indian Affairs, 6 as cited in Hawthorn, Tremblay, and Bownick 1967, 28). At last, Indians were to become *citizens like all other citizens*, precisely the White Paper liberal vision of where they 'belonged' in Canadian society – and they were to do so primarily through mainstream public education. The similarity with the intent of the White Paper could not be more striking. In the new order, hierarchical encapsulation would permanently exclude Aboriginal groups from genuine and equal political participation. The Hawthorn Committee foreshadowed and opened the political door to the possibility of the White Paper itself.

> The Government believes that its policies must lead to the full, free and nondiscriminatory participation of the Indian people in Canadian society. Such a goal requires a break with the past. It requires that the Indian people's role of dependence be replaced by a role of equal status, opportunity and responsibility, a role they can share with all other Canadians. (Chrétien and Canada, Dept. of Indian Affairs and Northern Development 1969, 1)[4]

The second part of the new policy direction proposed by DIAND at the time, which was reflected in the Hawthorn report, was to continue operating schools on reserves that were too remote to allow the busing of children to public schools. In these communities, *advisory* school committees would influence what happened in what remained, for the most part, federally operated 'Indian Day Schools.' Some DIAND officials, however, thought that these committees might even serve as the embryos of future school boards (The Administration of Indian Affairs, 49, as cited in Hawthorn, Tremblay, and Bownick 1967, 40).

Both complete integration of Indian youth into public schools and the continuation of on-reserve Indian Day Schools with purely advisory local school committees shared one key policy lynchpin – the decisions that mattered most would be made by the 'receivers,' (DIAND), not by

Aboriginals themselves. Some individuals in DIAND had an opinion favouring additional advisory input on education from status Indian groups at the regional level (Joint Committee of the Senate and House of Commons on Indian Affairs, Minutes of Proceedings and Evidence, No. 16, Queen's Printer, Ottawa, 1961, 5, cited in Hawthorn, Tremblay, and Bownick 1967, 27). But the Hawthorn Committee would prove to be one more external (non-Aboriginal) group that would comment on the receiver's prerogatives and conduct, and that would be the end of it. The process of policy – and educational – tutelage under DIAND receivership would continue, and leave First Nations with only the dubious power to *make suggestions* regarding the delivery of educational programs and services to First Nations students and communities.

And so it might have been if Pierre Trudeau and Jean Chrétien, then Minister of Indian Affairs, hadn't concluded in 1969, on the heels of the Royal Commission on Bilingualism and Biculturalism, and in the throes of passing the *Official Languages Act*,[5] that the time had come to 'normalize' relations between Aboriginal peoples and the Government of Canada. The normalization process would entail, among other things, repeal of the *Indian Act*, and termination of all special legal and fiduciary relationships between the government of Canada and First Nations people. Rather tepidly, the White Paper acknowledged the potential cultural contribution of Aboriginal peoples to Canadian society.

> Rich in folklore, in art forms and in concepts of community life, the Indian cultural heritage can grow and expand further to enrich the general society. Such a development is essential if the Indian people are again to establish a meaningful sense of identity and purpose and if Canada is to realize its maximum potential. (Chrétien and Canada, Dept. of Indian Affairs and Northern Development 1969, 12)

Aside from its distinctly 1960s rhetoric, the White Paper's acknowledgment of the importance of Aboriginal cultures is distinctly essentialist (Aboriginal cultures are what they are and what they were historically – end of story) and has more than a discernable paternalism, if not outright condescension to it. The tone and rhetoric of this statement, as well as its lack of any specificity about just what might be done to support Aboriginal cultures, is reminiscent of postmodernist deconstruction of the way in which 'culture' is often used within mainstream curricula.

> Culture has itself been implicated in a process of postmodern deconstruc-

tion. Postmodernist scholars have noted that culture is often viewed as what the inferior 'other' has. While some peoples have civilizations, philosophies, romance languages, or cultured societies; other peoples have cultures, dialects, worldviews, and tribal knowledge. Peoples with 'civilizations' are regarded as inherently superior to peoples with 'cultures.' (Battiste 2002, 16)

The White Paper was framed invitingly in conventional liberal sentiment about the primacy of *individual* equality.

This Government believes in equality. It believes that all men and women have equal rights. It is determined that all shall be treated fairly and that no one shall be shut out of Canadian life, and especially that no one shall be shut out because of his race. (Chrétien and Canada, Dept. of Indian Affairs and Northern Development 1969, 4)

Its bottom-line message to First Nations and their people, however, was 'termination' – repeal of the *Indian Act* and unilateral withdrawal by the federal government from its historic, and even treaty-entrenched, fiduciary responsibilities to First Nations.

In the long term, removal of the reference [to Indians] in the constitution would be necessary to end the legal distinction between Indians and other Canadians. In the short term, repeal of the Indian Act and enactment of transitional legislation to ensure the orderly management of Indian land would do much to mitigate the problem. (ibid., 9–10)

The White Paper and its threat of unilateral termination by the federal government of its special relationship with First Nations people in Canada galvanized them to a show of unprecedented unity equalled only once since – when Pierre Trudeau proposed to patriate the Constitution without Aboriginal input and without any guarantees that Aboriginal rights would be entrenched in it. Less than four years after the White Paper, they united to form the National Indian Brotherhood and vehemently rejected it. The first major act of the Brotherhood was to publish the report titled *Indian Control of Indian Education* (National Indian Brotherhood, 1972/1984). For the first time, most status Indian organizations in Canada spoke with one voice. They advocated for increased Aboriginal jurisdiction and control over education. This report called for the control by First Nations of education on reserves with provisions for complete jurisdiction and autonomy over education, and, to that end, called for First Nations representation on local school boards serving First Nations students. Their response to the White Paper was, in essence, 'no way' – but they singled out education as the platform on which to formulate detailed resistance to its termination agenda. Because of its subsequent significance to First Nations education, and federal 'Indian policy' in general, *Indian Control of Indian Education* (ICIE) deserves careful attention.

The report begins by recalling that in Aboriginal cultures, adults share responsibility for each child. Its authors call for education founded on 'pride in oneself, understanding of one's fellow man [*sic*], and living in harmony with nature' (National Indian Brotherhood 1972/1984, 1). They then articulate the values on which such education should be based.

> We want education to provide the setting in which our children can develop the fundamental attitudes and values which have an honoured place in Indian tradition and culture. The values which we want to pass on to our children, values which make our people a great race, are not written in any book. They are found in our history, in our legends and in the culture. We believe that if an Indian child is fully aware of the important Indian values, he will have reason to be proud of our race and of himself as an Indian. (ibid., 2)

In sum, the authors of ICIE summarize 'what Indians want' in the education of their children as the *reinforcement of identity* on the one hand, and 'training necessary for making a good living in modern society' (ibid., 3) on the other. In the view of the authors, the primary means towards these ends are closely linked: 'parental responsibility' and 'local control' (3). The authors expressly reject an 'either-or operation' (4), that is, an education that equips students to live *only* in a traditional Indian lifestyle, or *only* in mainstream society. Education is to be socioeconomically eclectic, and therefore culturally flexible and malleable – or at least accepting of considerable malleability in individual identity choices. We believe in education:

- as a preparation for total living
- as a means of free choice of where to live and work
- as a means of enabling us to participate fully in our own social, economic, political and educational advancement (ibid., 3)

ICIE pointed out the crucial characteristics of meaningful reassertion of Aboriginal control and jurisdiction over education. In our view, these characteristics include:

- in economic terms, growth in the capacity of Aboriginal education systems to prepare First Nations students to participate fully in the economic life of their communities and in Canadian society (Minister's National Working Group on Education 2002) and, in particular, to participate as equals in the Canadian economy (Royal Commission on Aboriginal Peoples 1996b, 608);
- in political terms, control of Aboriginal education is central to building the capacity of Aboriginal nations and their communities to exercise various forms of self-government (Royal Commission on Aboriginal Peoples 1996a); and
- in cultural terms, abandonment of the ways in which the non-Aboriginal mainstream Canadian society imposes cultural hegemony on Aboriginal communities.

Much in this statement accords well with Schouls' emphasis on the desirability of a relational pluralist perspective which recognizes that individuals and communities interactively fashion and refashion their cultural and intellectual identities over time, identities capable of mutual adaptation and co-evolution on the part of both Aboriginal and non-Aboriginal persons and communities. This statement of purpose explicitly rejected what Battiste (1998) calls 'manufactured identities,' based on Eurocentric assumptions which ignored and marginalized Indigenous world views, knowledge, and thought.

However, the authors of the ICIE failed, in our view, to take meaningful account of the impact of diseconomies of scale on the ability of 'local' First Nations communities to shape and direct their own distinctive educational programs. By treating 'local control' as a synonym for 'Indian control,' the authors ignored the inability of small communities to develop curricula, provide supervision, develop and administer programs, and so forth. In doing so, they left First Nations communities and organizations to discover these realities over time in the 'school of hard knocks.' Over time, First Nations communities joined together into tribal and educational councils, but the idea persisted – and persists today – that 'real' Indian control is 'local,' at the community level. Small First Nations communities continue to guard jealously most practical aspects of curriculum, school administration, and supervision, when the best interests of their students would be served by sacrificing local control to obtain meaningful functional and program control over what goes on in community schools.

The authors of ICIE maintained that the government's fiduciary responsibility in education – and hence in other areas of treaty and historical responsibility – were ongoing. Furthermore, this responsibility applied to all status Indians, whether they lived on a reserve or not. 'While we assert that only Indian people can develop a suitable philosophy of education based on Indian values adapted to modern living, we also strongly maintain that it is the financial responsibility of the Federal Government to provide education of all types and all levels to all status Indian people, whether living on or off reserves' (National Indian Brotherhood 1972/1984, 3). With regard to agreements involving funding and accommodation for Indian students studying outside of their own communities, the authors asserted again that it was the unqualified responsibility of the federal government to pay for such service, but insisted on the a priori right of Indian parents and their communities to decide how such money was spent.

ICIE left no doubt. Status Indians would stand their ground on federal fiduciary responsibility – and they would make education the centrepiece of that stand. Trudeau and Chrétien had two political choices available, flight or fight. They chose accommodation, although they failed to establish fiscal and policy frameworks that might have led to implementation of the major tenets of ICIE. On 23 June 1972, Jean Chrétien, then minister of Indian Affairs, delivered a speech to the Council of Ministers of Education of Canada (CMEC), in which he indicated that many of the key recommendations of ICIE would form the future basis for federal policy on Indian education (Indian and Northern Affairs Canada 1982, Appendix D). ICIE became the official policy of the Government of Canada in regard to Indian education, but the policy's implementation would prove more symbolic than real.

Devolution Debacle: Squaring Implementation Circles

Thus began a long and largely unsuccessful attempt on the part of the federal government to 'devolve' control over Indian education to local communities. DIAND summarized the departmental view of the essence of the new ICIE-inspired, post-Chrétien-speech policy in the following terms:

The education policy of the Department of Indian Affairs and Northern Development, adopted in 1973 and in keeping with its mandate and the expressed wishes of Indian people, is to support Indian people in ensuring their cultural continuity and development by providing Indian youth with the knowledge, attitudes and life skills necessary to become self-sufficient and contributing members of society. (ibid., 3)

The title and content of the DIAND report, *Indian Education Paper: Phase 1* (Indian and Northern Affairs Canada 1982) suggests that this paper was viewed within DIAND as the beginning of a new and more aggressive step towards devolution of control over Indian education to local First Nation authorities.[6]

Phase 1 begins by noting that 'The Department adopted its current policy on Indian education in 1973. This policy emphasized both the need to improve the quality of education and the desirability of devolving control of education to Indian society' (ibid., 2). The authors of *Phase 1* believed that four problems were at the heart of the failure of devolution over the preceding decade:

QUALITY OF EDUCATION
- Federal capacity in areas such as curriculum development, student and teacher support, and the monitoring of education standards was reduced as a result of the transfer of programs to bands.
- Indian education organizations were not supported or developed to assume the functions associated with provision of quality education.

INDIAN CONTROL
- 'Indian control' was not defined.
- Control was often transferred without adequate preparatory process.
- Deficiencies in the federal school system were not eliminated prior to transfer of control to Indian organizations.

EDUCATION MANAGEMENT FRAMEWORK
- The education management framework both in the Indian and federal school systems is inadequate when assessed against generally accepted management principles, and is significantly inferior to provincial structures.

FUNDING
- Implementation of the 1973 policy was approved on the basis that it would not result in incremental costs.
- Funding of Indian and federal schools is inferior to provincial funding levels, despite the relatively greater costs of meeting the special demo-

graphic, social, and economic circumstances of most Indian communities. (ibid., 2–3)

Although we believe the most fundamental and pervasive problem was the conceptualization of 'Indian control' itself, and that that 'problem' really encompasses all the others, we will discuss the problems identified in *Phase 1* in the original order they were presented by the authors. DIAND did systematically divest itself of the small curriculum and supervision capacity it had at the time. Indeed, as Yuzdepski (1983) points out, the government was determined to devolve control to First Nations groups with no additional expense. In the absence of 'new money,' funding for the administrative needs of band operated education authorities would have to come from dismantling the small program staffs that DIAND had in place at various administrative levels. Thus, in addition to inheriting schools and educational programs that were clearly substandard when compared to provincial norms, band operated schools which were, in most cases, former 'Indian Day Schools' that had been operated directly by DIAND prior to devolution, were thrust into the world with *no* program or administrative infrastructure whatsoever, and no resources to create such infrastructure. These communities found themselves completely alone and bereft of any means to develop the capacity to administer their schools coherently – much less in a way that would adapt provincial curricula to ensure 'cultural continuity and development.'

The real Achilles heel of Indian control, however, was Indian control. The authors of *Phase 1* rightly observed that 'Indian control' was never defined, not in ICIE, not in Jean Chrétien's 1973 CMEC speech, certainly not by DIAND's memorandum authorizing the creation of 'band education authorities,' and not by anything else emanating from DIAND or any other authoritative source. Worse still, the illusion fostered by ICIE that 'Indian control' and 'local control' were different sides of the same coin persisted tenaciously. This illusion translated into the facile proposition that if DIAND could pass direct management of the day-to-day affairs of schools to individual bands, authentic 'Indian control' would be achieved and DIAND would have successfully 'devolved' most of what really mattered in First Nations education to these bands.

Maintenance of the status quo rather than transformation of Aboriginal education was the main goal of DIAND, in spite of partial devolution of power to First Nations over education. 'Along the way, Indian control of education became synonymous with local control. Admittedly, the policy paper[7] was short on details in terms of what actually constituted Indian control. But local control as an objective was clearly enunciated in the document, and INAC cheerfully accepted this interpretation of Indian control because it·fit conveniently with its emerging policy on devolution' (McCue 2004,4).

What this simplistic view of Indian control failed to recognize, of course, was 'diseconomies of scale.' First Nations communities with small population bases (and that was the vast majority of them), would *never* have the resources to create their own curriculum, and certainly not their own cultural and Native language programs. They would never be able to provide professional supervision, and would be very lucky to even attract appropriately qualified principals. Only the largest First Nations communities could legitimately hope to engage in meaningful program and capacity development, and even they would be largely dependent on extraordinary funding and outside expertise in such matters. Nothing could change this inescapable dynamic of small units of organization having intrinsically limited resources for program and capacity development and professional infrastructure.

Over time, First Nations came to recognize that diseconomies of scale severely limited their ability to act meaningfully and coherently in educational policy and programming. As a result, many joined together in tribal councils, education councils, and associations, along with other venues of cooperation. Unfortunately, such collaboration has generally been less fruitful than it might have been. Nonetheless, it became more widely accepted that to accomplish anything coherent, much less culturally distinctive in education, cooperation among First Nations communities was required.

The *Phase 1* observations on the problematic 'management framework' for First Nations education raises issues within each of the other problem areas – and foreshadows repeated and increasingly vehement denunciations of the 'INAC management framework' (especially in education) by the Auditor General of Canada (2000a, 2004b, 2006), as well as equally persistent criticism by responsible parliamentary committees (see, for example Canada, Parliament, House of Commons, Special Committee on Indian Self-Government, and Penner 1983; Standing Committee on Public Accounts: 38th Parliament–1st Session 2005).

The very concept of a 'management framework,' raises the question of who is managing and who is being managed. If devolution is about passing on meaningful control to the local (or other First Nations entity) level, the question of the authenticity of the control conferred by such 'delegation' is hard to avoid. Delegated control is, at best, an oxymoron. Central authorities delegate *agency* – not autonomy (see Manzer 1994). The accountability of Parliament for the funds it distributes requires that Indian and Northern Affairs Canada (INAC), or whatever body is responsible for distributing funding for First Nations education, have a 'management framework' that assures reasonable value for the intended purposes of such investments. In other words, the relevant government department should have an effective management and accountability framework. Such a framework, however, runs directly contrary to the principle of 'inherent right' and is one horn of the perpetual 'divided accountability' dilemma of First Nations education. The *Phase 1* authors, who clearly recognized this dilemma, put it this way:

UNDER THE INDIAN ACT THE MINISTER IS RESPONSIBLE FOR INDIAN EDUCATION AND ULTIMATELY ACCOUNTABLE TO PARLIAMENT FOR BOTH THE EXPENDITURE OF PUBLIC FUNDS AND THE RESULTS ACHIEVED. RESPONSIBILITY FOR THE DELIVERY OF INDIAN EDUCATION PROGRAMS IS TRANSFERRED TO EDUCATION AUTHORITIES AT THE BAND LEVEL WHERE THEY SO REQUEST AND WHERE SUITABLE CONTRIBUTION AGREEMENTS ARE CONCLUDED AND WHERE BANDS HAVE HAD THE OPPORTUNITY TO ACQUIRE THE NECESSARY MANAGERIAL SKILLS. INDIAN EDUCATION AUTHORITIES ARE REPRESENTATIVE OF, AND RESPONSIBLE TO THE PARENTS OF THEIR COMMUNITIES WITH RESPECT TO EDUCATION POLICY SETTING, PLANNING, PROGRAM DELIVERY AND QUALITY. THE DEPARTMENT ADVOCATES ENHANCED INDIAN RESPONSIBILITY AND PARTICIPATION WITH PROVINCIAL EDUCATIONAL JURISDICTIONS. UNDER THE TERMS OF CONTRIBUTION AGREEMENTS, INDIAN EDUCATION AUTHORITIES ARE ACCOUNTABLE TO THE MINISTER FOR THE EXPENDITURE OF PUBLIC FUNDS. (27; all caps in original)

A decade after ICIE, the authors of *Phase 1* recognized that accountability for Indian education is irreconcilably split between Parliament and DIAND as its representative on the one hand, and First Nations communities and their band councils on the other. Added to that is the necessity of interacting with and conforming to (or at least pretending to conform to) provincial educational programs and curricula for a variety of reasons and purposes.

In addition to the deep and intractable conflict between parliamentary and community accountability, there remains the contradiction between 'devolving' control and authentic autonomy. This issue has become much clearer lately in the evolving literature and jurisprudence on inherent rights. Although the resulting literature and jurisprudence are becoming conceptually sophisticated, the bottom line contradiction is anything but complex: if a central authority 'devolves' power over something to a subordinate entity, that entity can exercise the power only as long as the central authority continues to delegate the power in question – and only in ways acceptable to the central authority.

In *Tradition and Education: Towards a Vision of Our Future – A Declaration of First Nations Jurisdiction over Education* (1988), the educational secretariat of the Assembly of First Nations found that Aboriginal communities had limited jurisdiction because the federal government had envisioned Indian control merely as managerial control of programs, not as a restructuring of Indian education. In short, meaningful power and authority remained with settler governments in spite of copious devolution rhetoric, with its supposed encouragement of community ownership, local discretion, and a decision-making structure more responsive to local needs.

Policy aimed at such devolution is managed through hierarchical encapsulation (marginalization and limitation of the autonomy of one group by another). In the context of First Nations policy, it renders First Nations ineligible to compete for higher or more significant forms of power within Canadian society by relegating them to the status of 'agents' of the federal government through devolved federal 'agency,' and a master-agent relationship. Devolution in the context of Aboriginal education legitimates inequality, which is viewed as necessary and appropriate within industrial paradigm assumptions (Bertrand and Valois 1980). Devolution takes for granted that Aboriginal communities should accept the norms to which they are subject instead of setting such norms themselves, which would involve both asserting their identity, and seeking to discover, modify, or achieve it.

The prospect of patriation of the Canadian Constitution in the early 1980s rekindled the First Nations' conviction that, despite Trudeau's admission on the heels of the *Calder* decision[8] that First Nations people might have more rights than the prime minister had suspected, his agenda on extinction and termination had never really changed. With a *Charter of Rights and Freedoms* that was likely to embody the essence of individualist liberalism looming on the horizon, First Nations leaders saw the spectre of 'White Paper liberalism' rising from its devolution ashes. Aboriginal 'rights' were simply off the radar of the patriation discourse.

George Manuel, then head of the Union of British Columbia Indian Chiefs, headed up First Nations resistance to this constitutional package offering no entrenchment of Aboriginal rights. In particular, he organized the 'Constitution express,' both a political pressure strategy, and at one point, literally a trainload (actually two) of First Nations leaders who converged on Ottawa on 26 November 1980 (Union of BC Indian Chiefs 2000). They went to the capital to protest what they regarded as yet another attempt at unilateral termination of federal recognition of Aboriginal rights and its fiduciary obligations to Aboriginal peoples. Several busloads of those who went to Ottawa on the physical 'Constitution express' went on to take their case to the United Nations, and Manuel and those on the train carried their case to Europe as well.

In the end, the efforts of Manuel and his compatriots prevailed, although for quite some time it appeared that their victory was largely symbolic, if not in fact Pyrrhic. Section 35 was added to the Constitution to entrench *existing* Aboriginal and treaty rights, but three conferences where the federal and provincial governments met with First Nations and other Aboriginal groups about constitutional entrenchment could not find agreement on defining the substance of that guarantee.

On the heels of a crippling recession in the early 1980s, the government of the day began posing a question that would soon come to be asked with increasing force and frequency: 'What are Canadians getting for the money their Parliament is investing in Indian affairs?' Keith Penner, Liberal MP for Cochrane-Superior, headed up a parliamentary inquiry into the state of Indian affairs in Canada, and, in particular, into the question of value for investment in the DIAND/INAC machinery. The Penner Committee was the first such government commission in post-ICIE, post-patriation Canada, although it would not be the last. Penner and his parliamentary colleagues produced a voluminous report, mostly in the form of sets of minutes from their hearings (Canada, Parliament, House of Commons, Special Committee on Indian Self-Government and Penner 1983).

The Penner Committee roared like a lion on the devolution question. Unfortunately, it gave birth to what had the earmarks of a mouse. The committee noted that Indian and Northern Affairs Canada was spending more than all foreign aid combined, but concluded that Canadians were getting very little value for that investment. The Penner Committee insisted that Indian Affairs be dismantled – and not from within.

In its place, the government should create a small body responsible for negotiating *global* fiscal agreements with First Nations groups. The committee cautioned that this dramatic change in the modus operandi of government interaction with First Nations would not remove the problem of grossly unequal bargaining partners. Nonetheless, at least it would dispatch Indian Affairs. In short, the committee members believed that the best thing Canada could do was negotiate sensible block-funding agreements with First Nations for all their programs, and let them allocate these resources themselves. Doing so would avoid passing all First Nations resource-allocation decisions of any consequence through the Indian Affairs bureaucracy, which managed to swallow the majority of the public investment in Indian (Affairs) programs.

The proposal to terminate Indian Affairs, of course, was much too radical for its time from several points of view. It would almost certainly have been perceived by First Nations leaders as one more thinly veiled attempt to push the termination agenda to completion. However bad the colonial, paternal *Indian Act* and its department might be, 'better the devil you know ...' What did emerge shortly after the Penner Report was an option provided by DIAND to bands and tribal councils for 'block funding,' or rather, two block-funding options: (1) Alternative Funding Arrangements (AFAs), which empowered the First Nations recipients to transfer monies along program lines (although not between capital and operations and maintenance) and could provide multi-year funding if desired by recipients; and (2) Flexible Transfer Payments (FTPs) which were similar to Alternative Funding Arrangements, except that they had no 'entrance requirements' in terms of band management readiness, along with less onerous reporting requirements. Flexible Transfer Payments allowed unexpended program funds to be transferred to other areas, (*although only with departmental approval*), required only a standard audit as opposed to a more detailed audit for AFAs, but imposed very detailed program requirements (Norman 1989).

The DIAND block-funding scheme was thus divided into a high-choice, intensive-audit-trail option, and a less flexible (despite its name), but also less audit-intensive option. At the time, DIAND officials hoped that this block-funding scheme would catch on and provide a viable and plausible way of at last closing the devolution circle by simultaneously ensuring that:

• The accountability of the chief and council to their Band members is enhanced ... [and]

- The Minister's accountability to Parliament remains intact. (Indian and Northern Affairs Canada 1986, 6)

In the end, the Penner Committee's findings resulted only in a little-trusted and subsequently very-little-used funding option.

Devolution, if not certifiably dead, had failed to take root in the post-patriation period. That outcome is hardly surprising, given all the things that were working against it – from organizational political economy to inertia, inadequate funding, and ongoing fixation on the local level as the primary legitimate locus for 'Indian control.' Most importantly, however, devolution began to 'wear' its oxymoronic nature more and more publicly. Devolved authority was not autonomy. It was increasingly recognized as nothing like an 'inherent right' to determine the nature of First Nations education, much less to determine the nature of First Nations themselves!

The concept of devolution is solidly grounded in the idea of hierarchy. Entities with authority can devolve, that is, delegate some decision-making discretion to subordinate units. They can also repossess it – or second guess it. Hierarchy is an integral part of industrial paradigm logic, and thus it is bound to rational or technological paradigm ways of thinking about education. It is completely opposed to symbio-synergetic-paradigm approaches for understanding society and to the integrative holism of inventive-paradigm understandings of the nature and purpose of education, understandings we have already indicated are much closer to traditional Aboriginal ways of understanding the construction of knowledge, the nature of humankind, and the place of human beings in the universe.

Devolution, moreover, is conceptually situated within the principles of 'White Paper liberalism.' Under 'devolved authority,' the government decides all that matters, sets programs, standards, parameters, and so forth. First Nations are there to implement government programs, 'not to create their own.' Flanagan[9] could live with this logic. Devolution simply does not offer a very promising strategy for renewing the relationships of First Nations with the Canadian state – in education or in any other program domain. As McCue recently summarized, the history of devolution:

Devolution, like local control of education, transferred a range of INAC programs from the department to communities with few if any intervening institutions or structures to assist communities with issues of capacity to tackle the programs' administrative and operational complexities. It also provided an illusion of control.

Devolution never equaled control – the programs and services that INAC and other federal departments devolved to First Nations were still controlled by Ottawa. Nowhere is this inadequacy and illusion more apparent than in elementary-secondary education. (McCue 2004, 4)

Post-1980 policies promoted Aboriginal control of education in the context of a model that privileged the integration of Aboriginal students into existing provincial delivery systems of educational services and programs. Aboriginal control of education was promoted as a means of encouraging political autonomy as well as economic development for Aboriginal communities – both considered at the time as critical elements of decolonization though devolution of power. The federal and provincial governments promoted self-government and control of education as a way to enhance the opportunity of First Nations people to enter the market society by liberating them from colonial constraints. However, the devolution concept of self-government provides only a form of neocolonialism, rather than decolonization. It denies Aboriginal peoples' capacity to formulate and pursue their own conceptions of person and society.

As a result, no real alternative options, along with attitudes, norms, values, perceptions, and beliefs have been targeted by any of the policy directions pursued with regard to Aboriginal self-governance in education. No substantive policy has emerged that aims to change and fundamentally renew Aboriginal and non-Aboriginal political relationships in the field of education. Instead, these policies pursue their quest to improve the efficiency and effectiveness of what was and is currently done without disturbing basic organizational features, and without substantially altering the way that Aboriginal and non-Aboriginal communities perform their respective roles in the power structure. These policies embodied no significant attempt to change the fundamental ways that Aboriginal educational organizations were put together, or the goals they were charged with achieving, especially learning and socialization goals, structures, and available roles in providing education to their people. Basically, policy-makers assumed that educational institutions governed by Aboriginals should be organized according to a simple template promoting accountability – at least in formal terms – with rules designed by a non-Aboriginal authority, notably provincial and territorial education ministries, an approach which obviously raises serious issues of legitimacy.[10]

It is no wonder that fifteen years of spin-doctoring failed to make devolution plausible as a mode of self-determination in either education or self-government. To the contrary, the policy thrust towards increased Aboriginal self-governance over education in the late 1990s and early 2000s has exacerbated existing fragmentation among Aboriginal communities. The notion of local control has mutated into a form that has deprived First Nations communities of the capacity to establish relevant, healthy, and sustainable education systems. These policy-driven dynamics of fragmentation continue to contribute to the plurality and dispersion of administrative authority, and to a looming authority crisis in Aboriginal education among both Aboriginal and non-Aboriginal communities. The capacity of local Aboriginal communities to cope with the dynamics of change and self-governance has decreased as the complexities and contradictions of fragmentation and diseconomies of scale have become more pervasive – and more significant, given the broader context of education in Canada and an increasingly globalized knowledge economy.

> Many First Nations students and communities face fundamental issues and challenges that are more prevalent for them than for other Canadians and may impede their educational achievement. For example, most First Nations communities are small, with fewer than 500 residents. Thus, their schools have difficulty providing a range of educational services. (Auditor General of Canada 2004b, 2)

Another fifteen years and several permutations on, block funding arrangements have largely failed to provide meaningful, useful education to First Nations students as well. But does any alternative to devolution exist if parliamentary accountability is not to be violated?

Aggregating for Service Delivery: Promises and Problems

Despite the ICIE legacy of fixation on the individual First Nations as the sole legitimate locus of authentic 'Indian control,' various groups of First Nations recognized over time that their only hope of making progress on a variety of policy and program matters ranging from curriculum development to special education and administrative services lay in collaboration. From the early 1980s, groups of First Nations communities across the country began working together through a number of cooperative structures, most notably education councils, tribal councils, and cultural centres.

Initially, DIAND was reluctant to recognize such second-level (as it later came to be called – an unhelpful misnomer at best)[11] activity because it entailed cost increases in a band operated regime that the government intended from the beginning to function without increased cost. Eventually, however, the sheer impossibility of individual bands undertaking certain kinds of administrative and coordinating activities (e.g., professional development, curriculum development, supervision, and, eventually although very belatedly, special education programming – institutional capacity-building still remains, for the most part, largely unaddressed) forced INAC to fund such organizations. Nonetheless, the scope of such inter-community collaboration needs to be significantly expanded if First Nations are to move closer to 'real' control over the education of their children. First Nations, as well as the government, will each have to pay a price for such collaboration, and we worry that neither party is convinced it can or should pay the required price. In our view, thoughtful, carefully planned collaboration is a necessary condition for meaningful control by First Nations people over the education of their young.

Given our conviction about the central importance of integrative, substantial, *functional* collaboration in First Nations education, at least in the sort of education that might plausibly claim to exemplify 'Indian control' in some meaningful way, we find Anderson's (2004) uncritical acceptance of the First Nations-as-locus-of-control in his contribution to the Union of Ontario Indians *Manifesto* chapter on second-level services troubling. In our view, it is a short conceptual distance from ICIE to Anderson's overall position on First Nations educational governance:

> First Nations communities are engaged in the process of developing their own system of First Nations education. This includes developing the many different agencies and institutions needed to support the delivery of a First Nation's educational agenda. First Nations communities and educators, not government administrators, must determine the nature and areas of responsibility of these second-level services.
>
> A relationship that guarantees an infrastructure that builds onto the current funding of First Nations schools, second-level services (support agencies) and First Nations institutions is needed for the delivery of all

educational services required to support First Nations students. (Anderson 2004, 2)

The real problem here is that Anderson and like-minded colleagues cling to the 'community base' language of ICIE. *Communities* are to develop *their own* systems of education. Then second-level services viewed as 'support agencies' should be waiting in the wings with a menu of appropriate services for each community's 'system.' What kind of school 'system' in any conventional use of the word, can a community of five hundred inhabitants operate? They can have a school, perhaps, but never *their own* school system. Even if a government were ridiculously generous in its educational funding to such a community, diseconomies of scale would forever prevent it from developing *its own* system.

And by what magic are 'support agencies' to arrive at the right time with the right expertise and support in the absence of larger, inter-community, long-term strategic planning? In our view, First Nations education and First Nations students, not to mention their educators, have already suffered far too much for too long from this kind of wishful thinking. Without careful planning by broadly integrative First Nations bodies, with representation from their constituent communities, the past is sadly foreordained to repeat itself. Program and professional development, when they occur, will be as it was in the past, not organized in any way. Such development will be project-based and hence sporadic, temporary, and without any enduring mark on the schools they are intended to serve. Institutional capacity development won't happen. First Nations education communities will be forever excluded from becoming learning communities that grow professionally, and will fail to develop appropriate teaching and support capacities.

A major problem with the ICIE legacy, in fact an integral part of its radically balkanizing and debilitating fixation on strictly *local* control, is that it promotes endless competition and turf wars over education among individual First Nations. Each community wants to *control* every aspect of education in *its* school, with the result that it controls next to nothing that counts. Instead of asking how we can collaborate strategically to improve the education of young First Nations persons in our area or cultural-linguistic group, those responsible for school operations and problems focus on protecting the 'turf' of *their* community school '*system.*'

Diseconomies of scale impose an inescapable no-pain-no-gain control paradox in First Nations education. That paradox, in fact, strikes to the heart of Indian/First Nations control issues. First Nations control of education cannot be addressed satisfactorily over the long term without conceptual and political 'closure' on just what is at stake in Aboriginal self-determination and how it might best be addressed. That is why we have structured our text within a broad socio-political framework.

Unless, and then only to the degree that individual First Nations are willing to, and are empowered fiscally and otherwise to collaborate in the *functional integration* of key educational infrastructure services such as curriculum development, administration, supervision, program support, and so forth, *First Nations control of First Nations education will remain an illusion*. ICIE had it fundamentally wrong. Furthermore, as McCue sagely notes, INAC was happy to embrace that error as a way of imputing First Nations approval to 'devolution' (McCue 2004, 4).

The political bottom line here is that First Nations must forfeit the pretense of comprehensive local control if they are ever to realize something resembling authentic Indian control. This is a hard truth but, in our view, an inescapable one. While some unusually large First Nations communities have been successful in establishing and maintaining some of the support services needed to provide reasonable control as a framework for exercising school-site-level discretion, none, to our knowledge, have been able to 'go it alone' and provide really satisfactory and distinctively First Nations educational programs and services. If First Nations control is the objective, *deep and comprehensive functional integration* will be necessary.

Schouls (2003) summarizes the broader dimensions of the diseconomies of scale problem in these terms:

> Many First Nations are small in both population and reserve size, making it difficult and perhaps unrealistic for some of them to administer the services and financial resources necessary for self-government. First Nations may therefore choose to delegate authority to political entities such as tribal councils in functional areas beyond their capacity such as policy development, higher education, and human resource training. However, it is First Nations at the band level that are invested with statutory political authority, and for this reason they are the focus of my attention. (54)

In our view, simply 'delegating' selectively certain support service functions to an education or tribal council, while clinging to the illusion of a local, community-based educational system, has not been and will never be sufficient to provide a platform for meaningful First Nations control of First Nations education.

It is essential that organizations which provide the functional integration of services to First Nations communities be created with respect for the wishes and sense of identity of the member communities. Equally essential is the need to invest such organizations with appropriate professional knowledge, expertise, and skills – to create and foster on an ongoing basis development of the *institutional capacity* to deliver the direction and support needed. This means that the architects of such collaborative institutions must especially resist the temptation to use them as venues for 'pork-barrel' appointments to key positions of unqualified but locally well-connected people.

While we are convinced that meaningful First Nations control over First Nations education will likely require development of school-board-like entities, we do not believe that such entities should be clones of provincial or state school boards – nor do we believe they should adopt the goals and purposes of public school boards in their entirety. Rather, they should take the most desirable and useful features of school boards (and that will be many, in our view), add elements that are needed to support the distinctive purposes of Fist Nations education, and adapt the entire package to their specific purposes and context.

'Aggregation' and 'deep comprehensive functional integration' are not neutral words. To the contrary, they are heavily value-laden. Aggregation and functional integration suggest 'power,' and power in First Nations hands suggests purposes – and the ability to choose them. Purposes are anything but neutral. We see purposes and the capacity to choose them as central to the aggregation and functional integration of First Nations educational-governance entities. These entities should set the context for First Nations education, or at least that part of it over which they might reasonably exercise control. *They* should limit or expand the range of First Nations control over their education system – within which ends and means are framed, alternatives pondered, and educational choices made.

Clear and well-articulated purposes permit the pursuit of certain values in ways of being, acting, and communicating. Aggregation and functional integration are background conditions necessary for authentic and meaningful First Nations control over First Nations education. They constitute second-order change that shapes, assists, permits, or inhibits particular courses of action. They are not, however, first-order change that transforms, fosters, or shapes major courses of policy action. The distinction between the two types of change is important. It differentiates between the operation of *self-governing* First Nations educational entities and that of 'agents' of policy crafted by others. We believe that such a distinction prevents the reader from mistaking second-order for first-order changes, from treating the suggestion of aggregated self-governed First Nations educational entities as an unseen hand that would magically 'cause' First Nations communities to pursue desirable purposes or goals and undertake similarly desirable action without awareness of why they do so and *without taking responsibility for their conduct and choices*.

The First Nations Education Resource Conundrum:
Evolving Funding Policies in the Context of Diseconomies
of Scale and Fragmentation

> ... we also strongly maintain that it is the financial responsibility of the Federal Government to provide education of all types and all levels to all status Indian people, whether living on or off reserves. It will be essential to the realization of this objective that representatives of the Indian people, in close cooperation with officials of the Department of Indian Affairs, establish the needs and priorities of local communities in relation to the funds which may be available through government sources.
>
> National Indian Brotherhood, 'Indian Control of
> Indian Education' (1972/1984), 3

Financial resources for First Nations 'education' are framed by the devolution conundrum. On the one hand these resources are, with rare exception, provided exclusively by the Government of Canada under its fiduciary and treaty obligations to First Nations peoples. Yet, following the underlying principle of ICIE, those resources should serve the educational purposes of First Nations peoples themselves. In the case of non-status Aboriginal peoples, the conundrum is even more pronounced. Resources for the education of non-status Aboriginal children flow from and through the normal funding and governance of publicly funded, provincially mandated education. Both are geared towards and dominated by the needs and values of non-Aboriginals. Fundamental disjuncture exists, in a word, between the funding source and the desirable locus of control, hardly a portent for success in a world where he who pays the piper does, almost inevitably, choose the tune.

ON PLAYING – AND FUNDING – EDUCATIONAL CATCH-UP

First Nations education in Canada was born in penury. As Miller (1996) points out, the churches that ran the residential schools made do with frequently unqualified and incompetent, and not infrequently abusive staff, in considerable measure because Ottawa simply could not or would not pay for qualified, competent, trustworthy teaching and supervisory personnel in the residential schools (419).

Broad agreement exists that First Nations people are, for the most part, collectively and individually victims of a major educational deficit that is one of the major legacies of the residential system and of the penury and myopia within which it was conceived and operated. First Nations students are systematically *behind* – and they are not catching up very fast! In fact, the Auditor General of Canada recently concluded in a now celebrated claim about the gravity and tenacity of the learning deficit in question that, at the current rate of progress in closing the gap between the educational achievement of First Nations students and mainstream Canadian students, another twenty-eight years would be required to complete the process (2004a, 1). What is more, Minnis (2006) argues that educational underachievement among First Nations students is closely linked to 'rentier' dynamics in funding First Nations education. Rentier dynamics consist of one-way income flows deeply enmeshed in a patronage system without benefit to funders on the one hand, and without need for any significant social consent on the part of either Aboriginal or non-Aboriginal communities on the other. They lead to low educational achievement, precisely because of the low status of education, and consequently the low regard in which it is held. Within such dynamics, Minnis argues, educational underachievement among First Nations students is likely to perpetuate itself even as it has done in the immensely rich rentier economies of the (Persian) Gulf states.

A curious paradox of 'remediation'[12] exists with regard to the question of assisting students who are systematically behind, students who would today be captured in the generic 'at risk' rubric, to 'catch up' with their mainstream peers. This paradox is directly reflected in debates about how best to spend scarce public resources to assist such students. Leaving aside racist arguments that some racial and ethnocultural groups in society lag behind in educational achievement *because they are less able and intelligent* than other groups, serious questions emerged in the 1960s and 1970s regarding education as a social and economic 'equalizer.' Researchers and policy-makers questioned the ability of education in general and schools in particular to contribute significantly to closing educational achievement gaps among identifiable groups in society. The renowned Coleman study (1966), the largest quantitative sociological study ever conducted in education, concluded that schools have very little impact on student achievement, that in fact, most systematic variations in achievement are largely accounted for by family background. Not until some years later, as other researchers reworked the Coleman data, with notably smaller levels of aggregation (Coleman and his colleagues had aggregated to the district level so that school-specific differences in measured achievement were largely 'washed out' in the resulting analysis) did it become evident that schools matter – *or at least that some schools matter to some extent with some students,* who come to school with limited mainstream social and cultural capital.

The remediation paradox lies in the fact that it is remarkably easy to lose sight of what seems an absurdly simple and self-evident proposition: those behind in the education race must run faster if they are ever to catch up. Despite this self-evident proposition, remediation, be it in the form of 'remedial programs,' 'life-skills courses,' 'basic-level' reading, literacy, numeracy, and so on, generally functions on the principle that one must 'meet the student where he/she is' and then move *more slowly* than normal through the material so he/she doesn't get lost. But as Levin trenchantly observed (1994), this approach means the student never catches up, instead falling progressively further behind, and eventually becoming a dropout or a pushout. Furthermore, as Levin notes in the same piece, all evidence to date shows that the most effective and efficient interventions available are those like his 'accelerated schools program' or Slavin's 'success for all students' program (1993), programs that have a good track record in helping at-risk students avoid early reading failure. Conventional remediation, Levin argues persuasively, is a self-defeating strategy because it substitutes sloweddown, watered-down, dead-end learning for the accelerated learning very young at-risk students need if they are to avoid crossing the critical threshold of definitive early reading failure, failure to read before the end of grade two. The same argument, of course, can be made for remediation at any level, including secondary – or even tertiary – study. As stated above, a secondary student who is behind has to 'go faster' than his/her 'on-track' peers if he/she is ever going to catch up. The main difference is that research shows that school systems will get the greatest 'bang for their remedial buck' if they invest heavily in programs that reduce early reading failure.

How is all of this linked to funding? Governments provide 'vertical equity' funding for two basic reasons, first, to compensate for unavoidable differences in per-pupil costs encountered by different school jurisdictions (for example, high fuel costs in boards whose schools are in remote areas with atypically long, cold winters, or higher-than-normal administration costs for boards that must operate many small schools spread over a large geographic area, a high incidence of poverty or limited English or French fluency within a board's student population, and so forth), and second as program stimulation incentives (such as additional money for junior kindergarten, when junior kindergarten is not required by law). Among programs that draw program stimulation funding in different provinces and states are various remedial programs. Most are built around the idea of 'slowing a program down' to a pace at which at-risk students can work. Since students can't remain in school indefinitely, this practice inevitably results in truncating the program to fit the 'ability and motivation' of 'slower' students. So far, we are attending only to programs and courses conceived as 'remedial,' not to 'special education,' although the boundary between the two is porous and disputed, and has been the subject of much controversy, for instance in regard to targeted federal 'Title' programs in the United States.

Ideally, remedial programs in First Nations education should be based on assessment of the *cumulative* learning and skill development of each child. Therefore, such remedial programs should include measures to improve the quality of care and stimulation provided to children during their infancy and preschool years, as well as opportunities First Nations children have to learn in school, at home, and in the community during their elementary and secondary school years. Comprehensive, multifaceted, and integrated approaches to 'remediation' and improving overall 'well-being' at all ages from birth to adolescence could go a long way towards bridging the current achievement chasm separating First Nations youth from mainstream Canadian youth. The Health Canada Head Start Program might well serve as a point of initial coalescence for such comprehensive remediation efforts, but we believe the ultimate control, articulation of, and direction for such programs needs to come from authentic, duly constituted *functionally integrated* First Nations education entities, since the task is ultimately an educative one.

There are really two ways governments can respond through vertical equity funding to the needs of at-risk students. They can target support on particular remedial programs (such as English as a Second

Language) in which case funding is made dependent on the types of programs a board offers and on the number of students enrolled in them (or credit-hours taken in them, etc.). Alternatively, governments can provide funding to cover such needs based solely on some proxy index of local need. To return to the limited English or French example a government might choose, instead of funding based on ESL/FSL programs offered, to fund based on census data showing the proportion of families with home languages other than English or French within a board's area of jurisdiction. The index, of course, could be much more complex and take into consideration not only household language but also household income, parental education, and so forth. The fundamental distinction, however, is between funding *program* on the one hand, and funding *need* imputed on the basis of some readily available indicators on the other. In the former case, boards have an incentive (assuming the funding *level* is adequate) to provide the targeted programs; in the latter case, the boards can do whatever they want with the money that comes to them in respect to the relevant 'at risk' indicator set(s).

For our purposes, this distinction matters. First, we observe that INAC has historically been much more reluctant than the provinces to provide vertical equity grants with respect to learning needs and problems (including special education). Second, enticing boards – or First Nations educational jurisdictions – to provide remedial assistance for at-risk students can be either program-specific (e.g., a 'success for all students' grant applicable only to programs that are either recognized by Slavin's organization or can prove that they are based on and operate within similar principles) or need-indicator-based, in which case boards can do whatever they like with the money – although governments are always free, as some do, to set some general limits or 'enveloping' to such use.

Now governments can react with funding in one of five ways to the existence of factors disposing students to failure that do not fall within the bounds of recognized physical or mental handicaps or exceptionalities:

1. they can ignore such factors entirely,
2. they can fund programs that offer traditional 'remediation' (slower presentation and truncated content),
3. they can fund programs that offer 'acceleration' with a view to helping students who are behind catch up with their more advanced peers,

4. they can fund based on indicators of need and leave it to boards to decide how to spend the 'compensatory' funding, or
5. they can use some combination of options 2, 3, and 4.

Option 1 is generally unconscionable, although it might be less so if overall funding were very generous or if the particular need area in question was regarded as not terribly more important than other needs that are funded. Option 2 responds to the need but is more of a symbolic than effective policy response, since this approach to remediation, as Levin argues, simply allows the learning-deficit gap of students in such programs and courses to *increase* over time. Option 3 seems like the obvious choice if the objective really is to help students who are behind 'catch up.' It has just one problem. Accelerated programs tend to be very teacher-work intensive (that is, they require much individual, one-on-one help) and hence are *very expensive* to run. They also require a significant, long-term commitment on the part of teaching staff involved in them, which is not something one can legislate, or even ensure with incentives. Option 4 is only as effective as the use the board makes of the money. Option 5 mixes the benefits and liabilities of options 2, 3, and 4.

HOW MUCH IS ENOUGH: THE (TORTUROUS) QUESTION OF ADEQUACY
Funding adequacy is a problem that has persistently bedevilled politicians, policy- analysts, and students of public and educational finance alike. No definitive standard of adequacy exists – any more than a definitive, universally-agreed-upon standard of vertical equity exists – or ever could exist. Various 'time-honoured' approaches, as well as some much newer ones, warrant brief consideration before we summarize the current state of DIAND funding of elementary and secondary education for First Nations students and, the findings and conclusions of the Band Operated [Funding] Formula (BOFF) Group work. Each approach to determining adequacy in the funding of education has particular strengths and characteristic blind spots. More than any single factor (at least in North America), judgments arising over the last fifteen years from education-finance litigation in the United States have forced renewed attention, innovative thinking, and policy experimentation regarding adequacy. American courts have increasingly refused to consider equity as something that can be dealt with in the absence of attention to adequacy – and for a very good reason. In the end, as Schaefer (1990) concludes, quality cannot be said to exist without equality,

and equality without quality is not worth having. Equitable amounts of inadequate resources remain nothing more than fair shares of penury.

Perhaps the most basic, as well as the oldest and most widespread way of assessing adequacy is simple comparison. Generally, such comparison is either with the past or with other jurisdictions presumed to exist in an at least roughly similar context and to confront comparable needs and unit costs. Thus, one might use past mean or median per-pupil revenues and spending of a school board as a rough barometer of current adequacy. The problem with this approach as Dror pointed out some forty years ago in the first version of what became a policy-analysis classic (1983), is that circumstances, needs, and opportunities change over time. Past performance might have been, by current – or any – standards, unacceptably low. Standards also change over time. Policy and funding based solely on past practice, then, run the same risks as a driver absorbed solely in what she sees in her rear-view mirror – particularly if that driver is unsure if she really liked where she has just been.

The second most common and pervasive 'comparison' approach to adequacy is to look at mean or median per-pupil revenues and spending levels in similar jurisdictions. Those who seek to assess the adequacy of a province or state's per-pupil funding and spending inevitably compare them to current revenue and spending levels in neighbouring provinces and states, or in contextually similar ones, or with *all* other provinces and states. Just as families and individuals are given to using 'how well we are keeping up with the Jones' as one litmus test of how adequate their revenues and spending are, school boards look over their shoulders at their jurisdictional peers for the same reason. Of course, the problematic assumption here is that needs, costs, and general context are more or less equally distributed among jurisdictions, which they clearly are not.

Beyond these two 'direct comparison' methods lie two other generic approaches to assessing funding adequacy: resource-cost approaches, and output-cost approaches. The resource-cost approach to funding builds a finance model from two bases, a unit cost for each type of goods and services accounted for in the model, and the number of such units a particular board of education is deemed to require. The product of the former and the latter gives the amount of money provided for each itemized service or commodity. Thus, for instance, if one assumed that the cost of providing basic half-day kindergarten instruction for a student in an 'average' school board was $4,000 and if a particular

board had 100 half-time kindergarten students, its basic funding allocation for kindergarten would be $400,000 ($4,000 x 100). Resource-cost
models can, in theory, be very simple or very elaborate, although they
have had a tendency both to be complex and to grow in complexity
over time.[13]

Where do the unit-cost assumptions come from in resource-cost models? They can come from two different sources: expert-panel judgment,
or empirical data on past and current cost – or from some combination of the two. However, the key point to remember with resource-
cost models is that they are founded solely on equity and adequacy
decisions about inputs to the educational process. By themselves, they
are completely disconnected from the outputs and outcomes of the
educational processes they support. Although some outcome-output
feedback doubtless occurs in the judgment of expert panels and education officials as they decide the overall shape of a resource cost model,
nothing in the model is designed specifically to link inputs to outputs.

Theoretical funding models that have attracted the most attention
(positive and negative) from widely respected writers in educational
finance in recent years have sought to *link funding to outcomes*, hence
their generic designation as output-based models. The quest for such
linkage should come as no surprise in the 'lean production' ethos that a
globalized economy has imposed on education as it has on most other
public service areas. With accountability as the policy byword of our
time, the 'best minds in the business' have been drawn increasingly to
the problematic of doing not just 'more,' but doing 'better' with less –
or at least with less than would have been spent under other funding
models and assumptions.

Linking funding to outputs, however laudable it may sound as a
policy goal, is much easier said than done, especially in the complex,
value-laden, and technically uncertain arena of education. The human
capital idea that one could generate production functions which would
provide fail-safe mathematical relationships between inputs and outputs has long since lost its credibility – and not just in education (see
for instance, Blaug 1968). Life is complex and intimately context-bound,
education particularly so.

Beyond complexity and contextuality, another fundamental issue
confronts those who would link funding to outputs. What kinds of outputs are desired – and, equally important at the political level, what
kind of outputs do those with power and influence in a government
think it can afford? For instance, is the most desirable system-wide

'output' to raise most (however most is defined) students to an *adequate* level of achievement (by whatever indicators of 'achievement' a government adopts), or is it to raise them to an excellent level of achievement? Is the performance standard to be one of minimum standard adequacy, or excellence?

Attractive as they sound in a mainly industrial paradigm and accountability-minded world, three major problems vex the ostensibly simple and laudable ideal behind output-cost approaches to adequacy including attempts to link educational resources to outputs. First, it must be decided which outputs will 'count,' second, the problems of how they will be measured, and the standard(s) that will be applied to the selected measures, are difficult and controversial. These choices strike to the heart of the most perennial and vexatious question in educational policy, and one that frames debate among differing educational paradigm stances: 'what knowledge is of the most worth?' Its inescapable corollary, moreover, is equally persistent and contentious: 'who should decide what knowledge is of the most worth and why?' Huge variation exists in relevant contexts within which education occurs, and in turn leads to considerable variation in educational goals and expectations among national, provincial/state, and local levels.

Closely linked to the second problem is a third, namely *whether money matters*, or *whether it is mainly how money is spent that matters*. Does how money is spent impact educational outputs similarly across variations in context (social, economic, and cultural changes, for instance, that occur over time within a school catchment area, and so forth)? In our view, money matters, but so does the way in which it is spent. That said, production function analysis has failed to establish any broadly generalizable relationships between resource inputs and educational outputs. At present, we are hard-pressed to go beyond the limited findings available from human relations-based research (for example, studies in education inspired by Hertzberg's seminal work in the area). Such studies confirm that in education, as in other areas of knowledge, the work itself and its intrinsic rewards, such as satisfaction, praise, and respect, are on the whole more powerful motivators than 'hygiene' factors such as working conditions, salary, and benefits. However, the best studies emphasize that the situation in education is more complex than either a simple hygiene/intrinsic-reward dichotomy along Herzberg's lines (see for instance, Dinham and Scott 1998; Holdaway 1978; Nias 1981), or the contextually specific conclusions of the 'effective schools' research movement. In short, we find the method and conclusions of Hedges,

Laine, and Greenwald (1994) on the 'does money matter' question convincing, and thus believe that *both* the amount of money available (at least up to some threshold of diminishing returns on additional marginal expenditures) *and* how it is spent matter with regard to educational outputs. Nonetheless, we do not believe any credible *general* prescription exists for how to spend money in education in order to achieve desired outputs effectively and efficiently regardless of context.

Champions of an output orientation to adequacy disagree about whether the standard against which funding adequacy should be measured is 'average performance' or 'excellent performance.' 'Average performance,' while potentially more affordable, has the albatross of mediocrity around its political neck. Excellent performance is more desirable within the assumptions and priorities of 'global competitiveness' in the industrial/post-industrial paradigm and its associated educational paradigms. However, excellence can be expensive, particularly if linked to an expectation that many or even most students are to attain a standard of excellence – or at least educational 'rigour.' The troubling question of 'average' versus 'excellent' or 'rigorous' performance cannot legitimately be avoided here. This question forms an important nexus of the equity-and-adequacy part of the accountability debate, though it is rarely formulated in quite such direct and brutal terms. This question of equity-and-adequacy is particularly crucial for First Nations as they move away from models of colonial domination, assimilation, and integration to facilitate education for the next generation that is culturally, linguistically, and philosophically relevant and empowering (Battiste 1998). Within such a perspective, what is the meaning of 'excellent' or 'average,' and what would be the cost of achieving one or the other?

Must we be content, given available resources, to raise most (51 per cent, 75 per cent, 80 per cent?) students to an average level of performance, or should we be intent on ensuring that a small cadre of 'the best and the brightest' who will become serious competitors in a globalized knowledge economy get the very best education possible without much worrying about the quality of the education their peers receive? Clearly, not everyone can be 'excellent,' much less at everything, unless we are willing to evacuate the word of all meaning.

Odden and Clune (1998) have proposed two fundamental alternatives in regard to output-linked assessment of adequacy. First, they say, one could 'cost out' 'average performance systems,' and then construct a resource-cost model based on this exercise. In this way, the costing results would 'feed back' into the resource-cost schedule. Alternatively, one could cost out 'a high performance school design and ensure that each district/school receives sufficient funds for such a program' (164). The advantage of the former is a semblance of equity based on 'average' performance and relative affordability. The advantage of the latter is its appeal to the excellence ethos of our time, while its main liability is a cost likely to be greater than that associated with an average-performance standard.

Verstegen (2002) neatly contrasts traditional concepts of adequacy founded on entitlement to a guaranteed *minimum* standard of education ('basic education') with the current excellence ethos in discourse surrounding resource adequacy in education.

> Antiquated finance systems rest on a conception of minimum education – not a quality or world-class education. In the past, once the vision of the basic or minimum education was crystallized through state constitutions, curricula, goals, objectives and/or exit exams – it could serve as a basis for the state-funding guarantee. This approach, however, resulted in at least two problems.
>
> First, there was no clear consensus on what students should know and be able to do to formulate a basis for determining costs ...
>
> Second, school finance systems are flawed in theory and practice: 1) they drive wide and growing gaps in education quality and equality among more and less affluent school systems, 2) funding targets are not anchored in research or cost studies ... but are instead determined on a political rather than rational basis. (756–7)

Such antiquated, minimalist approaches to adequacy, she insists, must be abandoned in favour of understanding adequacy as providing an alignment of finance systems and high educational standards. She offers six steps to realizing such alignment:

1. Establish goals or objectives expected for all standards that reflect Constitutional[14] requirements
2. Develop curriculum frameworks linked directly to those standards
3. High-quality resources (human and physical)
4. High-quality professional development
5. Student assessment based directly on curriculum
6. School finance systems linked directly to state and national standards, goals, and assessment systems. (ibid., 761)

While supporting the idea and ideals of aligning resources with high-quality educational output, Baker (2005) underscores the importance of context – and of 'controlling for' context in a funding formula. He brings readers back to enduring concerns over vertical equity – and to the inextricable relationship between equity and adequacy. He reviews evidence on 'compelling consistencies' with regard to the extraordinarily high costs associated with helping at-risk and disadvantaged students rise to average or high standards of achievement. Economies of scale, he notes, produce a sharp per-pupil cost drop that levels off between 2,000 and 6,000 pupils in a school district or board. Furthermore, the marginal costs associated with achieving defined outcomes for children from economically deprived backgrounds, Baker (2005) insists, likely fall between 35 per cent and 100 per cent above average cost and may increase with scale. The marginal costs of achieving outcomes for children with limited English proficiency are likely to be around 100 per cent above average costs (286). Worse still, scale, student needs, and input prices interact to influence costs multiplicatively. In short, Baker argues, the cost of compensating for social, economic, and cultural disadvantage, for helping at-risk students 'run' fast enough to 'catch up' in the educational race, tends to be very much higher than the marginal costs for disadvantage built into most state (and equally, we would maintain, provincial) funding formulae (286).

In light of these realities, Baker recommends reshaping finance plans in accordance with resource or outcome-cost data. He believes that jurisdictions should replace pupil weights and cost adjustments with a single, aggregate 'cost of educational outcomes' index. Such an aggregate index could represent a significant departure from the past practice of 'piling up' vertical equity adjustments more or less helter-skelter depending on political influence, 'squeaky-wheel greasing,' and simply perceived relative importance of various special costs and needs. Of course, an aggregate index could also be no more than a 'repackaging' of existing vertical equity grants, but we believe Baker's insistence on a holistic view of special cost and need adjustments to be a step in the right direction.

Notwithstanding our endorsement of such holistic linkage of cost and output, we recognize the complex, controversial, value-laden, and politically sensitive nature of both educational outputs and educational spending. Indeed, Hanushek has recently provoked broad and intense debate on whether current approaches to output costing amount to anything more than econometric 'alchemy' (Baker 2006; Duncombe

2006; Hanushek 2005). There is no escape in the end, as Baker (2006) notes, from the dependence of all public source funding for education on economic context and political will.

> In the end, the overall level or absolute standard of adequacy of any state's public educational system will continue to be derived from the political will of legislatures, under the watchful eye of courts, in the sometimes tenuous context of fluctuating state economies. (260)

To no less a degree, it is sobering to remember that the overall level or standard of adequacy within First Nations education is currently dependent on the political will of Parliament and of its electorate. That is the inescapable significance of 'Kymlicka's constraint' to the funding of First Nations education within the devolution conundrum.

THE CURRENT STATE OF PLAY IN FUNDING ABORIGINAL
EDUCATION IN CANADA

Currently, British Columbia and Manitoba provide designated funding for the education of Aboriginal students who are not eligible for funding from the federal government, that is, for non-status Indians and for Métis and Inuit students. As well, Alberta and Ontario have recently added funding for Aboriginal education to their transfer grants to school boards. Alberta instituted such funding in the 2004–5 school year. Originally it was based on census data, but is being transformed into a grant in respect of self-identified Aboriginal students, although school boards are not required to opt in to a self-identification basis for the grant.

Non-status Indian, Métis, and Inuit students normally find themselves within provincial school systems on the same terms and conditions as other students served by these boards. While such students may benefit from the Aboriginal culture and language programs funded by some provinces, they usually do so under the same terms as non-Aboriginal students.

Federal funding for Aboriginal education generally takes six forms:

1. funding provided directly to First Nations,
2. funding provided to First Nations aggregate bodies such as tribal or educational councils, or cultural centres,
3. funding provided to the Katavik or Cree School Board under special joint arrangements with Quebec,
4. funding provided in respect of specific treaty obligations,

5. funding provided to post-secondary institutions for specific programs related to First Nations education (e.g., Native teacher education programs or tutor training programs), and
6. special project funding.

In general, federal funding supports the following activities related to
First Nations education:

1. the operation of elementary and secondary schools in First Nations
   communities,
2. tuition for First Nations students whose parents or guardians live
   in a recognized First Nations community (band) but who attend
   a publicly funded school operating under provincial or territorial
   statute,
3. operations and programs of cultural centres,
4. post-secondary student support,
5. post-secondary Indian studies programs recognized for support
   under Indian Studies Support Program, and
6. a variety of targeted special purpose and special project programs.

First Nations organizations have recently concentrated increasing
attention on the question of the adequacy and general appropriateness of INAC funding of elementary and secondary education for First
Nations students. In 2003, the Assembly of First Nations (AFN) and
DIAND agreed to collaborate on a review of the funding formula 'currently in use' (reasons for the quotation marks will become evident) to
fund elementary and secondary education for the children of parents
who reside in a First Nations community. To this end, AFN and DIAND
established a joint task force the Band Operated [Funding] Formula
Working Group. The working group involved First Nations representa-
tives from across Canada and Department of Indian Affairs personnel
(Hull 2005, 1).[15]

Historically, it has been very difficult to obtain information on how
INAC/DIAND funds First Nations education, as Paquette has experienced repeatedly. In one attempt to obtain such information, he spoke
directly to Mr Doug Forbes of INAC who, at that time, was coordinating the BOFF Group. In a personal communication by telephone on
27 August 2004, Mr Forbes confirmed that, in practice, no national
funding formula was currently in use. According to Mr Forbes, each
INAC regional director general was responsible for determining how

available funds are distributed and how they are allocated among programs.

Having made that important caveat about the pervasiveness of regional discretion in educational funding for First Nations, we turn to a brief description of the findings with regard to funding of First Nations education that Hull provides in his draft report on the BOFF Group work, a report which was never issued publicly in any form, and which was expressly disavowed by the AFN.[16] According to Hull, DIAND developed a set of funding policies and a 'funding formula' for federal and band operated schools in 1988–9 (Hull 2005, 9).[17] Hull confirms the central importance of regional discretion during the 1990s (9). He also insists, however, that funding to the regions was provided within a 'national funding model' composed of five general areas:

- instructional services for band operated and federal schools,
- student support services, for students attending band schools or other schools,
- operation and maintenance of schools on reserves, excluding capital,
- band employee benefits, and
- band support and tribal council funding. (9)

Within its numerous limitations and data challenges, the BOFF study attempted to answer the key question driving its simulation, namely, what First Nations 'systems' *would* receive *if* they were public schools funded in accordance with the transfer grant scheme ('funding formula') in effect during 2003–4 in the province where they were located. Application of the British Columbia 'funding formula' (transfer grant scheme) to First Nations school 'systems' there results in per-pupil funding that, at $12,950, stands head and shoulders above funding yielded by application of the funding formula in any other province in the study. The Ontario grant plan would, under the study methodology, have yielded $10,996 per-pupil, the next highest amount, while the Manitoba funding arrangement would have generated $8,386, the lowest total per-pupil amount to emerge from the BOFF simulation.[18]

Among the findings of the BOFF Group study, the most eye-catching result is the 21.5 per cent greater per-pupil amount generated by simulating the yield of the BC funding scheme on First Nations school 'systems' in that province. The BC funding formula would also have yielded 349.5 per cent greater funding of 'differential cost factors' ('vertical equity') such as remoteness and diseconomies of scale. These two findings are consistent in direction if not in magnitude with the results of a simulation exercise using a similar methodology (although the simulations in the latter case were based on only two fictional First Nations schools) undertaken by Matthew. She calculated that 1999–2000 provincial funding to her 35 FTE (full-time equivalent) simulated elementary reserve school would have exceeded estimated DIAND funding by 41 per cent and funding to her simulated 100 FTE elementary–secondary school would have exceeded estimated DIAND funding by 70 per cent (Matthew 2000, 29). In both cases, provincial funding in respect of economies of scale (and special education funding) would have accounted for significant portions of these per-pupil differences (ibid., 26–31).

The Alberta funding scheme would have generated 21.7 per cent *less* per-pupil than estimated DIAND regional funding, the Saskatchewan scheme 14.1 per cent less, the Manitoba formula about 23.1 per cent less and the Ontario grant scheme only 2.3 per cent less. Thus, the overall findings of the BOFF exercise can be summarized in the following terms: application of the provincial funding schemes in provinces included in the study, using the simulation methodology of the study with all its limitations and data challenges, yields about one-fifth more per-pupil funding than estimated DIAND funding in BC, about one-fifth less in Alberta and Manitoba, about one-seventh less in Saskatchewan, and almost the same in Ontario.

A joint First Nations Education Council of Quebec (FNEC)/INAC comparative simulation study concluded that the four FNEC communities in the study would have received per-pupil funding 25 per cent to 38 per cent (mean 29 per cent) greater than DIAND funding attributed by the study to these communities. Furthermore, even if only MEQ allocations were considered (that is, if local taxation was excluded), the study concluded that the Commission Scolaire de la Moyenne Côte Nord would have received 17 to 28 per cent (mean 20 per cent) more funding than DIAND was calculated to be providing, and the Commission Scolaire Eastern Shores from 4 to 14 per cent (mean 7 per cent) more (ibid., 101).

Furthermore, the same study concluded that applying Quebec Ministry of Education calculations for 'in difficulty' and 'severe' high-cost special education needs students to FNEC data would have resulted in $2,920 per-pupil more, on average, than was currently available from DIAND for such students in a sample of eight FNEC communities (102).

Using the methodology adopted in the FNEC/INAC study, applying the funding parameters used to set funding available to the Cree School Board, eight FNEC communities studied would have been eligible for total per-pupil funding increases that ranged from 16.6 to 126.3 per cent. Using the same approach, the FNEC/INAC Tuition Committee calculated that applying the funding parameters used to determine funding available to the Kativik School Board would have generated per-pupil funding increases ranging from 106.4 to 183.8 per cent for the same communities (104, 106).[19]

In sum, recent work on funding adequacy in First Nations education in Canada has generally taken the form of comparison of per-pupil funding levels with other jurisdictions, usually provinces or provincial school boards. Such comparisons are difficult both conceptually and technically. In particular, they involve many 'apples and oranges' comparisons that result in 'rough justice,' force-fitting provincial and federal funding into the same revenue categories, along with numerous data availability and quality issues.

Even so, overall evidence *based on inter-jurisdiction comparison* seems to point in the direction of per-pupil funding for First Nations schools that is somewhat to substantially inferior to that imputed to provincial jurisdictions. That is far from always the case, however, as the BOFF data from Alberta, Saskatchewan, and Manitoba clearly reflect.

BETTER FINANCING FOR ABORIGINAL EDUCATION

General agreement exists about the inappropriateness of using direct comparison to provincial funding as the sole means of assessing the adequacy of funding for First Nations education – even among those who have used comparison indicators.

In Hull's (2005) conclusions, he explains the rationale for a needs-based rather than comparison-based approach such as that used in the BOFF Group study:

> The differences between DIAND and provincial models in the allocation of funds suggest that some areas may be under-funded, while others may be over-funded. It is also possible that the high funding identified in some areas, such as operation and maintenance, reflects the costs of providing these services in band operated schools and that provincial models would not provide adequate funding in these areas. *It needs to be remembered that provincial funding policies are not necessarily an appropriate benchmark for funding First Nations schools* [emphasis added]. In general, the flexible,

non-prescriptive DIAND approach to funding, together with multi-year block funding agreements, has made it difficult to link funding allocation to needs. *Funding levels for band operated schools should be based on a systematic approach to assessing educational needs* [emphasis in original]. (52)

Similarly, Breaker and Kawaguchi (2002), on the basis of their review of 134 reports relating directly and indirectly to infrastructure and funding issues in First Nations education in Canada, concluded that policy-makers need to '[r]ethink funding from formulae driven to needs driven [*sic*] and make systems accountable' (24). They note further that base funding should be augmented by an amount 'sufficient to compensate for chronic under-funding' (29) implicitly recognizing that the risk of academic failure associated with cumulative underfunding and lack of accountability requires that at-risk students have sufficient resources to 'catch up' in a schooling race in which they are already seriously behind.

In the same vein, the FNEC/INAC Tuition Committee recommended, among other things, that FNEC should embark upon a careful, extended assessment of their needs to provide a credible foundation for negotiations with INAC, which would lead to a comprehensive funding formula for FNEC and its member community. Specifically, the committee recommended that FNEC develop and negotiate with INAC a formula 'that would take into account each of the 21 factors that we have highlighted in this report' (FNEC/DIAND Tuition Fees Committee 2005, 138). Need factors would range from Aboriginal language teaching in bilingual or multilingual contexts, to isolation and diseconomies of scale, high incidence of special needs and at-risk students, vocational program needs, and culturally appropriate capacity-building including second-level services (127–36).

Needs, of course, are in the eyes of the beholder, inescapably subjective and contextual. With need perceptions, moreover, 'what you see depends on where you sit.' For instance, if one believes that the educational needs of First Nations students are limited to the knowledge and skills required to keep body and soul together for a limited number of years in their home communities, the 'educational needs of First Nations students' are minimal. If, on the other hand, one believes that First Nations students require the same distribution of knowledge and skills as mainstream Canadians, *plus* a considerable degree of functional competence in their own particular ancestral culture and language, *plus* the knowledge and skills to contribute productively to defining the identity, purposes, structure, and processes associated with the political and socio-economic life of their 'nation' and community, their educational needs are vast indeed. They are greater still in proportion to the large knowledge and skill deficit First Nations students currently face when compared with the mainstream Canadian student population.

First Nations education is not exempt from the dilemma that frames the resource politics of education in general, namely, balancing horizontal equity (levelling the resource playing field) and vertical equity (compensating justly and appropriately for special costs and needs), and providing resources adequate to the goals and purposes of the educational enterprise. Adequacy is where subjectivity in the form of informed human judgment comes into play in determining what overall level of funding is appropriate. Vertical equity is where subjectivity enters the lists on the question of fundamental fairness in distribution of resources among competing need claims. Neither adequacy nor vertical equity can be decided soundly without some vision of which needs matter and how much they matter, both absolutely and in relation to one another. That vision of student-need priorities inevitably requires a broader vision of educational purpose and priorities as a whole.

As we have noted, evidence on the adequacy of DIAND funding for First Nations education derived from comparison with other jurisdictions is mixed but, on the whole, suggests that such funding is likely less generous, or at least not significantly more generous, than funding of provincially funded schools in 'similar' contexts. Comparison with provincial funding, however, is not appropriate for determining adequacy of funding for First Nations education, or for Aboriginal education in general. In one way or another, adequacy – and vertical equity – should be determined on the basis of need, obviously with due respect for the capacity of the Canadian state[20] to pay, but on the basis of need nonetheless. A needs approach, moreover, is consistent with the repeated complaint by the Auditor General concerning the absence of a coherent cost and accountability framework in First Nations education (Auditor General of Canada, 2004a, section 5.48) and with the Auditor General's recurrent insistence on closing the 'gap' between First Nations educational achievement and that of mainstream students in Canadian schools (section 5.93).

What kind of needs should funding for First Nations education take into consideration, and what kind of perspective should it bring to bear on those needs? The list is a long one, and represents a dramatic departure from INAC/DIAND's tendency to minimize the number of needs it recognizes in its national and regional funding schemes. First, the entire spectrum of educationally relevant handicaps and exceptionalities needs to be funded adequately and appropriately, taking due account of dramatically higher incidence levels of such conditions in general, and especially of some of the most costly types of handicaps and exceptionalities in the First Nations population. Indeed, the lack until very recently of any funding of special education services for First Nations students studying in their home communities can only be described as scandalous, given the adoption and funding of mandatory special education services founded on the principle of an appropriate education at public expense for all children by every province in Canada during or before the early 1980s. We recognize that service delivery capacity in special education, as in every other program area in education, takes time, and that it would not have made sense for the federal government to have immediately funded at the full rate recommended in the FNEC study of special education cost conducted by Paquette and a colleague (Paquette and Smith, 2000). In spite of this fact, funding commitments by the federal government subsequent to that seminal work have been disappointing.

Nonetheless, we acknowledge that, in addition to varying per-pupil amounts designated by INAC at the regional level in respect of low-cost special education needs, INAC has recently introduced national program guidelines for funding of moderate and high-cost special education needs. In 2002, INAC commissioned a review of special education policies and funding (Hurton 2002). At that time, the amounts summarized in table 3.1 were reported as earmarked for low-cost special education on a flat per-pupil-amount basis (all students reported on nominal rolls drew such amounts – in the following year). No consistent policy on high-cost special needs was in place at that time. Several regions, however, were sponsoring special education pilot projects in the wake of the pioneering First Nations Education Council of Quebec pilot project, which had begun in 1997.

On the heels of impetus generated by pilot projects in several provinces, and of discussions with various First Nations groups (especially AFN), INAC put into place a set of national program guidelines on special education funding and, at least implicitly, standards. These guidelines are intended to provide a process for gradual phase-in, first of 'indirect' and then of 'direct' special education services for students with moderate to high-cost special needs. They are obviously also aimed at trying to ensure a degree of accountability for funds allocated

Table 3.1
Per-pupil low-cost special needs funding

British Columbia	$219
Saskatchewan	$500
Ontario	$216–26
Quebec	$216
New Brunswick	None

Source: Hurton (2002), 21–2.

Table 3.2
Maximum amounts payable under INAC national special education guidelines

Tuition rate for specialized schools (e.g., deaf/blind)	$65,000 per student
Tuition rate for regular schools (band, federal, or provincial)	$30,000 per student
Regular school transportation	$5,000 per student
Emergency transportation	$5,000 per student
Accommodation (includes room and board)	$50,000 per student

Source: Indian and Northern Affairs Canada/Affaires indiennes et du Nord Canada (2002), 14.

under these guidelines. In particular, detailed reporting is required first to obtain and then to retain funding provided under the guidelines. The guidelines allow service delivery under the aegis of 'First Nation Regional Managing Organizations,' an implicit recognition of the need for such bodies to achieve whatever coordination of effort and economies of scale are possible in the delivery of high-cost special education services. The current guidelines allow the maximum per-pupil amounts shown in table 3.2.

In sum, INAC *has* moved in the direction of national standards for special education funding in the wake of the pilot projects and the 30 September 2002 throne speech pledge (Governor General of Canada 2002) stating, 'The government will work with the recently created National Working Group on Education to improve educational outcomes for First Nations children, and *take immediate steps to help First Nations children with special learning needs*' (emphasis added). Unfortunately, the slightly more than $100 million per year being invested by INAC in First Nations special education remains, in our view,[21] disproportionately small in comparison to needs, at least on the basis of the calculations used by Paquette and Smith to estimate the costs of those needs by extrapolating from the First Nations Education Council of Quebec pilot project cost assessment they conducted in 2000 (Paquette and Smith 2000). The amount is disproportionately small even when due allowance is made for the necessity of orderly capacity-building in First Nations special education service.

Diseconomy of scale factors, particularly small school and class sizes and dispersion over geographical space of schools (we assume a quasi-school board model) require funding that is adequate and appropriate. Isolation and remoteness also require adequate, appropriate, and distinct recognition. Special language considerations such as bilingual or multilingual education, or programs to help students adjust to standard English or French need funding that is sufficient to the purposes of the programs supported. Moreover, support for these programs needs to be integrated carefully with support for other factors that put the education of First Nations students at risk. Adequate and appropriate professional development funding is needed, as is funding for system, in the sense of a 'school board-like' entity, creation and capacity development. Annual cost of living adjustments need to take proper account of changes in the cost of living, particularly in remote, isolated communities. Teacher salaries and benefits need to be comparable to provincial remuneration levels. In particular, pension fund support should be make it possible for teachers in First Nations schools who wish to remain in provincial teachers' pension funds to do so (see, for example, FNEC/DIAND Tuition Fees Committee 2005, 25). Adequate funding should also be available to allow First Nations school systems that wish to do so to second teachers and resource persons from school boards willing to enter into such agreements.

Changes are needed to current funding levels if First Nations students are to have a chance to 'catch up' with mainstream Canadian students, and catch up in a way that respects and reinforces their identity as Aboriginal persons. As the government undertakes to build, in collaboration with its First Nations partners, a funding model that takes adequate and appropriate account of these special needs, it should take into consideration Baker's (2005) points about the dire insufficiency of vertical equity adjustments in most provincial and state transfer grant programs (see discussion in the preceding section, 'How Much is Enough'), and particularly his point about the *multiplicative* interaction of factors that dispose students to educational failure.

We believe that the most promising and far-sighted long-term approaches to funding public sector education are those that attempt to 'cost out' systems that deliver high student performance on all valued goals for schooling (again, see discussion in 'How Much is Enough'). We recognize, of course, that these approaches are dauntingly difficult to put into practice for several reasons (see, for instance, Baker 2006; Duncombe 2006; Hanushek 2005). First, they require sufficient political agreement on what student performance outputs (knowledge, skills, attitudes, beliefs, moral commitments, and so forth) count most – and on how to measure or otherwise account for them. Here, the legendary temptation to measure what is most easily – and cheaply – measured must be resisted! Second, context will affect the appropriateness and efficiency of various programs and resources. What works well in Kahnawake, for instance, may be a disaster in Cat Lake or Red Deer. Should there be one master performance cost formula with regional and district variation, or separate formulae for each region, cultural area, or other basis of aggregation? Third, the very newness of such approaches tends to frighten governments from becoming the first to 'test the waters' of cost-based performance. Fourth, other interesting innovations continue to be proposed[22] and the question of how these might interface with cost-based performance approaches inevitably arises.

All this said, we believe that cost-based performance, suitably modulated to take account of regional and perhaps district level differences, offers the best way forward in funding First Nations education adequately, equitably, and efficiently. We also believe that some sort of 'aggregate need index,' with transparently clear, contextually adjusted, vertical equity components to recognize local need would be the best choice for a new approach to funding First Nations in Canada.

Developing and implementing such an index, or any other funding formula that takes appropriate account of the major cost drivers in First Nations education, will take considerable time, effort, and money. At the end of the day, however, such investment is necessary if appropriate funding is going to arrive where and when it is needed. To be sure, in this case and in all others, politics and economics will play an important role. As Baker recognizes with regard to educational funding in general, 'In the end, the overall level or absolute standard of adequacy of any state's public educational system will continue to be derived from the political will of legislatures, under the watchful eye of courts, in the sometimes tenuous context of fluctuating state economies' (260). One could paraphrase this insight for First Nations education in Canada in the following terms, 'In the end, the overall level or absolute standard of adequacy of any First Nations educational system will continue to be derived from the political will of the Parliament of Canada, under the watchful eye of the courts, in the sometimes tenuous context of fluctuations in the national and world economy.' We would encourage an additional qualifier, 'and with open and continuous collaboration on the part of First Nations.'

This line of argument leads us back inevitably to what Turner characterizes as 'Kymlicka's constraint,' namely that, for better or for worse, implementation of Aboriginal rights and resources for their realization are, and will remain in the hands of mainly non-Aboriginal politicians and judges. The sum total of what we have said on the question of adequacy should by now have signalled clearly to readers that we believe substantial 'new money' is needed if First Nations education is ever to provide an efficacious environment for First Nations students to 'catch up' to their non-Aboriginal peers. To be sure, some First Nations will require substantially less and others substantially more than whatever a legitimate needs-based funding formula delivers in the way of overall average increase but, in our view, the needed overall increase will be substantial – if enabling Aboriginal students to 'catch up' is a real and not merely a symbolic policy goal.

Like a host of writers before us, moreover, we insist that these new resources must flow to First Nations education systems – real systems, not sham ones – and they must not disappear into the INAC bureaucracy. Having made these central points with regard to future funding of First Nations education, we wish to introduce an equally central cautionary note, one which flows from 'Kymlicka's constraint.'

We devote a chapter of this book to ethics and reserve most of our discussion of ethical issues for that chapter. In the context, however, of asserting the need for substantial new resources in First Nations education, we cannot ignore the need for strong commitment to the ethical use of those resources. As we noted earlier, the Canadian electorate is not and will not be disposed to fund waste, corruption, and lack of fiscal accountability. In our view, no substantial new funds will be made available to make 'catch up' possible without *convincing* assurance (transparency in planning, policy, and appointments, commitment to strong ethical standards, openness to stringent auditing procedures, and so forth) that those funds will be used efficiently and honourably for the intended purposes as defined by First Nations. If such funds are made available, moreover, they will be quickly rescinded at the first evidence to the contrary. If they are to survive and become effective instruments of educational 'catch up,' First Nations school systems will need to commit unequivocally to an ethos of servant leadership rather than self-serve leadership. Such systems and those who work in them, as well as those involved in their governance, have but one overarching purpose, the educational success their students.

Money by itself will not transform First Nations education into an excellent, effective, and efficient means of closing the achievement gap between First Nations and mainstream Canadian students. Money does 'matter' – but only when it is used appropriately and efficiently. First Nations education organizations, both those currently in existence and more school board-like future entities, will need to commit to and engage in transformational capacity-building if they are ever to become effective in closing the First Nations educational gap in a way consistent with their 'nations' aspirations to define themselves in the future. Nothing less than a 'quantum leap' forward will suffice. To say this in no way denigrates the good and occasionally heroic work that has been done in the past and continues at present in various places. We do believe, however, that the magnitude of the educational gap between First Nations and mainstream Canadian students speaks volumes to the need for a quantum leap in organizational capacity in First Nations education.

Of course, organizational capacity is generally built 'one brick at a time,' not in large quantities. The key lesson here as we see it, is one of keeping one's 'eye on the ball.' Even in moderately complex organizations, and many First Nations educational organizations already fit that description, such coherence means above all else, that *leaders, both administrators and those involved in governance, need to commit to strategic planning that includes the most ambitious programs of appropriate organizational capacity building feasible in their circumstances.* The crisis in which First Nations education currently finds itself leaves no room for 'muddling through' in the hope that things will one day get better. They will not. In fact, the surest way for First Nations education to further marginalize itself on the larger political agenda is for those with power in such organizations to refuse to commit to intensive restructuring and capacity-building within a context of transparency and ethics.

Paquette (1986) wrote at some length in an earlier monograph about both the desirability of local First Nations taxation for school purposes, and about practical means for dealing with great differences in potential local revenue-raising capacity among First Nations. Local and area contribution, in our view, are important tools in crafting and preserving local and area accountability. No policy philosopher's stone we know of can produce the same sense of local and area accountability in the absence of some discretionary control over locally generated resources, that is, *without some local and area taxation for educational purposes*. Such contributions, moreover, offer the only plausible antidote to the rentier ('rent-seeking') behaviour and the educational achievement malaise that seems to accompany it, even in national economies where the 'rents' are exceedingly high as in the Persian Gulf states (Minnis 2006).

We understand that not all First Nations are on an even playing field in terms of their ability to tax for educational purposes. However, we believe that the solutions offered in Paquette (1986) remain viable, notably the various approaches to ensuring horizontal equity used in the world of public education generally. These approaches to equalizing spending power for a given tax 'effort' could be adapted to First Nations education, although they would inevitably raise their characteristic problems, problems that are both theoretical (e.g., *comparability* of bases of taxation) and 'technical' (e.g., equalization of 'bases' of local and area taxation for school purposes).

Of course, meaningful local and area autonomy over revenues for educational purposes inevitably carries with it a certain tendency towards inequality. Invariably, governments cannot afford to equalize 'totally' the spending power of local school boards. The result is some degree of inequality in spending power. For this reason, *we recommend that reliance on purely local resources for First Nations education, while substantial enough to entail a sense of direct, real, financial accountability at the local and area level, should be limited.* Only an overall, average reliance on local resources sufficient to catalyze a sense of local ownership should exist, not reliance strong enough to disequalize in a substantial way. Practically speaking, we view about 10 per cent of resources from local First Nations resources as desirable. Moreover, that 10 per cent should be an average with the poorest communities paying nothing, and the most financially able communities paying substantially more. But a local share should be in place, and should be embraced by First Nations interested in building a real accountability consciousness at the local level.[23]

Depending on the course of evolving First Nations self-governance in general, First Nations area, regional, and, perhaps even Canada-wide governance might emerge. In such a case, depending on the revenue capacity of such aggregate self-governments, it may be feasible, and certainly would be desirable from an Indian responsibility and control point of view, for these governance entities to contribute more than 10 per cent of overall revenues for First Nations education.

Whatever the future revenue capacities of eventual 'upper tier' First Nations governance, if and when it emerges, we believe strictly *local* share should never exceed 10 per cent, because excessive reliance on purely local (that is, community-level resources for community-level purposes whose amount and allocation is decided at the community level) is associated with strong inequities in per-pupil spending power.

No one-size-fits-all funding formula is likely to be possible in First Nations education in Canada. Nonetheless, transparency and equity require *common funding principles*, and that requirement demands some sort of national formula, be it de facto or explicit. Whatever the nature of that formula, it should be transparent, information on its elements should be readily available for scrutiny, and comprehensive data on its component revenues, *even where education revenues are part of some form of global block funding*, should be readily available and accessible to the public. Parallel performance data on both educational outcomes and process performance at the education system level should also be collected, collated, and easily accessible. These requirements accord well with what we believe is a need to adopt a flexible, relational pluralist stance towards specific self-government and education system arrangements.

We believe that the structural and fiscal reforms we have proposed would go far to meeting the primary criteria for funding reform identified in the recommendations of the Minister's National Working Group on Education in its final report (2002), specifically in the following recommendation:

> The Minister and First Nations, working with departmental and other officials, identify the real and projected costs of a First Nations holistic education system with a special focus on:
> - costs associated with First Nations jurisdiction and jurisdictional issues in education;
> - costs to establish and maintain a First Nations community and regional education infrastructure;
> - costs of a quality First Nations education, including:
>   - assessment, review and remediation of student achievement levels;
>   - additional new dollars to offset the inequities and changing requirements, such as the salaries and compensation benefits of teachers and staff in First Nations schools;
>   - educational facilities that are safe, well-equipped, well-maintained

and culturally appropriate, and reflect Indigenous knowledge in the physical structure of the building (e.g., including space in schools for parents and elders, as well as for early childhood development);
- o [appropriate] education dollars from First Nations communities to the provinces and territories for students attending provincial and territorial schools;
- o First Nations developed and approved language instruction and curricula;
- o culturally relevant curricula for all subject areas that are developed and approved by First Nations;
- o curricula and resources designed to address the identified weaknesses in mathematics, sciences and literacy; and,
- o the development of culturally appropriate pedagogical methodologies and evaluation. (40–1)

Our recommendations project these principles onto future restructuring in which First Nations assume increasing program, governance, and financial responsibility for education of First Nations children and adults.

Finally, before concluding our treatment of funding issues with some thoughts about what our framework and principles mean for funding Aboriginal education outside the First Nations context, we wish to highlight one small but potentially important area to which we have already alluded in passing. We believe that the larger purposes of First Nations education, notably academic parity with Canadian education in general, within a capacity to develop among students a sense of First Nations identity that allows full participation in the life and ongoing self-definition of the First Nations group with which they identify, requires *both* excellent First Nations teachers *and* excellent non-First Nations teachers. Excellence among *both* constituent teacher groups is needed to nurture 'word warriors' in Turner's sense. In order to attract teachers from provincial systems of education, particularly master teachers with distinguished teaching records, First Nations must not only be able to match provincial salary and benefit scales and absorb differential living costs, they must also be able provide pension benefit levels sufficient to allow teachers to remain in (or opt into) provincial teacher pension funds. This is no small matter. One promising and yet little-explored mechanism for drawing 'star' teachers and resource persons from provincial systems into First Nations systems for a period of time is secondment – but secondments require the seconding agency to be able to pay the entire costs of that secondee's salary and benefits, *including employer pension fund contributions.*

To this point, almost all of our attention in this section has focused on funding of First Nations education. What are the implications of our conceptual framework and of our understanding of the current state of the literature on education finance for non-First Nations Aboriginal education, that is, for education of 'non status' students identifying themselves, or identified by a parent or guardian, as Aboriginal? We believe these implications are, for the most part, threefold. First, provinces ought to recognize appropriately the supplemental costs of providing culturally and linguistically appropriate education for Aboriginal students and of assisting them in reaching achievement parity with their peers. Some provinces, notably British Columbia, Manitoba, Alberta, and Ontario already have funding earmarked for Aboriginal programs. Second, we believe that such funding should be targeted specifically for Aboriginal students and should be 'enveloped,' that is, boards should be required to demonstrate that they have spent the amount received under such programs in ways that benefit Aboriginal students. Third, as part of overall accountability requirements, boards should be required to report annually to their provincial ministry of education on the use they have made of such funding, and on results achieved. In particular, such reporting should include annual reporting on appropriate benchmarks that reflect growth in the Aboriginal student population both on mainstream learning and socialization goals and on Aboriginal culture, language, and identity goals.

Earmarked funding for Aboriginal education raises the issue of Aboriginal 'alternative schools.' In general, such schools have been either the product of board-level initiatives or quasi-private schools. Our position is that alternative schools are useful only if and to the degree that they serve the overarching goal of Aboriginal education, that is, academic parity with Canadian education, within a capacity to develop among students a sense of Aboriginal identity that allows full participation in the life and self-definition of the Aboriginal group with which they identify. In particular, we are concerned that many such programs appear to fall prey to the 'remedial' trap of providing education that allows Aboriginal students to progress academically more slowly than their mainstream peers, and thus ensure that the gap that separates them from their peers grows rather than shrinks over time. Such programs foster 'falling behind' in students rather than 'catching up.' We would like to see direct provincial support for such programs because we would like to see direct, publicly accessible reporting by boards to provincial ministries on the goals, purposes, processes, strategies, and achievements of these programs. As in the case of board programs addressed to Aboriginal students in general, boards should be required to report to provincial ministries on appropriate benchmarks that reflect annual growth in the Aboriginal student population both on mainstream learning and socialization goals, and on Aboriginal culture, language, and identity goals.

4 Post-Secondary Education

In general, Aboriginal post-secondary education occurs within two fundamental and deeply intertwined constraints:

1. with the exception of a limited number of Aboriginally operated but tenuously funded institutions and programs,[1] post-secondary education occurs under provincial control and in institutions, mostly publicly funded, that operate under specific provincial legislation; and
2. the participation and success of Aboriginal students in conventional post-secondary education (PSE) programs are both significantly limited by a range of circumstances, including:
   a. inadequate elementary and secondary level preparation,
   b. financial incapacity,
   c. the social and emotional consequences of unstable childhood and adolescent environments,
   d. culture shock experienced by many Aboriginal students in post-secondary milieus,
   e. perceived and real anti-Aboriginal bias and hostility in post-secondary institutions, programs, and milieus,
   f. programmatic initiatives designed mainly to improve accessibility and retention of Aboriginal students, while the achievement, knowledge, histories, and perspectives of Aboriginal peoples remain too often ignored, rejected, suppressed, marginalized, or underutilized in universities (Battiste, Bell, and Findlay 2002, 82),
   g. overall lack of presence and valorization of Aboriginal knowledge and ways of being in post-secondary education conceived within industrial paradigm assumptions, and

h. perceived lack of usefulness or relevance of post-secondary
achievement to the lives of Aboriginal peoples.

The fact that the majority of post-secondary institutions and programs in Canada are established and regulated by provincial legislation, and that most obtain core funding from provincial legislatures,
means that such institutions and programs are shaped by provincial
policy agendas and priorities, and thus by the values and understandings that create and sustain them. For the most part, Canadian post-
secondary institutions operate within assumptions associated with
Bertrand and Valois' (1980) rational and technological educational
paradigms to prepare students for life in a sociocultural and economic milieu firmly rooted in the industrial/post-industrial paradigm. In
democratic forms of government, policy agendas are driven by majority interests, not minority interests – particularly when the minority in
question is as demographically fragile as the Aboriginal population of
Canada (however quickly that demographic is growing, and however
important it already is in certain regions of the country). 'Kymlicka's
constraint,' after all, is but a corollary of this larger principle.[2]

Cryptic and skeletal as the provisions in sections 114 through 120 of
the *Indian Act* are for First Nations elementary and secondary education, they at least provide some direct statutory authority for federal involvement in such education. No such direct authority exists in the case
of post-secondary education. The result is that federal support for First
Nations post-secondary education is even more tenuous than federal
support for First Nations elementary and secondary education. Indeed,
such support has always been dependent on annual discretionary appropriations by the Treasury Board, although such appropriations have
arguably become institutionalized over time. Support for non-First Nations Aboriginal education has been largely provincial, as in the case of
Saskatchewan's support for the Gabriel Dumont Institute.

Abundant evidence exists to demonstrate the gap between Aboriginal post-secondary completion and that of the rest of the Canadian
population. Mendelson (2006) provides a particularly telling analysis
based on post-secondary completion rates as of the 2001 census. Figure
4.1 shows one of the most troubling trends of educational attainment
statistics in that work.

In this 'fresh graduate' cohort from the last census for which data
were available at the time of the Mendelson study, Aboriginal males
lagged over 10 per cent behind the rest of the population in having
had some post-secondary education (PSE) with no certificate, while Ab-

Figure 4.1 Aboriginal and total population PSE completion, by gender
20–24-year-old cohort, at 2001

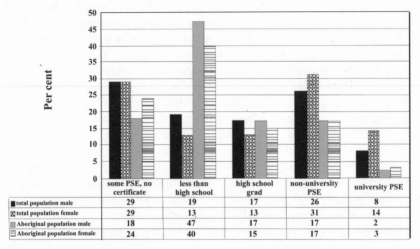

	some PSE, no certificate	less than high school	high school grad	non-university PSE	university PSE
total population male	29	19	17	26	8
total population female	29	13	13	31	14
Aboriginal population male	18	47	17	17	2
Aboriginal population female	24	40	15	17	3

Source: Mendelson (2006), 14, fig. 10.

original females lagged about 5 per cent behind both male and female
peers in the total population. The percentage of both Aboriginal male
and female young adults with 'less than high school' was more than
twice that of the total population of young adult males and females,
respectively. Aboriginal and total population percentages with high
school diplomas only were roughly comparable. About 17 per cent of
young Aboriginal adults of both genders reported having completed
a non-university PSE program, in comparison with 26 per cent of total population young adult males and 31 per cent of total population
young adult females.

As is widely recognized, disparities in university degree completion
are particularly troubling. Eight per cent of young adult males in the
general population reported having completed a university degree,
while only 2 per cent of young adult Aboriginal males reported having
done so. Fourteen per cent of young adult females in the total population reported having completed a university degree, while only 3 per
cent of Aboriginal females reported the same. As Mendelson shows,
great regional variation exists in these overall national patterns (the dis-
parity in post-secondary attainment is particularly worrisome on the

prairies), but these are the disturbing PSE completion disparities for all of Canada as of 2001.

Provincial governments have been involved, in a small way, in trying to promote equitable access to and success for Aboriginal students in provincially recognized universities and community colleges.[3] In addition, despite the perennial shortage of resources for this purpose, post-secondary institutions have created a wide variety of programs intended to enhance the participation and achievement of Aboriginal students in the courses they offer. For instance, many institutions are attempting to increase the numbers of Aboriginal faculty and staff, to recruit Aboriginal students proactively, and to intervene early in student aspirations and decision-making (promoting university study as a realistic goal among students still in Grade 10 or 11). However, the consensus among post-secondary institutions is that much more is needed.[4]

Federally Chartered Institutions?

The Aboriginal Institutes Consortium recently proposed that the way forward in establishing effective First Nations governance in post-secondary education is for the federal government to exercise its power to charter degree-granting institutions. The consortium points out that the federal government has actually chartered three such institutions, Queen's University, the Royal Military College, and McGill University. The Consortium argues that despite the fact that section 93 of the Constitution assigns education to the provinces, and despite the fact that aside from these three exceptions, all degree-granting institutions have been established under provincial legislation, the federal government *could* charter an Aboriginal university if it chose to do so (The Aboriginal Institutes Consortium 2005, 32).

We believe that the First Nations University of Canada takeover (for a full discussion of this topic, see 'The First Nations University of Canada' section in chapter 7) suggests strongly that the federal government should *not* charter an Aboriginal university for the foreseeable future. Although we support, in principle, the establishment of an autonomous Aboriginal university, the events surrounding the First Nations University of Canada demonstrate that the time has not yet arrived for a First Nations entity to engage autonomously in university governance. In our opinion, it would be an egregious and costly mistake for the federal government to charter such an institution at this time.

In any case, whatever level of government charters a university, it can only build and retain credibility as a university-level institution by adhering to standards and norms that support university study, research, and student and faculty life. Academic freedom and arm's-length distance between governance and academic administration are non-negotiable components of university life, study, and research. A federal charter as opposed to a provincial one changes nothing with regard to this reality.

As we noted at the beginning of this chapter, Aboriginal post-secondary education occurs within two fundamental constraints: first, post-secondary education of Aboriginal students occurs within institutions chartered and controlled by provincial legislation; second, participation and success of Aboriginal students in such programs are limited by various circumstances, particularly a lack of fit between Aboriginal needs and conventional post-secondary programs.

These two restraints have led to two INAC funding programs: student funding and program funding. We turn now to the question first of post-secondary funding in general, and then to the question of funding for Aboriginal post-secondary education in particular.

Post-Secondary Funding

As with elementary and secondary school funding, we begin this section with an overview of some classic issues surrounding the funding of post-secondary education, all of which now have relevance to funding post-secondary education for Aboriginal students. Like elementary and secondary funding issues, the central questions in post-secondary funding tend to be intertwined and not easily separated from one another.

Theoretical Underpinnings

Since the 1960s, human capital theory has posited that both knowledge and skills are means of production as fundamentally important as the classic land-capital-labour triad. The three-legged stool of production now has a fourth leg, human knowledge, skill, and ingenuity. That argument has strengthened as the world has moved rapidly into a globalized, knowledge-based, and increasingly technology-driven economy. The central human capital problem was how to quantify the importance of education in productivity and wealth creation, and additionally, how to assess the relative importance of different educational levels and sectors in that regard.

Perhaps the most persistent and continually contested issue in post-secondary funding is who should pay, or more precisely, how the cost of post-secondary education should be shared among those who benefit from it directly and those who benefit from it only indirectly. The debate on this issue has historically turned on rates of private versus social and public return from the investment in post-secondary education, as opposed to private, public, and social rates of return on elementary and secondary education. This is hardly the place for intense examination of the rate-of-return method employed, either with or without recent approaches using more longitudinal bases for the estimation of returns. Still, we cannot address the relative moral and political claim of post-secondary education on the public purse (as opposed to elementary and secondary education), without sketching the general shape of the debate.

In the simplest terms, private rates of return seek to estimate average future returns over a working lifetime to given increments in educational attainment, either in general (e.g., a university bachelor's degree over secondary school completion) or specifically by discipline or program (e.g., a medical degree over secondary school completion). Using various methodologies, mostly regression-based, such studies seek to estimate average future returns for the educational level in question over the next lower milestone level of attainment (e.g., a university degree over a secondary school diploma, or a secondary school diploma over elementary completion). 'Returns' are increases in after-tax income less opportunity costs (including tuition, fees, foregone after-tax income, and so forth) associated with completing the educational attainment milestone in question. Table 4.1 compares key concepts for each rate of return measure.

Social rates of return attempt to quantify the marginal benefit to society as a whole of important educational attainment milestones, as opposed to private benefits to students. They do so by comparing 'the resources committed to education and the additional production observed at the community [society-wide] level. In particular … [they] take … into account the additional production expected when the general level of education rises' (Appleby, Fougère, and Rouleau 2002, 4). Thus, social rates of return attempt to calculate the difference between salaries to teachers and institutional overhead costs plus the total value of goods and services not produced as a result of student involvement

Table 4.1
Social, private, and public returns to post-secondary education

AGENT	SOCIAL The Community	PRIVATE The Student	PUBLIC (fiscal) Governments
Costs	**Direct costs:** Total value of education expenses: salaries paid to teachers, maintenance expenses of institutions, and cost of capital. **Indirect costs:** Total value of goods and services not produced (approximated by the total value of gross income not received).	**Direct costs:** Total value of tuition fees and related expenses. **Indirect costs:** Income not received (net of tax) during education/training leading to attainment milestone in question (opportunity cost), less financial assistance given to student.	**Direct costs:** Subsidies paid to students and institutions. **Indirect costs:** Value of taxes not collected on income foregone during education/ training.
Earnings	Additional production for all of society, approximated by the additional gross earnings received by the most highly educated (including all private benefits).	Additional earnings (net of tax payable) received by a post-secondary graduate compared to those of someone with a lower level of education.	Total value of tax collected on additional earnings received by the most highly educated.

Source: Adapted from Appleby, Fougère, and Rouleau (2002), 6, table 1, cited in Lemelin (1998), 105–6, table 5.1.

in the level of education in question on the one hand, and additional production in the form of marginal increases in gross earnings by those who attain the educational milestone in question on the other.

Public rates of return estimate costs and benefits *to governments* of a particular educational milestone. For public rates of return, costs are subsidies paid to students and institutions, and the taxes associated with the forgone income of students, while 'earnings' are the total value of taxes collected on additional income received by those who attain the educational milestone in question.

It would be an understatement to say that the rate of return methodology is controversial. In all rates of returns, the results obtained are based on past relationships between costs and earnings that are extrapolated into the future. Recent work with time-series data can thus be reasonably expected to more accurately map onto future relationships between costs and earnings rather than single-point-in-time, 'snapshot' data, but no methodology can predict or compensate accurately for unexpected structural changes in production or the means of production. For instance, even the most sophisticated time series methodologies could not have accurately estimated in advance changes in rates of return to certain types of post-secondary programs associated with the widespread deployment of robotics and other labour-saving technologies over the last fifteen years.[5] In short, rates of return are a blunt instrument with which to predict future benefits from current educational investment, but they are the best instrument economists of education are likely to have for the foreseeable future.

One other caveat is worth mentioning here. Not only are rates of return specific to time, they are also specific to place – and they are even specific to groups and genders within a country. For example, the rate of return for a bachelor of science (or even more specifically, a bachelor of science in physics), is highly dependent on the economy of the country for which it is calculated. Thus, a bachelor of science in physics will normally have a higher rate of return in a country where considerable research in physics is taking place, rather than in a country with a predominantly agrarian economy. Returns to whole levels of educational attainment vary from country to country in this way, so that rate-of-return studies have shown low rates of return for tertiary and even secondary education in developing countries. Psacharopoulos (1990) notes that social rates of return for primary education in developing countries are typically about 25 per cent, while social rates of return to tertiary education have generally been only around 12 per cent (372). Rates of return differ by gender, and presumably would differ among demographic groups in society as well. For example, Monk (2000) compared returns of 'white' and 'non-white' American college students (of each gender) across a matrix of institutional quality indicators. In short, one must be circumspect in applying and interpreting rates of return.

All these cautions considered, some rate-of-return trends have proven fairly resilient over time and place, at least in developed countries. One in particular has proven pivotal in framing the post-secondary funding discourse. In general, *private* returns of university-level education have been consistently and significantly higher than *social* returns of university education (Psacharopoulos 1981, see especially table 1, 327–8). Furthermore, the social returns to elementary and secondary education are great enough that, aside from some consistent but also 'shrill' and non-mainstream critique from the political right, few question a dominant role for the state in funding elementary and secondary education. In post-secondary education, however, private returns are sufficiently high that popular opinion, and hence public policy, have both long held that students should pay a significant portion of the cost of their post-secondary studies. Over time, growing stress on limited public resources in tandem with particularly high returns to *certain types* of post-secondary programs has resulted in two widespread changes in post-secondary funding. First, given the much greater importance of private returns in post-secondary education on the one hand, and the growing inability of the state to meet its obligations, especially in the face of skyrocketing health costs on the other, public policy reflects growing public opinion that post-secondary students *should* pay a greater portion of the cost of their post-secondary studies. Second, given that the private benefits of some of the most costly post-secondary programs (such as medicine) are much higher than the returns to other post-secondary programs, tuition and fees have been deregulated in many jurisdictions so that post-secondary institutions can differentiate them according to program cost.

Such deregulation raises questions of fairness, and especially of equity of access to the programs with the highest earning pay-offs. These questions ultimately can only be answered by taking into account the entire fiscal universe impacting on the cost of post-secondary studies. Thus, before one can conclude that passing more of the cost on to students and deregulating tuition and fees are unfair, one needs to look at the availability of scholarships and bursaries, at adjustments for student and family 'ability to pay,' at student-loan costs and terms, (including provisions for loan forgiveness under certain conditions), at what constitutes an acceptable ratio of earnings to post-secondary study debt for graduates, and so forth. It is ultimately the whole package of student costs and supports that shapes accessibility, at least as much as the availability of post-secondary funding alone can influence it (Leslie 1985). Broader issues of equity of access and results in elementary and secondary education, of course, influence which demographic groups are better positioned to compete for valued post-secondary placements. In this regard, available evidence suggests that Aboriginal students remain far behind all other identifiable groups in Canadian society in their readiness to compete for places in post-secondary programs (see, for instance, White, Maxim, and Spence 2004b). Post-secondary funding, in short, raises complex and difficult-to-answer questions both at the normative and quantitative level.

If post-secondary funding typically raises numerous and troubling questions, the funding of Aboriginal post-secondary education does so with particular scope and tenacity. That said, with one vital exception, the funding problem of post-secondary Aboriginal education shares many commonalities with post-secondary funding in general. Indeed, suitably adjusted for the historical and contemporary realities confronted by Aboriginal students, the main ingredients in the public policy discourse on post-secondary funding serve quite well for framing discussion on the funding of Aboriginal post-secondary education.

The vital exception is the degree to which one accepts and interprets post-secondary education as a treaty or even 'inherent' Aboriginal right, as opposed to simply a social policy choice on the part of government. In general, Aboriginal peoples, especially First Nations, have insisted that post-secondary education is either a right guaranteed by the educational provisions of the 'numbered treaties,' or that it constitutes an 'inherent right' because, prior to contact with Europeans, Aboriginal people educated their young successfully for the social, political, and practical realities of life in their historical context, and post-secondary education is now as necessary to function successfully in contemporary Canada as pre-contact traditional education was for its time and context.[6] However, the federal government has consistently viewed its support for First Nations post-secondary education as qualitatively different from its support for First Nations elementary and secondary education. The government considers post-secondary education a matter of 'social policy' rather than a matter of statutory, treaty, or moral obligation (Indian and Northern Affairs Canada/Affaires indiennes et du Nord Canada 2005, 35) – and, of course, it has consistently denied any particular responsibility for the post-secondary education of non-status Indians and Métis.

We draw from three sources in our critical analysis of the current state of funding for Aboriginal post-secondary education: the literature on post-secondary funding in general, evidence of current funding practices in Aboriginal post-secondary education specifically, and our broader conceptual framework along with its implications.

The Current State of Funding

As our analysis of current post-secondary programs addressed specifically to Aboriginal students revealed, almost no examples exist of *targeted* provincial funding in support of post-secondary programs addressed to Aboriginal students, with two exceptions. Saskatchewan's support for FNUC and the Gabriel Dumont Institute are the two important exceptions to this general rule of provincial disengagement from *direct* support for Aboriginal post-secondary programs. (In the spring of 2010, both the Governments of Canada and of Saskatchewan announced cancellation of their funding for FNUC [White and Church 2010]. See chapter 7 for further discussion of this issue.)

As we also noted in the context of our discussion of current program offerings addressed to Aboriginal students, this lack of *targeted* funding from the provinces does not mean that the provinces are contributing nothing to such programs. What it means is that, to date, *provinces have generally left it to post-secondary institutions to decide what supports and what course and program adaptations are needed* – and to find the resources for such accommodations within the established sources for their operating expenditures, notably block and special funding, tuition and fees, or through supplementary revenues generated by entrepreneurial activities.

In general, post-secondary administrators believe that resources available to them from these already overextended revenue sources are inadequate to meet Aboriginal support and program needs. For their part, provinces are reluctant to engage in micromanaging Aboriginal programming by providing post-secondary support grants for specific types of Aboriginal support, given that post-secondary institutions are much better placed to know what types, qualities, and levels of services and programs are needed. The current situation thus appears to be gridlocked in a permanent 'standoff' between the need of institutions for supplementary resources to offer and maintain quality Aboriginal programs, and the unwillingness of provincial governments to target funding for such programming.

INAC has a long history of supporting First Nations post-secondary students and programs. However, that history, like most of INAC's involvement with First Nations education, has been a troubled one. INAC's post-secondary funding lacks even the vague and implicit authority the *Indian Act* provides for funding First Nations elementary and secondary education. Given this lack of *direct* statutory authority, INAC depends on annual Treasury Board authorizations of its post-secondary funding resources, a precarious foundation for such funding.

INAC's post-secondary support takes two forms, student support and institutional support. The ministry has set two formal objectives for its Post-Secondary Student Support Program (PSSSP):

1. To support Treaty/Status Indians and Inuit to
   a. gain access to post-secondary education, and
   b. graduate with the qualifications and skills needed to pursue individual careers, and
2. To contribute to the achievement of Indian self-government and economic self-reliance. (Indian and Northern Affairs Canada/Affaires indiennes et du Nord Canada 2005, 1)

From the inception of DIAND/INAC, support for status Indian post-secondary students until 1987 (most sources say 1991, but that year is incorrect) funding was strictly enrolment-based. INAC simply applied a formula to existing post-secondary enrolments. The formula covered the costs of tuition, books, and eligible living expenses (Indian and Northern Affairs Canada/Affaires indiennes et du Nord Canada 2005, 1). Eligible enrolments were not capped or limited in any way. In 1987 William McKnight, then minister of Indian Affairs, announced in a letter to chiefs and councils that the post-secondary assistance program as it existed under the 'E-12 Guidelines' would be reviewed, a review which in fact occurred between 1987 and 1989 (Canadian House Of Commons, Standing Committee on Aboriginal Affairs 1989). According to INAC, that review process included consultation with the Aboriginal community during the last six months of 1988.

What raised indignant protest from First Nations groups and attracted brief media attention at the time were 'interim changes' to the E-12 Guidelines. Overall, these changes had the effect of capping post-secondary support eligibility, thus forcing First Nations administrative entities responsible for funding post-secondary students (band, educational, and tribal councils) to 'ration' post-secondary support for the first time. One of us remembers vividly the paradoxical description of the rationale for these changes by an INAC spokesperson on CBC Radio news the morning they were announced in May of 1987. The spokesperson claimed that the changes were intended to encourage bands and other status-Indian organizations to take control of post-secondary education by prioritizing their support and hence, although the spokesperson made no mention of it, exclude some potential students from support and delaying support for others. According to the spokesperson, the reason for the policy change was to further the goal of Indian control of Indian education.

Following completion of the review in 1989, INAC post-secondary student support ceased to be linked to relevant cost drivers, such as tuition, books, travel, accommodation, and especially enrolments. Funding was based on ('benchmarked to') previous funding plus an arbitrary percentage increase determined by INAC which was unrelated to current cost and demand. Between 1992 and 1997, the Post-Secondary Student Support Program funding was folded into each INAC region's block funding, thus completely obliterating any implicit linkage to cost and demand. Since 1997, 'block funding envelopes have been capped with annual increases allotted according to Treasury Board directives' (Indian and Northern Affairs Canada/Affaires indiennes et du Nord Canada 2005, 1). In short, the Treasury Board provides what it deems appropriate for PSSSP, and if demand outstrips resources provided, First Nations funders can exercise their 'Indian control' by determining their own prioritization rules and queuing schemes.

No meaningful 'standards' are required with regard to provision of post-secondary support by First Nations funding agencies. They are required simply to 'provide financial assistance for post-secondary education to eligible treaty/registered Indians living on and off-reserve, ordinarily resident in Canada' (ibid., 8). Beyond that stipulation, First Nations funding agencies are required only to have written guidelines or policies available to the Members of Parliament and the public regarding such funding, and to provide an appeal process for administrative decisions regarding post-secondary student funding (ibid., 8–9).

INAC's Indian Studies Support Program (ISSP) provides financial support to post-secondary institutions or other organizations delivering post-secondary-level programs and courses for the development and delivery of programs specially adapted to status-Indian needs. INAC has assigned four objectives to ISSP:

1. To support Indian post-secondary education.
2. To improve opportunities for Treaty/Status Indian students to complete post-secondary programs of study.
3. To emphasize disciplines relevant to Indian self-government and appropriate labour markets, as determined in collaboration with Indian leaders and Indian educators.
4. To enhance Indian language, culture and traditions. (ibid., 2)

INAC sets an ISSP funding envelope up to a maximum of 12 per cent of total annual INAC post-secondary education spending (ibid., 2).

Four types of institutions are eligible to receive ISSP grants:

- post-secondary institutions (PSIs – degree, diploma and certificate granting institutions recognized by a province including institutions affiliated with or delivering recognized PSE programs by arrangement with a PSI);
- Indian post-secondary institutions (IPSIs – Indian post-secondary institutions that issue some sort of diplomas or certificates);
- Indian education organizations (IEOs – Indian education organizations such as band, tribal, or educational councils which purchase and manage special programs but do not have authority to grant degrees, diplomas, or certificates); and
- FNUC. (ibid., 2)

The Indian Studies Support Program funds post-secondary programs leading to a certificate, diploma, degree, or credit courses delivered by a post-secondary institution and 'specifically designed for/delivered to' students eligible for support under PSSSP (ibid., 3–4). A complete list of programs targeting First Nations and Inuit students has never been compiled, although according to INAC, 'special programs for teacher training, social work, health sciences, native studies and business management have developed all across the country' (ibid., 4). INAC's 2005 review of its post-secondary education support apparently identified 143 programs 'focussing on Aboriginal topics' (ibid., 4).

The education branch of INAC sets ISSP funding for each region annually. The important exception had been the First Nations University, which received what amounted to core funding in the amount of about $7 million annually (although it was not called that). Otherwise, access to ISSP is on a proposal-approval basis. Regional offices have three responsibilities in regard to ISSP, to:

- notify headquarters ... by December 31 of each year of multi-year commitments and proposed annual expenditures for the next fiscal year;
- establish a Regional Committee and regional management and administrative procedures in consultation with Aboriginal leaders; and
- communicate regional objectives, priorities and procedures to institutions and educational organizations by June 30 of each year; enter into and implement required contracts and funding arrangements; ensure that annual regional funding is within approved levels; monitor the delivery of education programs; and report annually by December 31 of each year. (ibid., 9)

Table 4.2
National post-secondary education funding levels, 1999–2000 to 2001–2002

National Funding	1999–2000	2000–2001	% Increase, 1999–2000 to 2000–2001	2001–2002	% Increase, 2000–2001 to 2001–2002
ISSP Funding	20,820,798	20,369,174	–2.0%	23,149,687	12.0%
PSSSP Funding	259,241,202	263,608,826	2.0%	262,314,313	0.0%
TOTAL PSE	280,062,000	283,978,000	1.0%	285,464,000	1.0%

Source: Adapted from Indian and Northern Affairs Canada/Affaires indiennes et du Nord Canada (2005), 8, table 2.

Despite the formal requirement that regions establish regional committees to 'define objectives and priorities within the region; review and rank program proposals and make recommendations to the Regional Directors General on proposals that meet ISSP funding requirements; and issue reports on the quality of the programs,' only the BC region has a functioning regional committee (ibid., 9).

Institutions and educational organizations propose, develop, and deliver eligible programs.[7] Multi-year agreements for such programs are allowed and a great many ISSP beneficiary programs continue to exist and draw ISSP funding over periods longer than one year.

As table 4.2 shows, INAC was investing more than a quarter of a billion dollars annually into post-secondary education at the turn of the millennium, of which about 92 per cent was going towards student support, and about 8 per cent was allocated to ISSP. Table 4.2 also reveals an annual overall increase in such funding in the order of 1 per cent over a time period when the annual all-item Consumer Price Index for Canada varied between 2 per cent and 3 per cent,[8] so that such funding increases did not begin to cover annual inflation even if demand had remained stable instead of increasing as it is currently.

Despite opinion being strongly polarized between First Nations organization administrators who participated in an INAC 2005 evaluation exercise on the one hand, and INAC participants on the other (see figure 4.2), the balance of evidence assembled in that review suggests a sizeable inadequacy of current INAC post-secondary funding in light of current demand and need. In fact the evidence presents a picture

Figure 4.2 Adequacy of PSSSP to satisfy all eligible claims

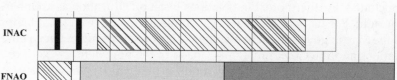

Strongly agree   Agree   Neither Agree [n]or Disagree   Disagree   Strongly disagree

INAC: Indian and Northern Affairs Canada
FNAO: First Nations Administering Organizations

Source: Adapted from Indian and Northern Affairs Canada/Affaires indiennes et du Nord Canada (2005), fig. 2.

of an approach to funding that is seriously out of date in general, and out of touch with the current reality of First Nations post-secondary education needs in particular. The evidence was so convincing that the authors of the report on the review (a process, it is worth noting, with significant INAC oversight) concluded that the current INAC Post-Secondary Education program lacks a 'contemporary policy framework' (ibid., 49), as well as a useful management data framework, and the support it provides falls well below 'standards set for other Canadians,' standards which the authors inferred from provisions of the Canada Student Loans Program (ibid., 51). The review concluded that INAC post-secondary funding is out of touch both with First Nations needs and with the times.[9]

The key issue in funding Aboriginal post-secondary education is the validity of First Nations claims that education, *including post-secondary education*, is both an inherent and treaty right that is therefore entrenched under section 35 of the Constitution. Here, First Nations organizations and the federal government are diametrically opposed by their interpretations. First Nations organizations insist that treaties with any guarantee of schooling should be broadly construed to include post-secondary education, because in the contemporary context, it has become every bit as essential to well-being and human development as primary schooling was at the time the numbered treaties were concluded. Furthermore, First Nations insist on education as an inherent right. For its part, the federal government (aside from the attempt of the Martin government to negotiate a new relationship between First Nations and the Government of Canada in the now defunct 'Kelowna Accord') has maintained that it funds post-secondary education for First Nations students as a matter of social policy, not fiduciary obligation (Indian and Northern Affairs Canada/Affaires indiennes et du Nord Canada 2005, 34). The difference in position on the source of the mandate for federal funding of First Nations post-secondary education couldn't be more fundamental, or more crucial.

The pivotal importance of the treaty/inherent-right claim is this: Aboriginal and First Nations students are eligible for Canada Student Loans (and the educational tax deduction if they or sponsoring parents have taxable income)[10] on the same terms and conditions as any other Canadian student. Furthermore, Aboriginal students are eligible for Millennium Scholarships on the same terms and conditions as other students – although almost no First Nations students obtain them.[11] Thus, *purely in terms of access to funding outside of family sources for tuition, student fees, books and materials, and living expenses*, First Nations students and Aboriginal students in general are no worse off than other Canadian students. Whether that support is adequate or not, and whether the resulting average student debt loads and debt-to-earnings ratios are appropriate in terms of 'equitable' access to post-secondary education are separate, though related issues. Reasonable student investment in education with relatively high private rates of return to them is also a separate issue. Figure 4.3 shows changes over time in average debt incurred by graduating baccalaureate-level students who borrowed from the Canadian Student Loan Program, and in the proportion of all graduates who borrowed from CSLP.[12]

The underlying issue is whether Aboriginal students in general and First Nations students in particular are entitled to additional or separate support mechanisms, and what that entitlement might be. Generally, Aboriginal groups claim that they have such an entitlement and that it takes one of two forms, treaty right or 'inherent right'– or both.

The Treaty Right Rationale

The treaty right argument generally runs along the lines that the origi-

Figure 4.3 Incidence and amount of student debt of bachelor's degree graduates from 1982 to 2003 (in 2003 real dollars)

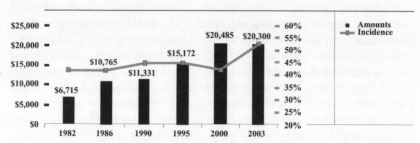

Source: Junor and Usher (2004), fig. 6.IV.1, using original data from Statistics Canada's 1982, 1986, 1990 and 1995 National Graduate Surveys (from Finnie, Student Loans), Statistics Canada's 2000 National Graduate Survey (custom tabulations) and Lang Research's 2004 Meta-Analysis of Post-Secondary Institutions Graduate Surveys.
Note: Because of change in methodologies, 2003 figures are likely 'slightly overstated' (Junor and Usher 2004, 281). The historical values in this figure are somewhat higher than those Finnie (2002) estimated (even allowing for different currency 'base' years).

nal school guarantee wording of the treaties should be given a liberal interpretation and taken to mean 'provide education necessary to survive and prosper in the new post-treaty socio-economic reality.' The strict wording of the treaties, however, binds the government only to provide 'a school in each reserve' (Treaties 1 and 2) or 'to maintain schools for instruction' (Treaty 3 and Treaty 5) or 'to pay such salaries of teachers to instruct the children of said Indians, and also to provide such school buildings and educational equipment as may seem advisable to His Majesty's government of Canada' (Treaty 9).[13] Neither party to the treaties could have foreseen the dramatic changes in educational standards and expectations that have occurred over time. In particular, neither party could have foreseen the rapid increase over the last century, especially since the Second World War, in levels of educational attainment necessary for an economically prosperous, socially fulfilling, and politically engaged life. Until the 1960s at least, an elementary education was sufficient for a man to provide a decent living for his family and to participate meaningfully in grass-roots politics. Since then, higher education has become essential for most women and men who expect to be economically self-sufficient and able to comprehend, as well as engage meaningfully with the political and policy processes that control and shape their lives in myriad ways.

So, should the educational clauses of treaties that contain one (and not all do) be interpreted strictly, as according a contractual and fiduciary right only to federal provision of elementary and perhaps secondary schooling, or should they be construed broadly according a federal guarantee of 'education necessary for you *as First Nations persons* to function and prosper in the larger Canadian society of the day'? Furthermore, should such a guarantee be 'read into' treaties that do not mention schools or schooling or into the situation of First Nations groups not covered by treaty? And if the first assumption is taken as correct, what quality of elementary and secondary education would such a minimalist guarantee encompass – a 'formally' equal education, with the same number of years of study available as in comparable provincial systems, or a *substantively* equal education, with similar outcomes on relevant achievement outcomes (and where would Aboriginal languages and cultures fit in such a comparability calculus)?

The Royal Commission on Aboriginal Peoples notes, 'Over the past two decades, the Supreme Court of Canada has ruled in various cases that broad, just and liberal interpretation of treaties is in order, with due regard for the historical context in which they were signed,' and then cites approvingly an elder who argues for a comprehensive and 'contemporized' view of education as a treaty right, a view broad enough to encompass 'state of the art' post-secondary education:

> Pauline Pelly, a Saskatchewan elder, voiced this view at the Federation of Saskatchewan Indian Nations treaty rights education symposium in October 1991:
>
> > Education was given to us. They promised us that you will be very smart, like the cunning of the white man. The highest education that you can get, that is what they promised to us. That is what we wanted.
> >
> > First Nations maintain that the spirit and intent of the treaties are as significant as the actual wording. The promise of a 'schoolhouse on every reserve' represented what was state-of-the-art education when the treaties were signed. And elders maintain that it was state-of-the-art education that Aboriginal peoples negotiated. Supreme Court interpretations have lent support to Aboriginal contentions that the representations of government at the time are as important as the actual words written down. (Royal Commission on Aboriginal Peoples 1996b, 506–7)

In a similar vein, MacPherson (1991) concludes that the legal obligations imposed by the treaty education provisions will likely be read broadly by the courts:

> I believe that the education provisions in most of the major treaties impose a legal obligation to do more than simply 'maintain a school.' If Simon and Sioui teach us anything it is that the ancient and usually terse language of treaties will be interpreted in light of modern needs. Accordingly, depending on the historical evidence in particular cases, phrases like 'maintain a school' might be interpreted to mean 'provide effective education' because at the time a treaty was signed the provision of effective education was articulated in the shorthand of 'maintain a school' mode. In any case, whatever the actual content of individual treaties (this will depend not only on statutory interpretation but also on the historical record) the important point is that there can be no doubt that when there is an education provision in a treaty it will be interpreted liberally so as to ensure that it operates in a meaningful way in the current context. (32)

If a really broad reading of treaty education clauses is correct – and if, therefore, the federal government is wrong in ascribing 'social policy' status to funding First Nations post-secondary education – just what would such a liberal interpretation guarantee? Would it assure completely funded access for all potential First Nations students to all post-secondary programs to which they can obtain admission? Or would it only imply *partial* funding for *some* First Nations students in *certain* post-secondary programs, and function more like a bursary program than a guaranteed 'full funding' program? Who will decide, and what are the implications of who decides for the nature of the decisions likely to come?

These are troubling questions which are likely to be answered only in the course of negotiating new relationships between First Nations and the Government of Canada. The pertinence of Turner's insistence on 'Kymlicka's constraint' couldn't be more obvious. The scope and details of any post-secondary guarantee read into the treaty guarantees, and the treaty relationship in general, will depend on adept, intelligent, informed 'word warriors,' but it will also depend on the values and priorities of the 'power brokers' in Canadian society, government, and the judiciary. Word warriors capable of facilitating answers to these questions favourable to the interests of Aboriginal students, as to questions that emerge from inherent-right claims, will indeed need to 'engage the

Canadian state's legal and political discourses in more effective ways' (Turner 2006, 99).

Given the uncertainty and evident dependency embedded in the treaty argument, and its obvious lack of direct application to Aboriginal groups not covered by one of the numbered treaties (non-status Indians, Métis, most First Nations peoples in Quebec and so forth), most Aboriginal groups argue in favour of the 'full funding' of all costs associated with post-secondary education for Aboriginal people by the federal government, without any 'rationing' restraints beyond the ability of Aboriginal students to gain admission to post-secondary programs. They also argue that an obligation of the federal government to fund post-secondary education for Aboriginal peoples stems not only from treaties and treaty-like relationships but also more fundamentally from the nature of education at all levels as an 'inherent right.'

The 'Inherent-Right' Rationale

Such attempts to ground an Aboriginal or First Nations post-secondary funding claim on 'inherent rights' raises the question of what might legitimately constitute an inherent right in the case of Aboriginal peoples. In particular, it begs the question of what courts might be willing to construe as an inherent right and, what they would be willing to support as a legitimate exercise of such a right. How likely is it that the courts would legitimate post-secondary funding as an inherent right of Aboriginal peoples? After all, the judiciary's position on the matter will be a crucial element in the political calculus surrounding ultimate acceptance or rejection of claims that funding of post-secondary study for Aboriginal students is part of Aboriginal 'inherent rights.'

MacPherson cites Pentney as a key scholar who argues for inclusion of education within the scope of Aboriginal rights. Interestingly, Pentney's argument for education as an Aboriginal right is grounded almost entirely in cultural difference, or 'different-ness' as he calls it. Specifically, Pentney insists that '... [p]rotection of the group's existence will be meaningless unless it is accompanied by protection of the group's activities and institutional structures and capacity for maintaining these by practices and education' (as cited in MacPherson and Canada, Dept. of Indian Affairs and Northern Development 1991, 33). Macpherson is palpably less optimistic, however, with regard to the judicial prospects for education as an inherent Aboriginal right rather than a treaty right.[14]

Education as an inherent right poses a grave and fundamental ambivalence, post-secondary education particularly so. In his insightful exposition of the legal difficulties and policy conundrums associated with applying the *Charter* to Aboriginal governments in the exercise of their inherent rights, Wilkins (1999a) summarizes succinctly what the Supreme Court has determined in *Delgamuukw*[15] and *Van der Peet*[16] to constitute 'Aboriginal' and hence 'inherent' rights.

> ... mainstream law protects and enforces as aboriginal rights only those traditions, customs and relationships that already existed in some form, and were of central or defining significance to the culture of the relevant aboriginal community before and apart from European influence. Practices or customs that 'arose solely as a response to European influences' – including, one must assume, any rights or powers conferred by settler peoples – 'will not meet the standard for recognition of an aboriginal right.' Any self-government rights that qualify for the constitution's protection [under s. 35] as aboriginal rights will, therefore, of necessity be inherent rights. (4–5)

Where might these key judicial decision criteria – exercised prior to contact, of crucial cultural importance, and not solely a response to European influences – leave 'formal' education in general and post-secondary education in regard to their potential claims to inherent-right status? On the one hand, there can be no legitimate doubt that Aboriginal peoples 'educated' their children prior to contact, if by education we mean something like 'transmitted the knowledge and skills and fostered appropriate values and beliefs for life within their time, culture, and environment.' The modality of the education, as has so often been noted, differed radically from that of European, school-based, 'formal' education. But in the broader purposes of preparing the young and initiating them into functional roles in their society along with nurturing values and beliefs to help them find meaning and order in their journey through life, pre-contact Aboriginal education surely paralleled the purposes of European education. Without doubt, education as practised in Aboriginal societies was of crucial 'cultural importance'; it constituted the very means by which each generation passed on its sense of what it meant to be a member of that society. The remarkable precision with which oral tradition passed down verbatim from one generation to another the great lessons and mysteries of Aboriginal culture testifies eloquently to the centrality of that aspect of education to the nature of Aboriginal culture. By virtue of its placement in time, pre-contact education was 'not solely a response to European influences,' it was completely devoid of them.

What of contemporary 'Aboriginal education,' the education that young Aboriginal people experience in our time? Except in its most abstract and overarching purposes, and even then, to what degree can such schooling claim roots in the education Aboriginal peoples provided their young prior to contact? Given the widespread disjunction of contemporary 'Aboriginal education' – even education administered by Aboriginal entities themselves – from Aboriginal traditions and culture (either historical or contemporary), to what degree could a claim be defended that it is 'of central significance to Aboriginal culture,' especially when the qualifier 'pre-contact' is understood to apply? Finally, given that the standards and comparisons by which Aboriginal education is evaluated are established by mainstream Canadian education, to what degree could one defend successfully in court the proposition that such education is not 'solely a response to European influences'?

Interestingly, the criteria Wilkins (1999b) summarizes seem to lead squarely to the 'parity paradox' of Aboriginal education: the need to conform to the broader standards and norms in provincial education systems on the one hand and the need to be substantially grounded in Aboriginal cultures and/or languages on the other. To the extent that Aboriginal education is grounded in Aboriginal cultures (historical or contemporary – and the distinction matters if one grounds one's political-theory framework in a relational pluralist stance as opposed to a cultural preservation and restoration stance) and/or languages it can legitimately be viewed as:

- carrying on 'traditions, customs and relationships that already existed in some form,'
- 'of central or defining significance to the culture of the relevant aboriginal community before[17] and apart from European influence,'
- not 'solely ... a response to European influences,' and
- not constituting a right or power 'conferred' by settler peoples.
  (Wilkins 1999b, 4–5; emphasis added)

Education that credibly balances Aboriginal content, especially culturally central content, with contemporary provincially sanctioned curricula or programs should be considered a legitimate exercise of an inherent right to educate, in our view. Consequently, it should be protected by section 35 of the Constitution – completely apart from the meagre and strictly permissive statutory provisions for First Nations elementary and secondary education in the *Indian Act*. Education that does not contain culturally central components, *even if administered by First Nations or other Aboriginal entities*, could not qualify as an inherent-right exercise, at least not by the criteria currently contained in the potentially relevant Supreme Court of Canada decisions. In this sense, education provided by non-status Indian or Métis school jurisdictions that balance credibly Aboriginal content, especially if it is culturally central with contemporary provincial curricula or programs, might also qualify as an exercise of an educational inherent right.

The crucial obverse corollary to this reasoning is that education that does *not* incorporate such a credible balance between culturally central content and mainstream curricula could *not* qualify as an exercise of an educational inherent right and therefore could never attract section 35 protection, *even if delivered by an Aboriginal entity*. This conclusion should be taken seriously by Aboriginal and especially First Nations jurisdictions that have often provided more lip service to culture than substantial and *credible* cultural components to the educational programs they administer. Such programs at the elementary and secondary level, and funding for them are almost as vulnerable as INAC support for post-secondary students and programs, since sections 114 through 120 of the *Indian Act* do not require the minister to do anything.

A CONDENSED HISTORY OF DIAND/INAC POST-SECONDARY FUNDING RELATED TO THE INHERENT-RIGHT CLAIM

Understanding the 'ontological,' political, policy status, and legal prospects of the inherent-right claim as applied to post-secondary funding requires a sense of historical context. Stonechild (2004) meticulously recounts the history of post-secondary education for First Nations students and of federal support for it from the earliest claims of the National Indian Brotherhood for federal support for 'The Education Right of the Mature Indian' embedded in a 1974 NIB proposal to the federal cabinet for drastic overhaul of the *Indian Act*. This seminal proposal 'would call for such funding to be statutory rather than discretionary, and as well *to be available to all Indians who desired it without regard to cost* [emphasis added]. Such funding would cover all costs related to higher education for Indian students, and there would be no limit placed on the number of students who could access the funding [in short, this proposal called for no rationing mechanism at all]' (84).

The federal reaction to this proposal was consistent with historic federal reticence in funding First Nations,[18] to say nothing of Aboriginal education: trepidation at the potential cost of such an unqualified right to unlimited resources, a cost burden the government estimated at close to $500 million dollars (in 1977 dollars, and thus close to $1.6 billion in 2005 dollars).[19] Despite its earlier endorsement of *Indian Control of Indian Education*, with its claim that 'it is the financial responsibility of the Federal Government to provide education of all types and all levels to all status Indian people, whether living on or off reserves' (National Indian Brotherhood 1972/1984, 3), the government rejected the 'mature-Indian' funding proposed by the NIB because it 'did not apply to all Canadians generally,' a response the NIB criticized as a refusal to honour treaty obligations (ibid., 85). This reaction on the part of the federal government implicitly denied the blanket NIB claim to an 'education right' on the part of all 'mature' (over fifteen years of age) Indians, regardless of treaty provisions.

The history of financial assistance for status Indian post-secondary students began in 1968–9, when DIAND assisted 250 students who could not obtain funding for their studies in any other way (Stonechild 2004, 104). In the wake of the White Paper, *Indian Control*, and the federal response, Indian Affairs began 'unilaterally' drafting guidelines (the 'E-12' guidelines) 'to formalize its discretionary funding of post-secondary students' (ibid., 105). Early provisions requiring contributions by students and student performance standards were removed in the face of objections from Indian organizations, and maximum eligible time for assistance was increased. From the beginning, then, the NIB and DIAND were gridlocked over whether or not E-12 guidelines should contain restrictive measures to ration resources channeled into post-secondary student support (ibid., 106).

In the face of rapidly increasing Indian and Inuit enrolment in colleges and universities, in 1977 Indian Affairs created the Post-Secondary Education Assistance Program (PSEAP) 'to encourage participation and to fund the maximum number of students who qualified for entrance' (ibid., 106). In 1978, Indian Affairs finalized its PSEAP funding guidelines. In their initial form, the guidelines provided unlimited funding for any status-Indian student who was accepted into a university program. For a brief moment in history, First Nations leaders had what they wanted in regard to post-secondary support, full funding without rationing. Even as DIAND embarked on this policy of unfettered access to university, however, it warned that such a policy with no rationing mechanism would be unsustainable over time, and that cutbacks would be necessary. In the wake of this 'full funding' approach, enrolment burgeoned, reaching 6,500 nationally by 1982–3, although completion rates remained significantly below national norms (ibid., 107).

Only after the dust had settled from patriation of the Constitution, and from the drama surrounding Aboriginal efforts to assure constitutional entrenchment of their rights in any patriated version of the Constitution, did DIAND move to cap funding for post-secondary student support. In May of 1987, shortly after the release of the Nielsen Task Force's scorching indictment of Indian Affairs and its programs, Bill McKnight, then minister of Indian Affairs, invited First Nations to participate in consultations aimed at improving PSEAP. INAC said it wanted to encourage Indian organizations to take greater responsibility for managing the program while making it more cost effective in light of the overarching goal of Indian self-determination. The government proposed to revise the E-12 guidelines to cap funding, and to force First Nations funding agencies to decide who got funding and who didn't, and to provide reasons for their decisions. Among other things, the initial draft revisions to E-12 would have reduced funding eligibility from 96 to 48 months, cut funding for adult upgrading education outside of that provided by a university or college, imposed funding on a priority basis, and ended the possibility of appeal on the basis that funding was unavailable (ibid., 126). The proposed revisions produced a brief tempest of reaction and media attention. Regardless, in June of 1987 McKnight imposed a cap of $93.7 million on Indian post-secondary funding, although in October of the same year he denied publicly that such a cap was actually in place (ibid., 128). Henceforth, Indian postsecondary students would compete against one another for a fixed amount of funding, and First Nations agencies would make the rules – and take local blame – for allocating such funding.

The 1986 and 1988 Auditor General's reports sharply criticized PSEAP. The 1988 report particularly took aim at inconsistent monitoring practices and errors, including errors in payments, and lack of documentation in student files. The report also called attention both to the lack of statutory basis for the program and the unclear delineation in policy of the respective roles of DIAND on the one hand and bands and tribal councils on the other (ibid., 129). McKnight again announced plans for consultations with First Nations to be held between May and December of 1988, with a view towards implementing a new policy by

1 April 1989. The planned policy revision would ensure greater local control by requiring local First Nations funders to develop their own operating guidelines (ibid., 130).

To offer context for Aboriginal constitutional discussions, the government had funded the Assembly of First Nations (successor to the National Indian Brotherhood) to establish the National Indian Education Forum (NIEF). This generously funded enterprise culminated in a report entitled *Tradition and Education: Towards a Vision of Our Future* (National Indian Brotherhood and Assembly of First Nations, 1988) which promised far more than it delivered. It did, however, set the semantics for 'First Nations jurisdiction' discourse over the next two decades. Unfortunately, its impact was minimal because of its lack of conceptual rigour and credibility. Indeed, its most enduring impact may well be the wholly unintended one of demonstrating how important such rigour and credibility are if Aboriginal peoples and First Nations people in particular are going to 'engage the Canadian state's legal and political discourses in more effective ways' (Turner 2006, 99).

With regard to the question of post-secondary support as an inherent right, the authors of *Tradition and Education* had little more to offer than an assertion that '[t]he data gathered and analyzed from the First Nations by three research programs [threads of inquiry related to primary, secondary, and post-secondary education] strongly affirmed that post-secondary education is an aboriginal right of First Nations' (National Indian Brotherhood and Assembly of First Nations 1988, 97). Aside from impressive vagueness about what such a right would entail other than 'direct federal funding sources for post-secondary education … controlled by individual First Nations,' the 'data' consist mainly of opinions from First Nations constituent groups gleaned from community survey instruments. Unfortunately, these survey instruments are not reproduced with the study report, or with an equally poorly documented Committee of Inquiry process, so they cannot be examined for biases or other problems. The embarrassingly myopic and conceptually anemic prescription (especially given the magnitude of resources consumed in the study) of the authors of *Tradition and Education* for post-secondary funding, as for most problems in First Nations education, seems to boil down to more money at the local level: 'While First Nations educational institutions are frustrated by fiscal restraint and constructive guidelines [it is not clear whether the 'constructive guidelines' existed and were frustrating, or their absence was frustrating; did the authors want more 'guidelines'?], First Nations are pursuing direct federal funding by proposing transfer of specific educational monies to the local level' (ibid., 98). It is hardly surprising that this exorbitantly overpriced study and report (INAC provided $8 million for the project) attracted little more than disinterest and disdain in the broader policy world, especially in the halls of INAC. The authors proved lamentably inept both as researchers and as 'word warriors,' and thus failed to 'engage' the Canadian state's relevant legal and political discourses in ways that would be taken seriously. The report did nothing to advance the cause of First Nations education in general, and of First Nations post-secondary education as an inherent right in particular.[20] At best, the report popularized 'jurisdiction' semantics, which many years later would be incorporated into the 'restoration of jurisdiction' efforts of a number of First Nations groups.[21]

Despite sporadic student protests against new and impending cuts to post-secondary funding that attracted little media attention or public sympathy, Pierre Cadieux, newly appointed minister of Indian Affairs, announced a new student funding program, the Post-Secondary Student Support Program (PSSSP, which was mentioned earlier), that has survived to the present day. Cadieux aggressively defended the department's funding of Indian students as 'generous and fair,' noting that the number of students supported by INAC had grown from 3,500 in 1977–8 to 15,000 in 1988–9, and that support costs had risen from $9 million to $130 million over the same time period (Stonechild 2004, 134). Cadieux seized the occasion to underscore that, in the government's view PSSSP, like PSEAP before it was a matter of social policy. It was not a treaty, and certainly not an inherent right: 'For the government, the position is crystal clear ... treaty references to education do not include post-secondary education ... The government has funded this special program to ensure that a significant number of Indian students attain university-level qualifications' (ibid., 136).

A November 1989 INAC retrospective evaluation of PSEAP revealed the Achilles heel of the program in terms of its 'social policy' goal, that is, ensuring 'a significant number of students attain university-level qualifications.' First, only one quarter of supported students were registered in universities. Most were in community college programs. Completion and graduation rates were abysmal – 'in a typical year, less than 15% of the students had completed their year's program' (ibid., 142). Those who did complete their studies tended to be in short-term community college programs. The non-completion rate was 76 per cent in social sciences, where well over half of the supported students studied. Participation in health and sciences accounted for only 2 per cent of students. University and college entrance programs had very high failure rates (ibid., 142).

Paralleling these disturbing indicators of academic failure was the emergence of a plethora of 'general vocational programs' that had little purpose, limited benefit for students, and dubious program content.[22] These programs siphoned funding away from students in reputable programs. In the new reality of rationing, caps, and a dearth of funding for increases in both the cost of living and enrolment, these programs made it more financially difficult for students in bona fide university or college programs to cope with living expenses, including travel and, increasingly, childcare.

Another crucial event had overtaken PSEAP funding in 1985. The provision in section 12 of the *Indian Act*, which had removed status from Indian women who had married non-status males while allowing status Indian males to 'pass on' status to their non-status spouses and children unmistakably violated section 15 of the *Charter*. Following the Lovelace decision by the UN Human Rights Committee,[23] the government passed Bill C-31 on 28 June 1985.[24] Designed to end gender discrimination under the *Indian Act*, although in reality it removed only one notorious instance of it, Bill C-31 made it possible for all women who had lost their status by marrying a non-status husband to be reinstated to both the official list of status Indians maintained by the minister of Indian Affairs and to the band membership list from which they had been stricken at the time of their marriage. The crucial importance of Bill C-31 for PSEAP was that it threatened to add over 50,000 reinstated women and their children to the rolls of potential PSEAP applicants.

THE LEGAL PROSPECTS OF INHERENT-RIGHT-BASED POST-SECONDARY FUNDING

Despite the Supreme Court of Canada's now often-repeated dictum that 'treaties and statutes relating to Indians should be liberally construed and doubtful expressions resolved in favour of the Indians,'[25] First Nations groups have been understandably reluctant to test the waters in court concerning the nature and extent of treaty, fiduciary, or inherent-right bases in law for First Nations education. We agree with Stonechild (2004) in his assessment that this reticence is attributable to fear of the implications and the finality of decisions on any of these three non-statutory legal groundings for education right claims.

With the federal government failing to enact appropriate legislation, the *Tradition and Education* report pointed out that: 'A test case seeking a declaration that Constitutionally the federal government has an obligation to resource education for First Nations citizens' could be pursued. It cautioned, however, that 'an adverse ruling is difficult if not impossible[26] to negotiate away.' Apart from the fear of the court arriving at a negative or narrow interpretation, the finality of such a decision and the implications that it might have for the gains made so far, give pause for thought about rushing into legal action. (185)

A Supreme Court of Canada decision against Aboriginal educational claims, and especially post-secondary education claims based on treaties, fiduciary obligation, *or* inherent right would effectively foreclose any future use of the impugned type of claim in negotiations with the federal or any provincial government. In this, at least, the authors of *Tradition and Education* spoke with insight. Defeat in litigation carried to the Supreme Court would be the death knell of the kinds of claims in question. Here as elsewhere in Aboriginal politics and policy, there is no escape from 'Kymlicka's constraint.' Whatever proportion of Aboriginal people may believe that elementary, secondary and post-secondary education is an inherent right, that won't carry much weight in policy unless the courts agree – or unless policy-makers believe they might.

Wilkins (2004) contrasts the current and evolving state of play in jurisprudence on treaty rights versus Aboriginal (inherent) rights:

One crucial indicator of the reasonableness [to courts] of a claim for constitutional protection is proof of the importance to the claimant community of the interest, practice, custom, or arrangement for which it is seeking protection. Courts now routinely accept that Aboriginal parties to treaties are entitled to expect the Crown to keep the treaty promises it made to them, *as the Aboriginal parties might reasonably have understood those promises at the time the treaty was made*. In respect of Aboriginal rights, however, the issue is more complex and more controversial. The Supreme Court's insistence in *Van der Peet* that Aboriginal rights (apart from Aboriginal title) include only that which has traditionally been 'integral to the distinctive culture' of the claimant community has come in for a good deal of astute and considered criticism, but it does reflect, if perhaps too clumsily or overzealously, a strong sense that the constitution should not be understood to give Aboriginal peoples (or anyone else) license to do just whatever they might want. If Aboriginal rights are unique to Aboriginal peoples, the sentiment is that such rights should protect only that which is unique to them as Aboriginal peoples. (296–7; emphasis added)

Even so, Wilkins reminds readers that the members of the Supreme Court, wisely sensing that they are on very unfamiliar ground, have been very cautious to cut themselves considerable slack for future decisions on Aboriginal rights: '... their intuitions about these matters are in many respects not yet refined enough or trustworthy enough to support general legal rules or firm doctrinal pronouncements ... that, in respect of these matters at least, there are more things in heaven and earth than are dreamt of in its jurisprudence' (ibid., 294). He concludes that potential Aboriginal rights litigants would do well to the extent possible to coordinate strategically the course, sequence, and pace of Aboriginal rights litigation. He recommends that Aboriginal parties start systematically with small, limited claims whose 'proportionality' and 'discreteness' are less likely to disturb judges' sense of impact on the existing constitutional and legal order, and then gradually move on to larger issues with potentially more expansive consequences. Moving in this way will allow the courts to gain a better sense of the issues at stake from an Aboriginal perspective, and of how to balance Aboriginal rights with essential elements of the Canadian constitutional and legal order.

Even as he does so, Wilkins reminds readers that litigation is light years away from Aboriginal traditions, that it is at best a blunt and dangerous instrument, and that negotiation is often preferable. 'Even participating in mainstream judicial institutions is to some extent a compromise of traditional Aboriginal ways. The greater the sense of compromise, the better the reason for Aboriginal peoples to avoid litigation, where the option exists (ibid., 306). Still, in a conclusion reminiscent of a lawyer's version of 'Kymlicka's constraint,' Wilkins 'invite[s] ... [Aboriginal section 35 litigants] to take realistic and deliberate account when and as they are able to do so in preparing their litigation, of the evident concerns and propensities of their non-Aboriginal judges' (ibid., 305).

In regard to post-secondary being regarded similarly to elementary and secondary education, the courts would almost surely follow the general reasoning and criteria set forth in *Delgamuukw* and *Van der Peet*. If that were the case, cultural content would be likely to emerge as a pivotal and difficult issue, especially given that most Aboriginal students, and First Nations students in particular, pursue fields of studies neither rooted in nor adapted to Aboriginal culture (historical or contemporary). They do so in public universities and colleges not aligned with or committed to Aboriginal communities. It is particularly difficult to envisage how the courts would construe Aboriginal participation in mainstream post-secondary education as 'a logical evolution of the activities traditionally engaged in' by any Aboriginal group prior to contact, the test that C.J. McLachlin, writing for a unanimous court in *Marshall and Bernard,* applied to the question of whether the plaintiffs' logging activities constituted *either* a treaty right *or* an exercise of 'Aboriginal title' entrenched by section 35 of the Constitution.[27] McLachlin focused mainly on the treaty issue; however, the court also rejected the claim to title following a traditional use rationale. While the degree to which the Supreme Court would follow the 'logical evolution' rule in regard to an Aboriginal/inherent-right (as opposed to treaty) claim is purely speculative at this point, it offers the only semblance of a 'test' the high court has offered to separate protected Aboriginal rights claims from unprotected ones. Even as the Court insisted on the 'logical evolution' principle, however, it cautioned that 'Ancestral trading activities ... are not frozen in time and the question in each case is whether the modern trading activity in issue represents a logical evolution from the traditional trading activities at the time the treaties were made.'[28] If the courts adopted this logical evolution principle as a binding precedent 'test' of Aboriginal rights claims in general, it would require a particularly broad interpretation to construe post-secondary education without significant Aboriginal cultural content as a logical evolution of traditional, pre-contact education.

In short, the reticence of Aboriginal groups to try to establish education as an inherent right by litigation seems particularly prudent with respect to post-secondary education. Even if they could prove to the satisfaction of the courts that post-secondary education is as fundamentally necessary to prosperity, personal fulfillment, and social and political participation as was pre-contact education, in its current state, Supreme Court reasoning would likely return to the question of cultural centrality. This would raise the question of the importance of the education to preservation, or perhaps even to contemporary redefinition of the Aboriginal culture(s) at issue in the case. A program that supported mainly participation in conventional courses in public universities and colleges would be unlikely to meet such a standard.

The end result of this juridical inherent-right calculus is uncertain at best, as well as potentially quite unsettling. At the post-secondary level, the inherent-right claim argument would be even more difficult to sustain than at the elementary or secondary level.

Or would the courts, given the latitude for case-by-case findings the Supreme Court has left available so far, find some unforeseeable reasoning to deal with the greater maturity and need for immersion in the world of ideas and skills to justify mainstream post-secondary programs in institutions as an integral part of the Aboriginal inherent right to education? If there is light to be found at the end of that tunnel, it perhaps comes from Turner (2006):

> What can an indigenous person who *is* trained in European philosophy *do* to play a more effective role in the relationship between the indigenous political leadership, which finds its roots in indigenous philosophy, and the European intellectual tradition, which is used in articulating the content of Aboriginal rights discourse in Canada? I believe there are two important roles a philosopher can play. The first is pedagogical. From my own experience, I have seen too many indigenous students come into university resisting the idea that learning European forms of knowledge, never mind critiquing European ways of thinking, is important for their intellectual development. Don't get me wrong – there are very good reasons for this resistance, and I don't think every person, indigenous *or* non-indigenous, is suited to this kind of intellectual journey. Indigenous professors are obligated to guide their students through complex intellectual landscapes so that they can begin to think for themselves how ideas relate to their indigeneity. Like all students, *indigenous students need to learn bodies of knowledge in order to be able to think effectively* [emphasis added]; and if indigenous students leave university without at least knowing the social, legal, and political history of the Indian-white relationship, they have failed to receive a good education and their chances of becoming effective indigenous intellectuals are severely limited. (114)

By an ironic twist of fate, could judicial reasoning lead to a conclusion that, *as a minimum condition* for becoming 'effective Indigenous intellectuals' and hence suitably equipped to *defend* and thus to participate in the development of their culture (after all, isn't that what Aboriginal peoples did in pre-contact times?), Aboriginal students require just the kind of deep grounding in *mainstream* disciplinary knowledge and skills that most programs in provincial post-secondary institutions offer? This sounds too far-fetched to be anywhere on the 'radar screen' of judicial reasoning, but may be no more unlikely than other bits of unexpected reasoning that have found their way into precedent-setting decisions.

Of course, even if the courts were to decide that Aboriginal post-secondary education could be part of an inherent right, all of the qualitative issues about the nature and scope of the education, and hence funding guaranteed, would remain. Would all Aboriginal students in all post-secondary programs (regardless of the quality and credibility of such programs) be funded, because any such study is a legitimate exercise of an inherent right? Or would rationing of funding by program quality, at least to the point of excluding the funding of dubious programs by questionable institutions, be taken as a legitimate exception to – *or even an integral assurance of* – an inherent right to post-secondary study?

To understand the inescapable relevance of this question, one has but to reflect on the history of INAC funding of First Nations post-secondary students. Initially, DIAND cheerfully funded any eligible student in any 'post-secondary' program. As enrolments increased and programs, particularly dubious transition programs perceived increasingly as 'opportunist' proliferated, and finally as the potential enrolment implications of Bill C-31 and First Nations birth rates far above provincial averages became obvious, INAC decided to enforce rationing by decoupling funding from the number of eligible applicants and 'devolving' to First Nations agencies the decision of how to allocate the reduced resources. Over time, as the pool of potential applicants increased and funding stagnated, First Nations funders have been increasingly constrained to ration available funding *both* by limiting the number of students funded *and* by limiting the amount provided for living expenses. The end result has been that Post-Secondary Student Support Program has evolved into what amounts to a bursary rather than a comprehensive student support program. Nonetheless, it seems likely that PSSSP continues to be *the* crucial enabler of First Nations post-secondary students for most individuals benefiting from the program. Of students surveyed in Phase 2 of the INAC evaluation study, 77.4 per cent reported that they would not have attended a post-secondary institution without PSSSP funding (Indian and Northern Affairs Canada/Affaires indiennes et du Nord Canada 2005, 33).

RCAP's Approach to Post-Secondary Education and Funding

In a manner consistent with its strong stance in favour of inherent rights in education and in governance generally, the Royal Commission on Aboriginal Peoples (RCAP) proposed a series of measures to improve post-secondary education and funding for Aboriginal and especially First Nations people.

RCAP recommended various measures, among which some are clearly reflected in the Association of Universities and Colleges of Canada study of current university and degree-granting college adaptations to Aboriginal needs (Holmes 2006, 14–33). Specifically, the commission (1996b) recommended:

> Public post-secondary institutions in the provinces and territories undertake new initiatives or extend current ones to increase the participation, retention and graduation of Aboriginal students by introducing, encouraging or enhancing
>
> (a) a welcoming environment for Aboriginal students;
> (b) Aboriginal content and perspectives in course offerings across disciplines;
> (c) Aboriginal studies and programs as part of the institution's regular program offerings and included in the institution's core budget;
> (d) Aboriginal appointments to boards of governors;
> (e) Aboriginal councils to advise the president of the institution;
> (f) active recruitment of Aboriginal students;
> (g) admission policies that encourage access by Aboriginal applicants;
> (h) meeting spaces for Aboriginal students;
> (i) Aboriginal student unions;
> (j) recruitment of Aboriginal faculty members;
> (k) support services with Aboriginal counsellors for academic and personal counselling; and
> (l) cross-cultural sensitivity training for faculty and staff. (515–16)

Each of these measures has obvious cost implications and provincial governments, as noted earlier, have not directly funded such initiatives. Individual post-secondary institutions are, to varying degrees, 'finding' money within their budgets to support some of them.

In addition, the commission recommended establishment, where numbers warrant, of Aboriginal colleges affiliated with chartered public universities (ibid., recommendation 3.5.25, 516) in the manner of the First Nations University of Canada. The commission also endorsed somewhat smaller, but by Aboriginal standards, 'large' colleges and technical institutes with more limited mandates, and spoke supportively of smaller, more narrowly focused and locally based programs offering university preparation or university-level study. In regard to such programs, the commission considered that 'The key to the success of smaller, Aboriginally controlled institutions is having cash in hand to shop for the best programs for their students' because '... [c]olleges and universities, eager to increase their student counts, tend to respond positively when there is financial assistance to support non-conventional delivery of courses' (ibid., 518).

Finally, the commission praised the potential value of adult education learning centres such as the Alberta Vocational Centre and Contact North in Ontario, and of 'non-profit institute[s] that offer ... training in communities or to a group of communities such as First Nations Technical Institute in Tyendinaga, Ontario, and the First Nations Justice Institute in Mission, British Columbia' (ibid., 518–19). These types of programs, of course, share financial dependence on client communities – and hence, on the ability of these communities to secure funding in support of them.

Not surprisingly, RCAP was strikingly parsimonious and vague in its comments addressed specifically to post-secondary funding. The RCAP commentary on post-secondary funding can be reduced to a reinforcement of central lines of critique of the ISSP program emerging from the INAC evaluation study (see discussion earlier in this chapter in 'The Current State of Funding' section):

> Aboriginal post-secondary institutions live on precarious federal and provincial funding. The department of Indian affairs [*sic*] provides the only stable financial support received by the Saskatchewan Indian Federated College. But as the college has documented repeatedly, this funding is far less than that received by comparable public post-secondary institutions. The other schools depend on small program grants, which are short-term, often project-specific and always subject to change. This instability unsettles operations and makes long-term planning difficult. Aboriginal post-secondary institutions must be recognized and given stable funding. (ibid., 519)

Beyond these very general observations, the commission recommended only that

> Federal, provincial and territorial governments collaborate with Aboriginal governments and organizations to establish and support post-second-

ary educational institutions controlled by Aboriginal people, with negotiated allocation of responsibility for

    (a) core and program funding commensurate with the services they
        are expected to provide and comparable to the funding pro-
        vided to provincial or territorial institutions delivering similar
        services;

    (b) planning, capital and start-up costs of new colleges and institutes;

    (c) improvement of facilities for community learning centres as re-
        quired for new functions and development of new facilities where
        numbers warrant and the community establishes this as a priority;
        and

    (d) fulfilment of obligations pursuant to treaties and modern agree-
        ments with respect to education. (ibid., 522)

As in the case of elementary and secondary education, RCAP made
the role of elders central in Aboriginal education by calling for 'opportunities for elders to exchange traditional knowledge with one another
and to share traditional knowledge with students and scholars, both
Aboriginal and non-Aboriginal, in university settings' (Royal Commission on Aboriginal Peoples 1996b, 529). Such 'opportunities' are potentially exciting and, in addition to valorizing traditional knowledge, are
conducive to the broader purposes and goals embedded in our conceptual framework and the assumptions and interpretations we bring to it,
in particular to creative and mutually enriching interdependence. They
are also likely to be very expensive, since they would engage universities in an area where they have little experience and capacity.

Finally, in its most radical, but also most financially challenging proposal on post-secondary education, RCAP proposed establishment of
an 'Aboriginal Peoples' International University,' 'with the capacity
to function in all provinces and territories, be established to promote
traditional knowledge, to pursue applied research in support of Aboriginal self-government, and to disseminate information essential to
achieving broad Aboriginal development goals' (ibid., 533). However
attractive the development of such an institution is in terms of our own
central criterion of marshalling scarce resources where reasonable economies of scale can be achieved, this proposal faces numerous obstacles
that render its implementation extremely improbable. Among the most
important obstacles is the likely prohibitive cost of establishing a 'full
service' Aboriginal university that could provide the diversity of programming that would be required to serve the needs and interests of
the entire Aboriginal community in Canada – and endless wrangling

over cost-sharing among the federal, provincial, and territorial governments. Every danger exists, furthermore, that governance and policy in such an institution could easily become a dysfunctional tangle of conflicting interests and priorities.

Still, the relevant policy communities both Aboriginal and non-Aboriginal should not deceive themselves here. This proposal likely offers the best available hope for reasonably comprehensive and integrated university study within an Aboriginal conceptual and governance framework. One way or the other, if such education is ever to become available, federal, provincial, and territorial governments will need to contribute. Doing so piecemeal is likely to be more expensive in the long run than doing so in a focused and 'centralized' way – if ethics, value commitments, and governance arrangements can keep those involved in such an enterprise focused on the common good rather than on partisan control and gain.

Funding of Aboriginal Post-Secondary Education within Relational Pluralist Assumptions

Given the uncertain potential legal and constitutional status of Aboriginal claims to a right, be it treaty or inherent in nature, to targeted funding for post-secondary education, post-secondary funding issues are closely wedded to larger claims to self-governance and self-determination rights emanating from Aboriginal ancestry. We therefore necessarily embed our recommendations regarding Aboriginal post-secondary funding in our vision of a suitable process for renegotiating relationships between Aboriginal and settler governments, especially the federal government.

First Nations and other Aboriginal governments should negotiate new relationships with settler governments on a case-by-case basis – although terms, conditions, and funding levels in existing agreements will inevitably shape expectations about what is possible and desirable in future agreements. Through such negotiations, however, it will be essential to maintain some overall sense of adequacy, equity, and fair play, as well as some standards with regard to who gets funded under what conditions, and on transparent and consistent use of funds.

In short, barring some large-scale transfer to Aboriginal governments of at-source revenues as discussed by Marc Malone in his 1986 monograph on financing Aboriginal self-government (a most unlikely outcome given that it 'short circuits' *in principle* parliamentary responsibility for funding allocations made under the authority of Parliament),[29] some central body charged with negotiating the terms and conditions of new relationships with First Nations and other Aboriginal groups (the latter being, regrettably, very low on federal priorities in regard to Aboriginal affairs) will be necessary. This type of federal negotiating body is precisely what the Penner Committee (Canada, Parliament, House of Commons, Special Committee on Indian Self-Government, and Penner 1983) proposed a generation ago. Much of the logic of such an arrangement has already been adopted in regard to land claims settlement with the creation of the Comprehensive Claims Branch (CCB) of the Claims and Indian Government Sector of INAC, although the branch and sector remain technically within the INAC structure. The reasoning of the Penner Committee for this body remains sound, particularly with regard to the desirability of divorcing the negotiating of new relationships from INAC and its legacy. While less than a complete break with INAC, the CCB was a significant break from its normal program operations, and recognized that a new entity with powers to negotiate new relationships was needed. Progress to date towards land claims settlement (see summary in Comprehensive Claims Branch 2006), however limited, is owing mainly to the creation of a negotiating body distinct from the normal operational branches of INAC. Nonetheless, the announcement by Prime Minister Harper (CTV.ca News Staff 2007) of the creation of an 'independent land claims tribunal' to expedite a largely stagnated land claims process is further evidence of the wisdom and prescience of the Penner recommendation to remove the negotiation of new relationships from its historic INAC context.

At one level, the challenge of assuring adequate and appropriate post-secondary support to First Nations is parallel to that of assuring similar elementary and secondary support. Whatever specific agreements are negotiated with First Nations, and whether or not education is part of a larger social service envelope, funding adequate to meet the costs of education at current prices and enrolment levels is needed. At the post-secondary level, the situation is more complex, given much greater variety in programming and associated tuition, fee, living expenses,[30] and transportation costs, greater complexity surrounding issues of quality and accreditation, and higher potential private returns to graduates.

While we believe First Nations (and other Aboriginal groups, for that matter) should be free to negotiate comprehensive agreements that establish appropriate, feasible political and policy 'boundaries' around them, we also believe that Aboriginal access to post-secondary education, given its central importance in a globalized economy, should not be left entirely to the vagaries of case-specific comprehensive negotiations. Particularly in light of the large gap in post-secondary participation and graduation between Aboriginal and non-Aboriginal students (with the exception of First Nations college and technical school qualifications in Ontario, New Brunswick, Newfoundland, and the Yukon) (Indian and Northern Affairs Canada/Affaires indiennes et du Nord Canada 2005, 22), a minimum threshold of post-secondary funding adequacy and equity needs to be hard-wired into comprehensive self-determination agreements. This should be the case even if particular negotiating groups are eager to 'trade off' such funding for other benefits.

In addition to tuition, fees, and living expenses, assumptions about appropriate rationing and student participation in absorbing post-secondary costs will remain pivotal issues in determining post-secondary funding adequacy. INAC PSSSP funding has stagnated as living costs and tuition have risen substantially over the last two decades, with the result that at least 10 per cent of eligible First Nations post-secondary applicants are denied funding solely because funding was not available to support them. On top of that, most PSSSP-supported students have to 'find' supplementary funding to remain in their programs of study (Indian and Northern Affairs Canada/Affaires indiennes et du Nord Canada 2005, 31).[31]

We believe that, however the issue of post-secondary education as a treaty or Aboriginal right may be resolved, legally or through negotiation, the Government of Canada should ensure funding adequate to support *all* First Nations post-secondary students accepted into any program recognized by accreditation standards applicable to public post-secondary institutions. In short, we do not view limiting placements, except in the case of repeated failure in a particular program by a given student, as an acceptable approach to rationing post-secondary student support resources. Limiting placements leads to arbitrary and inconsistent standards regarding who will be funded in what programs, and why.

That said, we also believe that rationing by requiring some contribution from students, whether in the form of student loans, bursaries, private resources, or otherwise, becomes defensible when and to the extent that First Nations post-secondary participation and completion rates and patterns approach those of mainstream Canadians. Given that we are far from that reality at the moment, rationing by requiring student participation in cost should *not* be part of the current approach to funding. Rather, it should be phased in over time to the degree that First Nations participation and graduation patterns approach those of mainstream Canadian students, due allowance being made for higher Aboriginal participation rates in programs of particular relevance to Aboriginal students.

In short, we believe that once the dramatic gap between Aboriginal and non-Aboriginal students in post-secondary participation and completion begins to disappear, support for Aboriginal students, while it should remain more generous than post-secondary support available to the general population, should not entirely relieve Aboriginal students from participation in the costs of their post-secondary study – and the sense of responsibility that such participation in costs can promote. We take this position for two reasons: first, for the same reason we believe Aboriginal governance entities should tax their members and residents for school purposes, because such contribution provides the only meaningful form of personal, direct, ongoing investment and 'ownership' in education; and second, because the higher rates of *private* return to post-secondary education apply at least as much to Aboriginal as to non-Aboriginal students. No reason exists not to employ tools such as means testing, targeted loan forgiveness, appropriate limits on overall individual student debt loads, and so forth to help keep the burden of post-secondary cost from becoming unreasonable for Aboriginal students. Doing so would serve other legitimate policy purposes as well, such as encouraging Aboriginal participation in particular professions or to practise professions, such as medicine, that are in high demand among Aboriginal populations.

With regard to institutional and program support, we believe that, *within limits*, flexibility trumps equity in the sense that innovative proposals and good programs deserve support in preference to poor or stagnated ones. The idea of regional adjudication boards is a good one, and deserves broader implementation in preference to the current practice of simply 'renewing' funding for previously funded programs in most INAC regions. We remain convinced that partnership with public institutions is a promising model for advancing programs of particular interest and relevance to Aboriginal peoples, while ensuring credibility and accreditation that will be recognized beyond Aboriginal contexts. In particular, we salute the efforts of First Nations groups that, as part of negotiating new relationships with settler governments to establish reasonable, useful political and policy 'boundaries' around their operations and governance, are also taking care to partner with non-Aboriginal post-secondary institutions to offer courses, programs, and generally recognized diplomas to their members. The Nisga'a Wilp Wilxo'oskwhl Nisga'a (House of Wisdom) (Nisga'a Nation 2001, 36–8) partnership network strikes us as a particularly hopeful example of the type of post-secondary partnering we believe should be encouraged and funded.

Two final post-secondary funding areas seem to cry out for comment. First, post-secondary institutions themselves are much better placed than governments to identify and prioritize program initiatives to address Aboriginal needs. That they should do so in consultation and cooperation with actual and potential Aboriginal client groups goes without saying. Still, it seems appropriate that provincial funding for publicly supported universities and colleges should reflect marginal costs of providing programs and services adapted to the needs and interests of Aboriginal students. It appears that provinces have been reluctant to provide such funding to date, and that situation needs to change. It is highly unlikely that post-secondary institutions would regard such funding, even if they were required to demonstrate that they had used it to serve Aboriginal needs and interests, as intrusion on their academic freedom. On the contrary, evidence from both AUCC (Holmes 2006) and ACCC (Association of Canadian Community Colleges 2005) studies suggest institutions would welcome such funding and sense a strong need for it.

The second major loose end in our discussion of post-secondary funding is the question of non-First Nations Aboriginal students, that is, non-status Indian and Métis post-secondary students. This is an issue RCAP struggled with, and we can do no better on the subject than the commission. In a better world perhaps, the federal government would be inclined to respond positively to long-standing assertions on the part of non-status Indians and Métis that it owes them a fiduciary obligation of care just as it owes such a duty to status Indians and Inuit. It would be naive to expect, however, that any federal government is going to risk greatly enlarging its potential liability to Aboriginal peoples by admitting in any legally binding way that it has such an obligation toward non-status Indians and Métis. We are thus at a loss to go beyond the RCAP recommendation in this respect: 'A [government and privately supported] scholarship fund be established for Métis and other Aboriginal students who do not have access to financial support for post-secondary education under present policies' (Royal Commission on Aboriginal Peoples 1996b, 510), except to suggest that a really major joint effort is needed here.

In sum, we believe that the ten key elements of more appropriate post-secondary funding for Aboriginal students are the following:

1. Negotiation should be preferred to litigation here, as in other aspects of Aboriginal self-determination and governance.
2. Overall standards of adequacy and equity, including bases of rationing available resources, program and student eligibility, and so forth.
3. Adequacy standards need to recognize:
   a. current prices of post-secondary tuition and fees, and
   b. current living expense and transportation prices taking due account of family responsibilities for parents and couples, and
   c. program quality issues – specifically by requiring minimal program quality standards and accreditation acceptable to public institutions.
4. No 'trading off' of adequacy of post-secondary funding against other benefits in comprehensive negotiations should be allowed.
5. *All* First Nations post-secondary students accepted into any program recognized by accreditation standards applicable to public post-secondary institutions should be funded (no rationing by limiting places, although rationing on the basis of repeated withdrawal or failure seems appropriate).
6. As First Nations post-secondary participation and completion rates and patterns approach those of mainstream Canadians, funding arrangements should require reasonable student contribution to post-secondary costs from student loans, other bursaries, private resources, or otherwise.
7. Appropriate mitigation of such contributions through measures such as means testing, targeted loan forgiveness, and appropriate limits on overall individual student debt loads.
8. Targeted provincial support to institutions for programs and services to address Aboriginal needs and interests.
9. Encouragement of intelligent, productive, dynamic partnership networks between First Nations post-secondary institutions and mainstream institutions.
10. A major national joint government/private effort to establish and generously endow a scholarship/bursary fund for non-status Indian and Métis post-secondary students.

Taken together and applied thoughtfully and purposefully, these elements offer the best chance of bringing Aboriginal post-secondary participation, achievement, and completion into line with the rest of the Canadian population and at the same time ensuring availability of high quality courses, programs, and services better tailored to Aboriginal needs and interests. These measures will result in greater costs in federal support of Aboriginal post-secondary education in the short term, but should reduce both direct and spillover social costs while increasing tax revenues over the long term as Aboriginal graduates take their rightful place in Canadian society and in the Canadian economy.

5 Up the Down Staircase in Two Dimensions: Local, Regional, National Control and Jurisdiction

The historical legacy of DIAND-imposed band council governance at the community level aligns perfectly with identification of Indian control as local control in *Indian Control of Indian Education* (National Indian Brotherhood, 1972/1984). This belief has taken on quasi-religious proportions over the years, despite the fact that most First Nations are too small to command the resources necessary to operate a meaningful education system. This ill-fated conjuncture has led to much confusion, frustration, and confrontation over appropriate levels of collaboration and the proper distribution of power and discretion in aggregate organizations such as tribal and education councils. Current policies in Aboriginal education ignore the potential relevance of aggregated institutions as crucial governance and bargaining agencies that could help transform power relationships between Aboriginal and non-Aboriginal communities in education. Such a concept refers to the process of relocating power to integrated but self-governing aggregate organizations. *Such integration can only be embodied in interconnected networks rather than in territorially based band councils.* However, to the degree that Aboriginal educational purposes, content, and patterns of delivery become increasingly interlinked through aggregated forms of self-governance, resistance and opposition by some Aboriginal power brokers is inevitable as Aboriginal education outgrows narrow, parochial ties to individual communities and local band councils, and acquires new visions, purposes, and meanings. Sadly, the end result of the myth of Indian control as local control, besides pointless discussion of 'second-level' and 'third-level' services, has often been factionalized internecine wars. Such dysfunctional confrontation dissipates goodwill and diverts energy from positive initiatives into battles for control and resources, unworkable governance structures, and mutual mistrust among all parties.

Such problems are far from unknown in the larger world of public education, as a rich literature on political economy, goal displacement, and bureaucratic dysfunction testifies (see, for example, Boyd 1982; Lawton, Freedman, Robertson, and Institute for Research on Public Policy 1995). Nonetheless, the severity and pervasiveness of organizational dysfunction in First Nations education is arguably much more pervasive. At the head of the list of reasons has to be Indian and Northern Affairs Canada (INAC), its threadbare statutory mandate for education, the structures it imposes on governance, and the balkanization that the band council system it put into place has encouraged. A closely related second reason would be the illusion fostered by the authors of *Indian Control of Indian Education* (ICIE) that 'Indian control' is a synonym for 'local control.' INAC has used that illusion to justify its practice of bypassing First Nations political organizations and going directly to communities on the rare occasions it has engaged in meaningful consultation with First Nations constituents. Other reasons include intense inter-community competition for limited resources, for control, however limited and illusory, and for much needed community-level employment that comes with such resources.

The Current State of Provincial and First Nations School Governance

Key aspects of provincial and First Nations school governance differ markedly from each other. Given the central point of our conceptual framework, that purpose should be embedded in social and educational paradigms, we shape our critique of governance in provincial and in First Nations schools within the broader question of purpose that lies at the heart of educational policy. Having said this, our principal focus in this chapter is on governance structures and processes (mainly educational) and on questions of jurisdiction and control. Nonetheless, questions of purpose and paradigm occupy an important place in that discussion since we believe that form should follow function.

Provincial School Jurisdiction and Control

Over the last twenty years, structures and processes for 'local control' of schools mandated in provincial education and school acts have become increasingly disconnected from meaningful control over own-source revenues. Of course, school boards and districts are under the jurisdiction of provincial law, so strictly speaking, they have no own-source revenues independent of those assigned to them by provincial regulations. Historically however, school boards in most provinces obtained an important part of their overall revenues from a tax rate they were permitted to levy on local property tax wealth. While the specific reasons and mechanisms for disconnecting school boards from their historical power to set property taxes for school purposes have varied over time and place, the common denominators have been provincial desire to control *total* educational spending, which provinces cannot do if local boards are free to set their own property tax rates and there is concern about inequities in spending power for similar tax efforts between assessment-rich and assessment-poor boards.

Out of this 'repossession' of control by provincial governments over local property tax revenues for school purposes has come a disturbing dilemma – a parallel disconnect of local school ratepayers from their school boards. Restructuring of provincial school boards over the last couple of decades has eroded the local control of public education by imposing larger board sizes in the wake of major amalgamations, and thus distanced elected trustees from those they represent. The most significant disconnect in the historic local control mechanism, however, has been the removal of or dramatic reduction in school board discretion over local property tax revenues for school purposes. This loss of control over autonomous revenues has predictably resulted in voter disinterest in school board elections.

On top of this new reality, an inherent contradiction exists between local bargaining power for the general limits of board employee salaries, work conditions, and benefits on the one hand, and provincial control of nearly all school board revenues on the other. Inevitably, power follows money. That is a significant part of why provinces have repossessed control over local property tax bases allocated to school purposes. Control over wealthy local property bases conferred great independence on certain boards, whatever their policy obligations to provincial ministries of education might have been.

Figure 5.1 shows a simplified[1] representation of public school governance, with particular focus on the flow of 'voice,' 'authority,' and 'accountability.' We use these terms in ways that differ from the meanings they may have in everyday language for most readers, specifically:

- voice is the right, conferred by law, to participate in decision-making processes relevant to policy without having the right to vote or participate in any final decision;
- authority is the right conferred by law to make decisions about a particular matter in an education system; and
- accountability is the legal responsibility for defined results (program accountability) or use of financial resources (financial accountability). Program accountability may be based on either effectiveness criteria (were results produced?) or efficiency criteria (were results produced at a reasonable cost?) or both.[2]

Two other terms require a working definition for our governance analysis:

- stakeholders are groups and individuals involved in the delivery of educational programs and services or who benefit from or pay for such services; and
- policy actors are stakeholders (group or individual) designated by law to exercise authority or voice at different levels of governance (e.g., school, school board, province) but do not include administrative bodies charged with carrying out policy crafted by policy actors (definitions adapted from Smith, Paquette, and Bordonaro 1995).[3]

We begin by noting the hierarchical framework of authority and accountability at the heart of provincial systems of education (leaving aside the question of how well it actually functions). This framework is derived from industrial paradigm logic, values, and approaches to structuring and making sense of education, all the more so as provincial governments and their ministries of education have reasserted control over program and financial accountability in recent years. Such logic, values, and approaches are characteristic of what Bertrand and Valois call the 'rational' and 'technological' paradigms of education. These educational paradigms thus situate themselves within the industrial (and post-industrial) structuralist understanding of social, economic, and educational purpose.

Residents of public school zones are voters and taxpayers at three levels of government: federal, provincial, and local. They have 'voice' in policy decisions, and in rules and regulations derived from these decisions, at all levels of governance, and they will balance their educational interests against their priorities regarding other policy interests

Figure 5.1 Simplified representation of public school governance voice, authority, and accountability

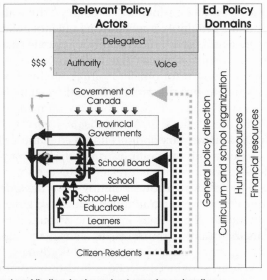

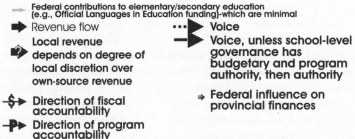

Source: Adapted and extended from Smith, Paquette, and Bordonaro (1995).

and those assigned by the Constitution or by statute to each level of governance. Despite the constitutional allocation of responsibility for education to the provinces, all three levels of government are involved in elementary and secondary education policy. The federal government is involved directly only in a very small way, through incentive programs such as the Official Languages in Education program that provides federal funding to provinces in support of official-language education, especially French-language instruction outside of Quebec but also some funding in support of English-language instruction in Quebec. Indirectly, however, the federal government has great impact on the overall fiscal capacity of provincial governments to support education, health, and other social programs. This powerful influence on the fiscal capacity of the provinces is currently a matter of great political interest and conflict, as shown by the contentious debate surrounding 'fiscal federalism.' Nonetheless, most citizen-residents do not consider programs like federal support for official-languages education as very important to their voting behaviour in a federal election. Therefore in figure 5.1, the school voice arrow to the Government of Canada level is slender, and the resource arrows indicate a very small direct federal contribution to elementary and secondary education. However, if equalization payments and tax point transfers to provinces are considered, the federal government has greater influence on provincial finances, indicated by the gray arrows pointing from the federal level to the provincial one. This strong (and much contested) federal power over the fiscal capacity of the provinces makes the citizen-resident voice in federal elections important with regards to elementary and secondary education.

Residents also vote in provincial elections and thus combine their public education preferences with other provincial policy preferences when deciding how to cast their ballots. Public schooling is not the only or even most important issue on the minds of most voters when they vote in a provincial election (today, health care would be considered the most important issue by the majority of voters). Even so, it is a more important concern in a provincial election, which is why there is a much more substantial voice arrow from residents to their province than to the Government of Canada. Similarly, much more provincial spending goes to schools through local school boards, a reality we capture schematically in a more substantial set of revenue flow arrows.

School boards traditionally paid for a significant share of the operating costs of elementary and secondary education from their own-source revenues (they did so by setting local tax rates on board property tax assessments for school purposes). As noted above, however, provinces have been 'repossessing' this authority to set school property tax rates. Given this situation, we superimpose a question mark on boards' own-source revenue flow to schools (◀✓).

We represent financial accountability by arrows with dollar signs superimposed on them (–$➤), and program accountability by arrows with the letter P on them (–P➤). In theory, program accountability comes from teachers and school-level administrators. Schools are accountable both financially and through the programs they offer to their boards, and boards are similarly accountable to provincial governments through their ministries of education. In short, program accountability 'upward' closes the accountability circuit with resource flow 'downward.' It does so in two layers, an external provincial layer and an internal board one.

The orderly symmetry of this dual-layer (inner and outer) circuit has been disrupted as provinces have removed or reduced school boards' power to set tax rates on their local property tax base. In particular, since school boards have lost control of their own-source revenue, the lines of fiscal accountability to the province have tightened, with school boards becoming more of an 'administrative agent' of the province than an instrument of 'communal autonomy' through community 'confederation' (Manzer 1994).

The key point here is that by voting, citizen-residents have a voice in choosing members of both provincial governments and school boards. They may also have a voice in choosing school council members. Except in Quebec and British Columbia, school councils have no meaningful accountability relationship to schools. In Quebec, school governing councils have statutory authority to approve school budgets, although final ratification rests with school boards. British Columbia has also recently added significant oversight responsibilities to its school councils. Even so, provincial systems of education provide residents with a voice in educational policy, allowing them to affect what happens in their area schools. Through provincial and local school board elections, that voice feeds into a fiscal and program accountability circuit that gives effect to their voice. Citizen-residents vote in elections that ultimately matter for their school systems in terms of resource flow and reciprocal lines of fiscal and program accountability.   ➔

First Nations School Jurisdiction and Control

Figure 5.2 shows a simplified[4] schematic representation of First Nations school governance, again focusing on the flow of voice, authority, and accountability. Band members are free to vote in federal elections. As is the case with other citizens, federal education programs, among them

Figure 5.2 Program and fiscal accountability links of local resident
to band education authority school

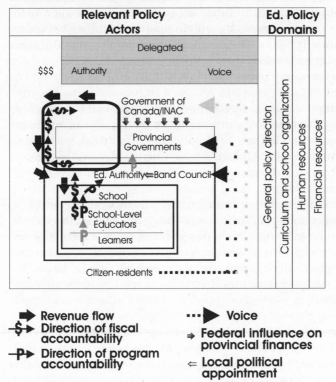

Global Context of Education: international policy
and program norms, economic and financial
fluctuations, and so forth

Relevant Policy Actors			Ed. Policy Domains		

Revenue flow

-$▸ Direction of fiscal accountability

-P▸ Direction of program accountability

···▸ Voice

⇢ Federal influence on provincial finances

⇐ Local political appointment

education programs addressed to First Nations learners, are one area of
potential interest, among a great many others, to First Nations voters
(although they are presumably of greater interest to those living in First
Nations communities than to most other voters in federal elections).
Given the diminutive weight of First Nations education in shaping
federal voter behaviour, the relative electoral 'voice' of First Nations
citizen-residents in federal funding and policy affecting the education
of children in their community school is small and tenuous (hence the
ephemeral 'voice' connection to the federal level in figure 5.2)

Nevertheless, nearly all of the financial resources for band-operated schools flow from the federal government through INAC. The political mandate for such appropriation and allocation of funds comes from the Canadian electorate at large, and thus flows in to the artificially closed system representation we offer for the sake of simplicity. Band members express their preferences with regard to education, but do so simultaneously with a host of other issues, concerns, and allegiances. They elect their band councillors, who in turn appoint members of the education authority. Thus, the electoral mandate of band-education-authority members towards their school(s) differs in two key aspects from that of members of provincial boards of education:

- band-education-authority membership is ultimately the product of an electoral process that combines education with the full spectrum of social, infrastructure, and local political issues that shape band council election results; education issues are thus diluted in band council elections unlike school board elections; and
- in band council elections, band members elect proxies (band councillors) to decide band-education-authority membership; control over band-education-authority membership by voters is thus *indirect*, in addition to being diluted (the reduced voice in education at the local level is shown schematically by a dot pattern in the voice line to the band council/band-education-authority level, different from that used to represent resident voice to the school board level in figure 5.1).

Significantly, non-resident band members are eligible to vote in band council elections, so their voting behaviour flows into our artificially closed system depiction of voice, financial accountability, and resource flow, diluting the resident voice in community schools at the band level even further.

The single most consequential difference between the dynamics illustrated in figure 5.1 and figure 5.2 is the lack of any significant *parallel* flow of own-source revenue and fiscal accountability at the community level. The resource flow and therefore the primary line of financial accountability is *from* INAC to the band and school(s). Fiscally, band education authorities are administrative agents (Manzer 1994) of INAC. The only significant line of resident voice to band schools is through the diffuse band electoral process and is, in all consequential ways, completely disconnected from the revenue flow from the federal government.

From the analysis presented above, it is obvious that parallel connections of political mandate and financial accountability from the individual resident to the local school are much more tenuous when the resident is a band member residing on a reserve (even taking into consideration the recent pattern of removing school board control over local property tax rates).

Band residents have little control over what occurs in their schools mainly because of the almost complete disconnect from the political/ electoral mandate, and thus from the lines of funding and financial accountability that empower and bind school administrators and personnel. Leaving aside very small fundraising activities, the federal government pays the band education authority in a way that keeps them almost completely insulated from band resident preferences regarding schooling in their community. This model provides bands and resident band members with very little meaningful control over what occurs in their schools.

Figure 5.2 exposes another critical difference from provincial publicly funded schools in the relationship between revenue flow, fiscal accountability, and program accountability. The revenue-financial-accountability circuit is between the federal government as represented by INAC and the local band and its education authority. But a significant part of the line of program accountability (if such a line can be said to exist at all), flows to the province, which is completely outside of the revenue-financial-accountability circuit for First Nations schools. There is no program accountability to INAC, which has always insisted that band schools, like federal Indian day schools before them, must conform to *provincial* curricula and standards. As McCue (2006) observed, 'every one of the SGAs [self-government agreements] referred to ... includes a clause or clauses that in effect say that the education that the affected First Nation(s) provides as a result of the SGA must be comparable to the provincial system, or that students must be able to move from the First Nations education program to a provincial school [at any time] without penalty (6).[5] Thus, in the case of First Nations schools, the line of program accountability diverges from the main revenue and fiscal accountability circuit. Instead of connecting to INAC and the federal government, it connects to provincial governments (shown as a gray arrow from education authority to province in figure 5.2) with standards established by their ministries of education.

Enforcement of such standards by provincial authorities is indirect and uncertain at best. Generally speaking, provincial ministries have no mandate to require that First Nations schools conform to their curricula, however much INAC may insist that First Nations schools are required to do so. Some provinces have more stringent private school registration procedures than others, and some First Nations schools choose to register with provincial ministries as recognized private schools, although nothing requires them to do so. Where First Nations are operating secondary programs, they must submit to some form of provincial 'inspection' in order to have their courses accredited by the province. Even in such cases, however, provincial inspection is often more pro forma than substantive. In the wake of more than a decade of deep cuts to their resources, provincial ministries are even less able to invest the time and energy needed for in-depth secondary accreditation work on rapidly proliferating First Nations secondary programs. In the end, provincial curriculum standards are enforced not by any direct provincial accreditation process but by post-secondary admission requirements.

The issue here is that *no one* seems to have much control over what goes on in many 'band-operated' schools. The federal government insists on some minimal audit evidence that money provided for education is being spent for education (unless the band has an alternative funding arrangement, in which case education is but one element of overall audit requirements), and otherwise is content to insist that band schools must conform to provincial curricula without enforcing this rule. Such a governance arrangement results in highly centralized power at the band level, exercised through an oligarchic community and area social structure. Within such community and area structures, direct authority is exercised by a limited number of individuals, who are free to privilege their allies and punish their opponents. Adding to this lack of inclusive voice, authority, and power in First Nations education, provincial governments have no authority, resources, or interest to ensure that their curricula and standards are adhered to in First Nations schools. In terms of program accountability, these schools are rudderless ships.

The status quo in First Nations governance reflects an assimilationist stance at a very deep level and in a particularly insidious way. One might aptly characterize the recent historic approach of INAC and the federal government to First Nations education as one of benign neglect. INAC funds the process without much attention to adequacy or purpose, and provides an unclear mandate to follow provincial curricula. Otherwise, in the guise of furthering Indian control of Indian education, First Nations are left to do what they want in their community schools.

Provincial curricula and standards prevail to the extent they can because they reflect the requirements of post-secondary professional,
academic, and trades gatekeepers. Left alone, First Nations – and other
Aboriginal peoples – will assimilate and adopt schooling that mirrors
both the processes and content of mainstream Canadian schooling. Let
them hang a First Nations shingle on their community schools if they
want, but the process is indisputably one of assimilation.

We conclude this section by calling attention to two closely related
concepts cropping up with increasing frequency in critiques of Aboriginal and especially First Nations governance. We believe these concepts
are part 'red herring' and part oxymoron, and generally misleading
given the assumptions within which they appear to be framed. The
concepts are 'second-level' and 'third-level' services. Anderson (2004)
describes 'second-level services' in this way:

> Many efforts to work within federal programmes have enabled several
> agencies, institutes and organizations to develop and deliver services (in
> a limited capacity) for First Nations students. These service organizations
> deliver high school programmes, engage in curriculum development,
> teacher training, professional development for teachers, college and uni-
> versity courses, special education services and advisory services. INAC's
> policy on second level services provides some funding for these agencies,
> but not all organizations fall within the fiscal criteria. (2)

With regard to support services (or programs), the cause of high-quality Aboriginal/First Nations education is not well served by following the siren call of local control embodied in radically local models of
school governance. First, contracting out support or programs is not an
option for most First Nations communities. They don't have sufficient
resources to fund such programs *either* internally *or* on an external basis. The option of mounting many support programs is only available at
levels of aggregation higher than the community level.[6]

Second, support services related to educational programming are
more likely to be effective if they are designed and implemented within
the vision and mandate of First Nations educational jurisdictions themselves, rather than within the values and corporate culture of some external contractor or service provider. In our view, diseconomies of scale
and cultural distinctiveness alike argue against using a contracting
out model for programs (or services) connected to First Nations education.

Following this logic, we believe that functional aggregation of community-level units is both desirable and necessary in First Nations education, although it can raise serious challenges, particularly in areas where First Nations cultures, languages, traditions, and developmental aspirations differ strongly from one community to another. Logically, too, such collectives should occur at two levels. The first should be an area level similar to the school board in provincial systems, and the second at a regional level, analogous to the provinces in public schooling. Just what the boundaries and horizons of these two jurisdictional levels ought to be is both unclear and potentially very controversial. Perhaps the only certainty here is the relational pluralist insight that one-size-fits-all answers are likely to be futile and destructive. Finally, some agency with authority to allocate federal (and eventually First Nations) funding to regional First Nations education authorities will continue to be needed to assure reasonable equity and adequacy across the spectrum of First Nations governing arrangements.

The advantage of combining to provide such services is hardly news. Despite perennial resilience of the myth of local control as a synonym for Indian control, individual First Nations have been working together through various associations, tribal councils, and education councils for decades. What we believe is new here is the insistence on something more than voluntary participation when such participation suits immediate community educational and political priorities. *What is needed is functional integration, resulting in school-board-like aggregations within regional First Nations education jurisdictions.* Pursuing the illusion of Indian control in the guise of community control can only continue to facilitate the breathtaking failure of First Nations education, which the Auditor General keeps reminding Canadians about on a regular basis.

Disconnected Layers of Governance I: INAC and First Nations

By this point it should be evident that layers of governance are completely disconnected in First Nations education. It is useful to think in terms of two layers of disconnected governance. These two layers are distinct but superimposed on one another in the same way that computer drawing programs allow users to draw on separate layers, with the final result being a composite of all layers viewed simultaneously.

The INAC-First Nations layer of disconnected governance is the one which we have focused on thus far. Figure 5.2 presents a part of this layer, outlining the INAC-to-*individual*-First Nations dimension. Figure 5.3 illustrates the conflicting relationships *across* the two layers of First Nations educational governance.

Figure 5.3 Layers of governance relationships in First Nations education

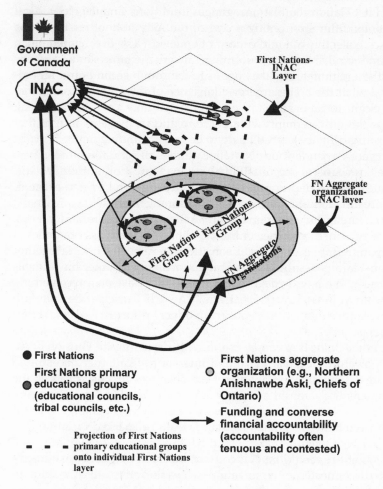

● First Nations

First Nations primary
● educational groups
(educational councils,
tribal councils, etc.)

First Nations aggregate
○ organization (e.g., Northern
Anishnawbe Aski, Chiefs of
Ontario)

Funding and converse
◄──────► financial accountability
(accountability often
tenuous and contested)

— — — Projection of First Nations
primary educational groups
onto individual First Nations
layer

First, the INAC-to-First Nations layer includes all First Nations with band-operated educational programs (elementary, secondary, and post-secondary). Figure 5.2 can most usefully be thought of as a breakdown of a single band-school-to-INAC governance relationship in the top layer of figure 5.3. As we have noted, bands frequently join together in aggregate organizations such as tribal councils, educational councils, and band associations to pool capacity for certain limited purposes in education and in other social policy areas. As shown in figure 5.3, these aggregate organizations often join together in even larger aggregations, ultimately forming organizations such as the Chiefs' Committee on Education (CCOE) or the National Indian Education Council (NIEC) initiatives, sometimes becoming a part of the Assembly of First Nations (AFN) or Assembly of First Nations of Quebec. First-level aggregations sometimes link directly to each other for specific purposes and activities, although more often they are linked through second- and higher-level aggregations. These connections vary from purely nominal to authentically collaborative.

The most obvious points with regard to the First Nations-INAC layer are those made in the preceding discussion surrounding figure 5.2. First Nations are dependent on INAC for almost all educational revenues but the lines of fiscal accountability back to INAC are notoriously tenuous, and the lines of program accountability are virtually non-existent. Given INAC's requirement that First Nations schools follow provincial curricula, the line of program accountability, if any can be said to exist, is to the provinces and their ministries of education. Less obvious but equally important is the point illustrated in figure 5.3. First Nations are joined in aggregate groups that compete with one another for recognition, credibility, and limited federal funding. They often receive support, as figure 5.3 indicates, *both* from INAC and from member bands, a funding-source duality that pulls them in very different and conflicting directions.

The other point that can be made with regard to the First Nations-INAC structure of governance and lines of accountability illustrated in figure 5.3 is that the Canadian state seems to be positioned as the only potential guarantor of stability for First Nations. Therefore, any new forms of First Nations self-governance that might emerge without active support by the Canadian state would be marked by instability and disorder. One might argue that the power structure regulating the interactions between First Nations and non-First Nations institutions overseeing education is acquiring new collaborative attributes due to INAC's policy of devolution of powers to local First Nations governance entities. However, these apparently new attributes emerging within the current governance system may only obscure its original and enduring contours. To regard the devolution of power at the local level as the formation of a new self-governance system for First Nations education fails to recognize that the process embodies continuity from the past. The aggregated forms of governance in figure 5.3 exist to supplement, not to replace, the long-established institutional structures of authority dominated by INAC. The department's promotion of the devolution of power to the local level has not created any new political space for First Nations to exercise real control over their education systems.

Figure 5.3 can be used as a starting point to rethink the current governance model of Aboriginal education, a web-like process of self-governance of education, and thus to confront the challenges of fragmentation. Such a model of governance would have to employ rule and norm systems (translated into mechanisms of governance and a shared concept of human good) that would direct educational issues through both hierarchical and networked connections across levels of aggregation. These levels of aggregation would need to encompass all the diversity of First Nations communities along with the individuals who would participate in the self-governance of education. In order to overcome the current fragmentation of First Nations communities, such a governance model would require authority over education that would be reasonably decentralized without being fragmented to the point of incoherence, with authority that would flow both horizontally and vertically through clearly defined participatory and accountability channels. The success of such a governance model would depend on all parties accepting the virtues of collaboration and the need to reverse the worst effects of the current fragmentation due to the promotion of Indian control as community control. It would also depend on the capacity of First Nations and non-First Nations communities to foster conditions conducive to agreement on shared values along with consensus about developmental aspirations.

Whatever the difficulties, what needs to be developed is new aggregated governance in First Nations education forming a functional network that is connected both horizontally and vertically. Such aggregation requires a substantive common understanding regarding the ends First Nations education should pursue. The purposes of such an exercise by First Nations would logically have to be (1) to agree upon reasonable limits for First Nations pluralism, particularly as it impacts education; and (2) to reduce the negative impacts of fragmentation dynamics, which tend to emphasize self-interest at the expense of community interests and the common good of First Nations students.

Disconnected Layers of Governance II: First Nations Aggregation

The aggregation layer (bottom layer in figure 5.3) adds a level of confusion, competition (often perverse), and strained lines of governance that is largely unique to First Nations education. The key problem with First Nations educational aggregates is readily apparent upon careful consideration of figure 5.3. From the individual First Nations level to the highest levels of aggregation, First Nations organizations involved in education are, almost without exception, entirely dependent on INAC and the federal government for their revenue. INAC serves as judge and jury on how First Nations education should be provided, but it is a large, bureaucratized judge and jury whose priorities are guided by no educational vision or policy priorities. Furthermore, aggregate First Nations organizations involved in education are often dependent *both* on INAC funding mediated by the priorities and decisions of band councils *and* on funding directly from INAC itself. Bands often agree to provide support for certain educational tasks of an aggregate organization, part of whose essential and core funding also flows directly from INAC. Such organizations must steer a course between conflicted, and often ill-defined, band council priorities and ambiguous and volatile INAC priorities, as these are translated into funding at the First Nations level on the one hand and at various levels of aggregation on the other.

The fact that many First Nations aggregate organizations have a broad range of mandates, interests, and functions outside of education increases the potential for conflict in this arrangement. The 'aggregate organization' layer in figure 5.3 can best be thought of as a thick multi-substrata layer in which many aggregate organizations assist with several aspects of reserve services. For instance, they might have an educational substratum, social services substratum, an infrastructure substratum, and so forth – although adding this additional dimension to figure 5.3 would hopelessly confuse it. Retaining core funding often requires applying repeatedly to new INAC 'project-based' funding initiatives with clever titles such as 'Gathering Strength' or 'New Paths.' Furthermore, unless they are exclusively focused on education, they must constantly revisit the same delicate balancing act in regard to all the competing areas of social and/or infrastructure policy in which they are involved, not just education.

Of course, it can be argued that that is just the kind of thing governments do, authoritatively allocating limited resources across complex, competing claims. The situation here, however, is fundamentally different for three reasons. The first reason is the cross-jurisdictional role of INAC, which is almost completely insulated from the First Nations electoral voice, as the final arbiter of what gets funded, a role it occupies even in situations where bands opt into alternative funding. The second reason, as we demonstrated in our discussion of educational voice and authority relationships, is that no clear mechanism exists to translate local electoral voice in educational matters into authoritative decision-making at the local level. *The local educational voice is always diluted in the totality of local band council politics.* Further, it is the band council that determines who gets to participate in aggregate organizations, not band education authorities, even in the case of participation in purely educational aggregate organizations. This situation has little in common with that of school boards embedded in provincial education systems.

Finally, conflicting priorities across different levels of First Nations aggregation complete the picture. What might be very important at one point in time for first- or second-level First Nations aggregates in British Columbia or Ontario may have relatively limited immediate importance in the Prairie provinces. Then there is the question of national Indian politics, which has its own enduring stresses and fault lines. The relationship between Quebec First Nations and the Assembly of First Nations can best be described as collaboration when common interest encourages it. All this occurs only within the domain of status First Nations and Inuit stakeholders. The conflicts of interests and priorities are much greater once non-status Indian and Métis groups are added to the mix.

Considering these structural problems hardwired into the situation of First Nations education, what lessons can be derived from the history of attempts at constructive cooperation through aggregation, particularly higher-level aggregation?

First Nations (Education) Organizations: Local, Regional, and National

Many First Nations are small in both population and reserve size, making it difficult and perhaps unrealistic for some of them to administer the services and financial resources necessary for self-government. First Nations may therefore choose to delegate authority to political entities such as tribal councils in functional areas beyond their capacity such as policy development, higher education, and human resource training. However, it is First Nations at the band level that are invested with statutory political authority ...

Schouls, *Shifting Boundaries* (2003), 54

Schouls (2003) reminds his readers that First Nations are central to analysis and understanding of First Nations self-government and self-determination options because:

- they have long-established relations with the Canadian government;
- they have a distinct constitutional status and are the bearers of Aboriginal rights, including that of Aboriginal self-government however recognized or implemented;
- they have a continuing or former identity as an Indian Act band that provides members with common experiences and perceptions;
- they have a unique location and a land base that infuse their identity;
- they have a governing structure [albeit an imposed one];
- they provide both political and social settings in which individuals can gain and maintain their personal Aboriginal identities; and
- they have fiscal resources enabling them to carry out community activities. (54)

Despite the disconnected layers of governance discussed in the preceding section and the diseconomies of scale associated with their generally small size, First Nations constitute the first-level building blocks of any second- and higher-level aggregations, including those wholly or partly involved in education. *It is First Nations as a whole that must create, authorize, sustain politically and financially, and ultimately evaluate (explicitly by deciding to continue to support them) aggregates that provide a wide range of infrastructure and support services beyond the reach of individual First Nations.*

In a wide variety of ways over the past few years, First Nations and their aggregate organizations across Canada have been searching for means to increase their control (jurisdiction) over education.[7] In our view, most have done so without any plausible mechanism for fixing the disconnected layers of governance endemic to the current organization of voice and authority in First Nations education. Indeed, it would be beyond their power at the moment to unilaterally impose any solutions to the disconnected layers of governance because the control of resources rests with INAC. Nonetheless, this renewed drive for control framed within the inherently collaborative idea that jurisdiction is important because it confirms that individual First Nations as well as their aggregate organizations are aware that, given the reality of large diseconomies of scale in First Nations education, meaningful control can only occur through collaboration. This thirst for jurisdiction also signals some awareness of the compromises and power delegation necessary in functional collaboration at various levels of aggregation.

The INAC minister's National Working Group on Education (2002) focused on jurisdiction as the central concern of its first recommendation:

> Putting jurisdiction for First Nations education in the hands of First Nations is a critical first step to making our vision a reality.[8] Therefore, we recommend that:
> 1. Canada commit to jurisdictional discussions with First Nations concerning lifelong education for First Nations learners on and off reserve. This shall include capacity building at the community and regional level that would encompass a strategy and resources for implementation. Steps should be taken immediately to enhance or develop First Nations organizations that would facilitate this process. (11)

The Working Group saw the following process as a potential way to implement this jurisdiction:

- prepare options for establishing First Nations jurisdiction;
- establish benchmarks and an operational plan for transfer of jurisdiction;
- support First Nations to determine the appropriate option for jurisdiction;
- respect the diversity of First Nations, the existing and evolving models of jurisdiction in First Nations education, and the current regional negotiations on jurisdiction in First Nations education; and
- conclude the transfer of jurisdiction within a five year time frame. (11)

We wholeheartedly agree with the principle that First Nations should control their own education through governance arrangements that align the political voice *in education* of First Nations members with authoritative decisions and the allocation of all values in First Nations education, including financial ones. Nonetheless, we find misleading the proposition that INAC can transfer a jurisdiction, which it clearly does not currently have, if jurisdiction implies meaningful control of what counts in education. The central point of the Auditor General's recurrent criticisms of INAC with respect to education is precisely that INAC has no control and that program accountability does not currently exist.[9] One cannot transfer what one does not have.

No lucid minister of education would dare assert that she was in charge of an educational jurisdiction in the face of such sweeping assertions of lack of direction and control on the part of a provincial Auditor General, certainly not in the present educational policy environment. In general, jurisdiction in Aboriginal and in First Nations education is yet to be established. It needs to be built from the ground up, and we should have no illusions about it being conveniently available for transfer, delegation, or devolution from INAC. The language of transfer here is not helpful because it brings with it the false sense of a simple bureaucratic procedure, which is anything but the truth of the matter. In that respect, the first four elements of the Working Group's (WG) proposals for process seem strangely out of sync with the fifth – and with the rhetoric the WG used to frame its core position on jurisdiction.

Education and Self-Government Agreements Currently in Effect

At least fifteen self-government agreements with specific education provisions are currently in effect across Canada. Most of these agreements involve First Nations in the Yukon and the West, although the only agreement in effect bearing exclusively on education is the *Mi'kmaq Education Act* in Nova Scotia.

Signed in 1997 by the Mi'kmaq First Nations of Nova Scotia and the federal government, the *Mi'kmaq Education Act* was subsequently ratified by participating Mi'kmaq First Nations and given force mainly by federal[10] and some provincial legislation.[11] Despite considerable lore surrounding the fact that this Act is the first of its kind, the agreement itself contains surprisingly little that is new, very little that separates Mi'kmaq jurisdiction from the INAC boilerplate language on program equivalency, and no substantive guarantees with regard to resourcing beyond what is provided for in the recently renegotiated funding schedule. McCue (2007) has aptly captured the broad educational policy implications of the Mi'kmaq agreement in these terms:

> The agreement that eventually became a federal act soon thereafter (Bill C-30: The Mi'kmaq Education Act) established the Mikmaw-Kina'matnewey (MK) as the education body in Nova Scotia that would deliver education programs and services to the participating Mi'kmaq communities. To date, the funding and resources that the MK receives annually from the federal government has not enabled it to mount anything similar to the 2nd and 3rd level education programs and services that the

provincial government provides to its provincial schools. Nor has its small staff (7–8) succeeded in creating a Mi'kmaq education system. This experience must provide a caution to First Nations involved in SGA negotiations. (7)

The main provisions of the Mi'kmaq agreement bearing on jurisdiction, accountability, and control are the following:

1. band councils exercise jurisdiction, not Mikmaw-Kina'matnewey (MK), the aggregate organization (Her Majesty the Queen in Right of Canada and Mi'kmaq Bands in Nova Scotia 1997, 8, s.3.1.2);
2. to that end communities individually will make and administer laws with respect to elementary and secondary education (8, s.5.1.1) and post-secondary support (8, s.5.5.1);
3. band councils may delegate jurisdiction to a *community* education board (8, s.5.3);
4. MK is constituted strictly as a service-support organization and has no rights or obligations regarding supervision or accountability (8, s.3.1.3 and s.5.7.1);
5. the agreement is a contract, and although not prejudicial to potential treaty or inherent rights in education or overall federal fiduciary responsibility, has no status beyond that of a contract recognized explicitly in a statute (8, s.4);
6. members of participating bands are not entitled to similar educational benefits from DIAND/INAC (non-duplication of services, 8, s.5.6.5);
7. education laws of participating First Nations have precedence ('paramountcy') over federal and provincial education laws (9, s.6.3); *but*
8. '… [T]he participating communities shall provide primary, elementary and secondary education programs and services comparable to those provided by other education systems in Canada, so as to permit the transfer of students between education systems without academic penalty, to the same extent as the transfer of students is effected between education systems in Canada' (8, s.5.4);
9. Section 5.2 of the agreement provides that, in the case of conflict, participating First Nations education laws prevail over 'any other law respecting primary, elementary or secondary education in the Province …' but, since a participating community can only enact laws 'to the extent provided by the Agreement' (s.5.1, 3), a com-

munity could presumably not develop and implement a curriculum that would not permit 'transfer of students between education systems without academic penalty.'

The particular formulation of the INAC program equivalency requirement contained in section 5.4 of the Mi'kmaq agreement is marginally less constraining than formulations encountered in other agreements (see table 5.1 for a summary of the salient points of these agreements).[12] Section 5.4 at least recognizes that transferring from one education system to another in Canada may involve some academic penalty, to the extent that program content and pedagogy differ from one system to another and that this degree of penalty is largely unavoidable. Beyond this limited concession to an evident and ubiquitous reality, section 5.4 imposes the same requirement (or fiction) of programming identical to that offered in provincial schools – at least in its outcomes – at all levels of schooling from primary through the end of secondary.

Furthermore, the fact that the Mi'kmaq agreement invests all meaningful control and jurisdiction at the individual First Nations level and casts the MK council solely in the guise of a support service provider with no meaningful *control* over anything of educational significance ensures continued balkanization of programming, supervision, and administration with all its attendant evils, particularly in a context of extreme diseconomies of scale.

Table 5.1 summarizes education and taxation provisions of existing self-government and education agreements. The main features of these agreements reflect a certain degree of compartmentalization of Aboriginal and non-Aboriginal communities. These agreements restrict the efforts of Aboriginal groups to give public expression to their distinctive identities and concepts of 'flourishing.' They also limit the ability of Aboriginal groups to organize their educational affairs in terms of their traditions and values, and to protect their integrity and existence over time by controlling education within Canadian society. This subordination of 'Indian control of Indian education' to non-Aboriginal program standards remains the most important and intractable source of political conflict between Aboriginal and non-Aboriginal groups for this issue.

These agreements do not reflect an effort to discover norms and values that all can accept, which could be used to regulate both Aboriginal and non-Aboriginal common interests. They cannot be understood as legitimate attempts to reformulate the relationship among federal

Table 5.1
Education and taxation provisions of self-government and education agreements currently in effect

First nations entity	Date concluded	Effective date*	Key education provisions	Direct taxation provision(s)
Nova Scotia				
1. Mi'kmaq Education Agreement	1997	1998	• transfer to provincial schools 'without penalty' to the same extent as the transfer of students is effected between education systems in Canada' • jurisdiction, control, and law-making authority invested in individual First Nations • in the case of conflict with 'any other law,' the First Nations law prevails but only if it is within what is provided for in the agreement • band councils may delegate jurisdiction to a community 'education board' • aggregate organization (MK) is simply a support-service provider	
Yukon				
2. First Nation of Nacho Nyak Dun	1993	1995**	• provision of education programs and services for citizen-residents choosing to participate but not in facilities out of the community	• property tax • direct personal tax on citizen-residents and under certain conditions of other persons and entities on 'settlement land'
3. Champagne and Aishihik First Nation	1993	1995**		
4. Vuntut Gwitchin First Nation	1993	1995**	• no explicit program equivalency requirement	

Table 5.1 (*continued*)

First nations entity	Date concluded	Effective date*	Key education provisions	Direct taxation provision(s)
5. Teslin Tlingit Council	1993	1995**	• control over ancestral culture and language education matters • possible voice in Yukon government curriculum and supervision relating to education in their community	
6. Selkirk First Nation	1997	1997		
7. Little Salmon/ Carmacks First Nation	1997	1997	• provision of education programs and services for citizen-residents choosing to participate but not in facilities out of the community	• property tax • direct personal tax on citizen-residents and under certain conditions of other persons and entities on 'settlement land' • Yukon committed to 'sharing tax room' with First Nations
8. Tr'ondëk Hwëch'in First Nation	1998	1998	• no explicit program equivalency requirement • possible sharing by request with Yukon government design, delivery, and administration of curriculum and supervision relating to education in their community • right to negotiate mandatory membership on school entities involved in education in the community	
9. Ta'an Kwach'an First Nation	2002	2002	• can provide various educational programming including adult and vocational, and Native language and culture • mainly looks to Yukon-wide agreement to provide details	• for future negotiation in context of Yukon-wide self-government agreement

Table 5.1 (continued)

First nations entity	Date concluded	Effective date*	Key education provisions	Direct taxation provision(s)
10. Kluane First Nation	2003	2004	• no equivalency requirement • very sparse on details of educational jurisdiction in the absence of a future Yukon-wide agreement	• for future negotiation in context of Yukon-wide self-government agreement
11. Kwanlin Dun First Nation	2005	2005	• control over ancestral culture and language education matters • can provide various educational programming including adult and vocational, Native language and culture	
12. Carcross/Tagish First Nation	2005	2006	• possible voice in Yukon government curriculum and supervision relating to education in their community • no explicit program equivalency requirement	
NWT 13. Tłıchǫ land claims and self-government agreement	2003	2005	• strong and reiterated program equivalency provisions • delivery of programs envisaged as flowing from 'intergovernmental service agreements' (IGAs) – hence by intergovernmental collaboration ('single mechanism') • notwithstanding, programs will 'respect and promote' language, culture and way of life	• although envisaged in the SGA, the shape and scope of taxation powers will depend on future negotiations • any future direct taxation powers must not prejudice the NWT's ability to set 'economic and fiscal policies' for the Territories as a whole

Table 5.1 (*continued*)

First nations entity	Date concluded	Effective date*	Key education provisions	Direct taxation provision(s)
			• also, Tłı̨chǫ law (but not Tłı̨chǫ community law) has precedence over federal laws except laws of general application, and over territorial laws except when they implement federal obligation under international agreement	• taxation, for local purposes
14. Sechelt	1986	1986	• power to make laws in relation to education	
British Columbia 15. Nisga'a Lisims Government	1999		• provision of education programs and services • curriculum, examination, and other standards to permit transfer between school systems and to provincial PSE • certification of Nisga'a language and culture teachers • certification of other teachers within provincial norms • create and manage PSE institutions but within provincial norms and standards	• extensive direct taxation powers within sophisticated principles on own-source revenue capacity • decennial (or more frequent by mutual agreement) renewal of own-source revenue capacity principles • possible taxation power by subsequent agreement over persons other than Nisga'a citizen-residents on Nisga'a land • possible coordination with taxation of Canada and British Columbia

Table 5.1 (*concluded*)

First nations entity	Date concluded	Effective date*	Key education provisions	Direct taxation provision(s)
16. Westbank First Nation Self-Government Agreement	2003	2003	• transfer to provincial schools 'without penalty' 'to the same extent as the transfer of students is effected between education systems in Canada' • jurisdiction and law-making authority vested in First Nation • can create administrative bodies	• although envisaged in the SGA, the shape and scope of taxation powers will depend on future negotiations

* Year indicated is the year in the agreement came into effect under federal legislation.
** Section 5(1) of the *Yukon First Nations Self-Government Act*, S.C. 1994, c. 35 s. 5(1) indicates that these self-government agreements came into effect on the day the Act came into effect, which was 14 February 1995. The Regulatory Impact Analysis Statement published with the list of Statutory Orders and Regulations included at the end of Schedule II of the act, however, implies that these self-government agreements became effective on the day the act received royal assent, 7 July 1994. We are indebted to Marianne Welch for this detail.

and provincial governments, Aboriginal schools and communities. The bases of educational agreements on Aboriginal control and jurisdiction are devolution of relatively low-level managerial powers and provision of provincially sanctioned curriculum (some of the best reputed Aboriginal schools are unsurprisingly those that have stepped outside the boundaries of provincial programming; see, for instance, Bell 2004). Existing self-government agreements and their limited vision of Aboriginal self-government, leave wide areas of Aboriginal sociocultural, educational, and economic life to be remotely regulated through non-Aboriginal institutions. It could be argued that these agreements on devolved power over education impose the principle that First Nations control of education must be bound strictly within the paradigm that frames federal and provincial policy. Organizational principles embedded in these educational and self-government agreements that regulate the use of power by Aboriginal and non-Aboriginal groups conflict with Aboriginal values and conception of life that are not broadly shared in Canadian society. In doing so, they fix the decision-making balance strongly in favour of non-Aboriginal groups and make it impossible to establish meaningful policy boundaries around Aboriginal governance in general and the governance of education in particular.

Some Pervasive Policy Issues

The most obvious and debilitating issue in First Nations education has changed little over the last forty years. Although the reality lived 'on the ground' in First Nations schools is often far different, First Nations education is required to mimic provincial education sufficiently closely so that students can transfer to provincial schools without penalty *at any time*. The current INAC national guidelines impose this requirement on all band-operated or federally operated schools – whether or not the First Nation in question has concluded a self-governing agreement with a specific program equivalency clause.

> In the case of band-operated or federal schools, the Council shall ensure that programs comparable to provincially recognized programs of study are provided, and that only provincially certified teachers are employed. The Council shall also ensure that education standards allow students to transfer without penalty to an equivalent grade in another school within the school system of the province in which the school is located. (Indian and Northern Affairs Canada 2003, 4)

Financial accountability for First Nations schools is to the federal government through INAC, while program accountability – although nearly non-existent – is nominally to the provinces and territories. The marriage to provincial and territorial curricula is even more integral for other Aboriginal students, who must study in publicly funded schools operated by public (or separate) school boards or districts.

INAC's efforts to 'square the circle' of scrambled accountability in the face of increasingly virulent Auditor General criticism has focused on periodic reviews of programs delivered by First Nations in community schools.

> An independent evaluation of each band-operated and federal school is to be undertaken every five years. This evaluation must include, at a minimum, a review of the curriculum, an assessment of instructional quality and standards, and a review to determine if community and school objectives have been achieved. The Council will ensure that the school has a plan in place for the implementation of the recommendations of the school evaluation report. This plan will be updated each year. (Indian and Northern Affairs Canada 2003, 4)

Such reviews are meaningless in the absence of common goals, purposes, standards, and vision. Some reviews conducted by highly qualified, conscientious contractors may be both full of insight and potentially highly useful. Other reviews done by persons with few or no credible qualifications or scruples may be worse than useless – they may whitewash completely unacceptable practices and very low standards. The point is that nothing anchors the INAC program review mandate in any consistent standard, so the mandate is only as valuable as the ethics, qualifications, and competence of the reviewers. Furthermore, even highly qualified and conscientious reviewers may differ greatly in what they consider to be of central importance for their reviews. In the absence of any meaningful oversight, nothing assures that changes recommended in such reviews will be implemented. In short, the whole process is completely lacking in credibility as an evaluation and development tool.

The relationships among aggregate entities involved in First Nations education (what INAC usually calls 'First Nations Management Organizations') and in particular, the elusive 'hierarchy' of aggregation in First Nations education continues to thwart not only efficient and effective support services but also governance, administration, and supervision in general. Workable lines of governance and accountability at the regional as well as the local level are prerequisites of real improvement in efficiency, effectiveness, and outcomes. Finally, some meaningful (functional) aggregation at the Canada-wide level, however contrary to the grain of recent experience it may run (e.g., the distance of First Nations aggregate organizations in Quebec from AFN and CCOE/NIEC) is, in our view, *the only plausible vehicle for establishing comprehensive jurisdiction over education on the part of First Nations,* despite the huge challenges in coordination and collaboration. This conclusion flows directly from the relatively small scale of First Nations education *as a whole* across Canada.

Funding remains a contentious issue. More than that, funding is a central element in the governance-accountability-aggregation policy problem. So long as program accountability is effectively separated from financial responsibility, little deep change in First Nations education is likely. Central to the funding question is that of own-source revenues, at all levels of First Nations governance, and at all levels of instruction.

Embedded within the funding quandaries of First Nations education is INAC's imposition of a non-duplication-of-services principle. This principle is disingenuously framed within the label of parental choice, a misnomer that is paradoxically misleading. In some regions, in the case of communities that offer a secondary program, INAC will fund secondary students studying outside of their community *only at the level provided for students enrolled in the in-community program.* However, funding for in-community programs fails to recognize supplementary costs (transportation, lodging, and so forth) associated with attending school away from home. INAC argues that this is 'parental choice.' Really, this policy is a thinly disguised way of forcing communities as whole – not individual parents – to decide where secondary students will be allowed to study. In short, far from being an instrument of parental choice, this policy removes parental choice by allowing only for *community-wide choice.*

Although it has a specious aura of efficient allocation of scarce resources, this non-duplication-of-services policy is a serious barrier to meeting individual student needs. If the goal is really better achievement for most students, the policy is inherently inefficient because it denies many students access to the best education for their needs. For many students, in-community secondary education, particularly in later grades, is simply not effective for a variety of reasons, including

- lack of appropriate secondary program and course offerings in the community program

- dysfunctional family
- dysfunctional personal associations in the community
- medical conditions requiring monitoring that are not available in community, or
- parent(s) or guardian(s) is/are studying in a postsecondary program

We believe this policy of systematically underfunding secondary students studying away from home if their community has a secondary program is particularly destructive and ultimately inefficient in furthering the legitimate ends of First Nations education. After all, diseconomies of scale will continue to mean that most First Nations communities will not be able to offer comprehensive secondary-education programs at the community level. That does not mean, however, that funding provisions should impose on First Nations communities a Hobson's choice between no community secondary programming at all on the one hand, and only offering to all students what can be provided at the community level on the other.

Finally, given our stance on the centrality to good governance and administration of ethics, fair play, and transparency, we find it ominous but unsurprising that only one self-governance document, the Nishnawbe Aski Agreement in Principle (AIP) (Participating members of Nishnawbe-Aski Nation and Her Majesty the Queen in Right of Canada 2006), contains any wording dealing with ethical issues. Despite considerable attention to key transparency issues – notably conflict of interest, freedom of information, and privacy – the relevant terms of the agreement would, if ratified, apply only to member First Nations and not to their aggregate organizations and would provide no assurance of appropriate access to information on the part of the broader Canadian public. These terms also fail to ensure that future enabling amendments to the federal *Access to Information Act*[13] and *Privacy Act*[14] would allow exceptions to access to information requests only when the privacy of individuals would be threatened or where such exceptions serve simultaneously the public good and bona fide interests of First Nations education entities acting in the best interests of students.

Overall, the lack of attention given to ethical and transparency issues in the educational provisions of both in-draft and in-force self-government documents are symptomatic of a general lack of attention to ethics and transparency in First Nations education – in fact, it entrenches them.

6 Breaking the Gridlock: Challenges and Options

Educational reforms are not a prerequisite for self-government; the two go hand in hand.

Royal Commission on Aboriginal Peoples,
Vol. 5, *Renewal: A Twenty-Year Commitment* (1996c), 3

The Demographic Challenge

It is no secret that the segment of the Canadian population growing most rapidly by natural increase (as opposed to immigration) is Aboriginal people. Two results of great educational significance result directly from this high rate of natural increase: the Aboriginal proportion of the Canadian population is on the rise, and it is significantly younger than the Canadian population in general. The median North American Indian age in 2001 was 23.5, while the median age for non-Aboriginals was 37.7 (Statistics Canada 2003a, 20). What is less well known is that recently birth (fertility) rates have declined considerably for First Nations and especially for Métis people, while remaining very high among the Inuit.

Borrowing from several sources, White, Maxim, and Spence (2004a) succinctly summarize most of these trends. We build on what is of interest to us in their analysis as we chart and contextualize the demographic challenge faced in Aboriginal education. Figure 6.1 shows growth in the total population reporting Aboriginal ancestry over the twentieth century. Growth over the thirty years prior to the 2001 census is particularly striking. Even so, these numbers likely underestimate the total Aboriginal population because not all persons of Aboriginal

Figure 6.1 Population reporting Aboriginal ancestry (origin), 1901–2001

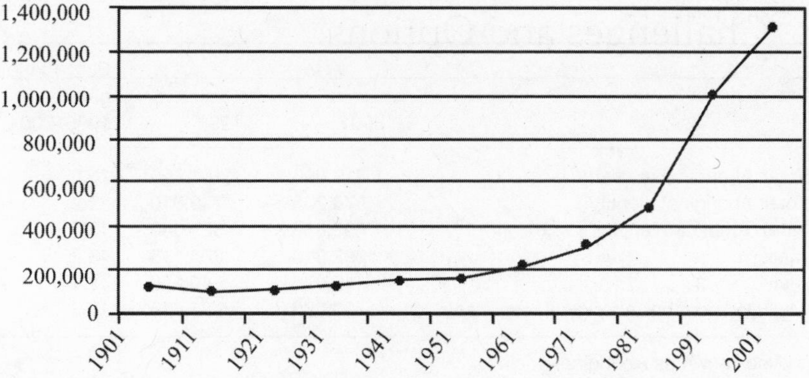

Source: Statistics Canada (2003a), first chart.

ancestry self-identify as Aboriginal for census purposes, and because both historically and recently not all Aboriginal communities have chosen to participate in the census process.

Table 6.1 compares respective numerical and percentage growth in the principal Aboriginal groups in Canada between the 1996 and 2001 censuses. Overall, Aboriginal population growth was about 20 per cent during that period, with the 'North American Indian' population growing by about 15 per cent, the Métis population by 43 per cent, and the Inuit population by about 12 per cent over a period when the entire population of Canada grew by only 4 per cent (Statistics Canada 2003a).

A significant component in the rapid growth of Canada's Aboriginal population in the late 1980s and early 1990s can be attributed to Bill C-31,[1] which restored Indian status to First Nations women who had lost it as a result of marrying non-status spouses prior to that legislation. Bill C-31 also restored status to the children of such women, but with the controversial restriction that these children are not able to pass on status to their own offspring. Furi and Wherrett (2003) summarize the demographic impact of this legislation in these terms:

In the first five years (1985–1990), the status Indian population rose by 19% as a result of the amendments. Women represented the majority of those who gained status, particularly of those who had status restored. By

Table 6.1
Size and growth of the population reporting Aboriginal ancestry and Aboriginal identity,
Canada, 1996–2001

	2001	1996	Percentage growth 1996–2001
Total: Aboriginal ancestry[1]	1,319,890	1,101,960	19.8
Total: Aboriginal identity	976,305	799,010	22.2
North American Indian[2]	608,850	529,040	15.1
Métis[2]	· 292,310	204,115	43.2
Inuit[2]	45,070	40,220	12.1
Multiple and other Aboriginal responses[3]	30,080	25,640	17.3

1 Also known as Aboriginal origin.
2 Includes persons who reported a North American Indian, Métis, or Inuit identity only.
3 Includes persons who reported more than one Aboriginal identity group (North American Indian, Métis, or Inuit) and those who reported being a Registered Indian and/or band member without reporting an Aboriginal identity.
Source: Statistics Canada (2003a), 20.

31 August 1995, the status Indian population had risen from its 1985 level of 360,241 to 586,580. This was an overall increase of 61.4%, 27% of which came from new registrations. In 2000, registrants of Bill C-31 made up 17% of the Indian register ...

Although Bill C-31 registrants helped to increase the status Indian population significantly, by the early 1990s the percentage of change in the status Indian population began to return to levels observed before the 1985 amendments. Whereas Bill C-31 registrants had accounted for 48% of the growth in the status Indian population in 1988, they accounted for only 2% of the growth in that population in 2000. (n.p.)

The fallout (including the demand for education support, which has major financial implications for the federal government) from gender inequities arising from the patrilineal succession provisions of the *Indian Act* may not be fully felt. While Bill C-31 rectified one particularly egregious instance of such discrimination, the loss of status by women who married non-status men prior to Bill C-31, it left others untouched – and presumably vulnerable under section 15 of the *Charter*. In particular,

• status men who married non-status women prior to Bill C-31 coming into effect transmitted their status without restriction to their spouses and any children of that union while, even in the wake of Bill C-31, status women who married non-status men prior to the passing of the bill cannot pass on their status to their spouses;

- more significantly in terms of potential demand for educational service and post-secondary support, the children of status females married to non-status males cannot pass on their status to their own children.

Should litigation result in judicial determination that the 'legacy' of patrilineal gender discrimination in the *Indian Act* contravenes the *Charter* (a partial but potentially significant step in that direction has already occurred in *McIvor v. The Registrar, Indian and Northern Affairs Canada*, 2007 BCSC 827), another bulge in the registration of status Indians and hence in Aboriginal population can be expected, particularly as the grandchildren of status mothers and non-status fathers demand registration to take advantage of health and education benefits associated with Indian status. Given that most of these individuals do not live on reserve, the impact from such a registration bulge would almost certainly be in demand for post-secondary support rather than for increased elementary and secondary services in First Nations communities.

In 2009 the British Columbia Court of Appeals ruled on the *McIvor* case appeal. It found subsections 6.1(a) and 6.1(c) of the *Indian Act* to be unconstitutional and of no force and effect but suspended application of its decision for one year to give Parliament an opportunity to enact corrective legislation (see *McIvor v. Canada [Registrar of Indian and Northern Affairs]*, 2009 BCCA 153). These were the subsections that had prevented status First Nations women who married non-status men prior to proclamation of Bill C-31 on 17 April 1985, but who had their Indian status restored under Bill C-31, from passing their status on to their *grandchildren*. Although Bill C-31 allowed them to pass on status to their children, the status of their children was limited in that those children could not pass on status to their own children.

As this book was in final editing, the Minister of Indian affairs, Chuck Strahl announced that the government would enact legislation to correct this aspect of *Indian Act* gender discrimination. In doing so, he announced that the government estimates some 45,000 people will thus become eligible for registration as status Indians (Galloway 2010). The impact of this decision will be pervasive, including a substantially

Figure 6.2 Estimated births per woman, by Aboriginal identity group and total Canadian population, Canada 1986–1991 and 1996–2001

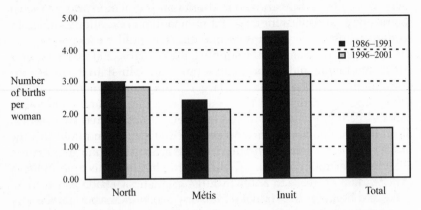

Source: Norris and Siggner (2003), as cited in White, Maxim, and Spence (2004a), 7.

increased demand for post-secondary support for status Indians in the years to come.

Figure 6.2 shows that best available estimates reflect Aboriginal fertility rates in decline since the late 1980s, although North American Indian and especially Inuit rates remain well above those for Canada as a whole, and above the 'natural replacement' rate of just over two children per woman. Interestingly, fertility rates for Métis, the fastest growing group according to the data used in table 6.1, have declined to the natural replacement level among the Aboriginal groups as they are classified by Statistics Canada.

Recently, Statistics Canada made projections for Aboriginal population growth to the year 2017. This involved numerous obstacles beyond those found in typical demographic projections, including problems with obtaining reliable past estimates of Aboriginal fertility and mortality. Furthermore, Aboriginal fertility varies substantially not only among different Aboriginal groups but also by geographical region.

The Statistics Canada study explored three different scenarios, a low-growth scenario (relatively speaking), a medium- and a high-growth scenario. Five sets of fertility rate assumptions were used, including the continuance of the 2001 estimated baseline rates, various degrees of decline in Aboriginal fertility, and rates above those from 2001 for the Canadian population as a whole, in combination with 2001 mortality levels. In all three scenarios, the Aboriginal population was projected to grow at about twice the rate of the Canadian population as a whole, so that by 2017, the Aboriginal population would be (depending on the scenario and exact assumptions) between 1,390,200 and 1,431,800. Although they would continue to be more youthful than the rest of the population – and hence have a larger proportion of members in the school age and traditional university undergraduate and community college age cohort – there would be a reversal of the recent historical trend towards declining median age: 'In 2001, children under the age of 15 years represented one-third of the total Aboriginal population (32.9%). If fertility continues to decline moderately, the proportion of children will decrease to 28.6% by 2017' (Statistics Canada 2005b, 8).

Figure 6.3 shows the Statistics Canada projection of Aboriginal population growth to 2017 by specific group and for all groups in a medium-growth scenario. Although the study projects Aboriginal population growth will continue to vary considerably by region, little doubt exists that Aboriginal population growth alone, even without expanding participation rates, signals an increase in demand for schooling and post-secondary education for Aboriginal peoples over the next decade. According to a medium-growth scenario, Statistics Canada predicts a population of 35.2 million for Canada as a whole by 2016, one year earlier than the projections shown in figure 6.3. If both sets of projections prove reasonably accurate, the Aboriginal component of the population of Canada would rise by almost 1 per cent from just over 3 per cent in 2001 (Statistics Canada 2002, 28) to just under 4 per cent by about 2017 (Statistics Canada 2005a).

First Nations demographic growth is a major reason why the current morass in First Nations education and its governance should not be allowed to continue.

Connecting Severed Layers of Accountability – Why Accountable, Transparent, Ethical, and Adequately Resourced First Nations Jurisdiction Matters

We have already shown that First Nations education is disconnected from program accountability, and that current self-government agreements and agreements in principle have done little to remedy this.

Figure 6.3 Aboriginal population by group, Canada, 1996, 2001, and 2017

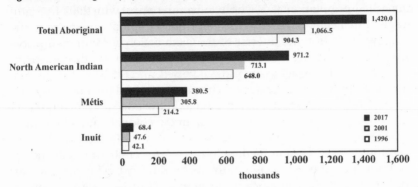

Source: Statistics Canada (2005b), 27, chart 3-1.

On the contrary, the pervasive INAC boilerplate policy of program equivalency in most self-government agreements and INAC's National Program Guidelines have cemented these disconnected layers of accountability in place for the foreseeable future.

Disconnected Layers of Accountability Prohibiting Bicultural, Bilingual Programming

McCue (2004) summarizes the net impact of these disconnected layers of accountability on First Nations jurisdiction in education:

> So, regardless of the amount of jurisdiction that the SGA provides to the First Nations (at least, in the ones examined), the affected communities must ultimately adhere to the provincial curriculum and provincial standards to educate their children. In effect, what these SGAs are saying is that, yes, a First Nation can have jurisdiction in education, but that jurisdiction must ensure that the status quo regarding the curriculum and education program are [sic] maintained in First Nations schools. There is no explicit recognition of First Nations jurisdiction in this regard. Provincial curriculum continues to be the baseline standard for First Nations education. (6)

This state of affairs matters because, *even if the governance challenges and problems associated with diseconomies of scale were successfully resolved, this commitment to provincial curricula as the baseline for First Nations schools renders the development and implementation of bicultural and bilingual education programs impossible.* We wish to be clear about why the INAC program-equivalency requirement, in addition to lending credence to the monstrous falsehood that First Nations education currently is equivalent to provincial education, effectively neuters efforts to implement such programs. Furthermore, as Battiste, Bell, and Findlay (2002) noted, this INAC program-equivalency requirement can be construed as a 'serial obstruction or evasion of Aboriginal knowledge and its producers so as to shelter and sanitize a destructively colonial and Eurocentric legacy'(83).

If the Auditor General is near to the mark in asserting that closing the achievement gap between First Nations and mainstream Canadian students will take twenty-eight years at the current rate of progress (2004a, 1), *wording that contributes to the illusion of program equivalency* in the status quo is much worse than 'unhelpful.' The fiction that students from most First Nations schools could transfer to provincial schools 'without penalty' seems not only Machiavellian but also a direct interdiction of the best chance available for achieving qualitative (not exact program) equivalency with provincial education.

The requirement that students should be able to transfer to provincial schools *at any time during their school career* 'without penalty' means that First Nations communities, schools, and aggregate education entities are prevented from establishing bicultural and bilingual education programs precisely *because* the education they offer is *substantially different* from mainstream provincial English- or French-language schools.[2]

Why are bicultural and bilingual programs so important to improving the quality of First Nations education? First, because most Aboriginal students can only learn effectively in an environment that integrates their culture and evolving identity into the image of 'the educated person' that it reflects, rewards, and reinforces.[3] In other words, First Nations education must enhance Aboriginal consciousness to show what it means to be a First Nation, empowering and enriching individual and collective lives (Hampton 1995). The single most alienating element of mainstream education for Aboriginal students is its rejection, even here and now, of 'Aboriginalness' as being compatible with an 'educated identity,' not to mention the rejection of its compatibility with scholarship or erudition. Despite some encouraging exceptions and progress in certain school systems and institutions, mainstream education still appears to have little room for 'Indianness' in an 'educated Indian.'

To become authentically 'Indian,' First Nations education will need to be rebuilt on inventive paradigm education and on its underlying social purpose assumptions, rather than on provincial or territorial programs of study. To a surprising extent, even in the twenty-first century, current INAC policy demands that First Nations education closely follow– or at least pretend to follow – provincial and territorial education. As a result, it builds normative expectations of an educated Indian on the degree to which the Indian has *shed* his/her Aboriginal identity in favour of mainstream academic accomplishments and polish. In this enduring cultural supremacism, Turner's 'word warrior' is at best an impossible dream.

Second, available evidence suggests that education employing Amerindian languages for instruction *is simply more effective in facilitating academic growth among First Nations students than official language education.* This superiority is manifest across the varying states of survival as living languages in which Amerindian languages currently exist. To say this does not diminish the formidable challenge of designing and implementing such programs, especially ones that are high quality (see, for instance, discussion in Burnaby 1980, especially at 265) in a language-restoration context (St Clair and Leap 1982), and especially in the context of 'semilingualism' (Leap 1982, especially 151). Rather, it acknowledges that they have a better track record, particularly when it comes to helping Native students pursue studies in appropriate academic language registers at the post-secondary level. The evidence consistently suggests that bilingual education – especially 'transitional' programs that start with instruction in Aboriginal languages and then switch to instruction in official national languages over time – produce more positive academic outcomes than programs that impose 'submersion' in official language instruction from the beginning.

The evidence that reinforces this state is twofold. First, the ubiquitous failure of immersion in mainstream language and culture curricula to promote participation and academic achievement among Aboriginal students similar to that of non-Aboriginal students. This failure cannot be explained away by pretending that educators still haven't discovered appropriate 'remediation' strategies for Aboriginal students, but that they will do so someday.

Second, academic outcomes have consistently improved where the will and resources have been found to mount bilingual and bicultural education programs for Native students. The most recent summary of American research on the question will be discussed below. Aside from a federally sponsored review of the state of Aboriginal languages in Canada and ways of saving them from extinction (Task Force on Aboriginal Languages and Cultures 2005), no parallel work is available in Canada.[4] Still, the major patterns of sociolinguistic evolution in the context of Aboriginal language survival and use in Canada and the United States would appear to be quite similar in most respects; although a larger proportion of Aboriginal children in Canada grow up, or have done so until very recently, with an Aboriginal language as a viable mother tongue. However, even in the case of Cree, Ojibwe, and Inuktitut, the only Aboriginal languages not in immediate danger of extinction in Canada, language erosion is taking place at a phenomenal rate, with a growing number of communities sliding rapidly 'upward' along the Fishman scale of language erosion ('intergenerational disruption') ranging from use of language in higher levels of government and education (Stage 1) to use by only a few elders (Stage 8). Schools alone cannot save endangered languages. To survive as living entities, languages must survive in the community as well as in schools. Towards that end, we find the Fishman model of response to language disruption as adapted by the Task Force on Aboriginal Languages and Cultures (see table 6.2) a promising blueprint for arresting the decline of Aboriginal languages in various stages of disappearance (Task Force on Aboriginal Languages and Cultures 2005, 85).

Evidence in the most recent American research on bilingual education leaves little doubt that it is a promising and powerful strategy to foster academic engagement and achievement in Aboriginal students, although it is difficult and costly to implement. The main points of McCarty's analysis can be summarized as follows:

> Despite a growing proportion and number of Native children who come to school with English as a primary language, 'Native students are often stigmatized as "limited English proficient" and, as a group, fare poorly in school.' As a result, 'contemporary Native American bilingual education programs have the combined goals of revitalizing endangered Native languages, incorporating local cultural content, and promoting children's English language learning and school achievement.' (McCarty, in press, 2)

Beyond the now legendary 'Rough Rock Demonstration School' experiment in the 1960s, the Rough Rock English-Navajo Language Arts Program (RRENLAP) organized elementary classrooms

Table 6.2
Suggested interventions based on different stages of language endangerment

Stage 8:	Only a few elders speak the language.	Implement Hinton's (1994) 'Language Apprentice' model, where fluent elders are teamed one-on-one with young adults who want to learn the language. Dispersed, isolated elders can be connected by phone to teach others the language.
Stage 7:	Only adults beyond childbearing age speak the language.	Establish 'Language Nests' after the Maori and Hawaiian models, where fluent older adults provide preschool childcare so that children are immersed in their Indigenous language.
Stage 6:	Some intergenerational use of language.	Develop places in community where language is encouraged, protected, and used exclusively. Encourage more young parents to speak the Indigenous language in the home with and around their young children.
Stage 5:	Language is still very much alive and used in community.	Offer literacy in the minority language. Promote voluntary programs in the schools and other community institutions to improve the prestige and use of the language. Use language in local government functions, especially social services. Give recognition to special local efforts through awards, etc.
Stage 4:	Language is required in elementary schools.	Improve instructional methods utilizing TPR (total physical response) ... TPR-storytelling ... and other immersion teaching techniques. Teach reading and writing and higher level language skills ... Develop two-way bilingual programs where appropriate, where non-speaking elementary students learn the Indigenous language and speakers learn a national or international language. Develop Indigenous language textbooks to teach literacy and academic subject matter content.
Stage 3:	Language is used in places of business and by employees in less specialized work areas.	Promote language by making it the language of work used throughout the community ... Develop vocabulary so that workers in an office can do their day-to-day work using their Indigenous language.
Stage 2:	Language is used by local government and in the mass media in the minority community.	Promote use of written form of language for government and business dealings/records. Promote Indigenous language newsletters, newspapers, radio stations, and television stations.
Stage 1:	Some language use by higher levels of government and in higher education.	Teach tribal college subject matter classes in the language. Develop an Indigenous language oral and written literature through dramatic presentations and publications. Give tribal/national awards for Indigenous language publications and other notable efforts to promote Indigenous languages.

Source: Reyhner (1999), v–xx, adapted from Fishman (1991), 88–109. Available online at http://jan.ucc.nau.edu/~jar/RIL_Intro.html.

around learning centers and culturally relevant themes. Classroom instruction was complemented by summer literature camps in which students, teachers, and elders jointly engaged in research, storytelling, drama, and art projects centered on local themes ... Longitudinal studies show that after four years RRENLAP students' mean scores on local tests of English rose from 58 percent to 91 percent. Overall, students who experienced sustained initial literacy instruction in Navajo made the greatest gains on local and national achievement measures. (McCarty, in press, 6)

Perhaps less counter-intuitively, at least from the perspective of assimilationist logic (see discussion of assimilationist versus non-assimilation logic in Jerry Paquette 1989), 'RRENLAP students also were assessed as having stronger oral Navajo and Navajo literacy abilities than their non-bilingual education peers' (McCarty, in press, 6).

The Navajo bilingual education program at Rock Point, Arizona yielded similar results.

... Rock Point offered initial literacy in Navajo and a secondary-level applied literacy program involving research, word processing, and publishing in two languages. Rock Point students consistently outperformed their peers in conventional programs, and students' gains were cumulative. (McCarty, in press, 7)

Similarly, in 1976 a public school program on the Hualapai reservation in Arizona started from scratch, including the development of an orthography for a language that previously had been strictly oral, increased oral English abilities, school attendance, and graduation rates (McCarty, in press, 7).[5]

In a most 'un-American' policy move that could only happen in Hawaii, the tiny state designated Hawaiian and English as 'co-official' languages in 1978. The educational legacy of this official bilingualism merits close attention – especially given student immersion in a language-restoration context. Particularly telling was parental insistence on the availability of secondary education in Hawaiian.[6]

Seven years after its implementation in 1987, students from a Navajo immersion program at Fort Defiance

... performed as well on local tests of English as comparable students in English-only classrooms; immersion students performed better on local assessments of English writing, and were well ahead in mathematics. On standardized tests of English reading, immersion students were slightly behind, but closing the gap (Holm and Holm 1995). The program has evolved into a full-immersion primary/intermediate school, and Navajo-immersion students continue to outperform their peers in mainstream English classrooms (Romero and McCarty 2006). These students are consistently accomplishing what a large body of research on second-language acquisition predicts: They are acquiring Navajo 'without cost' to their English language development or academic achievement, while developing oral proficiency and literacy in a second, heritage language as well. (McCarty, in press, 12)

The list of bilingual education success stories synthesized by Mc-Carty is long and impressive. One more will suffice for our purposes here, because it illustrates that, even in difficult situations, effective educational steps can be taken to arrest Aboriginal-language extinction. McCarty (in press) mentions the particularly difficult Aboriginal-language context in California, where none of the fifty Indigenous languages are spoken by children any longer. In such circumstances, Native-language groups have opted for a 'master-apprentice model' (the model proposed by Fishman as the best response when only a few elders can speak a language – see table 6.2).

By 1999, 55 master-apprentice teams were in place, representing 16 languages (Hinton 2001, 218). The teams' work is often complemented by immersion camps involving children, parents, and elders. Sims (1998) examines these efforts for the Karuk, a tribe in northwestern California with 2,300 members but only a few elderly Native speakers. In addition to master-apprentice teams, Karuk language camps involve intergenerational participation in language-learning activities embedded in everyday life. The staff reports the rapid rate at which children learn and use Karuk, language transfer to other contexts, and positive new intergenerational relationships (Sims 1998). Public school classes also involve teachers and students in collaborative learning of Karuk. (McCarty, in press, 13)

Like self-government agreements, bilingual education is not a 'silver bullet' for the problems of chronic alienation and underachievement associated with Indigenous education. Even where reasonably adequate resources are available, it is difficult to implement. Nonetheless, it offers the most promising way forward – if the ultimate goal is parity of achievement consistent with Turner's ideal of 'word warriors.'

Meaningful Aboriginal and First Nations jurisdiction matters because:

1. the most effective approach to closing the gap between First Nations and provincial education is to move forward with bicultural and bilingual education in a way that respects the contexts *and cultural aspirations* of various First Nations and First Nations regions (the same is true, although more problematic at a practical level for other Aboriginal groups);
2. distinctive Aboriginal education requires Aboriginal content and perspective, not cloned provincial curricula;
3. despite an *almost* non-existent group of non-Native educators fluent in an Aboriginal language, Native cultures and languages are, by definition, the intellectual property and heritage of Aboriginal people; therefore
4. in most cases, First Nations and their aggregate entities require a quantum leap forward in capacity to develop, organize, and implement such bilingual programs, and while efforts to do so need to take account of diseconomies of scale, only First Nations educators (for the most part) can ultimately develop, supervise, and staff such programs; and
5. progress towards effective bicultural and bilingual First Nations education can only be made once the prohibition against such programming imposed by requiring that students be able to transfer to provincial schools at any stage of their school career without penalty is lifted, and the layers of accountability in First Nations education are connected.

Aboriginal education needs to be rendered accountable to its constituents, particularly parents and community members. This is not policy alchemy, although certain aspects of it imply radical change. Nor is this approach a recipe for disconnecting Aboriginal education from provincial curricula. We are convinced, however, that the current policy of requiring nominal program equivalency reflects the rational educational paradigm which, according to Bertrand and Valois (1980), promotes *transmission* of knowledge, credible ways of thinking, and accepted cognitive structures that marginalize 'Aboriginalness' as incompatible with an 'educated identity.'

Instead, we believe that the road to quality for Aboriginal education, and for First Nations education in particular, is not lockstep program equivalency at all grade levels, but rather bicultural and bilingual programming with intelligent and appropriate provisions for the eventual transition to official language instruction at appropriate times in student development.

Accountability, ethics, and adequate resourcing – towards meaningful jurisdiction

Accountability implies transparency, especially ready access to appropriate information by stakeholders and the public. It requires adherence to high ethical standards so that the primary stakeholders, namely parents and community members, as well as concerned members of the public can have such access. This is the antithesis of an educational governance structure that sustains the power of an elite and unaccountable minority to make decisions on the majority's behalf.

Although we deal extensively with issues of transparency and ethics elsewhere, some observations related to connecting layers of accountability are necessary here. Organizations where decision-making takes place under a cloak of secrecy or without adequate paper and data trails, are, by definition, unaccountable. Furthermore, accountability *to* Aboriginal constituents means that they should be able to obtain relevant policy and performance information upon request in a reasonable amount of time and at an affordable cost. These processes should be subject to limitation only by bona fide student interests or other interests protected by federal and provincial freedom of information and privacy legislation. Given the important role of the federal government in funding First Nations education, and the resulting interest that Canadian taxpayers have in it, members of the Canadian public should also have broad access to information rights with regard to First Nations education. We see Aboriginal self-governance in education offering a vision of political life among Aboriginal communities not as struggle over position, power, and financial rewards, but as a form of self-determination – a political process that would enable all members of Aboriginal communities to direct their own educational affairs in accordance with the aspirations, developmental goals, and purpose they collectively accept. As Moon (1993) observes:

> The concept of moralization and transparency reflect a worldview that emphasizes the conventionality of social relationships, practices, and structures, a worldview in which less and less is taken simply as 'given', as 'natural,' or as ordained by the gods. Once we recognize that all relationships can be questioned and must be justified, we can insist that they express the judgments of the citizenry. (194)

Meaningful jurisdiction in the sense of 'Indian control over Indian education,' cannot occur in the absence of accountability, policy, and governance bound unflinchingly to ethical principles and standards, along with adequate resourcing. Although these are necessary conditions for meaningful jurisdiction, they are not sufficient in themselves. Meaningful jurisdiction cannot occur without collaboration in efficient aggregate organizations at all levels. In this sense, the vision of purely *local* control put forward in *Indian Control of Indian Education* (National Indian Brotherhood 1972/1984) is a mirage, and has no practical use in the realities of First Nations education. While it may be useful for inspiring work aimed at authentic First Nations control, ICIE does not present a practical vision of how such control might be achieved.

Control and Aggregation

Diseconomies of scale make control dependent on successful aggregation, efficient and effective aggregation which produces desired educational outcomes for First Nations and for Aboriginal education. We define control as a First Nations citizen-resident voice *that effectively shapes educational policy and practice on the one hand and has influence over educational resource flow and accountability for it on the other* (see figures 5.1 and 5.2). We are referring to political participation that enables all interested individuals to think as public beings, to make public claims about educational purposes, programs, and services, and to provide reasoned argument towards those ends. Such participation balances values shared in the present with traditions in the Aboriginal communities with whom they identify. This type of political participation is similar to the global sense of purpose framed by the symbiosynergetic paradigm which is 'the symbiosynergy of persons and communities,' of the 'total person.' Such participation does this in the belief that persons as holons are whole only when fully united with a society transformed into a meta-community (Bertrand and Valois 1980, 277). Just as the citizen-resident political voice is given policy and accountability effect in provincial education through local and provincial levels of governance, the citizen-resident political voice can only shape First Nations educational policy, resource flow, and accountability through political and governance structures, which promote decision-making based on non-hierarchical 'mutualism' (see our discussion in chapter 2, in 'The Inventive Paradigm' section). This structure reflects the consensus-based political decision-making which was integral in traditional Aboriginal communities and societies. The reason for aggregation is simple: most communities can never hope to command the resources necessary to create and sustain any kind of functional, integrated, and efficient educational system on their own.

To exercise meaningful 'Indian control over Indian education,' individual communities must engage in reverse 'devolution,'[7] surrendering control over administration, management, and supervision as well as program and infrastructure support to aggregate organizations. *Without surrendering control upward* (control which is generally non-existent beyond a very limited scope), *First Nations cannot have any meaningful control over education*. The cruel alternative to the upward delegation of authority is remaining mired in amateur educational and administrative practices. When fragmented among a large number of tiny communities, local control is ultimately sham control.

INAC has come closest to imposing what we have in mind for functional aggregation in its recent national program guidelines on special education. While not actually requiring that First Nations collaborate within aggregate organizations for special education assessment and program delivery activities, the INAC national guidelines recognize that, given the profound diseconomies of scale affecting special education services and programs, many First Nations will choose to organize into regional entities for special education. To provide some policy framework for such entities, INAC defines national minimal requirements for 'First Nations Regional Managing Organizations' (FNRMOs). Only organizations meeting these criteria can administer special education programs and funds delegated to them by participating First Nations. The guidelines stipulate that an FNRMO will

- have a documented management framework outlining the governance structure;
- have documented support from its member First Nations (band council resolutions, letters, etc.);
- have documented policy guidelines, both general to the FNRMO and specific to First Nations special education;
- have a work plan, including a budget and evaluation component;
- provide second and third level services; and
- demonstrate economies of scale. (Indian and Northern Affairs Canada/Affaires indiennes et du Nord Canada 2002, 9)

'Flow-through organizations,' those that simply transfer resources, are specifically prohibited from FNRMO status, which keeps them from acting as intermediaries in special education services and programs (ibid., 9). The guidelines identify three phases of development for an FNRMO, ranging from provision of indirect services while building capacity, to providing a complete range of special education programs and services. While these requirements hardly constitute a rigorous operational definition of FNRMOs and deliberately (according to the guidelines) leave much latitude for local adaptation, they nonetheless set out a basic expectation that coherent governance and policy will frame First Nations special education activities – and that many First Nations will find it necessary to aggregate for special education purposes.

FNRMOs offer a prototype of functional aggregation, one that needs considerable work to include accountability mechanisms, allowable governance practices, and so forth. They do not, however, signal broad recognition on the part of INAC and the federal government that aggregate First Nations education organizations need to work within coherent policy frameworks and relationships.

To exercise meaningful jurisdiction over education, First Nations *must* devolve, upload, or cede administration, supervision, and programming to aggregate entities. The function of such a governance structure is closely related to the idea of 'cohesive diversity' as expressed by Bertrand and Valois (1980) in their discussion of the symbiosynergy of heterogeneity and the universal recognition of the 'complementarity of differences' (see chapter 2, in 'The Inventive Paradigm' section). Aggregate entities, whether or not they are called 'school boards,' must be the primary vehicle of control and jurisdiction, and thus need to act like school boards while avoiding the pitfalls of bureaucratic dysfunction to which school boards can fall prey.

Those bodies which provide funding need to take account of first-level aggregation (school board-like entities) as the main locus of power and administrative capacity in First Nations education. In particular, the inherently dysfunctional conceptualization of aggregates as mere service providers to individual First Nations needs to end, and with it the funding and funding mechanisms predicated on it. A new balance between community and regional autonomy is needed – and with it a new approach to funding that takes account of a more important role for First Nations aggregate organizations, particularly regional amalgams that serve the same purposes school boards do in provincial and state education.

Various barriers to First Nations taxation for schools and other purposes have arisen over time, particularly in relation to self-government and self-government agreements. We cannot review the entire literature on the subject here, but we cannot overlook some of the issues in that literature of central importance to the funding of First Nations education.

Key First Nations Taxation Issues

Folk wisdom has long held that 'he who pays the piper calls the tune.' That relationship is why First Nations self-taxation matters. Since First Nations citizen-residents believe that they have no voice in determining revenue flows for education in their communities and furthermore, that the money that supports education is not *their money*, the basis for a meaningful accountability relationship is severed.

As a policy goal, self-determination is directly opposed to perpetuating dependency. That is what makes fiduciary responsibility a double-edged sword. Unilateral withdrawal of support for social programs like education for First Nations people that are grounded in both treaty and inherent-right claims, as the federal government attempted to do in the White Paper exercise, would be, by all moral 'ideas in good currency' (Pal 2006, 100, 116), simply unacceptable. However, because federal policy in First Nations education aims to establish boundaries around the ability of First Nations (and other Aboriginal peoples) to determine their future, 'own-source' revenue is essential. Grants from settler governments, however justifiable and necessary in the short term they are on the grounds of fiduciary responsibility, can never be the basis of meaningful self-determination.

The question of First Nations taxation is one of fiscal, legal, and moral relationships. In summarizing the relevant literature on fiscal relationships, MacKinnon (1998) lays out six principles with which we agree:

1. fiscal relationships must be functional
2. fiscal relationships must be contextual
3. fiscal relationships must be measurable
4. new fiscal relationships must be flexible but certain
5. resources are essential to success [to which we would add 'effective and efficient use of resources']
6. fiscal relationships are based on mutual respect and benefit [a relational-pluralist way of regarding them]. (3–4)

MacKinnon also identifies three types of obligation that can lead to the provision of fiscal resources: contractual, constitutional or legal, and moral (ibid., 6). We would add that moral legitimacy underpins all three types of obligation, and they all involve reciprocal responsibilities.

A recent report commissioned by INAC called *Fiscal Realities* offers a perspective on First Nations taxation issues that corresponds with our own thinking in interesting ways. We do have reservations about certain aspects of this report, and are disappointed at the lack of attention in it to aggregate organizations and their role. However, we consider it to be a refreshingly plausible and balanced look at a way forward for First Nations taxation, one that is in harmony with our interpretation of current tax theory.

Figure 6.4 reflects our starting point regarding the paradoxical relationship between meaningful self-determination and federal fiduciary responsibility over the long term. The 'vicious circle' on the left side of the diagram illustrates the malaise and hopelessness associated with perpetual dependence on 'other source' revenues, particularly revenues from the federal government. Despite its clever euphonic fit, we are uncomfortable with the label the *Fiscal Realities* authors used for the right-hand side of the diagram (moral virtue does not necessarily come from local taxation and development),[8] but we agree that self-taxation enables economic and social development – including the expansion and improvement of educational programming – beyond what can be expected solely from a federal transfer grant system.

Fiscal Realities (FR) (1991) identifies three reasons for cultivating and encouraging First Nations taxation:

> (1) Rapidly growing populations will drive up the expenditures needed to maintain current levels of service. (2) They will have to compete for additional federal funds against political pressure for tax cuts, increased spending on social programs and the cost increases associated with an aging society. (3) Self-government and economic aspirations require funds over and above those needed to maintain existing service levels. (iii)

Clearly, education is near the top of the list of services that will see spending pressure rise, given the First Nations demographics laid out at the beginning of this chapter. Available evidence also demonstrates that First Nations education is in need of a quantum leap forward in quality along with an increase in the quantity of services arising from growth in the school and post-secondary age population and from increasing participation.

Figure 6.4 Dependency versus wealth creation

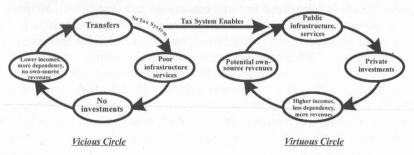

Vicious Circle   Virtuous Circle

Source: *Fiscal Realities* (1999), 37.

The idea of First Nations taxation in general, and First Nations property taxation in particular, no longer sounds as improbable as it did when one of us first advocated it over two decades ago (Paquette 1986). As *FR* authors note, at the time of writing, fifty-eight First Nations were levying property taxes on their communities, from which they were generating an estimated $20 million annually (*Fiscal Realities* 1999, 1). Even so, all parties familiar with the issue understand that taxation has been anything but an 'easy sell' among First Nations, who generally see it as an abrogation of federal fiduciary responsibility rather than as a tool of self-determination and development. Nonetheless, even the Assembly of First Nations has recognized that taxation power is worth exploring, although the terms under which they see such exploration taking place are unlikely to be acceptable either to the federal or provincial governments (ibid., 7).

Federal legislation currently regulates First Nations taxation of real property and, on a case-by-case basis, sales taxes (ibid., 1). Section 87 of the *Indian Act* continues to prohibit taxation of land or other real property being used by registered Indians living on reserve, although First Nations can pass a by-law imposing property taxes on 'designated land' leased by non-First Nations persons or entities. However, before it takes effect, the by-law must be approved by the minister of Indian Affairs on recommendation from the Indian Taxation Advisory Board.

We concur with *Fiscal Realities* that proceeding tax by tax and case by case is an ill-advised policy likely to serve no one's interest over the long term as relationships between First Nations and settler governments, are renewed. Leaving aside the specifics of the study, we wish to endorse their general guidelines for moving forward with First Nations taxation, with some specific comments and one caveat. We also call attention to their concern, which reflects our own, about the lack of adequate data to support First Nations taxation and to permit its harmonization with both federal and provincial tax systems.

We agree with the authors of *FR* that maintaining the integrity of the Canadian tax system is an essential goal as First Nations taxation is codified. In particular, First Nations taxation should be geographically based, harmonized with federal (and provincial) taxation, consistent with increased autonomy and self-sufficiency for First Nations, deal fairly and non-punitively with the interests of non-First Nations persons living or doing business on First Nations land, should not include indirect taxation, and should not offer GST exemptions to individual First Nations persons (ibid., 4–5).

FR (1999) proposes the following basic rights and powers for First Nations with regard to taxation:

- The property of Indians which is situated on reserves should remain exempt from *non-Indian* government taxation.
- Indian governments and their institutions will be exempt from taxation by other governments.
- Own source revenues are not to be used as a rationale for replacing existing funding arrangements unless the institutional infrastructure and level of service provision of a given First Nation government is reasonably equivalent to that of surrounding communities.
- The federal government will consider giving First Nations authority to levy all direct taxes.
- The federal government is willing to consider entering into arrangements to redirect a portion of federal tax revenues raised from Indian individuals on reserve to the First Nations government. However, in the case of the GST, this will likely affect the eligibility of low-income Indian citizens for the GST rebate.
- The extent to which non-First Nation members living on First Nation land will pay taxes to the Indian government is to be negotiated. (5)

With one exception, we see these principles as promising starting points for building a mutually beneficial taxation interface (for settler governments and First Nations). However, we take issue with the third point. Although it attempts to address an important principle, that First Nations that engage in taxation should not be penalized for doing so with respect to entitlement for grants and benefits from the federal government, it does so in a way that is either clumsily expressed or else simply inappropriate. We believe that, at least in education, *local* own-source revenues should never account for more than 5 per cent of the total operational budget, in order to avoid major inequities in per-pupil spending power. We also believe, however, that should regional First Nations organizations (for example, province-wide education authorities subsuming local 'boards') ever become a reality, a larger proportion of own-source area and regional (even Canada-wide) revenues would be appropriate and desirable. This raises the difficult question of aggregation and taxation in First Nations affairs, a subject that has not been much discussed – and one that may be less than appealing for both First Nations and the federal government – but one that we consider crucial and ultimately unavoidable.

Fiscal Realities (1999) also recommends that legislation to enable First Nations taxation

- clearly addresses First Nations concerns that developing own-source revenues will lead to the erosion of the federal fiduciary responsibility for Indians;
- specifies offsets and ensures incentives to generate own-source revenues;
- not penalize Indian bands who will be unable to raise significant revenues;
- provide increased political and economic autonomy for First Nation governments that create new taxation regimes. Fewer conditions should be attached to transfers and accountability provisions should be no more onerous than for other governments;
- provide certainty of funding over the long term;
- minimize the negotiation costs of assuming a tax authority, provide adequate tax powers, and pre-specify conditions of harmonization;
- specify support to First Nation governments in setting up tax administrations; and,
- provide investors, third parties, and other governments with a clear understanding of the eventual limits of First Nation tax authorities. It should assure them that First Nation taxation implies no increase in their tax burden or compliance costs. (41–2)

Again, we are in general agreement and note the autonomy-taxation link which we spoke of earlier. We agree that this link should be an important policy consideration in moving ahead with First Nations taxation. That said, given the need for comparable services and programming across communities, First Nations and their aggregates will necessarily set limits to such autonomy in education. We also believe that the first point needs to be adjusted in accordance with our observation that fiduciary responsibility is essentially incompatible over the long term with meaningful self-determination. The first point should be constructed around *fiscal capacity*. Enabling legislation should clearly address First Nations' concerns about the development of own-source revenues resulting in unreasonable and unjust reduction in entitlement to federal grants, benefits, and assistance. While many will not welcome the use of subjective standards such as unreasonable and unjust here, we see no viable alternative that would take account of vast differences in context, circumstances, and especially fiscal capacity across First Nations and their aggregate organizations.

At this point we are drawn back to the principle of he who pays the piper calls the tune. Unlike provincial school boards and districts that still have some significant own-source revenues over which they exercise meaningful discretion (although most school boards or districts in Canada no longer fit that description), First Nations aggregate organizations have *no* revenues to which they can lay claim, except those provided by participating First Nations or INAC. In terms of voice and control, it would be similar to a situation where provincial governments established *school-level* governance entities and transferred all funding for elementary and secondary education directly to them, while leaving it to them to decide whether they wanted to form, join, or withdraw from aggregate organizations. These school-level entities would also have to decide how much money they wanted to provide to such organizations, as well as the mandate, terms, and conditions under which the organizations would operate. The analogy would be more accurate if it was generally agreed that such aggregate organizations would have no purpose – and no authority – beyond providing the services agreed upon by participating schools. This would lead to chaos, sustained by endless inter- and intra-community power struggles. In a policy world where money talks, most pipers try to play the tune their benefactors choose, and the potential exists that the final result is no tune at all.

To avoid these debilitating problems, leverage available economies of scale, promote functional integration of First Nations community schools as well as secondary and post-secondary support services, and improve the quality of education in First Nations schools, the federal government must create appropriate financial incentives for First Nations. Such incentives should help create and sustain aggregate educational organizations that provide program development and implementation, administration, management, and supervision for the communities they serve. They should not merely serve as platforms for service delivery at the behest of individual communities.

The lack of outright fee-simple ownership of land and real property by First Nations citizen-residents poses some challenges with regard to taxation for education and other public service purposes. Some workable alternatives are already in use in those First Nations that have opted into taxation, notably taxation of property leased by non-First Nations members, and sales taxes. Neither of these is ideal – but then, no one tax is ever 'ideal.' Taxation of property leased by non-First Nations members, while it can be both just and useful, is not the equivalent of self-taxation by First Nations people themselves; and it is self-taxation that has the highest valence in terms of promoting a sense of ownership and responsibility at the local level. Sales taxes for education are rare, for the obvious reason that huge differences exist in the ability of school boards to raise revenues based on a sales tax (urban boards in large cities could raise sizeable amounts, while rural boards would not be able to raise any significant per-pupil amount). In any case, we are aware of only one jurisdiction in North America that has ever authorized school district sales taxes, Louisiana.

Numerous alternatives to taxation of real property are available. All that is required is the will to use them. One can imagine a 'property usage benefit' tax in lieu of property taxes. Such a tax would require occupants of band housing to pay a tax based on an assessed 'usage benefit' that occupants derive from their occupancy of the property. This approach would allow taxation of land and buildings on reserve in proportion to their estimated 'benefit value,' while avoiding the semantics of fee-simple ownership. Is it property taxation by another name? Perhaps, but if the goal is to inject significant own-source taxation revenue into First Nations education and draw the local interest that comes with a sense that 'it's *our* money they're spending in the schools,' then why not?

Other viable alternatives to property taxation for education would include user fees on various community services. The most challenging alternative would be income taxation. As *Fiscal Realties* notes (1999, 25), and as everyone associated with First Nations politics is well aware, advocating self-taxation is politically risky for First Nations leaders. The risk is particularly high where policy changes would expose the income of band members who work for First Nations organizations that meet current Revenue Canada criteria for exemption from federal and provincial income taxes to taxation by their own governments. A number of self-government agreements bear witness to the courage some First Nations leaders have shown in selling tax alternatives to their constituents. To date, however, these alternatives have all been relatively painless for First Nations members. To provide significant local and area support for education, as well as other public services and infrastructure, self-taxation will need to become just that – taxation of First Nations members by *their* government in support of *their* public services and infrastructure, including education.

As First Nations expand the scope of self-taxation, they and their federal partner will need to create suitable equalization measures to ensure that communities which currently have little tax potential are not denied access to quality education for their children simply because they cannot generate significant revenues in support of education at the local and/or area level. As Paquette noted two decades ago, any reliance on local taxation in First Nations education will require a powerful equalization mechanism to prevent truly 'savage inequalities' (Paquette 1986, 95–6) in spending power and 'level the playing field' in First Nations education. While a handful of First Nations might fund a substantial part of their educational spending out of own-source revenues, the overwhelming majority could not. Nonetheless, we remain convinced that even a 'token' proportion of funding from own-source revenues is better than none at all when it comes to fostering and entrenching a sense of local ownership and responsibility at the community and regional level. To avoid unacceptable inequalities arising from different local revenue-generating capacities, we would recommend what the Crombie Commission recommended to the Ontario government in 1996 in regard to their school boards, that *no First Nation or First Nations education entity should be able to raise more than 5 per cent of its total operating budget from local revenues* (1996).

Assurance that greater overall reliance on own-source income will not create or entrench a multi-tier education system among First Nations should go far to alleviating resistance among First Nations members and resultant political risk for First Nations political leaders who seek to pursue the educational and other service and infrastructure benefits of self-taxation.

All that being said, various barriers to First Nations taxation are unlikely to vanish anytime soon. In general, the current land base of First Nations is small and fragmented, and only a fraction of that base is or will be of commercial, residential, or recreational value. In addition, most First Nations are situated in remote or rural areas with few resources, little or no infrastructure, minimal business activity, and low incomes (*Fiscal Realities* 1999, 24), and are generally plagued with an intergenerational culture of dependency and helplessness, truly a 'vicious circle.'

All this being duly noted, if poor, remote, dependent First Nations (which form the majority of reserves) are ever to improve their economic situation, they, their aggregate organizations, the federal government, and provincial governments must move beyond 1970–80s rhetorical flailing at an elusive 'economic base' – as if prosperity were a treasure to be dug up, or a lottery to be won. Some of this movement is taking place within the context of land claims settlements and self-government agreements. Still, we believe fundamental changes in attitude, initiative, vision, and direction are needed from the level of First Nations communities to that of settler governments. As well, financial institutions, especially (though not exclusively) the First Nations Bank, need to rethink their role in First Nations business development.

Despite numerous barriers and challenges to First Nations taxation, we don't see meaningful self-determination for First Nations being possible in the absence of it. *Self-taxation* is especially necessary for education as well as for other public services and infrastructure. Adoption of self-taxation is ultimately a matter of values and determination, not a technical problem, but it does have technical aspects and implications.

With regard to the technical aspects of the issue, we endorse the position taken by *Fiscal Realities* (1999), that much more clarity is needed at all levels of government regarding the harmonization of First Nations tax formulas with federal and provincial taxation regimes (30), and that good software for estimating First Nations tax potential must be developed and made available to them (21). We would add that such software must be flexible enough to consider various alternative sources of taxation that particular First Nations might feel work better in their specific situations, and should include modules specifically aimed at assessing self-taxation capacity. The need to be able to estimate both traditional equivalent-to-property-tax revenues from leaseholders on First Nations land and more divergent and innovative possibilities, which could include 'bit taxes' on telecommunications use, or a spectrum of land-use taxes ranging from camping and ecotourism, to parking use, argues not only for flexible software – but also appropriate software development and good technical support over the long term.

These technical issues, however, are purely instrumental. The bottom-line issue is the will of First Nations people and the governance bodies they create to invest in improving *their* schools and *their* education, as well as their commitment to improving *their* infrastructure and social services.

How might First Nations educational taxation relate to other forms of taxation? It relates through the necessity of integration among individual First Nations into *functional* aggregate organizations that represent a working level of educational governance to which First Nations devolve (upward), policy-making authority and program, administrative, and supervisory responsibility.

We do not wish to show a prejudice against self-government agreements or discussions and negotiations about self-determination moving in the direction of a 'municipal model' of governance. Nonetheless, we believe that an arrangement in which aggregate education organizations can levy taxes that are collected by either individual participating First Nations or, where they exist, by aggregate governance bodies, is a sensible way forward. Any arrangement would have to balance the need for distinctively educational governance over taxation for educational purposes with the need for efficiency in tax collection. The need for such a balance argues strongly for only one First Nations aggregate taxation mechanism, where general governance and education entities coexist. Just as school boards have had varying degrees of discretion in setting tax rates on their property tax bases but have relied on municipalities, counties, or other non-educational entities to collect those taxes, First Nations educational aggregates could set taxes for educational purposes, and assume direct moral and political responsibility for those decisions, but rely on general governance entities to send out statements and collect the amounts owed.

One promising sign in the self-government agreements generally, although it is very limited at present, are clauses dealing with limited sharing of resource revenues. The sharing of resource revenues returns to Malone's (1986) key point about the importance of 'resource-sharing at source' by First Nations governance entities. Such individual agreement-specific provisions on resource revenues do not readily connect to the much broader vision of resource-sharing evoked by Malone. They also don't provide much light at the end of the tunnel for region-wide or national First Nations governance entities either generally or in education. Nonetheless, they underscore that both First Nations and settler governments recognize that resource-sharing – as opposed to exclusive reliance on federal discretionary transfers – is an essential ingredient not just in 'self-government' but in the more modest relational pluralist agenda of simply establishing meaningful boundaries around First Nations self-determination, whatever the governance model may be.

For most First Nations, meaningful autonomy in education as well as other social policies will require more own-source revenues than can be raised simply by taxing non-Aboriginal enterprises leasing First Nations property and self-taxation. Unless other resources are available to First Nations which are not controlled by the Treasury Board and INAC, there can be no meaningful policy boundaries around First Nations in general and First Nations education in particular.

Progress on further resource-sharing will depend on the commitment of First Nations governance organizations to the highest standards of ethics and fair play, but that is the subject of another chapter.

Special Education

Special education offers a unique challenge within the context of First Nations education. First, the *Indian Act* accords no rights to appropriate education to any First Nations students, much less to First Nations students with special needs. Second, past practice has left First Nations students with special needs in one of two situations:

- those with disabilities so severe they could not be accommodated in their community school(s) were sent to a provincial – or private – institution which served the needs of students with the disability in question (e.g., schools for the blind, deaf, severe behavioural disorders, etc.);
- students with disabilities that were not severe enough to warrant accommodation in an institution outside of the community were enrolled in the community school with only minor, ad hoc adjustments (or none at all) in program and pedagogy to take account of their special needs.

Until recently, most First Nations children with mild or moderate special needs had no support unless they happened to live in areas that had certain programs in place. If the child was fortunate, he/she would be enrolled in a school run by a First Nation that funded special education services by taking money from other budget lines, or was part of the pilot project in special education undertaken by the First Nations Education Council of Quebec (FNEC) in the late 1990s, or was part of a project run by the First Nations Education Steering Committee (FNESC) in British Columbia. Otherwise, the child was usually thrust into a regular community school classroom without any program adjustment or support. The corollary to this reality for special needs students was that their teachers were placed in the same regular classroom without any of the supports or resources taken for granted today in schools under provincial jurisdiction.

On top of that, few classes in First Nations schools are regular classes in any way that would make sense to teachers in schools under provincial jurisdiction. This reality is borne out by the widely accepted although poorly documented high incidence of mild to moderate disabilities in First Nations student populations. In the broader world of special needs study, it is well known that the proportion of students with disabilities increases along with family and community stress as socio-economic status decreases. In work one of us was involved with near the end of the FNEC special education pilot project in 2000, 47 per cent of children enrolled in schools participating in that study had been identified with a condition which affected their ability to learn. The lesson is hard to avoid, and the implications of cost related to it are daunting. Incidence rates among First Nations students across the whole spectrum of educationally relevant exceptionalities are several times higher than in the population as a whole, where the total incidence rate for all exceptionalities is typically only about 10 per cent. The particularly high incidence of fetal alcohol syndrome among First Nations populations renders the task of educators in First Nations schools especially challenging – all other things being equal, which, of course, they are not.

In spite of the dismal record of indifference on the part of the federal government and of First Nations educational service organizations to varying degrees, some disconnected efforts have been made to provide elements of support (such as the 'tutor escort' program, which funded minimal training for First Nations community members wishing to become educational assistants). Overall, however, nothing existed – or exists today in most First Nations – which could be compared to the guaranteed right to appropriate education at public expense in provincial education systems. This tragic status quo in special education continues to be a blight on First Nations education.

The blight will persist for some time to come. It will continue for at least two reasons. First, even if First Nations education were not awash with highly fragmented and fractious governance and plagued with acute diseconomies of scale, considerable time as well as substantial resource investment would be required to develop the capacity to provide special education assessments and services comparable to those available currently in provincial school systems. Second, the lack of appropriate education for every child has negative consequences on the intergenerational cultural and social capital (we obviously intend to include Aboriginal cultures and languages as an essential part of such capital in this context) available to support education for succeeding generations. Parental education correlates closely with student academic success. To use a concrete example, adults with learning disabilities that have been adequately addressed during their school careers have a much better chance of supporting their own children's learning and their motivation, than parents whose disabilities have simply been ignored and who have eventually failed or been pushed out of school.

The current INAC national guidelines on special education recognize the capacity development issue in two ways: first in the 'layered' phasing of development of First Nations Regional Managing Organizations (FNRMOs) from an indirect service and development phase to one where they become responsible for the complete range of special education assessment and service activities (Indian and Northern Affairs Canada/Affaires indiennes et du Nord Canada 2002, 10–11); and second, by its restriction until June 2005 of '100% the funding to deliver both direct and indirect special education programs and services' to FNEC and FNESC (ibid., 5), the two groups that pioneered special education among First Nations aggregate organizations, and hence have the greatest developed and demonstrated capacity.

As in other educational policy areas, money is not enough in special education. Even in abundance, it cannot eradicate lack of capacity and certainly cannot do so overnight or in spite debilitating diseconomies of scale. No amount of money can empower a community of 500 persons in a remote corner of the Canadian north to formulate a comprehensive and appropriate policy on special education, or hire and retain a complete staff of professional support personnel. Here, as elsewhere in First Nations education, the only promising way forward is *functional* aggregation, in which individual First Nations cede power, including fundamental policy decision-making power and resources to aggregate organizations.

Extrapolating from a costing exercise on the FNEC pilot project in 2000, Paquette and Smith (2000) estimated that something in the order of a quarter billion dollars would be needed to provide to all First Nations special needs students studying in their home communities the level of service comparable to that being provided in FNEC communities at that time (24). As of 2004, INAC reported that it would be investing $101 million in special education for First Nations students nationally (Indian and Northern Affairs Canada 2004). Even allowing for the need to escalate investment in First Nations special education gradually as the capacity to use special education funds develops among FNRMOs, the amount being provided is reflective of service levels well below current provincial norms *when the very high incidence rates in First Nations student populations is taken into consideration*, and is well below any reasonable estimate of overall assessment and service need in First Nations communities.

Mould-Breaking Aboriginal Schools

For those familiar with President George W. Bush's Education 2000 program in the United States, the title of this section will have either positive or negative connotations, depending on whether one considers the 'mould-breaking schools' initiative a good or a bad thing. The term, however, seemed useful to us because, abstracted from its highly politicized American context, the idea of schools that 'break the mould' of typical schools in comparable contexts has particular pertinence and value in Aboriginal, and especially in First Nations education.

That pertinence stems from the pervasiveness and rigidity of the mould. Within First Nations education, the mould is the INAC requirement that First Nations schools conform to provincial curricula. As we have noted several times, programming in First Nations schools must be, at least theoretically, structured so that students can transfer at any time to provincial schools without penalty. Given that fact, it is hardly surprising that mould-breaking schools and schools that offer unusually high 'added value' when compared with other similarly situated Aboriginal and First Nations schools, are relatively hard to find.

Not only are such schools likely to be rare given the policy within which First Nations education must operate, but also identifying them is difficult, given the lack of comparable 'performance' data and serious cultural bias and appropriateness issues around the application of provincial assessment instruments to Aboriginal student populations.

No body of research exists that clearly identifies a pool of mould-breaking, high value-added Aboriginal schools, much less research that identifies characteristics and practices in those schools that are closely associated with varying degrees of 'recognition and teaching of Indigenous knowledge' (Battiste, Bell, and Findlay 2002, 93), and high academic performance across a variety of potentially significant variables. Even allowing for the problematic aspects of investigation that compose what is referred to as 'effective schools' research (for a superb review of the problematic nature of both effective schools leadership and effective schools research, see Dantley 1990), we know much less than in education generally, and very little at all with certainty, about what contributes to academic performance in Aboriginal schools, and in schools with predominantly Aboriginal enrolment.

Several years ago, against the backdrop of this research void, the Society for the Advancement of Excellence in Education (SAEE) commissioned a multiple case study of ten Aboriginal schools (all, unfortunately, in Western Canada) said by knowledgeable informants to be providing education superior in quality to that offered by most Aboriginal schools. Although the study was framed within assumptions derived directly from the effective schools literature, its underlying methodology opened it up to complexity and ambiguity, the impact of context on what was helpful in each school, and the reality that there is no one best way of doing anything in Aboriginal schools. In this way, the authors avoided the pitfalls of a narrow 'best practice' mentality and its assumptions.

It is self-evident in qualitative research that one finds what one sets out to find, at least to some degree. Conscientious and ethical researchers always remain open to the possibility that their initial hypotheses, hunches, or instincts may prove wrong but, following a widely used research theory metaphor, you can only find what is illuminated by the theoretical and methodological 'lamp' you are using. Thus the overall findings of the SAEE study reflect the effective schools agenda from which the study sprang.

Despite the rich diversity in approaches and circumstances, a number of common characteristics distinguished these schools. The elements of their success are similar to those in the research literature:

- Strong leadership and governance structures, often with long tenure
- High expectations for students

- Focus on academic achievement and long-term success
- Secure and welcoming climates for children and families
- Respect for Aboriginal culture and traditions to make learning relevant
- Quality staff development
- Provision of a wide range of programs/supports for learning. (Bell 2004, 13)

Leadership provides a case in point of how the case study methodology employed by the SAEE team 'opened up' the rather narrow effective schools leadership agenda to the broad leadership complexity in the schools studied.

Most principals had been at the school for some years. While their leadership styles varied widely, their role in promoting and sustaining a common vision, focus and energy was a dominant factor in their school's success. Models of decision-making within the schools ranged from consultation to full power-sharing by staff, students and community, all of whom have the right to veto a proposal. (ibid., 13)

The same complexity was evident in all the general findings of the study. Governance structures varied widely, as did concepts of 'high expectations,' long-term success, and appropriate assessment for students, along with respect for Aboriginal culture and traditions, as well as of their proper place in the overall curriculum. In short, despite its grounding in the positivist, recipe-oriented logic of the effective schools research tradition, this study was not shackled by a quixotic one-size-fits-all quest for stereotypical effective schools findings. However, some commonalities important to our analysis did emerge from this study and our consideration of Amiskwaciy Academy. These merit brief discussion.[9]

Overarching Lessons from SAEE Case Studies and Amiskwaciy Academy

We drew several lessons pertinent to our analysis from the SAEE studies. These lessons are relevant to our own conceptual framework. We make no pretence to having strong empirical grounds or the ability to make sweeping generalizations. Still, these are the insights that strike us as worthy of note, and they offer some of the most plausible solutions for Aboriginal education in Canada.

The single most striking consistency in these case studies was the focus among those who participate in the governance, administration, and operation of these schools on respect, responsibility, and the moral virtues of honesty, integrity, and fairness, and the importance of the trust and transparency that consistent exercise of these virtues produces. These schools are dominated by an ethos of 'servant leadership,' where all those involved in operating and supporting them asked consistently and what they could do for students, not what their involvement in the operation of the schools could do for them. It will become evident in our discussion of ethics and values that this is no small matter.

The approaches and styles of leadership varied greatly from one school to another, and we believe that is as it should be. Research on leadership has never determined one leadership style as the best for all occasions. What is important is the intelligent and purposeful adaptation of a given leadership style and substance to the context and characteristics both of the formal leader and of those around her/him who may be able to share, extend, and enrich it. What is evident in these schools is this intelligent adaptation of leadership style to the context of the community and its school, the character and characteristics of the formal leader, and the capacity of staff members to share in leadership of the school – within an ethos of 'servant leadership.' Central to that ethos are high expectations for both student achievement and responsibility.

Another important consistency is widespread recognition among those who work in these schools first of the importance of Aboriginal culture in the school program, second, the centrality of ancestral languages in that culture and its preservation, and finally, the manifold difficulties associated with establishing successful language programs in an environment of limited resources, great diseconomies of scale, and multiple languages fragmented into numerous dialects and adapted to writing in multiple orthographies. Even those schools, such as Reindeer Lake, that serve a culturally and linguistically homogeneous community, find it impossible to develop 'immersion' or 'language transition' programs, mostly because of a lack of resources both human and financial.

Furthermore, several of the case studies show the legacy of a binary, 'linear trade-off' mentality (for a thorough discussion of such beliefs, see Paquette 1989a, 1989b) in Aboriginal education is far from dead, even in schools doing quite a good job of educating Aboriginal students. Fundamentally, this view of the relationship between mainstream curriculum and programming on the one hand and Aboriginal culture and language on the other sees the two in direct competition. The more time, energy, and resources that are poured into Aboriginal culture and language, the less are available for the really important job, learning the mainstream curriculum. This view accepts as given the superiority of the world view and value assumptions underlying mainstream curriculum. It is unmistakeably reflected in the comments of parents and administrators in some SAEE study schools, who fear that anything more than minimal focus within the school program on Aboriginal culture and language will necessarily detract from mainstream academic performance and success. Such a view dismisses the possibility of synergy between Native language and culture programming, especially instruction in a Native language in the early years of schooling and subsequent success in school and in life. Yet ironically, the American experience with Native-language immersion programs suggests that not only do such synergies exist but also that the majority of at-risk of Aboriginal students stand to gain the most from them (see the discussion of Native bilingual and bicultural education in the United States in chapter 6, under the section 'Disconnected Layers').

It seems clear that most of the SAEE schools, and certainly Amiskwaciy Academy (an alternative school within the Edmonton public school system) step significantly outside the strictures of provincial curricula. In doing so, they move outside of the INAC policy requiring students to be able to transfer at any time to provincial schools without penalty. Moreover, they do so in ways that those involved in their governance and administration recognize as likely to promote student growth academically, morally, and spiritually.

It is no accident that large schools, especially those with access to significant own-source revenues, figure among those singled out for excellence in the SAEE study. Ultimately, size matters in a world where diseconomies of scale are real. Furthermore, the ability to nurture a strong sense of community ownership in a school is significantly enhanced by own-source revenues. Nothing can substitute for a sense of 'it's our money they're using in that school' to foster a feeling of direct ownership for what goes on in a school across a broad base of community members. Of course, there is the brutal reality that schools with access to significant own-source revenues can buy more. The generous facilities and abundance of materials and learning resources at Chalo (Bell 2004, 97–119) would be impossible without such resources. One way or another, the leaders in every SAEE case have engaged with the issue of community ownership in their schools.

The SAEE cases suggest that 'good' Aboriginal schools use learning materials and programs eclectically but also purposefully, and that they adapt them to their particular context and needs. These cases do not suggest that blind adoption of externally produced materials is of much use in the Aboriginal context. In a similar vein, a very mixed picture with regard to assessment in these schools suggests precisely the same principle. Adaptation must be employed with due caution about the potential harm that can be done by the mindless implementation of culturally biased assessment instruments.

The SAEE cases underscore the importance of qualified and committed staff, along with competitive remuneration and benefits as necessary tools in hiring and retaining them. Because of their competitive handicaps in attracting qualified staff, many First Nations schools must provide significant financial incentives over and above pay and benefits scales in public boards to attract and retain really good teachers. These staffing handicaps, particularly the physical, mainstream cultural, and professional isolation mean that First Nations, like inner-city schools, must provide significant 'war pay' to attract high-quality staff who will remain long enough to make continuity and consistency possible. Reindeer Lake reminds us of the countervailing reality that the income tax exemption for status-Indian teachers working in First Nations schools is a powerful incentive for such teachers to continue working in them, which also means weak First Nations teachers often remain as well. It is therefore reassuring that a number of the First Nations schools in the SAEE study had implemented specific measures to avoid both the appearance and reality of nepotism in hiring staff. Finally, as a number of the SAEE cases attest, if hiring and retaining good staff is critical in Aboriginal schools, hiring and retaining excellent – and culturally sensitive – special education support staff is of equal or even greater importance.

The SAEE cases are unanimous in emphasizing the importance of school-community relations. First Nations schools stand or fall as 'community schools.' To the extent that they succeed in engaging parents and other community members (especially elders) in their work and mission, First Nations schools have a chance to make a difference in the education and lives of their students.

Finally, although it is an isolated instance in the SAEE set of cases, the governance structure for the Southeast Educational Centre (SEC) seems particularly promising. Although no current governance structure can eradicate the drastically mixed layers of program and financial accountability in First Nations education, the SEC structure avoids at least some of the most catastrophic pitfalls associated with them. Specifically, chiefs need to be *directly* involved in financial oversight and accountability for aggregate organizations in which their bands participate, with no exceptions. Boards of governors should only set policy, and not interfere with the day-to-day administration and operation of the school they 'govern,' and never utilize their position of influence to further their own personal welfare or that of friends and family. The welfare of students should prevail over political economy considerations. That is what 'servant leadership' is ultimately all about.

Finally, students need a voice in decisions that affect their well-being. Every organization responsible for educating Aboriginal students, especially aggregate organizations which serve students from multiple communities, should have an ombudsperson with credibility and persuasive force in the organization. The ombudsperson should speak not only for the interests of community members and parents but also and especially for the interests of students.

First Nations School Boards – or School Boards by Another Name

The emergence of functional equivalents to school boards in First Nations education seems inevitable to us: without bodies that are similar to school boards in the wider world of public education, the future of First Nations education itself is very uncertain. Whether such bodies are called 'school boards' or something else is unimportant. Whether they follow the precise form and function of provincial school boards and districts does not really matter. But they must provide a platform for functional collaboration in the general style of school boards. They also must conform to *at least* the degree of openness, transparency, and financial and programmatic accountability associated with modern school boards. In our view, the emergence of First Nations school boards is far more inevitable than is the emergence of higher-order aggregations in First Nations education (e.g., regional bodies encompassing such boards, or a national Ministry of First Nations Education). By First Nations school boards or equivalents we do not mean individual First Nations school administrations, but rather functional aggregates serving a large geographical area and substantial First Nations enrolment base.

Such school boards, or school boards by another name, would need to provide the following services, functions, and responsibilities. These can be roughly divided into those that pertain mainly to the board area as a whole, those of mutual importance to member First Nations and the board, and those of interest to the board in terms of its relationship with 'third-level' aggregate organizations and/or INAC.

A. Services, functions, and responsibilities pertaining mainly to the board area as a whole:
- program standards
- general system-wide student assessment
- system-wide special needs student assessment
- uniform, standard, and fair processes and policies regarding Individual Education Plans for students identified as having special needs
- regional administration including, where appropriate,
  - tuition fee agreements
  - inter-institutional relations and agreements
- service contracts
- maintenance of records at the regional level
- public relations at the board level
- ensure free access to information on a basis that conforms to current federal and provincial standards
- provide appropriate and adequate insurance coverage
- set policy on member honoraria

B. Services, functions, and responsibilities of mutual importance to individual First Nations and to board area as a whole:
- general program support
- program and materials development and support for Native language and culture programs
- set and ensure compliance with board policy
- organize and provide special education services
- hire and deploy special education support personnel
- hiring, firing, promotion, deployment, pay and benefits of personnel
- ensure adequate and appropriate supervisory support for both professional and non-professional employees
- oversight and coordination of evaluation for teaching, administrative, and other professional personnel
- oversight and coordination of evaluation for non-teaching personnel

- administer finances and guarantee financial accountability
- general human resources
- negotiate contracts and agreements with employees and employee groups
- ensure appropriate and adequate pension coverage for employees
- manage the career ladder
- build and maintain school and related facilities
- administer post-secondary funding on behalf of participating First Nations
- organize, coordinate, and fund student transportation
- set and enforce standards for record-keeping at local and board level
- set and ensure enforcement of board-wide ethical and professional standards
- provide and adequately fund a credible, effective, and efficient ombudsperson service for the board area as a whole

C. 'Supra-board' services and connections (to third level First Nations aggregate governance organizations where they exist and/or INAC):
- negotiate and update terms and conditions of adherence to and participation in third-level aggregate organizations.

Services, Functions, and Responsibilities Pertaining to the Board as a Whole

School boards are quintessentially 'educational' organizations. In our view, their most fundamental purpose is to set and maintain program standards – and to ensure that every child receives an appropriate education, regardless of the special needs they have. That is why we have set responsibilities to ensure program standards, system-wide student assessment (general), and system-wide special needs student assessment, along with standard and fair processes and policies regarding Individual Education Plans for students identified as having special needs as the first four board-wide obligations for future First Nations school boards (FNSBs).

In addition to these basic responsibilities and service obligations, FNSBs will need to conduct regional administration of education in general, including administration of tuition fee agreements involving students from member communities where it's appropriate. To ensure consistency and fairness from one member community to another in their relationships with external institutions and agencies, they will also enter into and administer inter-institutional relations and agreements on behalf of member First Nations.

As the aggregate body responsible for the provision of all education-related services to students from member communities, FNSBs will negotiate and administer contracts for services *both* at the community and the board level. Assignment of exclusive responsibility for contract negotiation and administration to FNSBs will help ensure consistency and fairness in the provision of services and in the award of contracts.

FNSBs will need to ensure that records at the regional level are maintained accurately and efficiently, are stored securely, and are readily available and accessible to organizational and school employees who have legitimate need of them. They will also need to engage in public relations at the board level on behalf of member communities. This public relations function will involve everything from maintaining suitable websites to dealing with media on relevant issues. To ensure transparency and accountability to its constituents and the general public, FNSBs will have to maintain access to information services that conform to current federal, provincial, and municipal standards. Towards this end, they will need to ensure cost efficient and reasonably swift access to both board-level and community-level records of interest to community constituents and the general public. Only this will maintain a real sense transparency and accountability.

FNSBs should be responsible for all aspects of insurance involving member schools and students from member communities. Again, the objective of centralizing insurance in an FNSB is to ensure both cost efficiency and adequacy of coverage. The experience of school boards under provincial jurisdiction has shown that liability insurance can be both expensive and difficult to obtain given the substantial damage awards that courts have given to student victims of negligence in recent years.

FNSBs should also set member honoraria and the terms and conditions for such payments. Where member band councils have voted for funds to support FNSBs (which would be almost everywhere), area chiefs or their delegates should be directly involved in deciding honoraria and their conditions. Furthermore, these terms and conditions should be a matter of public record, and be readily available for scrutiny. They should at least be available on a board's website and as part of a board's annual financial statement. These official statements of terms and conditions for honoraria should disclose *all* benefits enjoyed by those involved in governance as a result of their involvement.

Services, Functions, and Responsibilities of Mutual Importance to Individual First Nations and the Board as a Whole

FNSBs must not only set programs, they need to support them adequately. Program support will require FNSBs to make difficult choices in allocating precious resources among various kinds of program support. Such support should range from traditional 'program consultant' positions to innovative modes, such as online discussion groups and relevant online courses. Even more challenging than general program support will be FNSB support for Native language and culture program development. While we do not believe that FNSBs should completely supplant cultural centres in this regard, we believe that area FNSBs should decide what is needed to support Native language and culture programs in their schools, and should bear primary responsibility for assuring the availability of adequate and appropriate materials and professional support in this regard. We view cultural centres as most useful to First Nations education as service providers to FNSBs, not as autonomous program and material developers. The 'center of gravity' of educational materials and development in support of Native language and culture programs needs to shift to FNSBs as the agencies that will ultimately bear responsibility for them.

FNSBs will also need to set board policy, both in the sense of strategic intent for board operations and regulations, and with regard to how education will be administered and managed in member communities. Policy is embodied in strategic intent, not in rules, regulations, and other instruments created to give effect to that intent. FNSBs will need to 'keep their eye on the strategic intent ball' if they are not to lose themselves in the futility of producing disconnected rules to put out temporary operational fires. The proper role of governance is always to set *strategic intent*, not to meddle in day-to-day operational matters.

One of the most challenging responsibilities that FNSBs will have is to organize and provide special education services in unique contexts. But the difficulty of providing special education services in those contexts is an important argument for the relevance of FNSBs. Only school board-like agencies are capable of organizing and providing such services in the face of the challenges of small schools and significant cultural differences from mainstream education. These differences matter greatly in assessing exceptionalities, crafting appropriate Individual Education Plans (IEPs) to meet the special needs associated with them, and finally in ensuring that the IEPs are followed in the schools where they matter. In such circumstances, it goes without saying that FNSBs must shoulder the responsibility for hiring and deploying special education support personnel.

From our perspective, FNSBs must be ultimately responsible for the hiring, termination, promotion, deployment, and remuneration of personnel throughout the system. Only with human resource responsibility centralized at the board level can some degree of fairness and equity in this crucial area be ensured. Even so, the centralization of human resource responsibility at the board level should not mean that community voice in the choice of both professional and non-professional personnel serving in their school(s) should be silenced. On the contrary, we believe that discharging their responsibility to provide the best possible service in their schools will require FNSBs to establish policies and procedures that will involve member communities directly in the selection of those who work in the schools. Nevertheless, it will be the board and its agents that bear responsibility for the final decision in the case of disagreement regarding school personnel. As boards with ultimate political responsibility and accountability to *all* member communities (with their unique responsibility in education, FNSB members should be elected by *direct* universal, adult suffrage in their respective communities). FNSBs and their officers would have powerful incentives, short of compromising the organization's vision and guiding principles, to avoid confrontation over staff appointment and deployment.

FNSBs should provide adequate and appropriate supervisory support for both professional and non-professional employees. In the first instance such support involves providing a policy framework, and resources to enable school personnel to work together harmoniously and efficiently to fulfil the board and school mission. Beyond this support function, FNSBs need to oversee and coordinate the evaluation of all school personnel, including teachers, administrators, support staff, and maintenance workers. Obviously, as is the case in provincial school boards, school administrators will be key players in these evaluation exercises. In addition, FNSBs will need to ensure regular evaluation of their own office staff – and act appropriately based on the results.

Financial resources in education are nothing less than a sacred trust. Whatever the source, they are made available in good faith that responsible governance and educational leadership will use them to the best of their ability to support the mission of the school system and its schools to further the welfare, and especially the academic achievement of students. In no sense are such resources ever the property of a local 'educational fiefdom' intended to benefit educational leaders and especially governors at the expense of student well-being and achievement.

FNSBs need to 'administer finances and assure financial accountability,' with diligence, good faith, and adherence to the highest moral and ethical standards. They need to do so because *that* is their most sacred trust. For that reason financial administration in FNSBs must be honest, honourable, and transparent, as well as technically efficient and correct.

At the centre of FNSB responsibility for human and physical resources is a need to negotiate contracts and agreements with employees and employee groups. We are well aware that First Nations educational organizations have been very reluctant to allow the unionization of employees, and generally have done everything in their power to resist it. This is hardly surprising in the fiscal environment in which they exist. Nonetheless, there are some advantages to unionization, even for an employer. In a unionized environment, the employer and employees both know the general 'rules of the game' in their relationship during the term of a contract. That is not the case in an environment in which each employee is hired as an individual bargaining agent. In any case, we are convinced that FNSBs, as larger, more stable First Nations education service providers will inevitably face bids for unionization, and some of these bids will eventually be successful. We believe that is not necessarily a bad thing for FNSBs which will necessarily assume responsibility for negotiating contracts and agreements with their employees.

If education generally is beset with the problem of 'flat career ladders,' First Nations education is doubly so. In a typical First Nations community school, the only opportunity for promotion to a position of added responsibility is usually to the position of principal or vice-principal if the school is large enough to employ one. Creation of FNSBs would permit at least some flexibility in creating meaningful 'career ladders.' They would have to utilize the services of some program consultants and community-level personnel. These positions would provide at least the rudiments of a career ladder. Of course, the temptation to proliferate consultancies or department positions which do not respond to real student need must be resisted. FNSB efforts to establish career ladders should *never* be at the expense of student well-being and academic achievement.

Just as FNSBs will need to set high standards for board level record-keeping, they will need to set and enforce standards for record-keeping at the community level as well. Transparency and accountability require accurate record-keeping. While record-keeping is not an end in itself in any educational organization, it is an inescapable part of conducting the business of education in an accountable manner.

Only FNSBs can set and enforce area-wide ethical and professional standards. Ethical and professional standards, of course, overlap considerably. Furthermore, professional standards for teachers are generally set either by regulation or a set of standards issued by a college of teachers. In the case of teachers, most FNSBs are likely to borrow extensively from provincial standards, although they will likely find good reason to adapt them to their particular circumstances. It will fall to FNSBs to specify ethical standards for board governance and operations, administrators, and non-professional employees. Not only is this a major undertaking, it is the heart of the importance and purpose of FNSBs. An FNSB with no commitment to a code of ethics is unworthy of the trust it holds or the resources it commands. Each FNSB must lay out a clear, binding, comprehensive, and reasonable code of ethics. It then needs to hold its governors and employees accountable to it.

We have used the word 'enforce' or its equivalent several times in this section. In addition to its problematic nature outside of a positivist cause and effect view of the world, 'enforcing' a rule or principle, like 'enforcing' a law, depends ultimately on cooperation and acceptance by those one seeks to constrain with it. Furthermore, we recognize that 'enforcing' rules, or compelling compliance by force, is not a way of doing things that is in harmony with most Aboriginal traditions (nor is it aligned with a good deal of contemporary management theory either). Even so, we note that a number of the existing self-government agreements and their enabling legislation grant to First Nations signatories the power to impose fines and even jail terms as punishment for non-compliance with First Nations laws. The bottom line is that, in the realities of contemporary Canada, policies and the rules created to give effect to them require enforcement mechanisms to compel those who would not otherwise comply. For instance, a code of ethics with no enforcement mechanism is nothing more than a set of pious platitudes. If FNSBs are to become widely respected as ethical organizations, they will need to do three things: establish a code of ethics that both their constituent communities and all of Canadian society respect, nurture the values, principles, and practices that frame that code, and appropriately sanction those who transgress it.

*'Supra-Board' Services and Connections (to Third-Level First Nations
Aggregate Governance Organizations Where They Exist)*

In the best scenario, FNSBs will be an interconnecting part of a comprehensive First Nations educational governance arrangement. As such,
they would relate to their member communities and to regional, third-
level First Nations aggregate organizations as well. They would do so
the same way school boards in large provinces relate to regional Ministry of Education offices and ultimately to their provincial Ministry of
Education itself, although we would hope in an ethos of 'servant leadership.' We are under no illusions that arriving at a functional, well-
articulated governance structure such as this will be easy or quick. On
the contrary, we recognize manifold obstacles to it, including the vested
interest of those who benefit most from the current fragmented and
balkanized structure of First Nations education in Canada.

In any case, any foreseeable school board-like entity will need to
deal both with the federal government and, to a lesser extent, with provincial ministries of education. Obviously, in the absence of a transformative change in the overall governance of First Nations education
regionally and nationally, nothing in the FNSBs will put an end to the
disconnected layers of accountability which have troubled it for so
long. Even so, larger, more stable and more sophisticated second-level
FNSB entities are urgently needed. If solidly committed to appropriate
mission statements and bound to ethical and educational principles,
these entities stand a much better chance of making a significant mark
on the education of First Nations students than individual First Nations
or the current tangle of second-level aggregate organization programs.

We began this discussion by insisting that First Nations school
boards should provide a platform for functional integration. An inescapable corollary to this is that these boards must ground themselves in
principles and practices that will prevent them from becoming hotbeds
of classic school board dysfunction. It is no secret that school boards
can be highly dysfunctional, succumbing to the worst facets of empire-
building and self interest. In the worst cases, school boards lose sight
of servant leadership entirely, replacing it with self-serving leadership.
Ultimately, strong values, principles, and ethics are all that stand in the
way of such dysfunction. States, provinces, and countries that operate
national systems of education can impose various forms of accountability on local school jurisdictions. Nevertheless, all the compliance

mechanisms in the world cannot transform the values and culture of a school board. It is for this reason that various American states have instituted draconian forms of educational receivership for school districts that add little value to the intellectual development of their students. Beyond a certain point, the culture and values of an organization become so entrenched that the only way to change them is to knock down the organization and start over, as certain states have done by adopting a strategy taken from zero-based budgeting theory. In some cases, these states require all board employees to reapply for their positions, and to do so with the understanding that most will not be rehired. Once complacency, despair, and self-interest have eaten through the entire functional framework of the organization, there is little to do but tear down and start over.

If FNSBs are to help close the educational gap between First Nations students and mainstream Canadian students in a way that affirms and reinforces the very best in Aboriginal identity, they cannot afford to be seduced by the baubles of governance perks and empire-building. On the contrary, they must focus tirelessly on nurturing a generation of 'word warriors' – as well as numbers warriors, information warriors, science warriors, distinguished artists, and so forth.

Regional and National First Nations Aggregate Organizations

We believe that the best interests of First Nations students would be served by a fully articulated First Nations educational governance system with local, board, regional, and national levels – but only if the leadership and administrative culture is as we have described above. Everyone involved, however, recognizes that this solution is a 'hard sell.' It is a hard sell at one end of the governance spectrum, because individual First Nations communities are reluctant to give up what they regard as their rightful control over education in their communities. The fact that this control is largely illusory does not lessen their reluctance. Contributing to unwillingness to cede or 'devolve upward' (perhaps 'uploading' would be a more suitable term) authority and responsibility to aggregate organizations is the reality that some people benefit at the local level from the limited control they do have over education (especially over educational resources) in the community.

At the other end of the spectrum, a fully articulated First Nations educational governance system is a hard sell because of the huge vested interest and inertia within INAC as an institution. As the Penner Committee (Canada, Parliament, House of Commons, Special Committee on Indian Self-Government and Penner 1983) stated nearly a generation ago:

> The only way to produce legislation acceptable to Indian people is to create an entirely new ministry. The ministry would act as the governmental interface in all matters respecting the development and reconstruction of band government. The working relationship which the ministry would be designed to produce is one of cooperation and support. (Citing Union of British Columbia Indian Chiefs [2000], 60)
>
> ...
>
> 14. The committee recommends that a Ministry of State for Indian First Nations Relations, linked to the Privy Council Office, be established to manage and coordinate the federal government's relations with the Indian First Nation governments. (ibid., 61)

Despite this prophetic warning, a generation later, all of the federal government's energies aimed at creating a new relationship with First Nations, from education, economic development, and self-government to land claim settlements, have been channelled through DIAND/ INAC. Successive governments of different political stripes have consistently failed to heed the Penner Committee's warning. Notwithstanding a litany of discontent on the part of virtually every federal committee and agency that has scrutinized INAC and its operations over the years, it continues to be the spearhead of federal government efforts to renew its relationship with First Nations. Surely there is a message here about the low priority of such a renewal in the larger federal scheme of things.

The political economy both of current First Nations educational organizations and INAC militate against fundamental reform or anything resembling McCue's (2004) proposed national First Nations Ministry of Education (actually, McCue proposes such a ministry for Ontario alone, but that seems improbable to us on the grounds of diseconomy of scale) (12). In light of this reality, the prospects for a comprehensive structural and operational integration of First Nations education across Canada appear bleak, and the prospects of such an integration occurring outside of an INAC-dominated framework are minimal at present.

Nonetheless, our purpose is to deal with what ought to be without losing track of what is likely to be in the process. In our view, given the reality of diseconomies of scale on the one hand and the need for very specialized language and culture program development skills on the other, First Nations students across Canada would be better served by a Canada-wide functional integration of First Nations education than they are by the present patchwork arrangement. For this to succeed, six conditions must be met:

1. meaningful control of each level in the system would be in the hands of First Nations leaders focused mainly or exclusively on education,[10]
2. funding, including own-source revenues, would be adequate to the tasks at hand at each level,
3. only tasks and functions better accomplished at higher levels of aggregation would be assigned to those levels,
4. decision-making in every member organization would be transparent and open to public scrutiny and, towards that end, all member organizations would implement access to information policies and procedures similar to those in provincial and federal access to information legislation,
5. every member organization and all those who work in them would be required to adopt and enforce a common national code of ethics – to which they could add elements of local pertinence, provided they do not conflict with or subtract from the common national code, and, finally,
6. in the spirit of 3 and 5, member organizations, those who lead them, and those who work in them would commit without reservation to full and honest collaboration on those tasks best accomplished collaboratively at higher levels of aggregation, and set aside purely local and parochial interests to that end. Aggregate organizations, and especially the First Nations Ministry of Education, must never become captives of local interest.

Building on these six principles, on material progress towards institutionalizing First Nations own-source income at all levels of aggregation, and on the removal of INAC as the policy architect in First Nations education, real movement towards an authentic, Canada-wide First Nations education system is possible. Failure to adhere to these principles not only makes progress towards an authentic First Nations education system unlikely but also dooms the overall future of First Nations education to a bleak fate, regardless of a few successful schools and projects.

What might such a First Nations education system look like, and where would it come from? Figure 6.5 offers an outline of what overall governance and funding relationships might look like in the context of a First Nations Ministry of Education. At first glance, figure 6.5 does not look much different from figure 5.3. Nevertheless, it differs in several significant ways.

First is the addition of a First Nations Ministry of Education circle in the lower First Nations educational governance layer. Second, a large 'third-order' level of aggregation to represent a potential Canada-wide First Nations government (represented by a large circle) that has been added in the upper layer, now called the First Nations 'federal government layer.' Finally, INAC has been replaced with a body specifically mandated to negotiate, maintain, and update renewed relationships with First Nations and, depending on the extent of federal involvement with them in the future, with other Aboriginal groups across Canada as well.

Of great importance in this new scheme of First Nations educational governance is that the direct funding and fiscal accountability connection from INAC to first-level First Nations educational aggregate organizations has disappeared. It has been replaced by a funding and fiscal accountability connection to the First Nations Ministry of Education and by occasional connections to a future First Nations Canada-wide confederation. The latter connections would be analogous to occasional, often ad hoc links from provincial ministries of education to other provincial ministries to further common objectives.

Figure 6.6 shows potential fiscal and program accountability relationships in this new governance scheme. It may look similar to figure 5.2, but further examination reveals that it is strikingly different in a number of critical ways. The most fundamental difference is the existence of a First Nations Ministry of Education (FNMOE). Along with the logic contained in the five principles discussed at the beginning of this section and the critique we have put forth regarding funding and program accountability issues, the insertion of an FNMOE into the framework introduced in figure 5.2 has significant impact on voice, authority, fiscal accountability, program accountability, and funding flow.

First, as in figure 6.5, INAC is no longer the intermediary between the federal government and First Nations for education or for any other governance issues. Second, the FNMOE is situated within a hypothetical (represented by the question marks following it) Canada-wide First

Figure 6.5　First Nations Ministry of Education general governance and funding/fiscal accountability relationships

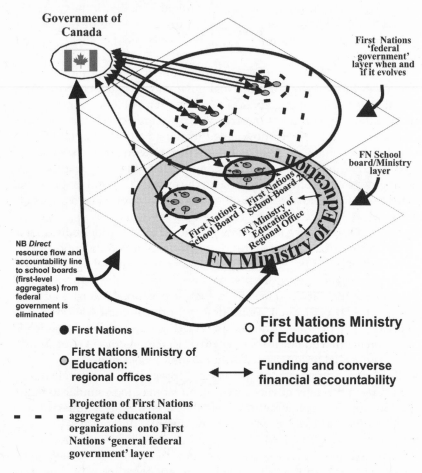

Nations confederation. Third, First Nations citizen-residents' voices now matter in education, not only at the community level, but also at the board, regional, and Canada-wide levels. Furthermore, assuming some school board-level taxation for educational purposes, direct funding flow from First Nations citizen-residents to their school boards exists, establishing a financial accountability dynamic from the school board to residents of member communities.

Figure 6.6 Voice, authority, revenue flow, and accountability under a First Nations Ministry of Education

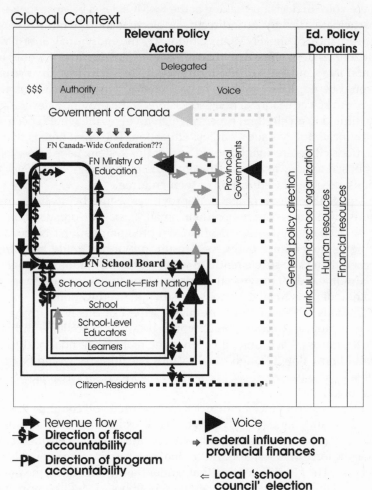

Notes:
1. INAC gone.
2. Canada-wide confederation not necessary but desirable.
3. Voice now in ed. authority, school board AND FN Min. of Ed. – options as to how voice into MOE would occur.
4. Assuming local taxation for school purposes revenue flow and fiscal accountability at local level.

Not only would First Nations citizen-residents have voice in school board-level decisions in this new arrangement, but also they would have voice in decision-making at the FNMOE level because they would participate, directly or indirectly, in electing those who make up the governance of the FNMOE. Obviously, the individual First Nations citizen-resident voice would be relatively small because it would be diluted in a Canada-wide electoral process. Nevertheless, their situation would be no different from the situation of provincial citizens whose voice in key educational policy decisions at the provincial level is greatly diluted in an electoral process which involves the whole spectrum of provincial policy issues, not just education. The point here is that First Nations citizen-residents would, under this system, have some voice as opposed to none at all as is currently the case in high-level policy decisions affecting the education of their children.

Under this new arrangement, provinces would be dealing not with individual First Nations or their small aggregate organizations, but with a relatively large and broadly representative First Nations educational governance body. As a result, provinces would be more disposed than they are currently to work with First Nations through their FNMOE to adapt provincial curricula along with other appropriate accommodations to First Nations jurisdiction in education.

Perhaps the single most promising aspect of this new arrangement is that program accountability would be almost parallel with funding flow and fiscal accountability, since the majority of non-local funding would now flow through the FNMOE. The ministry would be responsible in turn for *both fiscal accountability and program accountability* at the national level.

Of course, provincial ministries of education will continue to set curriculum and standards for provincial school boards and schools, and these curriculum and standards will continue to have considerable persuasive force on the shape and content of programming in First Nations schools. The key difference is that, under this arrangement, the program accountability of true First Nations school boards will be primarily to the FNMOE through its regional offices, and those offices will bear the main responsibility of liaising with provincial ministries of education with regard to program matters of interest to First Nations education. To us, this seems to be a much healthier dynamic than the current situation, in which all the parameters of educational programming are set by the provinces with little consideration of the various contexts in which

First Nations education occurs, and where INAC mandates First Nations educational entities to follow provincial curricula.

The obvious danger in the arrangement we propose is the potential for goal displacement. The possibility of this occurring increases at each level of aggregation, and is particularly menacing at the FNMOE level, given its structural and operational distance from grass-roots First Nations educational activity. The worst case scenario is even greater dysfunction than the status quo. It is for that reason that we have been so insistent on the importance of a strong commitment to ethics in general and to an ethos of servant leadership in particular at all levels in the organizational structure *and its governance*. In keeping with our emphasis on the importance of cultivating own-source investment in First Nations education by First Nations people, we believe that future First Nations governments should contribute from their own-source revenues to the FNMOE and the programs it runs, and its transfer grants to First Nations school boards. Such contributions from First Nations governments should reduce the probability of dysfunctional isolation in the FNMOE and its regional offices from the interests and priorities of local First Nations groups.

One of the major potential pitfalls in this type of integrated organizational structure is that conflicting political economy agendas could paralyse the organization as a whole. That could result in creative energies and goodwill being drained by endless internecine warfare over political economy crumbs. To avoid this catastrophic result, ethics and commitment will be required in great quantity, but they alone will not be enough. Eventual federal legislation creating an FNMOE, in consultation with the provinces and territories, should be carefully designed to incorporate the same kind of balance between central and local jurisdiction that has been built into provincial education legislation. In the same vein, such legislation should also clearly articulate student and parent rights as well as the powers and obligations at each level of organizational aggregation. In particular, the FNMOE should set overall program requirements, regional FNMOE offices should collaborate with First Nations school boards in adapting and tailoring these overarching program requirements to the realities of First Nations education in each region, and in each First Nations school board within that region. First Nations school boards should be responsible for the final adaptation and implementation of these program requirements to the area they serve.

Figure 6.6 illustrates what we believe should be the pattern of re-source flow in such an organizational structure. First, we believe that the First Nations communities which make up the school boards should raise up to 5 per cent of the total operating budget of their school board by local taxation. Second, should some sort of Canada-wide First Na-tions governance evolve, a significant portion – no less than 20 per cent – of its total revenues should be committed to education through the FNMOE (one branch of this ministry would coordinate First Nations post-secondary programs and services). The remainder of FNMOE funding, including its transfer payments to First Nations school boards, would come from a block transfer from the federal government. Only in this way can the alignment of program and fiscal accountability shown in figure 6.6 be realized. This is the only way *true* 'Indian control of Indian education' will ever take place.

Moving in this direction requires a substantial capacity-building en-terprise at all levels. Capacity is an integral component of getting done the things that matter in an organization, the core of its ability to ful-fil its official purposes. It resides first and foremost in the knowledge, competencies, abilities, and values of those who work at all levels with-in an organization but also involves appropriate and functional struc-tures and relationships. Capacity can atrophy as well. As Dror (1983, 42) pointed out, historically high levels of performance in an organiza-tion relative to its formal purposes ensures little for its future, unless management and staff succession and induction is orderly, regular, and appropriate – including the ability to adapt to changing contexts.

The inescapable corollary is accepting the legitimate costs associated with such capacity-building. Much of that investment will have to be made by Canadian taxpayers through the federal government; howev-er, a considerable portion of it must be borne by First Nations and their aggregate governance entities if First Nations citizen-residents are ever to have real ownership in this new order. The ultimate goal here is not permanent fiduciary dependence but significant movement towards meaningful and authentic self-determination in education.

Nevertheless, a couple of questions need attention here. Are Cana-dians and their government ready for such a radical new relationship with First Nations in regard to education? Probably not, but before they conclude that they are not and move on to other matters, they should ask themselves whether they want to continue investing over a billion dollars annually into an enterprise that, despite the occasional suc-cessful experiment, has done little but attract outrage for more than a generation from the parliamentary committees that have examined it, along with the Royal Commission on Aboriginal People and the Auditor General of Canada. Unless a new relationship is formed to address First Nations education, then that is probably just what Canadian taxpayers are fated to do.

Are First Nations also ready to put aside local differences, local priorities, and especially the quest to capture as large a slice as possible of the federal educational support? Probably not, but before they reject the idea out of hand, they would do well to consider the possibility that the Canadian taxpayer may not be inclined to continue to support First Nations education in its current form and that radical change in the organizational framework within which that education occurs may be more likely than not. It is not inconceivable that if significant progress in reducing the educational gap between First Nations students and mainstream Canadian students does not occur in the near future, the federal government could choose to divest itself of any direct involvement in the process, regardless of fiduciary responsibility. Precedents for such an act exist. That was precisely what the whole White Paper exercise was about. And that is what one of the current prime minister's most influential ex-advisers on First Nations matters has been recommending for some time (Flanagan 2000).

To put it bluntly, the alternatives to reinventing the structure and governance of First Nations education in the way we propose may not prove very attractive even over the medium term to First Nations citizens and leaders. They may leave little room for any meaningful First Nations language or culture component in education – which would almost certainly be the case if in the end the federal government 'bailed' on First Nations education and turned over the responsibility to provincial ministries of education, not an implausible hypothesis if the interminable series of highly critical parliamentary committee hearings and Auditor General reports continues. It is hard to see what would be good for First Nations children in that case, at least from any but the most hard-core assimilationist perspective. Such a prospect is not far in the current political context, given the general state of exasperation in Ottawa with INAC in particular and 'Indian affairs' in general.

We believe, therefore, that the last, best hope for First Nations education is complete reinvention along the general lines that have been proposed here. Despite enormous exasperation with the status quo on the part of all stakeholders, especially Canadian taxpayers and their parliamentarians in Ottawa who have not ceased to decry the lack of accountability since the Penner Committee report, little has improved. We strongly suspect that this frustration is shared by young educated First Nations people who have managed to succeed despite the current order of things in First Nations education. Given this broader context and the abject failure of incremental reforms in First Nations education, we believe that it is worth taking, to borrow a famous expression from Quebec political history, the *beau risque* to craft a better, brighter future for First Nations students across Canada.

It is worth the risk to First Nations leaders because only such a fundamental reinvention of First Nations educational governance is likely to make much difference for their children and grandchildren. Furthermore, given the current state of affairs, we believe that First Nations leaders have little to lose and much to gain by embarking on this project. For Canadian parliamentarians and for the citizens and taxpayers of Canada, the approach we have described offers a chance to establish order, fiscal accountability, program accountability, appropriate education, and a plausible form of 'Indian control of Indian education' where all these have lacked in the past.

Are we optimistic that some version of this reinvention of First Nations education will occur soon enough to redeem it from federal abandonment? At best, we are cautiously hopeful. First, anecdotal evidence suggests that a small nucleus of young, educated First Nations people is emerging and that within that nucleus, the old way of conducting 'Indian politics' has lost credibility. Indeed, the emergence of some of the most progressive self-government agreements is tangible evidence of a new generation of First Nations thinkers and leaders interested more in the pragmatic issues of self-determination than on winning a battle of principle with the federal government. Second, even within neoliberal values, the return on investment in such a scheme, provided that it sees the light of day using the principles and values we have outlined, would almost certainly be very favourable if it contributed to stemming the Aboriginal tide that is inundating the Canadian penal system, particularly in some provinces (Aboriginal people are over-represented in the Canadian prison population by a factor of at least five to one nationally. The proportion is much higher in Saskatchewan and the Yukon, and appears to be growing rapidly) (Statistics Canada 1998; on relative over-representation among youth in custody, see Statistics Canada 2003b).

Adding to doubt about how such reform might take place are serious questions about where one might find a political nucleus around which efforts could coalesce. The most plausible choices are the CCOE (the Chiefs' Committee on Education, National Indian Education Council), the NIEC (National Indian Education Council), and ultimately the Assembly of First Nations (AFN) in collaboration with the Assembly of First Nations of Quebec (AFNQ). Indeed, one possible reading of the AFN's 2005 statement on First Nations education is a plea for systemic reform (Assembly of First Nations 2005). Unfortunately, if that was its intent, it is a sadly myopic, muddled, and muted plea that is still mired in naive and discredited ICIE rhetoric about building Indian control upwards, community by community.

> First Nations education must be developed from the community up. In order to be meaningful and relevant, education solutions must be developed by communities. The AFN's role involves supporting First Nation communities and regions through the coordination of national policy development initiatives, and by advocating on behalf of First Nations in the national context. (4)

From this view, the AFN has little importance as a group around which a Canada-wide First Nations system of education might be created. Rather, AFN's only real importance is as a political 'bagman' for a balkanized amalgam of community schools and second-level educational service aggregates, whose only role is to provide just-in-time service to communities when and only as long as they desire such service. This is a recipe for disaster with inevitable results that are all too familiar. It is nothing more than the failed and now disgustingly rancid recipe from the past, warmed over one more time. If the objective is ultimately to provide First Nations students with high-quality education truly comparable in standards with provincial education but within appropriate linguistic and cultural frameworks, First Nations education cannot continue to be organized like so many autonomous Greek city states who only work together when they feel like it for as long as they are disposed to do so.

If what really counts in First Nations education is not providing First Nations students with a high-quality, culturally and linguistically appropriate education but instead maximizing control and resource flow at the community level, then the systemic reform we propose will generate little interest among First Nations educational or political leaders. We are convinced, however, that the ICIE 'Indian control equals community control' recipe has long since exhausted whatever credibility it might have had, particularly with Canadians and their elected officials, but also with thoughtful, well-educated young First Nations individuals. One way or another, the days of the current systemic disarray in First Nations education are numbered. Either First Nations leaders will seize the last chance they are likely to have to bring order to their educational house, or that house will disappear sometime soon into the provincial education colossi.

None of this should be interpreted as disparaging local initiative and ownership in schooling generally or in First Nations education. On the contrary, we have emphasized repeatedly the importance of such ownership and of encouraging it in every way possible. Nevertheless, abandoning community units to their own devices, communities that are minuscule by contemporary economy-of-scale standards in education (for a summary of current evidence on the subject, see Baker 2005) can hardly count as encouragement. Among many other things, effective and efficient aggregate organizations need to learn from and be an instrument of sharing good practice[11] at the local and community levels. To insist on this important aspect of 'organizational learning,' in no way diminishes our critique of the structural and operational impasse in which First Nations education is currently mired. It is a radically balkanized and thoroughly out-of-control mess. By all accounts, except for a handful of lighthouse schools driven by altruism, strong local commitment to quality education, and high ethical standards, the status quo is nothing like 'Indian control of Indian education'; rather, it is institutionalized chaos and conflict, classic organizational 'gridlock.'

We realize that First Nations leaders must concern themselves with many matters besides education. Nonetheless, education is central to any meaningful vision of First Nations self-determination. Furthermore, no escape is possible from the reality of diseconomies of scale in education. The bottom line is that small, community-size non-systems of education have no hope of ever commanding the resources necessary to develop and implement high-quality education programs or the necessary bilingual and bicultural programs. Amalgamation within the broad functional integration that we are proposing is really the only way out of the current state of generalized gridlock. For that reason, we believe that our current results-oriented government would be inclined to invest in this chance to improve substantially the quality of First Nations education, and at the same time, reap some of the benefits of meaningful Indian control of Indian education.

Cultural Centres

Since 1971, the federal government has funded a 'Cultural/Educational Centres Program' (CECP) through DIAND/INAC, under authority of the Treasury Board. Currently, over 100 centres share approximately $8.2 million in total funding. This program funds First Nations tribal/district councils, Inuit communities, and First Nations/Inuit non-profit corporations 'to preserve, develop and promote First Nations and Inuit culture and heritage, through the delivery of programs and services developed at the community levels. This is accomplished through the funding of established centres, which develop and operate cultural/educational programs for First Nations/Inuit people to participate in, and for the general public to experience' (Indian and Northern Affairs Canada/Affaires indiennes et du Nord Canada 2004).

The objective of the program is to make it possible for First Nations and Inuit people to operate cultural/educational centres in order to pursue 'any or all of the following objectives, consistent with the program philosophy' (ibid.):

- to revive and develop traditional and contemporary cultural skills of First Nations and Inuit people;
- to conduct and/or facilitate research in First Nations/Inuit heritage and culture;
- to increase First Nations/Inuit peoples' knowledge and use of their traditional languages;
- to develop First Nations/Inuit linguistic learning resources;
- to develop and test culturally-oriented educational curricula, methods and materials for use by established and other programs;
- to promote cross-cultural awareness in mainstream educational programs and institutions;
- to develop and increase access to new and more accurate information about First Nations/Inuit heritage; and
- to improve the opportunities for the public to become knowledgeable about, and sensitive to, the historical and current role of First Nations/Inuit people in Canada. (ibid.)

The problem with the cultural centres, in our view, is that they were initially established and continue to exist 'off to the side' of First Nations education. Although they have been an important source of culture- and language-specific learning materials for many years, with a few exceptions (primarily associated with large community and school size), they have no enduring relationship with First Nations schools or educational aggregate organizations. The situation is hardly surprising, given the nature of most First Nations aggregate educational organizations as tenuous amalgams of just-in-time service providers. Although the analogy is far from perfect, it is similar to the situation that would exist in provincial education if educational publishers in Canada had to cater to individual schools that set their own curriculum and were free to buy whatever they wanted to support it. The ensuing chaos would rapidly drive major publishing companies away from the Canadian educational market.

What is needed here are dependable connections between First Nations education providers and developers of First Nations-specific cultural and language learning materials. Strong, predictable connections have always existed between educational publishing houses and provincial ministries of education – although the nature of those connections has evolved over time. Given the complexities and challenges imposed by rapid language decline on the one hand and by radically different language families often segmented into dialects with widely varying orthographies on the other, sporadic, project-driven ad hoc materials are simply a waste of time and resources. Publishers of Aboriginal culture and language materials need to know what Aboriginal boards and schools need and want. Before the publishers can know, Aboriginal school authorities must have some idea themselves, and that can only happen in the context of the integrative, functional aggregation we are proposing. In short, whether cultural centres continue to be the main source of First Nations culture and language learning materials – and we have some doubts as to whether they should, given the multitude of other activities ranging from cultural tourism to developing materials for mainstream schools in which various cultural centres have become involved – strong and stable connections from Aboriginal culture and language publishers to Aboriginal education 'end users' are urgently needed. Here, as elsewhere, order must replace chaos if First Nations schools are to become veritable incubators of 'word warriors' in Turner's sense, to say nothing of culture warriors, number warriors, policy warriors, and so forth.

Of course, none of this will turn the production of Aboriginal culture and language materials into a profitable enterprise, so the generous federal subsidy of such materials will continue to be central to their development and production. That said, better to subsidize what qualified curriculum leaders in bona fide Aboriginal education systems need than to subsidize what independent cultural organizations absorbed in a multitude of other culture-related activities decide they want to produce. The production of educational materials, at the least those materials that support core curriculum, should be demand-driven, not supply-driven. To use materials to support core curriculum simply because someone decided to produce them and managed to obtain a subsidy to do so is not very sound policy or pedagogy.

Enduring Problems and Worsening Paradoxes in Native-as-a-First-Language Education

In Canada, Native-as-a-First-Language education, be it in an active language context or a language-restoration context, presents major challenges. A multitude of languages, dialects, and writing systems compete for space and scarce resources on the educational agenda – although these problems pale before the plight of California with its fifty-odd distinct Aboriginal languages, virtually all in the final stages of disappearance (Reyhner, Cantoni, St Clair, and Yazzie 1999). Diseconomies of scale make it particularly difficult to develop programs and resources, including human resources, to support strong Indigenous language programs in Aboriginal schools.

Furthermore, as Aboriginal languages disintegrate, the psychological, cultural, and intellectual 'space' separating them from schools and schooling rapidly increases. It is no accident that the very first recommendation of the Task Force on Aboriginal Language and Culture was to strengthen and reinforce the links of Aboriginal languages to 'the land' (Task Force on Aboriginal Languages and Cultures 2005, ix). The ties that bind Aboriginal languages to the land from which they came are deep and strong. It is one thing to be functionally fluent in an Aboriginal language within the context of day-to-day life in an Aboriginal community; it is quite another to be completely comfortable with the discussion of traditional pursuits by elders using the same.

Several requirements are necessary for a language to remain viable over the long term as a living language. First, a language can only survive as a living language if it lives both in the community and in the school. Schools are never sufficient by themselves as 'hothouses' or 'artificial life support systems' to keep languages alive, any more than communities, peoples, or nations can keep them alive if they are not used as school languages, and arguably as languages of instruction in the early years of schooling, at least. These requirements are troubling enough. But there is yet another requirement for survival beyond the status of a 'boutique' or 'closet' language over the long term in the socio-economic, political, and technological realities of our time.

The prospects for long-term survival of closet languages seem particularly bleak at present. The shape and texture of national societies deeply intertwined and hardwired together in a globalized economy is rapidly reducing cultural and linguistic diversity across the world. Science and especially technology are reshaping human ways of thinking, acting, and being, with a relentless and irresistible omnipresence that kneads and moulds human consciousness – and with it, language. Languages that fail to adapt rapidly to technological change, appear doomed to irrelevance and rapid extinction.

This need to adapt rapidly and efficiently to new technologies is particularly ominous in the case of Aboriginal languages, whose roots and context are so far removed in almost every way from the most powerful technologies of our time. The distance between contemporary mainstream Canadian society and Aboriginal cultures in world view, values, assumptions – particularly assumptions about what really counts in life, in psychology, in ways of acting and ways of being, in everything that Bertrand and Valois (1980) capture in their adaptation of the idea of 'socio-cultural paradigm' (60) is stunning. They could only be greater if they were diametrically opposed to the value of the moral virtues of honesty, honour, and integrity, which is not the case. It is one thing to have words for 'telephone,' 'fax,' and 'computer' – but it is quite another to have developed technological terminology, even quasi-dialects, to discuss everything from current changes in microchip design and fabrication to the latest developments in genetic engineering. Just as failure to use a language within the community – and especially within the home and school – foreshadows the rapid decline and disappearance of a language, so too does the failure to adapt to the 'lived reality' of society. Aboriginal communities, societies, and peoples cannot insulate themselves from contemporary Canadian society so that they will not have to discuss, read, and write about science, technology, and law in a multitude of ways on numerous levels. Languages that fail to adapt to these realities cannot continue to exist as living languages in any meaningful sense. An important corollary that is worth noting even in our time is that, whatever the historical status of a language was as a strictly oral entity, and however much elders may have resisted the imposition of a writing system on a particular language, strictly oral

languages cannot possibly survive given the press of science, technology, and law on daily life.

All of these observations can be distilled into three inescapable policy
propositions with regard to Aboriginal languages in education:

1. 'half measures,' in the sense of limited, ad hoc, poorly planned and
   poorly resourced second-language programs have no hope of stop-
   ping the rapid disappearance of Aboriginal languages in Canada –
   including those currently considered least threatened;
2. preserving or restoring Aboriginal languages as living languages,
   where that is a goal, is incompatible with the INAC policy of requiring that students be able to transfer to regular official language
   provincial schools without penalty at any time during their schooling career because it prohibits the use of Aboriginal languages as a
   medium of instruction and thus all forms of language transition (instruction in an Aboriginal language during the first years of schooling with transition to instruction in an official language later) and
   immersion programs; and
3. only the kind of large-scale functional integration in First Nations
   education that we are proposing can mobilize and focus the resources needed to support educational programs capable of arresting the rapid decline and disappearance of First Nations languages
   as living languages.

It has become a cliché that Aboriginal languages have no homeland
other than the land in which they evolved. Unlike European languages in Canada, Canadian Aboriginal languages are extinguished on a
global basis when they disappear in this country. They have no other
motherland. Indeed, the finality embedded in this linguistic observation is perhaps easier to accept with resignation for having become so
commonplace.

At the end of the 1980s, one of us published a couple of articles dealing with questions around the synergy between minority and Native
culture and language programs and mainstream learning (Paquette
1989a, 1989b). Paquette needed to signal why he believed the survival
of (evolving) Aboriginal cultures was important to mainstream society, an acknowledgment likely much needed after his insistence on the
need for all surviving languages to be able to deal with mainstream
technology, science and law. The first of these articles (1989b) drew a
sharp reply from C.A. Bowers. One aspect of the critique in that reply

shocked Paquette. Despite long involvement with First Nations people and education and deep respect for the broadly shared Aboriginal principle of respect for Mother Earth, Paquette drew criticism from Bowers for saying nothing in his first article about the importance of maintaining a reasonable balance between nature and the human presence on our beleaguered planet. We do not wish to repeat that mistake here.

One of the main reasons we attach importance to the survival of key elements of Aboriginal cultures and languages is because they offer a much-needed counterbalance to blind faith in the power of science and technology alone to provide fulfilling lives in a better world. Should that badly needed corrective voice be lost, not only do our children and children's children risk a much poorer and less fulfilling existence, they risk having no existence at all. That seems to be a very powerful reason for wanting to sustain and promote Aboriginal values which are embedded in the languages that frame their cultures.

Converting Aboriginal languages to written languages changes them and will continue to change them. Injecting a lexicon of Euro-Canadian science, technology, and law into them on even a relatively limited basis will change them at least as profoundly. The only available alternative, however, is their extinction as living languages. Given the pervasiveness of science, technology, law, and economics in all of our lives, languages that cannot accommodate at least a lay discussion of these seminal fields of human activity are doomed to irrelevance. As a result, they would be perceived as not worth the effort required to preserve them as living languages, even by native speakers.

The central paradox with regard to Aboriginal languages is that, on the one hand, they embody and provide texture and meaning to values badly needed in the contemporary world. On the other hand, they *must* adapt quite substantially to the realities of contemporary Western science, technology, law, and economics if they are to have any relevance for children who ultimately *must* grow up and function in Canadian society at large – even if they live in a remote Aboriginal community. Isolation, after all, isn't quite what it used to be in this age of satellite telephone, television, and broadband Internet access.

A chronic but rapidly worsening practical problem has plagued school-based Aboriginal language programs from the beginning. From their inception, schools wishing to embark on Aboriginal language programming have found it difficult to attract instructors who combined necessary fluency in the target language with ability to teach it effectively within a school context. Those who have the greatest fluency are also least comfortable with schools and schooling. With rapid attrition of fluency in all Aboriginal languages, the gap between fluency and the ability to work in a school environment is widening in most areas. While linguists and Aboriginal language teacher development programs can be of some help here, they cannot ultimately bridge the school fluency gap alone.

There is no silver bullet solution to this growing gulf between a diminishing number of fluent speakers, for the most part very elder speakers, and the school context. The window of opportunity for bridging that gulf is closing. We are under no illusions that even the most dynamic and efficient First Nations education system can quickly or easily reverse this trend. Yet we do believe that the best chance that First Nations have of making some headway in bridging the gulf between language competence and school savvy is ultimately just the kind of broad-based functional integration we are recommending. In the end, only large school systems can hope to command resources that can seriously impact this estrangement between language fluency on the one hand and a sense of belonging and being able to work effectively in a school context on the other. It is no accident that the most consistent complaints of Native-language teachers in the SAEE study reflect the central complaints of Native language teachers from the very beginning of such programs: a lack of resource materials and a lack of opportunities to share professional development.

Elders Are Precious Links to the Past, Not Miracle Workers

The Commission recommends that 'Elders be reinstated to an active role in the education of Aboriginal children and youth in educational systems under Aboriginal control and in provincial and territorial schools' (Royal Commission on Aboriginal Peoples 1996b, 528). In all societies that value their history, elders are precious living links from the past to the present and, through the young people they influence, to the future as well. The particular importance of elders in Aboriginal cultures and of the transmission of the values and world views at the heart of those cultures are widely recognized. We can add little of value in that regard, except to insist on a few points that are relevant to our overall framework for understanding and critique of Aboriginal education policy.

First, no people, including Aboriginal peoples, can live in the past, nor should they attempt to do so. That is part of the reason we believe

that the insights offered by relational pluralism to Aboriginal governance in general and Aboriginal education in particular are so important. What counts in terms of building useful, effective, and suitably
permeable boundaries around Aboriginal cultures is not freezing them
in time but rather empowering them to evolve according to the will
of Aboriginal peoples. Children cannot and should not relive the lives
of their elders; rather they should carry forward in time the best values
and principles their elders embody. Everyone concerned, however, especially elders themselves, must recognize that children, as they move
into the autonomy of responsible adulthood, will interpret and apply
those values and principles in light of their own understanding, wisdom, and conscience.

Second, elders are not miracle workers. They cannot accomplish
pedagogical miracles. While bringing elders into a language classroom
can stimulate learning in a number of ways, it is no substitute for an
intensive, coherent, and appropriately resourced Aboriginal language
program, if the goal is to preserve or restore functional fluency in an
Aboriginal language. Among the ways in which elders can be very useful in supporting language programs are the following:

1. Elders who share orally with delight and enthusiasm the richness
   of their experience are living antidotes to a destructive stereotype of
   Aboriginal persons which designates them as 'non-verbal' people
   who speak mainly with body language rather than verbal language;
   such elders become living witnesses to the orality at the heart of
   Aboriginal cultures, and thus debunk the popular myth that Aboriginal peoples take no delight in language and communication
   – and therefore are maladapted to schooling which is all about language and communication.
2. Elders can model good use of ancestral languages and hence moti-
   vate students to invest the time and intellectual effort to learn them.
3. Elders can challenge students in their ancestral language to think
   through difficult issues in that language – this, after all, was an important agenda for traditional legends and myths in the first place
   – and thus give living witness to the reality that intellectual activity
   and moral reasoning are very much part of Aboriginal cultures.
4. Elders can engage with non-Aboriginal teachers in discussion
   and symposia on matters of mutual interest, thus highlighting for
   students that there *are* such matters and that points of intellectual
   crossover and convergence *do* exist.

Finally, perhaps the most delicate subject we feel compelled to discuss in this work is that, in any culture including Aboriginal cultures, status as an elder is never licence for exemption from moral and ethical standards, particularly in what the late Thom Greenfield referred to so often as the 'moral enterprise' of education. Education, after all, is ultimately about shaping the values and principles of the next generation. Under no circumstances should any exception be made in the case of an elder to the standards of moral and ethical propriety required of every teacher in contemporary schools. In section 3.5.29 of volume 3 of its report, the Royal Commission on Aboriginal Peoples recommended that '[e]lders be treated as professionals and compensated for their educational contribution at a rate and in a manner that shows respect for their expertise, unique knowledge and skill' (Royal Commission on Aboriginal Peoples 1996b, 528). We agree. The necessary corollary is that they be held to professional standards of conduct and to the same expectation of moral rectitude as teachers both inside and outside of the school context.

Urban Aboriginal Education Revisited

The Federation [of Canadian Municipalities (FCM)] believes that any amendments to jurisdictions and systems of accountability must be addressed by all orders of government. We understand that different circumstances will require different forms of Aboriginal self-government. Whatever the shape, however, constructive intergovernmental relations and institutional harmony are necessary conditions for the successful realization of Aboriginal self-government.

J. Les, 'Approaches to Aboriginal Self-Government in
Urban Areas' (1994), 175

C.A. Knockwood (1994) recounts a survey for an urban self-government study entitled *The First Peoples Urban Circle: Choices for Self-Determination*, which was conducted by what was then the Native Council of Canada (NCC). That study solicited opinion from urban-dwelling Aboriginal people as well as from current service providers to urban Aboriginal people and Aboriginal as well as non-Aboriginal political stakeholders in six cities: Vancouver, Saskatoon, Winnipeg, Thunder Bay, Montreal, and Halifax. The study organizers wanted feedback on four generic models of urban Aboriginal self-government. The models proposed in the survey were:

1. an urban reserve with complete separation from urban or provincial
   government, and a direct tie to the federal government;
2. several or many autonomous Aboriginal service agencies with no
   common governing body (the status quo model);
3. a city-wide Native Aboriginal body which would set rules for Aboriginal services like education, health, housing, and policing; and
4. a community or neighbourhood in which Aboriginal people formed
   the majority and run [sic] their own schools, housing programs,
   health, and policing. (Knockwood 1994, 163)

Of these possibilities, number 3 is most problematic to us. How a 'city-
wide Native Aboriginal body' could ever 'set rules for Aboriginal services like education, health, housing, and policing' while those services
continue to be provided by municipalities and provincial school boards
is not clear. While such a body could well offer advice to municipal
and school board authorities on the services they provide to Aboriginal
people (as various stakeholder groups, including Aboriginal groups,
already do on a regular basis), it is obvious to us that it is unacceptable
to municipalities and school boards to have any outside agency dictate
rules to them, much less rules that would apply only to persons who
(presumably) self-identify as Aboriginal. Taken at face value, Knockwood's option 3 is implausible.

In a somewhat different taxonomy of possibilities, Young (1994) discusses (1) urban reserves, (2) First Nations 'hosting' of non-Aboriginal
communities on their ancestral land, (3) urban institutional development similar to Knockwood's idea of autonomous Aboriginal service
agencies, (4) urban governments with authority 'delegated' by existing
First Nations governments, and (5) 'provincially based approaches' in
which province-wide aggregate bodies exercise some forms of governance within urban contexts (156–62).

Although urban reserves already exist in a number of places in
Canada, they proved singularly unpopular among respondents to the
Knockwood/NCC survey, with only 11 per cent of participants favouring such a model. This is hardly surprising, especially with the question cast in terms of the qualifier 'with complete separation from urban
or provincial government, and a direct tie to the federal government.'
As Les notes, speaking on behalf of the Federation of Canadian Municipalities in the quotation at the beginning of this section, 'amendments to jurisdictions and systems of accountability must be addressed
by all orders of government.' Thus, any proposition regarding urban

Aboriginal governments that would bypass municipalities and school boards, to say nothing of provinces, is a political and likely a constitutional 'non-starter.'

A considerable number and variety of 'urban reserves,' already exist in Canada. These range from a full-fledged First Nations municipal structure in the case of the Sechelt Indian Band Council and the Sechelt Indian Government District Council in British Columbia (although the Sechelt arrangement remains unique in Canada) (Young 1994, 157), to large reserves in close physical proximity to major Canadian municipalities such as Kahnawake. In no case has a reserve been created within the boundaries of an existing municipality to accommodate a particular First Nations enclave within it, and it is difficult to imagine that happening in the foreseeable future. Such an urban reserve, like any designated Aboriginal neighbourhood, raises the spectre of creating Aboriginal ghettos or even institutionalized apartheid.

Taken together, the Knockwood and Young options appear to exhaust generic possibilities for urban Aboriginal self-determination, although the arrival of a functionally integrative organizational structure for First Nations education would add the possibility of some sort of affiliation of urban Aboriginal groups with that organization in regard to education. Indeed, multiple affiliations might be possible in the event that Métis and non-status Indians were to succeed in creating their own functionally integrative structures beyond the local and regional levels.

The key points to affiliation with higher-level Aboriginal aggregate organizations are first political, and second financial. It would be politically unacceptable for higher-level Aboriginal aggregate organizations to exercise any kind of direct decision-making power or authority in the operations of provincial school boards. This fundamental political reality precludes any legislative hardwiring of provincial school boards into something like a Canada-wide First Nations Ministry of Education. That said, we see no reason why legislative space could not be negotiated with relative ease between the federal government and provincial governments to allow school boards that operate schools serving mainly Aboriginal students to affiliate with higher-level Aboriginal aggregate governance bodies in order to improve the quality and appropriateness of educational services to Aboriginal students in such schools. Indeed, a much looser kind of affiliation might serve to improve the education *about* Aboriginal people that all students receive in provincial school boards.

Such affiliations would require resources to be meaningful and useful. School boards would require at least some budget capacity to enter into and sustain such relationships. More significantly, at least from a financial point of view, a participating First Nations Ministry of Education or other higher-level Aboriginal aggregate organization would need to have program, material, and human resources to render such affiliation useful and attractive to potential school board participants. These resources would cost a considerable amount of money. Furthermore, as in the case of all newly minted service programs, actual demand for the program cannot be assessed accurately until it is fully up and running.

Where would such 'new money' come from? Some would come from school boards and provinces, but likely only the amount necessary to negotiate and sustain school board participation in and commitment to such arrangements. Most of the money to support the resources required so that a First Nations Ministry of Education could have something of real value to offer affiliated school boards would need to come from federal bloc funding of the FNMOE itself. In addition, some money might become available from First Nations governments contributing directly to the FNMOE, its programs, and its transfer grant system.

In the event that one of the other models of urban Aboriginal governance should emerge, such as 'urban governments with authority "delegated" by existing First Nations governments,' the relationship of schooling within such an arrangement would be different from the relationship we propose. In the case of the 'delegation' scenario, schools within an urban enclave would ultimately be linked through levels of First Nations educational aggregation directly to the FNMOE. The connection would no longer be one of voluntary affiliation, but instead a direct functional integration (although not one of subordination in a traditional bureaucratic hierarchy). Nevertheless, we do not believe that alternative models of urban governance (beyond voluntary affiliation by provincial school boards) are plausible in the foreseeable future, and therefore they are not worth the time to consider at length here.

In any case, school boards have developed various forms of 'alternative schooling' to serve students, including Aboriginal students, who do not do well in conventional school settings. Among the more famous examples are 'cultural survival schools' developed expressly for Aboriginal students such as Wandering Spirit Survival School in Toronto, the Calgary School Board's Plains Indian Cultural Survival School, and the Saskatoon Native Survival School. By all accounts, these schools have made a remarkable contribution both to Canadian education in general and to the educational, spiritual, and moral development of Aboriginal students who otherwise would have fallen through very large cracks in the ability of provincial school systems to meet their needs (see, for example, Haig-Brown 1997). One of the most famous and successful survival school experiments in Canada is not run by a provincial school board, but by one of the largest First Nations in Canada, Kahnawake. The Kahnawake Survival School has two major goals, 'to promote and preserve Kanienkeha language, culture, values and history' and 'to develop the academic and technical skills needed to live and work in today's world' (Kahnawake Survival School 1995).

In addition to survival schools, native literacy programs such as the Native Women's Resource Centre program and the 'Council Fire' program in Toronto seek to meet the literacy development needs of Aboriginal people who have been failed by the schools to which they have been exposed, or who are currently falling through the cracks in the schooling they are receiving.

Finally, there is the unique case of Amiskwaciy Academy, which we have already mentioned. In our view, Amiskwaciy is an indication of what might be accomplished by schools that appeal to academic excellence within a context of Aboriginal knowledge, principles, and spirituality, a possibility that interests us as potentially fertile ground for nurturing future 'word warriors.' It also interests us for two other reasons, first because it is embedded in the Edmonton school system with its very strong tradition of school-based management along with the tolerance and encouragement of unique school identities, and second, because its program is open to non-Aboriginal students who genuinely wish to participate in it and who can produce convincing arguments to that effect. After all, why shouldn't a truly excellent, dynamic, and exciting Aboriginally based education program attract some non-Aboriginal students? Indeed, would its claim to excellence be markedly less convincing if it did not?

7 Values, Principles, and Ethics, as *sine qua non*[1]

[T]he capacity of any single Indigenous community to shape education on its own is limited. Changes in technocratic education and the end of cultural marginalization and educational alienation confronted by us require complex approaches involving partnerships and practice that straddle Indigenous communities. This requires a different way of thinking with key roles for Indigenous educators as catalysts, brokers, coordinators, and monitors as well as Indigenous forms of leadership that support all of the people's aspirations, not simply 'fattens' the leader ... Maori views include contexts of education such as economic, social, and environmental impacts, Maori tribal distinctiveness, access to language and culture, and access to natural resources. It also addresses responsiveness of education to Maori aspirations.

> M. Kēpa and L. Manu'atu, 'Indigenous Māori and Tongan
> Perspectives' (2006), 26

sine qua non: Etymology: late Latin, without which not: something absolutely indispensable or essential.

> *Merriam-Webster's Collegiate Dictionary, Eleventh Edition* (2007)

Unless solidly anchored in values, principles, and ethics respected in both Aboriginal and contemporary mainstream Canadian cultures, Aboriginal education, at least in any meaningful sense, is probably doomed. As discussed previously, many of the current social and educational problems in Aboriginal communities have roots in the painful adjustment of individuals and institutions to the values of material acquisition, competition, opaque decision-making processes, power, domination, and exploitation. Mutual recognition and support for shared 'prudential interests' (Margolis 1995, 15)[2] are necessary for a common commitment to sustainable biological processes and relationships for individuals, species, ecosystems, societies, and cultures. Within such recognition and support, the focus would shift from the separate evolution of both Aboriginal and non-Aboriginal societies (or the ongoing colonial imposition of 'Western' industrial monoculture) to the co-evolution of a sustainable environment. Ironically, as Bowers (2006) points out, to do so will require embracing biological and social-cultural *diversity* as a cornerstone of both non-Aboriginal and Aboriginal education. Individual self-defining values, attitudes, and lifestyles will have to be integrated into the underlying matrix of a globally sustainable ecosystem. In nature and form, both Aboriginal and non-Aboriginal education systems might become both scientific (but in the special sense of understanding and fostering the dynamics of sustainability in all aspects of human activities within an ecosystem) and spiritual (profound ecological awareness) at the same time. Values that have been imposed on current Aboriginal education entities include material acquisition, expansion, privatization of common goods, competition, and an obsession with technology and sciences. In overemphasizing these values, Canadian mainstream society has encouraged the pursuit of goals and practices that promote individualism, selfishness, and greed among Aboriginal communities.

At the profoundest level, a re-examination of current governance models in Aboriginal education needs to deal with the underlying value system and to recognize its deep ties to a long series of unworkable and unhealthy governance arrangements. While such emphasis on values, moral principles, and ethics may vary or entail different nuances of meaning for each Aboriginal community, most Aboriginal community members would probably agree, on careful reflection, that each of these things is an important dimension of Aboriginal self-determination and its feasibility.

Significant progress in Aboriginal self-determination, in the field of education and elsewhere, and especially in regard to the kind of functionally integrative aggregation we are proposing, will not be possible in the absence of deep trust on the part of the gatekeepers of Canadian power and resources. That is the essence of what Turner (2006) calls 'Kymlicka's constraint' (58). Negotiating new arrangements with appropriate 'boundaries' for authentic and sustainable self-determination can only happen in a context of mutual trust. This is true because, as

Turner insists, these gatekeepers are and will remain for the foreseeable future mainly non-Aboriginal. We do not mean by this that mainstream Canadian society should continue to impose its standards and governance on Aboriginal education. Rather, we wish to be clear that only mutual trust can break the cycle of dysfunction. The central quest, therefore, in renewing relationships between Aboriginal peoples and the Canadian state is for a self-determination mechanism that supports re-orientation of the Aboriginal ways of doing things so they are *simultaneously* responsive both to Aboriginal constituents and to certain ethical values of central importance in the larger Canadian society.

We begin with first principles here. Aboriginal education exists to provide a more efficient, effective, and appropriate education for Aboriginal students than provincial or territorial school systems can. However, experience to date in achieving that fundamental purpose has been anything but inspiring. Despite a federal investment in First Nations education that now exceeds $1 billion annually, the Canadian taxpayer is regaled every two to four years with an Auditor General's report deploring a striking lack of accountability for that investment and a desperate educational deficit on the part of First Nations people in general and students in particular. For those who are not interested in such issues, the plight of First Nations education then drops off the radar screen for another couple of years. For those who are interested, the policy 'space' between Auditor General reports (see, for example, Auditor General of Canada, 2000a, 2000b, 2004a, 2004b) is filled with sporadic reminders, often in the form of media reports, documentaries, and parliamentary committee evidence and reports[3] that, notwithstanding a handful of First Nations schools that may be more successful than most, not a great deal is changing in First Nations education as a whole.

In the end, educators and educational organizations can be derailed in one of two fundamental and related ways: by a lack of vision and purpose, and by a lack of ethical principles and commitment to them. To be sure, capacity and competence are issues of central and inescapable importance in the ability of any organization, educational or not, to achieve its formal goals, as well as matters of central ethical importance in their own right. When vision and purpose – or commitment to them and the values and principles they require – are lacking, the almost inevitable result is chaos that undermines the legitimate and productive interdependence across Aboriginal and non-Aboriginal societies. The resulting chaos can deter mainstream Canadian society from investing in any Aboriginal collective initiative that promotes educational self-determination for the common good of Aboriginal students. Efficiency and effectiveness within Aboriginal educational institutions will be possible only if they go hand in hand with a profound change in values and ethics. Shared values and ethics are not peripheral to Aboriginal self-governance in education but constitute its very basis and driving force.

The Nature and Importance of Ethics

> Organizations are not objects in nature; an organization is a moral order invented and maintained by human choice and will.
>
> T.B. Greenfield, 'Science and Service' (1993), 217

Main Entry: **eth·ic**
Pronunciation: **'e-thik**
Function: *noun*

Etymology: Middle English *ethik*, from Middle French *ethique*, from Latin *ethice*, from Greek *EthikE*, from *Ethikos*

1 *plural but singular or plural in construction*: the discipline dealing with what is good and bad and with moral duty and obligation
2 **a:** a set of moral principles: a theory or system of moral values <the present-day materialistic *ethic*> <an old-fashioned work *ethic*> – often used in plural but sing. or plural in constr. <an elaborate *ethics*> <Christian *ethics*> **b:** *plural but singular or plural in construction*: the principles of conduct governing an individual or a group <professional *ethics*> **c:** a guiding philosophy **d:** a consciousness of moral importance <forge a conservation *ethic*>
3 *plural*: a set of moral issues or aspects (as rightness) <debated the *ethics* of human cloning>
    Merriam-Webster's Collegiate Dictionary, Eleventh Edition (2007)

Ethics is a complex and contested concept and philosophical domain. Views of appropriate ethical standards on the part of leaders range from utter self-sacrifice and self-abnegation in the interest of serving others, even to dying in the place of another, all the way to radical hedonism – as the popular definition puts it, 'If it gives you pleasure and you can get away with it, do it, and don't worry about the consequences for others.' We cannot summarize the current state of moral philosophy in this context.[4] Nonetheless, the ethical issues surrounding Aboriginal and First Nations education in our day are so grave that we must critique them carefully and do so within a coherent position first on the nature of ethics and then on its importance. Such a position must take into consideration social and economic relations in society as a whole and more particularly within questions of the governance of First Nations education. To fail to do so would be to overlook what we regard as one of the two most fundamental challenges that First Nations education confronts in our time, the other being the question of fundamental vision and purpose, to which we turn our attention in our final chapter.

While our discussion will necessarily raise issues associated with all three definitions of ethics, our main focus will be on definitions 2a and 2b, that is, on ethics as a theory or system of moral values and as a set of principles of conduct governing an individual or a group – particularly, and unsurprisingly, as principles governing an individual in his/her relationship to and 'roles' within a group or groups. Indeed, one of the considerable moral epiphanies of our time is that one cannot sustain one set of moral values and ethical standards in private life and a completely different set in public and organizational life.

Ethics and Moral Objectivity

The history of ethics in Western philosophy has largely been that of a quest for moral 'objectivity,' for a set of principles that allow one to find 'reason' within a canon of universally acceptable virtues and, by implication, of universally unacceptable vices as well. Such rational principles upon which a 'universal' morality and ethics might be founded, however, have proven resiliently elusive, although not for want of effort by brilliant minds from Aristotle through Augustine and Aquinas to Hume and Kant, and, in our own time, Habermas, Rawls, and McIntyre (although McIntyre, reluctantly, tends ultimately to recognize the historical and cultural 'contextedness' of moral and ethical truth claims),[5] all of whom attack the problem from widely varying perspectives.

For a considerable portion of humanity, of course, questions of right and wrong, and good and evil continue to be resolved on the basis of belief in a code of morality 'revealed by God' or given by some great moral teacher. Nonetheless, however powerful and compelling such codes may be for those who accept their authenticity and authority, the fact that they are revealed or given does not establish them as universally acceptable or as capable of being 'reasoned to' in any way with which everyone, or even every reasonable person, would agree. Throughout history, but especially in our own time, the quest for a universal code of ethics grounded in an equally universal moral philosophy has failed. It has failed despite a quasi-universal 'longing' for a moral objectivity that transcends time, culture, and space, a longing so intense and so widespread that Margolis (2004) – the most articulate and prolific exponent of a new moral relativism which explicitly rejects all claims to 'privilege,' that is, universal moral truth claims[6] – has aptly labelled it the 'pathos of morality' (87–8).

If claims to universal moral and ethical principles have failed in the broader arena of moral philosophy, it is extremely unlikely that any attempts to suggest that such principles could be 'reasoned to' in the case of Aboriginal peoples could have any plausibility or intellectual 'traction.' *Indeed, the pervasive claim with respect to morals and Aboriginal peoples is one of Aboriginal distinctiveness and difference from mainstream Canadian culture and its moral and ethical values.* We will return to this claim later, particularly as it affects our interests in this work. Nonetheless, since this chapter is an ethical manifesto for Aboriginal education and governance, we need to provide a basic account of Margolis' reinvention of objectivity in morals and ethics. We are compelled to do so for three reasons: first, it represents, in our view, the only way forward in the quest for broad agreement in the area of ethics and morals; second, it offers the only credible place to stand for us, *as non-Aboriginal authors,* in this particular ethical manifesto exercise; and finally, Margolis' scheme resonates strongly with Schouls' view of relational pluralism, which we argue is a sound one for renewing relationships between Aboriginal peoples and mainstream Canadian society.

Margolis (2004) takes as his starting point that all moral truth claims are historically and culturally situated and contextualized. As humans, we can never escape the here and now of time and culture (11,); we are creatures, 'emergent artefacts,' of our respective *sittlichs*, that is, of our particular historical cultural community, with its particular beliefs, among other things, about right and wrong, virtue and vice – and of how moral truth claims are to be legitimated or vested with binding 'moral authority' within that cultural community. Within this perspective, ethical governance for plurality must be dynamic and it needs to be approached in the context of continuously renegotiated and renewed relationships (although this definitely does not imply adopting an 'anything goes' approach).

Because we are always bound by culture and history, our morality is also constructed out of *our* particular history and culture (Margolis 1995, 264; Margolis 2004, 34). That is why a single action can be assigned a vastly different moral significance by two different *sittlichs* whose moral visions collide. In the most extreme cases, for instance, the same act can be viewed as heroic martyrdom in one culture and savage terrorism in another. Furthermore, contests and conflict among moral visions are inevitable because of 'ineliminable moral diversity' (Margolis 2004, ix, 25, 110) among different societies as well as among different interests within societies, a diversity that makes any broad convergence in morals highly unlikely (110) and that assures both incompatibilities and 'incommensurabilities' (ix, 102, 119), which result in ongoing dialectical interplay (ix) of various sorts (from debate to all-out war) among competing moral visions.

Given the impossibility, then, of legitimating moral truth claims in any universal or absolute way – that is, outside of competing, often incompatible, and even incommensurable *sittlich* values – the best we can hope to achieve is sufficient agreement on moral matters to provide a modus vivendi among different societies and groups with competing moral visions. Margolis (2004) calls this a 'second best' morality, a *faute de mieux* (for want of anything better) morality (xvii, 24, 25); a crucially necessary modus vivendi, however, if diverse cultures are to coexist.

But how could we agree sufficiently on such a second-best morality so that it could serve as a working modus vivendi and why bother to do so in any case? Margolis' answer to both questions is strikingly pragmatic. We can only hope to cobble together a mutually agreeable second-best morality based on practical interests or what he calls 'prudential needs' or 'prudential interests' (Margolis 2004, 15). He sums up the case for prudential needs or interests as the ultimate foundation for second-best morality in this way:

> Once we give up appealing to supernatural, revealed, fictional, utterly utopian, indubitable, unrealizable moral resources, as well as obviously false and unconfirmable beliefs, preferring to proceed *rationaliter* (as among those who do not share our norms and values), there cannot be any compelling account of human interests that would ignore our hopes and fears regarding life and death in all its forms. These worries define the principal part of the content of our *prima facie* norms. They concern ourselves and all those we are likely to hold especially dear. There cannot be a fixed list of them, for they will vary from group to group, from one age to

another, from the sensibilities and technological resources of one society to another. And, of course, they will depend in good part on our organizing ideologies. Yet it is well-nigh impossible that some run of such interests will not play a decisive role in the moral vision of whatever society we choose to examine. (Margolis 2004, 14)

So, although he recognizes – and fears – the power of principle-driven commitment (16), Margolis (2004) argues that to find agreement among *sittlichs* with competing and colliding moral visions, at least agreement sufficient to provide a workable modus vivendi, we need to be guided by a 'compelling account of human interests ... [centred on] our hopes and fears regarding life and death in all its forms,' our own life and death, that is, and those of persons especially dear to us. To arrive at such agreement, we must accept the need to come to a workable dé-tente with '*those who do not share our norms and values*' (emphasis added). Furthermore, what 'counts' in negotiating the terms of détente among competing moral visions will vary depending on time, history, and the mix of cultures and ideologies involved. Still, the lives, safety, and well-being of family, kin, and community (including presumably future gen-erations) will inevitably count for much, Margolis argues, in sorting out acceptable terms among different or opposed *sittlichs*. Such negotiated, prudential-interest driven morality, Margolis (2004) believes, provides all the 'objectivity' we need – a 'weakened' objectivity (6, 52) in contrast to classic moral-objectivist claims, but a sufficient one – and all that we are capable of, in any case. This is very much a middling, muddling-through kind of morality, but, for all that, although clearly relativist, it is not 'anything goes' relativism either. Far from it!

Reaching acceptable terms of an agreement that are based on the hu-man interests shared among our respective *sittlichs* and that allow di-verse communities to flourish in a way they could never do alone is, of course, an imposing social and political project. An effort to reach mutually acceptable terms among different *sittlichs* can easily degen-erate into (or return to) a zero-sum/win-lose game, resulting in a re-newed hegemony of the strong over the weak rather than in more equal relationships. Yet renewing relationships between Aboriginal and non-Aboriginal Canadians will require consensus at least on those key assumptions shared among our respective *sittlichs*, especially our shared interest in an ecologically viable planet whose biodiversity can sustain human life and ensure our survival. Reaching agreement on mutually acceptable ethical principles to govern our interaction is the only way to a future of fruitful, creative interdependence – and to the change in moral climate between Aboriginal and non-Aboriginal groups that is necessary to achieve it.

Although Margolis (2004, 5) explicitly rejects Rawls' famous 'just distribution of goods' principle (1971, 302–3), he senses an obligation to provide some meaningful parameters around the general idea of prudential interest and in doing so 'recovers' at least part of the Rawlsian idea of fairness in the distribution of that interest. Margolis (2004) does so by insisting on *humanitas*, 'an unrestricted concern and respect for human life and its care: that is, the refusal to permit any part of the human race to be excluded or ignored in our moral deliberations' (113). He insists that *humanitas* is a viable basis for agreement precisely because it is 'vacuous,' that is, it carries with it no particular moral principles or 'privilege' of any sort – except that no group is beneath its ultimate concern and respect for human life.

Humanitas, Margolis (2004) then argues, requires that no society be subject to what he calls *summum malum*, the greatest evil:

> massive suffering, deprivation, or the like that marks the misfortune of a substantial population, where the grading of what will count as such is likely to be qualified *liberaliter* – that is, in conceptual terms, more generously than not, proportioned to our technological capacity and resources and expectations. I mean matters like the dire lack of food and water and shelter on a large scale; torture; natural disasters; the spread of AIDS and other terrible diseases; the dissolution of families; wholesale slavery; genocide; the loss of basic resources and the means of subsistence; war; constant unemployment; and the large-scale disorganization of ordinary life. (65)

The link to Bowers' (2006) central preoccupation with destruction of 'the commons' could not be more obvious. Where communal, regional, and intergenerational solidarity disintegrate in the face of rapacious individualism and *self*-interest, it is this litany of disasters that ensues (89–93). Within our capacity, then, *humanitas* requires that we do what we can to prevent and alleviate incidences of *summum malum*. Doing so, moreover, should not preclude us from doing what we can to ameliorate 'lesser forms of disadvantage, pain, and the like for smaller groups' (Margolis 2004, 65). We must do what we can to counter major threats to human life and dignity.

Humanitas, however, requires more than simply avoiding and ameliorating great evil. It requires that we do all we can to assure that every society achieves the minimum good, or *minimum bonum,* through a selection of *providentiae* (pragmatic, practical, prudential-interest goods). These need to be scaled to the *sittlich* history of a particular society and reflect that society's technological resources. Furthermore, this foresight must reflect a society's understanding of what is the least acceptable level of individual and societal life that is deemed adequate *(rationaliter)* for the survival of its offspring. We find this understanding to be particularly significant against the backdrop of Aboriginal education. Taken in this sense, *minimum bonum* requires an efficient, effective, and appropriate educational system, which provides an essential foundation for any healthy and prosperous society!

Another aspect of Margolis' emphasis on development (or what he terms 'capacitation') strikes us as particularly germane to the situation of Aboriginal education. Contrary to anything-goes relativism, Margolis (2004) argues that 'moral engagement' is a crucial part of the essence of human nature: 'Paradigmatically, [human] selves are moral *agents,* in the joint sense of judging themselves and others and of being the distinctive kind of creature about whom such judgments are rightly rendered – creatures who can judge and make commitments' (12). To be human requires us to reflect morally, to make moral commitments, and to judge the morality and moral commitments of others, nothing less! Moral neutrality is an abdication of our humanity.

It follows that ensuring the survival of a society's offspring necessarily entails the development of 'moral agency' in the young. To become fully human in Margolis' (2004) sense, the young need to be shaped as

> *(a)* moral agents … capable of knowing the lay of the entire world, both natural and cultural, in which they act; *(b)* [who, when] rightly informed … act with the knowledge that they cannot legitimate what they do, beyond the resources and limitations of one or another second-best morality; and *(c)* who … know they act under the conditions of an evolving history, their own *sittlich* formation, their partisan commitments, horizoned understanding, and the impossibility of avoiding conflict with the normative convictions and partisan commitments of other agents differently formed and informed. (86)

Human agency is a process of social engagement that allows members of a community to critically shape their own responses to problematic situations or important events. It requires individuals to continually re-focus their past and future ways of acting, being, interacting, and learn-ing. More precisely, Emirbayer and Mische (1998) define human agency as the 'temporally constructed engagement of social actors of different structural environments – the temporal relational contexts of action – which, through the interplay of habit, imagination, and judgment, both reproduces and transforms those structures in interactive response to the problems posed by changing historical situations' (970–1). This comprehensive definition encompasses three specific dimensions of human agency: interaction, projectivity, and practical evaluation.

Interaction refers to individuals' capacity to draw on past patterns of thoughts and actions in order to make the community relatively stable and resistant to fundamental change. Projectivity refers to the ability of individuals to reconfigure past thoughts and actions so they can better see future possibilities. Finally, practical evaluation refers to the individuals' ability to make practical judgments and choices from among possible alternative thoughts and actions in response to emerg-ing challenges, demands, dilemmas, and ambiguities. As Emirbayer and Mische (1998) point out, each of these three dimensions of human agency 'do not correspond in any simple, exclusive way to past, pres-ent and future as successive stages of action' (972). However, they claim that for each dimension of human agency, one temporal orientation (the past, present, or future) is the dominant one, shaping the way indi-viduals collectively respond to emerging educational challenges and to changes they make in their ways of being and interacting with others.

Following a logic quite in keeping with Emirbayer and Mische's con-cept of human agency (and one that accords well with the relational pluralist idea of the importance of balancing individual and group identities), Margolis (2004) argues that *humanitas* requires one more – albeit potentially divisive and controversial – point of departure, *nullum malum*, which holds that *sittlichs* should never impose any 'changeless rule or principle … to human nature or human reason that could possi-bly justify any moral injunction against living one's own life *rationaliter* – on the grounds of violating human nature or intrinsic reason or cog-nitively privileged norms' (22). *Nullum malum* implies that, unless real and palpable harm is done to others by the way in which one lives one's life, one should be free to live it in that way and, moreover, that any decision about what is harmful needs to be taken with due respect for the fact that different *sittlichs* within and outside of a society may differ dramatically on what constitutes 'harm to others.' Over time, according to Margolis, societies should develop greater tolerance for the divergent ways in which people conduct themselves.

Despite the importance Margolis attaches to the principle of *nullum malum*, he also recognizes that all human societies are inherently conservative (85), that all *sittlichs* tend to change slowly and be resistant to change and, furthermore, that, in general, they *should* be so (77). Nonetheless, he also cites Nazi Germany as an example to show that every *sittlich* is 'capable of morphing into a radical descendant of itself, one that, judged by its own lights *ante* [its preceding moral values and ethical standards], might have been thought to be utterly evil' (28). In a context in which members of a *sittlich* see themselves as victimized, the results can be catastrophic moral decline. This principle of slow, measured, well-considered change as opposed to ongoing transformation of societies and cultures as normally good is congruent with Bowers' idea of 'mindful conservatism' (2006, 117). Thus, while revolutionary change in morality is possible, it is exceedingly rare, and, in general and on average, that is not a bad thing, although clearly, from either a *summum malum* or *minimum bonum* point of view, some *sittlichs* may need to undergo transformative change.

We have not yet turned to the second question we posed at the beginning of our brief summary of Margolis' position on moral objectivity, that is, why bother with the strenuous work and often painful compromise needed to find mutually acceptable moral ententes among divergent *sittlichs*? Margolis contends that the answer to that question has undergone a quantum change in the wake of 9/11:

> We have reached a point in history at which the proliferation of contests of the 9/11 sort (just now identified) are so dangerous and destructive and so easy to match in a retaliatory way that the world cannot afford to neglect the chance to work out an answer that is at once coherent, pertinent, responsive, viable, reasonable, effective, practical, apt – and possibly even nonstandard in the way of tempering the pressure for further such confrontations. (xi–xii)

However difficult and improbable coalescence around such a second-best morality might be, we simply cannot afford to fail in our efforts to achieve it. Margolis (2004) continues:

> I think we cannot survive in our very dangerous world without a widely accepted morality, and what we now need is a proposal, fitted to a glo-

balized world, that tries to isolate those themes that are as close to being the least common (moral) denominators that we can imagine – completely without presumptions of cognitive privilege – and that we may fashion so as to be as tolerant of diverse, even conflicting, normative convictions as we can imagine and support. And 9/11 gives this a radical meaning. (xvi)

All of this, on our reading, resonates unmistakably with Schouls' view of relational pluralism (as discussed above). In particular, it resonates with the relational pluralist necessity of continually negotiating and renewing relations among different groups with different, often conflicting – and continually evolving – cultural identities (*sittlichs*, if you will). Finally, it is congruent with the relational pluralist insistence on doing so with mutual respect and with a sense of mutual dependence, or as Schouls (2003) describes it, 'mutually acceptable interdependence' (133), the same sense of mutual respect and dependence evident in the tradition the *Guswentha* or two-row wampum. That said, Margolis (2004) emphasizes that the pragmatism of morality grounded in prudential interest requires all parties to negotiate new political relationships (Margolis insists on the integral link among morality, law, and politics)[7] that embody new moral understandings and take into account *existing power relationships* (10, 19–20). This strikes us as being extremely close to the idea that Turner advances in the guise of 'Kymlicka's constraint.'

Finally, there are certain ethical values that are of central importance in the larger Canadian *sittlich* and that are indispensable in governing and administering effective, efficient, and appropriate Aboriginal and First Nations education. Coincidentally, these carry great weight in traditional Aboriginal cultures. Pre-eminent among these values are honesty, good faith, moral commitment and engagement, and responsibility, just the values, it turns out, that are necessary to renegotiate and renew political relationships and the moral understandings and commitments that underpin them. Turner's account of the two-row wampum leaves little doubt about the importance of honesty and good faith within the Iroquoian tradition. His account of the Condolence Ceremony extends and deepens that notion.

Renewal in political relationships, though, depends on an important proviso of the Condolence Ceremony – that keeping one's word within the public sphere is recognized by everyone to be of the utmost importance in securing and maintaining peace. Promises made in the public domain are elevated to the highest standards of diplomatic protocol. Of course, there are no guarantees that everyone will tell the truth, so even in diplomatic situations one is never sure the truth is being told. The indigenous approach to resolving this unavoidable human problem is to sanctify certain practices. Words are to be used in responsible ways and in certain situations they bind a person to keep a promise. This was especially true if there had been an exchange of wampum [to solemnize the promise]. (Turner 2006, 50)

By just about any conceivable applicable moral standard, then – whether it be Aboriginal tradition, the Aristotelian virtue legacy in any of its many and varied forms, Kant's categorical imperative, or the prudential interest of Margolis' second best, *faute de mieux* morality – effective, efficient, and appropriate Aboriginal education requires moral leadership. This leadership must be based on truthfulness, good faith, and the moral commitment of a conscientious stewardship that is focused on the development of Aboriginal youth and their maturation into responsible moral agents.

We note with interest and encouragement the code of ethics drafted by the Assembly of Manitoba Chiefs Youth Secretariat (2006) which focuses on just these values, and in particular, on the importance of an ethic of service to achieving some degree of meaning and fulfilment in life (and, we would add, in leadership and administration):

To serve others, to be of some use to family, community, nation or the world is one of the purposes for which human beings have been created. Do not fill yourself with your own affairs and forget your most important task. True happiness comes only to those who dedicate their lives to the service of others.

Challenges to Ethical Activity in Organizations: Self-interest versus Organizational Goals

With everyone sold on the good how does all the evil get done?
Saul Bellow, cited in Christopher Hodgkinson,
Administrative Philosophy (1996), 187

The arrogance of success is well known. Powerful people who are driven to turn their domains into empires begin to feel that they are above the rules, that what applies to ordinary people does not apply to them, and

they can use their power to suppress criticism and force their will on others, whether employees, customers, suppliers, or external watchdogs.
                    R.M. Kanter, 'How Leaders Restore Confidence' (2004), 41

Wotherspoon and Schissel (1998) observed disapprovingly that '[w]ith a few notable exceptions, there has been little attempt to integrate fully an understanding of Aboriginal issues with wider theoretical orientations' (3). A major part of what we seek to do in this chapter and throughout the book is to respond to that absence by bringing relevant 'mainstream' understandings from organizational and educational theory to bear on Aboriginal education. Aboriginal educational organizations are, after all, human organizations. Just as civilizations are not immune to decline, neither are human organizations immune to displacing their goals by focusing ever greater amounts of energy, time, and resources on goals that are different from, or even opposed to, the 'formal goals' of the organization. Even organizations with high commitments to idealistic values that are rooted in strong beliefs or principles that, for better or for worse, 'go beyond' reason, values frequently so strong that they provide reasons for which to live, to struggle, and even to die, often experience 'degradation' over time (Hodgkinson 1978, 1983). Ultimately, the only way to avoid, or at least postpone, such degradation is renewal of the ethics, vision, and purpose of those who govern and work in the organization. Otherwise, the organization becomes unsustainable, at least in terms of its official goals and purposes. Such renewal, indeed, is the main business of organizational leaders (Meyer 1986; Schein 1986). Ironically, renewal can be most difficult when things are going very well or very badly for an organization. When things are going very well, complacency and comfort make it hard to renew difficult commitments (Galbraith, 1992). When things are going badly, poor morale can trigger an ethos that is focused solely on what one can do for oneself and those close to oneself. In good times and bad, mindful conservatism is needed (Bowers 2006, 117).

Another key influence on the degradation of an organization's goals is the role political economy can play in promoting self-interest and even outright greed. 'Political economy is the study of the conflicting reward structures that society [and human organizations within it] can (and hence must) choose among' (Phelps 1985, 4). The political economy of an organization can easily sidetrack its formal goals. Boyd (1982) provides a particularly insightful and trenchant portrait of the political economy of public schools:

... to maximize the executive's [principals and senior administrators] benefits ... requires the executive to strike bargains with both employees and external groups in order to ensure that he or she can both meet the environments expectations and exploit it for resources. Thus, a kind of reciprocity with employees and key interest groups is created that ... tends to foster the maximization of budgets rather than profits (i.e., consumer or client satisfaction).

Second, consider employees. Perrow [1978] says that if we were to survey human organization members in terms of what they really are trying to do, we would ask such questions as:

> Can you minimize the personal costs of working in this place; can you manage to make the work fairly light; can you avoid unpleasant duties or clients ... can you manage to pick up office supplies or food from the kitchen ...? Can you get your friend or relative a job here? Most important of all, can you be sure of having a job here as long as you need it?

> ... Michaelsen [1977] concludes that a bargaining process between teachers and their principals and between principals and central office staff results in a generally agreeable arrangement all around: 'The needs of teachers and principals for control over their jobs most often take precedence over the needs of individual children and their families.' (115)

If anything, Boyd's insights have particular relevance for First-Nations education because there are few meaningful accountability checks and balances in place to thwart political-economy processes and interests. School boards, in the end, must respond in various ways to provincial standards and accountability processes. However flawed their responses may be, in the view of many critics, school boards cannot simply ignore provincial standards and accountability mechanisms. As the Auditor General has repeatedly pointed out, however, mechanisms to monitor accountability do not exist in First Nations education.

From the political economy perspective what counts in the organizational power game is not achieving educational goals but 'delivering the goods' to key members of the organization as well as other key stakeholders. The organization is a 'rice bowl' (Hodgkinson 1996, 168) and the prudent leader seeking to augment and consolidate his/her power makes sure, whatever else happens, that when the 'right' fingers reach into the rice bowl, there will be adequate rice for them to grasp. Her/his survival as leader depends on it!

From the rational choice paradigm perspective, a political economy analysis assumes 'that rational, self-interested individuals try to maximize their own welfare (or benefits) within the context of the institutional or organizational reward structure' (Hodgkinson 1996, 113). Public schools, like all publicly funded institutions, receive financial support from the tax-derived budget. They are thus insulated from any meaningful 'discipline of the bottom line.' In contrast to an optimistic human relations view of organizations, the political economy perspective suggests that employees all bring some degree of self-interest to their position and will focus their energies and attention on personal gain rather than attempt to find satisfaction and professional identity through exemplary work and fulfilling their organizational goals.

Thus the leader takes care of his/her own by lightening workloads, by tolerating sloth and incompetence so long as it doesn't become a public embarrassment, and by practising outright nepotism. The bargaining process that involves central office staff, principals, and teachers results in a 'generally agreeable arrangement all around' (Boyd 1982, 115). Students and their learning, of course, have nothing to do with this agreeable arrangement! The result is bureaucratic dysfunction at its worst.

We have already noted that in the case of First Nations education the gap in accountability between citizens and the administrative units responsible for providing education is exceptionally great. This is not surprising given the 'disconnect' that exists between citizens' voices on the one hand and meaningful program accountability and sustainability on the other. Given this disconnect, one would expect (all things being equal, which of course they are not)[8] substantially greater goal displacements to be taking place, that is, greater amounts of administrative and leadership attention and energies being spent on unofficial benefits and empire building than on public education (Lawton et al. 1995).

This is why a firm access to information policy is so critical to maintaining transparency in all aspects of an educational organization's operations. Administrators may behave differently if they know that parents and citizens, in general, and the press, in particular, can authoritatively requisition information and records to illuminate the aspects of administrative decision-making on just about any issue. It is quite a different situation if they are free from any access to information mandate. Recognizing that decisions can easily become a subject of intense public scrutiny places an overlay of accountability on administrative decision-making, an overlay that is lacking in the absence of an access to information policy that is subject only to minimal limitations.

One cannot, in the end, legislate morality. Conventional norms and morality, especially those that define what is to be expected from administrators within a particular organization, shape and sustain an organization's culture as well as the norms and morality of the organization itself. In addition to these norms, law and regulations provide bottom-line standards along with significant sanctions that can be applied against those who violate them. If one resorts to falsification of financial data or misappropriation of funds, for example, one needs to understand that possible sanctions could include dismissal, public disgrace, and possibly incarceration for a period appropriate to the gravity of the offence. The likelihood of anyone being exposed for such conduct is greatly increased when the norms of the organization are solidly aligned against it and when a strong access to information policy ensures that anyone seriously interested in a particular administrative decision, or the data underlying it, can obtain the relevant documents in a timely and orderly way. To reduce the temptation of committing financial wrongdoing and help achieve their formal goals, organizations should provide their staff with appropriate remuneration, benefits, and working conditions. While, as Herzberg (1966) demonstrated a half-century ago, these 'hygiene factors' cannot inspire a higher level of motivation, they can provide a minimal amount of security so that administrators and employees can focus their energies and efforts on achieving organizational goals.

Unfortunately, some administrators will be seduced by the prospect of using the power and knowledge associated with their position within the organization to garner illicit gains for themselves and those working closely with them. For that reason, formal legal sanctions that have teeth are necessary to discourage administrators who might otherwise be seduced by the possibility of such ill-gotten gains. For those administrators who flirt with such temptation, particularly in a public or quasi-public organization, few deterrents are more definitive than a strong culture of transparency buttressed by access to information regulations that allow no room for deviation from the spirit and letter of organizational transparency.[9]

The 'White Guilt' Paradox: Empowerment and Responsibility or Perpetual 'Fiduciary' Victimhood and Tutelage?

... human beings, individually or collectively, cannot transform or uplift themselves without taking full responsibility for doing so. This is a law of nature. Once full responsibility is accepted, others can assist as long as it is understood that they cannot be responsible. But no group in human history has been lifted into excellence or competitiveness by another group. No group has even benefited from the assistance of others without already having taken complete responsibility itself – complete to the point of saying that we appreciate your desire to help, but the help itself is unwelcome for the weakness it breeds.

S. Steele, *White Guilt* (2006), 62

It is hardly a secret that help and helpers can often be profoundly unhelpful, particularly when they are unwanted and unneeded. What is less generally recognized is that the targets of ill-conceived help can be ethically debauched in profound and disturbing ways by collusion with would-be helpers, particularly when the helpers' agenda is *their own* legitimation, expiation, and self-aggrandizement. No better account exists, as far as we are aware, of the mechanics and dynamics of this type of seduction than that offered by Steele in *White Guilt: How Blacks and Whites Together Destroyed the Promise of the Civil Rights Era* (2006). Steele provides a stunning exposition of such collusion and its lamentable consequences for American Blacks in the post–civil rights movement era. Although the history of Blacks in the United States is very different from the history of First Nations in Canada, the parallels and overlaps of Steele's analysis and critique with the overall situation of First Nations education and governance in contemporary Canada are equally stunning.

Careful mapping of Steele's argument in light of Margolis' second-best-morality schema shows that there are two conceptual hubs around which he builds his analysis and critique: a perverse conception of social morality or social justice on the one hand, and responsibility and accountability on the other. The perverse social justice that Steele attacks is built around dissociation from racism and its agenda for the white majority culture; in Steele's view, a dissociation that simply relegitimizes white moral authority. In a very closely related vein, Bowers (2006) laments the way in which such perverse social justice logic claims unique legitimacy for mainstream cultural approaches to knowledge grounded in radical individualism (151).

At first blush, dissociation from racism sounds like a laudable enough idea. For that matter, at least within the politically correct lexicon of our time, attacking social justice seems tantamount to opposing motherhood and apple pie in an earlier epoch. Steele deftly exposes, however, dissociative social justice framed within what he calls 'white guilt' for the 'poisoned apple' that it is. First, what does he mean by white guilt and why is that important?

> Because white guilt is a vacuum of moral authority, it makes the moral authority of whites and the legitimacy of American institutions *contingent* on proving a negative: that they are not racist. The great power of white guilt comes from the fact that it functions by stigma, like racism itself. Whites and American institutions are stigmatized as racist until they prove otherwise. (Steele 2006, 27)

Acknowledgment of such guilt puts an onus on whites and their institutions to demonstrate in an equally public way that they are no longer racist. Only in that way can they shed the stigma of racism and recover lost legitimacy and moral authority. Despite great historical differences, it is clear that both American Blacks and Canadian Aboriginal peoples suffered major oppression and injustice at the hands of whites and their governments and institutions. Equally clearly, both American and Canadian whites have publicly acknowledged the wrongness of these actions and most of them wish ardently to dissociate themselves from their racist pasts and the oppression that it visited upon racial minorities in North America, especially upon First Nations peoples and African Americans.

The Achilles' heel of white-guilt-driven social justice, according to Steele, is that, in their zeal to dissociate from the stigma of racism and the historical oppression that went with it – and thus recoup lost legitimacy and moral authority – 'whites' and their governments have been willing to accept, indeed to encourage and even foster, a lack of responsibility and accountability on the part of the oppressed minority. By funding various relief and pseudo-development measures and policies, most infamously and tellingly 'affirmative action,' mainstream governments have taken, or more accurately, have *reassumed* responsibility for the oppressed minority by 'taking charge' of ameliorating the conditions of their lives. Conversely, and by the same perverse social justice logic, they have prevented the minority from assuming responsibility and accountability for their actions and have absolved them from guilt for irresponsibility on their part – which, as both Steele and Margolis insist, is nothing less than to deny them the most essential element of their humanity, namely, *moral agency*.

The ironic key assumption in this perverse social justice logic is that whites themselves must repair the damage they did to the minorities they oppressed in the past. This logic has reinvented the paternalistic ethos of the 'white man's burden,' essentially warmed-up colonialism under a new rubric. Steele (2006) rages poignantly and eloquently against this perversity, so much so that it is hard to know what to cite to capture the full force of his argument in as few words as possible. Perhaps the following two quotations come closest to doing so.

> I have already discussed the narcotic effect of all this … this great infusion of moral authority gave blacks the power to imprint the national consciousness with a profound new edict, an unwritten law more enforceable than many actual laws: that no black problem – whether high crime rates, poor academic performance, or high illegitimacy rates – could be defined as largely a black responsibility, because it was an injustice to make victims responsible for their own problems. To do so would be to 'blame the victim,' thereby repeating his victimization. Thus, in the national consciousness after the sixties, *individual responsibility became synonymous with injustice* when applied to blacks. (55; emphasis added)

> No worse fate could befall a group emerging from oppression than to find itself gripped by a militancy that sees justice in making others responsible for its advancement. (62)

By using various slights of policy, partisans of such social justice engineer an illusion of rapid progress, but it is never a very convincing one. In fact, Steele (2006) argues, partisans *lower standards* for the victim group by expecting less from them, academically and intellectually as well as in other areas of responsibility. Unfortunately, as Steele (2006) points out, 'Double standards *always* stigmatize precisely those they claim to help' (116), while marginalizing and disempowering them.

Affirmative-action-style double standards can intrude into each aspect of education as well as its governance and administration – and thus poison it with the stigma of low expectations and incompetence. Elementary students who can't read, write, or do basic mathematics are told that it doesn't really matter because they have other 'ways of knowing' (Steele 2006, 119) or they can learn 'experientially' (this claim surfaces frequently in Aboriginal education) or 'intuitively' (120). Secondary students who can't write a coherent paragraph or do the most basic algebra are told that it doesn't really matter because they will get a post-secondary placement no matter what they can or cannot do at the secondary level. Furthermore, in the words of a post-secondary counsellor with vast experience in the area of First Nations education, students are 'spoon fed' throughout their secondary education so that they never really have to get organized and work hard – hard work, after all, is not part of their culture and, in any case, this should not be expected of victims. Of course, none of this will help them much, once they actually get into a post-secondary environment where no one has the time or inclination to spoon feed them. Thus the corrosive logic of victim entitlement and white (mainstream) obligation eats away at the natural human need to develop intellectually, morally, holistically, and spiritually. Steele (2006) captures this lamentable dynamic poignantly in regard to African Americans:

> There is no carnivorous white need standing between us and the pursuit of excellence. No pity. Thus, excellence is allowed to entice us with its own intrinsic joys and rewards; and we come in thrall to it. Suppose Marvin Gaye or Duke Ellington or Richard Wright or Kareem Abdul-Jabbar or Condoleezza Rice or millions of others (all people from humble beginnings born in the age of open racism) had let their pursuit of excellence be somehow contingent on the ministrations of white guilt, on the spiritually withering interventions of needy, morally selfish white people betting on the cliché of black inferiority rather than on the natural *human* longing for excellence that resides in us all? (65)

The same can be said of the Tom Longboats, Tina Keepers, Dan Georges, Basil Johnstons, Kim Andersons, John Borrows, Marie Battistes, and Dale Turners of the First Nations world. What would they have become if they had not heard the clarion call of excellence and instead 'bet ... on the cliché of ... [Aboriginal] inferiority rather than on the natural human longing for excellence?'

In governance, double-standard irresponsibility legitimates opportunism of the worst sort. As long as those in governance attend meetings once in awhile, they need not contribute in any meaningful way to the education of students in their system because they really can't be expected to do so. Finally, in the Cinderella logic of affirmative action, 'self-serve' leadership can become the norm, simply to be expected. If leaders are assumed to be beyond responsibility, why should they not simply look after themselves and that would be the end of it? After all, responsibility is for someone else, for those who have a *permanent* fiduciary (Steele [2006] does not use this term but it is a close synonym for the kind of tutelage relationship that he decries) responsibility for us – for the mainstream establishment seeking expiation of white guilt.

In this way, governments and institutions bent on social-justice-style reparation seek to avoid the supplementary stigma of 'victim blaming,' a high crime of politically correct social justice logic. Unfortunately, in the process, by creating programs and policies with low expectations, no accountability, and no requirements for responsibility on the part of beneficiaries, administrators, or those directly involved in governance, they provide a *perverse incentive* to continue playing the role of victim, to play the role of victim *for all it's worth*, to adopt a self-destructive, in fact, a dehumanizing role of perpetual 'victimhood,' to establish themselves firmly as the nation's official and, seemingly permanent, victims – or 'citizen-victims' (Steel 2006, 55).

All of this, of course, leads to what Steele (2006) characterizes as 'a kind of "upscale" corruption in which money changed hands and the government was told what it wanted to hear: that because we were black we knew the people we were working with, and because we were "innovative" we had the magic to steer them out of poverty. All we needed was more money, always more money' (119).

We have already noted the tension between the liberal emphasis on individual values on the one hand, and the emphasis on group values at the centre of what Schouls (2003) calls the 'identity approach' to cultural pluralism on the other. The danger, as Schouls recognizes, is that individual identity can be swamped or suppressed by group identity and, for this and other reasons, he regards the identity approach a dangerous one and insists that 'Aboriginal individuals in all their diversity must be given freedom to develop and contribute to community life without undue interference from their governing structures' (173). Steele (2006) carries the argument further. He insists that group identity can easily become a means to exploit 'white guilt.' Such exploitation frequently employs militant, if not an enraged insistence on permanent victim status in order to obtain what amounts to perverse incentive reparations and exactions. Those who engage in such exploitation justify it by a social morality based solely on dissociation from racism. Ironically, this type of exploitation empowers no one except for a small group of power elites. It ends by quashing individual freedom and stifling the moral agency that must necessarily accompany it. Worse, it can provoke blindness on the part of members of mainstream society to the reality that members of minorities targeted by this kind of social justice action *have* an individual human as well as one or more group identities. Steele (2006) calls this 'white blindness': 'People who are in the grip of white blindness, and thus unaware of their true motivations, always miss the human being inside the black skin' (136).

Freedom, after all, implies responsibility for exercising the moral agency that goes with it. It implies the impossibility of blaming all failure on reinvented colonial masters.

> Freedom becomes a great problem for an emerging group because of all the illusions the group falls prey to as it buffers itself from the humiliations and burdens of freedom. Instead of taking *full* responsibility for our underdevelopment, we convince ourselves that we should pursue social justice and that this will agent us into a competitive equality with whites. We avoid the terrifying level of responsibility that freedom imposes by arguing that *whites* should be responsible for our development. We even define full black responsibility as an intolerable injustice. Our understandable fear of freedom has led us to bank our fate on an absurdity: that we can develop by taking *less* responsibility for ourselves. We have defined freedom as a kind of heaven in which the inhabitants are forgiven responsibility. (68; emphasis in original)

The terrible result of this absurd belief that a minority *can develop* by taking little or no responsibility, either collectively or individually, is nothing less than willing complicity in reinventing colonialism and, with it, relegitimizing white or at least mainstream supremacy.

> So the very structure of the liberal faith – that whites and 'society' must facilitate black uplift – locks white liberals into an unexamined white supremacy. They can't really believe in blacks but they *must* believe in whites. Whites are agents; blacks are agented. (Steele 2006, 148; emphasis in original)

Perpetual victimhood, in short, can become hardwired into minority–majority relationships and with it comes the bedrock assumption that mainstream society and its institutions are *agents* while historically oppressed minorities are fated to be forever *agented* – that is, forever dependent on mainstream 'agents' who, by 'taking responsibility for them,' do more or less the same thing, albeit perhaps in vastly different ways, as Indian 'agents' did until the 1960s. When viewed as a permanent and immutable basis for all relationships between First Nations, fiduciary obligation translates into permanent dependency, in short, into being forever *agented*.

The key, of course, to breaking the gridlock of dependency on whatever amount of guilt-driven sense of noblesse oblige on the part of mainstream society Aboriginal groups can garner at any given instant in time *is to take control of education and its governance by taking full responsibility for them* and for what can reasonably be viewed as results endogenous to their activities. The same, of course, is true of areas of governance other than education as well. On the centrality of jurisdiction for meaningful control, Cornell (2002) says:

> Why does jurisdiction matter? First of all, it puts the development agenda and control of the necessary resources in indigenous hands. Without jurisdiction, indigenous Nations are subject to other people's agendas. You can't ask people to be accountable if you don't give them decision-making power. Whoever is making the decisions has the accountability. To reserve decision-making power in one place and then tell someone else that they're accountable is to kid yourself. Jurisdiction marries decisions to consequences, which leads to better decisions. (2)

Meaningful movement towards greater equality of opportunity and authentic amelioration of the social, economic, cultural, intellectual, and political circumstances of an oppressed minority requires that resources be focused on capacity development, on what Margolis (2004) calls 'capacitation,' or developing capabilities. Meaningful movement cannot be based on phoney 'results' that are produced by double standards and the evasion of responsibility on the part of minorities themselves for acting coherently, honestly, diligently, transparently, responsibly, and accountably to ameliorate the efficiency, effectiveness, and appropriateness of the education *they* offer to *their* young. A necessary corollary is that when things go well, such responsible 'servant leaders' should obviously accept responsibility for their part in successes. When things go badly, however, *they need to accept responsibility publicly for their part in what has gone wrong*; they cannot blame every problem and each failure on a colonial past and on the residential school legacy, as if these were sufficient to confirm their perpetual victimhood and incapacity to assume responsibility. Indeed, as Steele (2006) insists with regard to American Blacks, they cannot consider it 'an intolerable injustice' (68) to expect them to assume responsibility!

Social justice, at least in the sense of majority responsibility for solving the problems of historically oppressed minorities, is the opposite of developing the capacity of minorities to take full responsibility for their own welfare, although paradoxically it is usually proposed by its advocates as a plausible surrogate for such development, in fact, as the only 'just' approach to assisting beleaguered victims of historic oppression. Steele's (2006) stinging and insightful critique in this respect with regard to the situation of American Blacks in the post–civil rights era seems to us to reflect the ongoing gridlock in Aboriginal education in Canada today. As Steele (2006) writes: 'So white liberals and American institutions (along with a corrupt black leadership) keep seducing blacks with social justice as though it were also developmental' (63).

Evidence for the parallelism is not hard to come by! From its inception DIAND version of 'devolution' placed zero emphasis on capacitation. As we pointed out earlier, Yuzdepski (1983) noted a generation ago that DIAND's implementation of devolution consisted mainly of two things: first, of divesting DIAND itself of the tiny bit of educational program development that it had acquired, and second of 'turning over the keys' to the First Nations communities across Canada. The central assumption and main stipulation in this transfer, again as Yuzdepski (1983) notes, was that 'devolved' education *would not cost any more than federal-day-school education because there simply was no 'new money' available* (41, table 1). No provision whatsoever was made to begin the process of making a quantum leap from having no educational leadership and governance to a broad-spectrum capacity for a large-scale functional integration of educational programs and services for First Nations learners. Furthermore, no resources were available for that purpose even if First Nations leaders had desired to move in that direction – and, of course, they did not want to do so because they were completely in the thrall of the *Indian Control of Indian Education* (NIB 1972/1984) mirage of Indian control as local, that is, community-level control.

Far from encouraging meaningful development, the federal government through DIAND pursued its well-known divide-and-conquer strategy by insisting on and reinforcing its direct links to each individual First Nation and largely washing its hands of accountability linkages with First Nations aggregate organizations. Such organizations, the federal government reasoned, were really 'creatures' of individual First Nations and whether they were functional, dysfunctional, or even mainly shams being exploited as 'cash cows' by local First Nation power elites should not concern DIAND since its direct legal obligation under the *Indian Act* was clearly to the individual First Nations and not to First Nations aggregate organizations.

Nor is there any persuasive evidence that this disempowering encouragement of irresponsibility on the part of DIAND/INAC has changed much over time. On the contrary, we find it singularly discouraging that our exhaustive review of self-government agreements, agreements-in-principle, and the *Mi'kmaq Education Act* revealed only a single mention of fundamental transparency issues such as access to information and conflict of interest, and that single mention was only in an agreement-in-principle *and would bind only individual First Nations, not First Nation aggregate organizations* (see our discussion in chapter 5, 'Some Pervasive Policy Issues')!

Finally, if there were any doubts about the presumption on the part of the federal government and INAC about the incapacity of First Nations to assume full responsibility for control of their education, their unflinching policy requirement that students in First Nations schools be able to transfer *at any time without penalty* should put them quickly to rest (again, see our discussion in chapter 5, 'Some Pervasive Policy Issues'). Not only would it be a mistake to expect responsibility and accountability from First Nations aggregate organizations, First Nations are surely not to be trusted to make decisions about the nature of the educational programming for their young – only provinces are up to deciding such things. Furthermore, since all responsibility for deciding the substance of educational programming for First Nations students rests with the provinces, and should continue to rest with them in principle, *developing First Nations capacity for educational programming* is really a moot question and would be a waste of resources! In this disempowering, neocolonial vision, irresponsibility or non-responsibility on the part of First Nations for what really matters most in education is normal and desirable – no need here to bother oneself much about truly *functional* aggregation and certainly no need to 'fantasize' about regional and even national First Nations jurisdiction in a truly meaningful sense.

At this point it seems helpful to review in some detail the case of the First Nations University of Canada, perhaps the highest-profile example to date of great aspirations and expectations in First Nations education colliding with the realities and priorities of self-serve rather than servant leadership.

**The First Nations University of Canada: Colliding Visions –
National University or Local Fiefdom?**

The First Nations University of Canada (FNUC) grew out of the Saskatchewan Indian Federated College (SIFC), originally established by
the Federation of Saskatchewan Indian Nations (FSIN) in 1976. Its inception resulted from the efforts of John and Ida McLeod who joined
forces with Ida Wasacase (Cuthand 2006a) to put the creation of a First
Nations university on the FSIN agenda. The result was the *Saskatchewan Indian Federated College Act*, which was passed by the legislative
assembly of the FSIN in 1976. SIFC subsequently became affiliated with
the University of Regina as a federated college. From nine students in
1976, enrolment increased to just over 1,000 students by 2005, at which
time the institution claimed 3,000 alumni from across Canada and beyond (Wheeler and Henning 2006).

Over time, as the SIFC leveraged its affiliation with the University
of Regina, FNUC became the uncontested flagship of Aboriginal administered post-secondary institutions in Canada, offering university
level programs (from certification to masters' degrees) in community
development and health sciences, English and Indian languages, communication arts, literature, business and public administration, and
social work. These programs were offered on three campuses in Regina, Saskatoon, and Prince Albert (First Nations University of Canada
2006a). The FNUC also managed to attract a number of distinguished
Aboriginal scholars, including Eber Hampton, who served as president
from 1991, and Denise Henning, who served as academic vice-president. Both individuals served until shortly after a tumultuous takeover
of FNUC on 17 February 2005.

During an annual winter festival on 17 February 2005, Morley Watson, the chair of the FNUC board of governors and the FSIN vice-
chief,[10] 'took over' the Regina campus of FNUC in a move described by
two former senior FNUC administrators as a coup d'état:

> Watson was acting in his capacity as chair of FNUC's Board of Governors
> when he and his entourage of security guards, personal supporters, a lock-
> smith and a few chiefs stormed the FNUC executive office. He promptly
> suspended three senior officials and launched a forensic financial audit
> based on 'evidence' housed in a 'sealed envelope,' which he refused to
> show anyone until months later. Simultaneously all seven finance and
> four human resources staff members were evicted, the downtown interna-

tional and special programs office staffs were dragged out, and strangers with four portable hard drives invaded the technology area and copied the central server drive containing faculty records, research and e-mails, and student records. Once emptied, the office locks were changed.

The coup d'état played out like a Movie Channel sci-fi flick, Vice-Chief Watson yelling out orders to the executive assistants, dragging staff members to the board room and lining them up for questioning in a manner reminiscent of a sentencing court in a Third World dictatorship. (Wheeler and Henning 2006, n.p.)

Mr Watson effectively took control of FNUC administration himself, suspended, fired, or 'chased off' twenty senior managers, faculty, and staff and appointed three persons tightly linked to FSIN (including his own sister-in-law) in key financial posts at FNUC. Surely this episode must stand out as an alarming intervention in the administration of a university by its governing body. Just based on what happened and how, this incident flies in the face of all current norms and standards set out for university governance. In particular, it flies in the face of norms for maintaining a seemly distance between boards of governance and members of collegial 'senates' who determine academic standards and freedoms. These bodies are deliberately held at arm's-length from university boards of governors (Booth 2001). FNUC, however, and its context were unique among Canadian university-level institutions in ways that went beyond its identity as a First Nations university affiliated with a major provincial public university.

So what happened? University colleges have varying relationships with their parent universities. Some are bound tightly to their parent institutions in just about every way that matters, sharing the same academic policies that include appointments and tenure, obligatory compliance with senate decisions and policies, and union and collective agreements if they are part of a unionized university. Others are entities unto themselves in a number of these areas. In at least one Ontario university, for instance, affiliated colleges have their own collective agreements and can create their own policies regarding appointments and tenures even if such policies are radically opposed to standards generally held in esteem by university administrators and faculty alike.[11]

Still, nothing quite parallels the situation in which the FNUC found itself. As a First Nations university, it was at once a creature of the FSIN and responsible for developing and nurturing programs both for its Saskatchewan First Nations constituent groups and First Nations across Canada. Embedded within a large, unionized provincial university, many of its central priorities and concerns were not in sync with University of Regina's board of governors and senate or with the union that represented its faculty. The FNUC was thrust into the world of universities with a unique identity crisis.

To begin with, the FNUC vision statement asserts that 'as First Nations, we treasure our collective values of wisdom, respect, humility, sharing, harmony, beauty, strength, and spirituality.' With regard to more traditional academic values, the vision statement says:

> The First Nations University of Canada provides an opportunity for students of all nations to learn in an environment of First Nations cultures and values. The university is a special place of learning where we recognize the spiritual power of knowledge and where knowledge is respected and promoted. In following the paths given to us by the Creator, the First Nations have a unique vision to contribute to higher education. With the diversity and scope of the First Nations degree programs, the university occupies a unique role in Canadian higher education. The university promotes a high quality of education, research and publication. (First Nations University of Canada 2006b, n.p.)

That said, from its inception FSIN tended to regard SFIC as an institution under the total control of the Federation. For example, it established a thirty-one-member board of governors for the institution and appointed only elected FSIN officials and students (Wheeler and Henning 2006). This odd board-of-governors composition was in notable contrast to the usual practice of establishing university boards of governors that represent broad swaths of 'public interest' and augured badly for the future of governance–administrative relations at SFIC.

Governments, of course, generally appoint members of boards of governors but traditionally they do so with a view to ensuring that such boards represent a range of legitimate interest in university-level education and governance. In particular, it would be unthinkable for a government to appoint either a member of a provincial legislature or an acting civil servant to a university board of governors.

At the time of the takeover in 2005, the thirty-one-member FNUC board of governors consisted of twenty-three elected First Nations officials, including two FSIN executive members, two FSIN senators, one FSIN member-at-large, fourteen tribal councils, and three independent bands. Sixteen chiefs figured among voting members of this astonishingly large, and thus intrinsically unwieldy, governing body. In addition, visitors with only observer status from the Universities of Regina and Saskatchewan, the federal government, the Saskatchewan government, three student associations, and a single faculty member attended board meetings (Wheeler and Henning 2006). To say that such a composition was politically charged and politically suspect in terms both of academic freedom and of commitment to the public interest (Aboriginal or general) would be an obvious understatement.

The aftermath of the 2005 takeover is, in many respects, as unsettling as the event itself. As with many a coup d'état, the aftermath was a 'reign of terror' characterized by heavy-handed suppression of all opinion contrary to the new administration and all questioning of the takeover and its rationale. According to the former dean of the Saskatoon campus and the former academic vice-president of FNUC, faculty members who expressed disagreement with the takeover were ordered to 'refrain from defamatory comments, insubordination and actions and comments that entirely undermine the functioning of the institution' (Wheeler and Henning 2006, n.p.). A scheduled keynote presentation by Dr Blair Stonechild to the First Nations Forum on Post-Secondary Education was cancelled by FSIN. Students on the Saskatoon campus who protested against the takeover were threatened with disciplinary action. A forensic audit failed to turn up evidence of any substantial financial irregularities alleged as the basis for the takeover. Indeed, it is now alleged that the person who attested to the irregularities, Greg Stevenson, was the brother of Wes Stevenson, then vice-president of administration of FNUC, and that Greg Stevenson and his wife were paid $4,000 for the affidavit containing the accusations against his brother (ibid.).

The takeover has been costly for the FNUC, to both its financial stability and its credibility. Given the very large costs of the forensic audit, replacement salary costs for suspended administrators and faculty, lost research revenues, and other resulting costs, FNUC was saved from insolvency only by special 'top-up funding' from INAC (Wheeler and Henning 2006). The AUCC (Association of Universities and Colleges in Canada), at the direct request of the president and vice-chancellor of the University of Regina, delayed its investigation into whether FNUC had violated its terms of membership by allowing the FSIN direct political interference in its administration and in suppressing its academic freedom (Hawkins 2006, 5). This evaluation will soon take place and strong evidence suggests that such interference did in fact occur (Turk 2006), which would confirm that the AUCC membership requirement of non-interference by the governing body in the university's administration and academic freedom was indeed violated.

The financial, legal, and credibility fallout from this extraordinary event will take years to settle. One small but significant piece in that much larger puzzle, however, has already been put into place. An arbitration panel has ruled in favour of Dr Stonechild in his grievance against FNUC for having cancelled his address. The panel concluded that 'Vice-Chief Watson had a responsibility not to assert personal considerations as a reason for making decisions about the activities of an academic member .... [and that he] failed in his obligation to refrain from interfering in and to defend the academic freedom of a faculty member. In this respect, we find that the Employer violated the collective agreement.' The panel further emphasized: 'We think that any finding that academic freedom has been infringed is a serious matter, and serves to emphasize the importance of the Employer taking seriously its responsibility under the collective agreement to "safeguard and promote" academic freedom' (University of Regina Faculty Association 2006).

Universities cannot be creatures of government and remain universities, even if governments are heavily interested and invested in public (and for that matter private) university programs and operations in many ways. Academic freedom forbids it. When university-level institutions are forced to become malleable tools of political interest and dogma, they cease to be universities in any recognizable sense of the word. Unless and until FNUC can provide convincing evidence that it is, in the words of its vision statement, 'a special place of learning where we recognize the spiritual power of knowledge and where knowledge is respected and promoted,' it will sadly occupy the position of pariah among Canadian university-level institutions, regardless of the outcome of the AUCC hearing on its membership status. It is difficult to believe that the takeover will prove to be anything but a pyrrhic victory for its authors, and it is difficult to foresee how the fruits of that victory will prove to be anything more than 'ashes in their mouths.' To take control of a First Nations university in this way can hardly serve the interests of First Nations students in Saskatchewan.

How did all of this come to pass? The perspective and insight provided by a former senior administrator at FNUC show that, at the time of the takeover, the FSIN power elite believed that they were in imminent danger of losing control over FNUC, and hence of losing the ability to exploit FNUC as a lucrative cash cow that they had become

accustomed to milking for their benefit. Based on the main lines of critique that emerged during an interview with this senior administrator,
we were able to conceptualize the main elements in the FNUC leadership that led up to the 2005 takeover (see fig. 7.1). The administrator
told us that the immediate precipitating crisis was fear of losing control
of FNUC as it began to morph into a truly national institution:

> The first thing that was occurring at the national level is that one-third of
> the funding that INAC received for post-secondary education was taken
> right off the top and given to First Nations University of Canada. Now
> [when] the name change occurred [in the transition] from SFIC to First
> Nations University of Canada, I don't think that FSIN realized what that
> meant. That meant that it was a First Nations University for the entire
> country, not just Saskatchewan. So, at AFN [Assembly of First Nations]
> and at the meetings at the national level for Aboriginal education, First
> Nations educators [asked] the question – and they were demanding to
> know – why [were] *they* getting this funding when we have all these other
> institutions and programs that are going on – [and why was] there no
> representation outside of Saskatchewan? Now this was going on – I know
> [they] had been approached at AFN as well … the educators were in an
> uproar and were demanding representation.[12]

The second ingredient in the FSIN power elite's impending loss of
control over FNUC and its financial resources took the form of a rather
xenophobic reverse-racist reaction to the growing non-Saskatchewan
presence among FNUC faculty, especially among the senior academic
leadership:

> … the second thing that was going on was that, at the Saskatchewan level,
> all of a sudden we have an administration and faculty that are from other
> nations. So we have a new math professor … from the Six Nations people,
> Mohawk; … a president who is Chickasaw from Oklahoma; … and a vice-
> president academic who … is Cherokee and Choctaw from Oklahoma.[13]

Worse still, was the political economy perspective of FSIN elites that
led to a dangerous sense of parochialism:

> JP: So is this just garden-variety parochialism or is there something more
>   going on there?
> INTERVIEWEE: Ah, it's parochialism and jealousy!

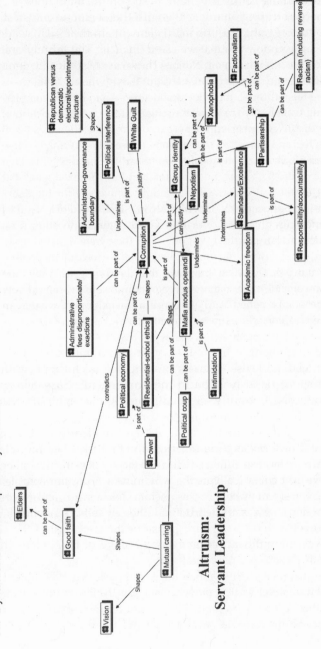

7.1 Dynamics of leadership and dysfunction

**Altruism:
Servant Leadership**

**Political Economy Web of Dysfunction:
Self-Serve Leadership**

JP: Parochialism and jealousy?

INTERVIEWEE: When I say jealousy, ... [I mean the kind expressed as] 'and by God we're not going to let somebody else get ahead of us, so we're going to pull you down so that we can feel equal.' And here we are, not only are we hiring at a First Nations University talented and gifted scholars and faculty from other nations but those [who are here] we're supporting them through their doctoral degrees – and they're completing [them]. And oh, my God, we're not going to be needed any more. *We outgrew FSIN.* [Emphasis added.]

JP: Fear!?

INTERVIEWEE: That's exactly it, absolutely it! Fear! We are losing what we have.[14]

If all this was not enough to provoke strong FSIN reaction to its increasingly endangered control over FNUC, there was one other reason identified by the administrator:

> ... the third thing that was going on was that we were getting national recognition for our research, national recognition for our special projects and our success and retention, and [the concern was] 'Oh, my God, they're getting the recognition and we're not!' And that's my opinion of what was going on, and so it was on three levels, not just two.[15]

All of this immediate sense of crisis prior to the takeover, however, did not arise spontaneously. It had profound roots in a deeply dysfunctional political-economy web of self-interest that had somehow engulfed the noble ideals from which SFIC had sprung (see fig. 7.1).

There is a cruel irony in the way the group identity, solidarity, and sense of cultural preservation championed by the SFIC founding elders dissipated over time into a political economy of self-interest. Perhaps the 'unkindest cut of all' was the way in which the same value of mutual caring for the members of this social reference group devolved into a dysfunctional and self-destructive ethos of self-interest for and among the power elite of the group. Consider the comment of the administrator explaining the founding vision of SIFC:

> The vision at that time [of SIFC's founding elders] was that we want[ed] to see our children and grandchildren ... not have to live in poverty, to educate our future, and to do that within a First Nations perspective so that we have cultural survival. You know, if you think about those ad-

ministrators … [they] are big-picture people – and that's what they do well … the visioning process … and connecting all of the big-picture items together and how that might look. I see that as maybe most of the elders at that time.[16]

By what unfortunate alchemy did the altruism of that big-picture visioning and the underlying legitimate concern for group welfare and well-being devolve into self-serving leadership? Figure 7.1 offers several troubling and convergent answers distilled from meticulous coding of this interview. Legitimate partisanship can be poisoned by narrow factionalism and xenophobic fear of all 'others,' including and especially others from First Nations outside the area represented by the local First Nations aggregate organization and its interests. In this way, 'where you are from' and 'who you are connected with' begin to take precedence over knowledge, skills, and work ethic.

There were a lot of people who felt that they were owed jobs because they had earned a master's degree and therefore they should be [hired]. One particular person who became a really active player and who evidently applied for every position that became available whether she was qualified or not for that position [felt that] because she was a graduate from First Nations University with her master's degree that she was owed a position. There were a lot of people like her who had applied for positions and weren't granted [them] because we were going through a normal vetting process and we had standards that we had to follow in our policies. Of course, then it became, 'Well they don't want to hire Saskatchewan because those American Indians are in charge, you know.' And … so that was one thing that was a big problem and those people were also some of the outspoken ones that … made very racist comments … that you can read about in any of these newspaper articles and letters to the editors – [they] were writing such scathing things that were very degrading to First Nations people as a whole … and making very racist statements … Then that whole … picket that took place … where … they [Watson's supporters] had an individual that was going into offices and telling folks that if they didn't go up and support this protest that was being put on, that their name would be duly noted and reported to the vice-chief.[17]

The predictable victim of this situation was academic freedom itself, a value that FSIN leadership clearly did not understand nor consider to be of any importance. As in any Mafia-like environment, the most important value becomes keeping everything in the family by assuring a collusion of corruption and a corruption of collusion.

> JP: Now what about the board and its relation to [the Federation]? ... You've talked a lot about the interference from the Federation in various forms. Where did the board fit in to all of this and were they really the same people? Was the board a distinct entity from the Federation or was it simply all ...
>
> INTERVIEWEE: Okay, the board was a majority [of] chiefs. However, FSIN chiefs and grand chiefs are not selected by the First Nations people themselves. They are selected by the elected chiefs.
>
> JP: Alright.
>
> INTERVIEWEE: Okay, so, stop and think about that in the terms – I hate to say this – but in terms of the Mafia.
>
> JP: (Laughing quietly as if in a moment of 'shock of recognition') Excuse me, I can't help laughing – this is a term I've used frequently in similar situations ...
>
> INTERVIEWEE: But in terms of the Mafia! (spoken with insistence)
>
> JP: Yeah! Yeah!
>
> INTERVIEWEE: 'You scratch my back, I'll scratch yours, and we've got so much information on each other that you dare not cross the line because if you do you're going down with me.' (Pause, sound of writing) When the media kept calling me – and I mean hounding me – I had to change my phone number. I was so hounded by the media that it was just like, you know, phfff, meat. (Hearty laugh) And I just kept saying, 'Follow the money – or the lack thereof – and you're going to find out.'[18]

Where are the deepest roots of this self-serve dysfunction? Here Lord Acton's famous epigram seems unexpectedly apropos. Truly, power corrupts and absolute power corrupts absolutely. We are human beings and we require checks and balances on our individual and collective power or we will slip all too easily into the madness of absolute power. In the Aboriginal world, for that matter, the traditions of voluntary rather than obligatory followership and consensus-based decision-making are particularly strong – altogether antithetical to the arbitrary exercise of absolute power for personal and elite peer-group gain! Unfortunately, it was to exactly such absolute power exercised with impunity that the residential school introduced generations of First Nations students. Indeed, it is probable that the vision these students grew up with of power and especially of leadership within mainstream society was almost entirely shaped by the exercise of unchecked autocratic power within residential schools. This vision of power is directly opposed to the concept of academic freedom within a university environment. Often, it is not understood, as the administrator points out:

> So, in my opinion, the chiefs have an image. What does that image look like? I don't know. I can't describe it for you because I'm not them. But they definitely have no concept or comprehension of what a university [is] and how it's supposed to run. In my opinion, their idea of education came from the residential school experience. And if that's the kind of management ... that's the kind of management that I saw happen ... [It] was a very colonialistic, very residential-school type of management that occurred ... So, when I say I'm angry and I'm hurt, [it's] because of what happened, because of what happened to my faculty and what happened to the students that I care a great, great deal about. But at the same time, I know where they were coming from because I've seen it in my own family – the lack of understanding. They had no idea what academic freedom meant.[19]

Ironically, the board of governors of FNUC had approved a 'Carver model' of governance that should, in theory, have prevented exactly the kind of egregious interference in the operation of FNUC that the takeover embodied. The Carver model is based on contemporary standards of separating governance from administration. Its starting point is the principle that the role of governance is to set policy while the role of administration is to carry out policy and run the day-to-day operations of an institution. In the end, the underlying principle is that governing bodies deal only with the CEO of an institution and are strictly precluded from interfering in the day-to-day operations of it.

> INTERVIEWEE: ... the Carver model – they had a board policy [on] governance that they had voted on in November 2003. Prior to that time they operated as a management model – okay.
>
> JP: That could mean many things!
>
> INTERVIEWEE: Well, basically ... what it means is that they were able to interfere at any time – the board could interfere at any time. A Carver model is that the only employee of the governing body is the president [or the CEO]. They cannot interfere with any of the rhetoric or day-to-day operations of the institution. They do not manage. The president manages and implements policy ...[20]

The administrator never used the term white guilt, or anything close to it. However, what is being described is the paralyzing effect of what Steele (2006) identifies as white guilt, that is, a loss of any sense of moral authority on the part of the 'white' government, including its judiciary and police branches. This loss of authority became glaringly evident at the time of the takeover.

> [The FSIN] didn't heed the rulings from the attorneys on the governance policies ... The police were even called – because it was clearly against the law for the chair to come in and take over the institution. [Then] the police came and Dr Hampton was in a meeting in Moosejaw. He was called back from the meeting. He drove back from Moosejaw to get there and ... [when he arrived, he arrived to] a vice-chief standing there scream-ing at the top of his lungs ... Now I wasn't even on the campus and I'm grateful. But I had my-uh-admin assistant who was there and who had to close her door because she was terrified. She closed it and locked herself in her office because she was terrified. And-uh-the police came. They [the police] came into the office and Dr Hampton said, 'This is the chair and the vice-chief, however, according to our governance policies, he does not have the right to manage.' ... And they said, 'Hey, it's your problem. This is First Nations stuff. It's your problem.' And then walked out and ... left. They [the FSIN] were already in the process of changing the locks on the building.[21]

In this way, the police in effect 'washed their hands' of egregious violations of both official FNUC policy and the *Criminal Code of Canada*. Either they feared the danger of an eruption of major violence or con-cluded that they simply did not have the 'moral authority' to deal with the situation – or both. As well, the University of Regina failed to take any effective steps to halt the FSIN from hijacking student and other confidential data, including and especially cutting off FNUC from Ban-ner, the backbone of the campus data system.[22]

If any bright side exists to the FNUC takeover, it would appear to be that the episode offers a striking, high-profile example of what hap-pens when First Nations education governance becomes an exercise in self-serve rather than servant leadership, an example that is very hard to hide, to make go away, or simply to wait out. Precisely because FNUC was the flagship of Aboriginal administered post-secondary education in Canada on the one hand, and because it was embedded in the academic standards, governance, union, grievance, and contractual apparatus of the University of Regina on the other, no concurrence of interest among key stakeholders in this drama is likely to prevent a very public examination of what went wrong in FNUC governance and in its relationship to administration. Stakeholders of all sorts will want to know what led to Vice-Chief Watson's actions and to tacit support of those actions by FSIN and its constituent organizations. Those who were most directly harmed by the takeover are likely to ensure that the details are vented publicly in the courts and in the press – for years to come! The inability to hide this disaster may yet prove salutary, precisely *because* of its very high profile and the impossibility of covering it up.

The FNUC takeover witnessed the 'colliding visions' (to borrow one of Steele's striking expressions) between two institutions. It was a head-on collision between those who sought to marry strong academic standards and academic freedom with a strongly culturally embedded post-secondary program framed within research values appropriate to a research-oriented university institution and those for whom a First Nations University was a local FSIN fiefdom and a convenient source of income for its parent organization.

One final consideration in this debacle is the source of FNUC funding. FNUC received $7 million annually from INAC; in fact, in addition to being by far the largest beneficiary of INAC's Institutions and Education Organizations Program (also ISSP), FNUC was the only post-secondary institution to receive such funding on an annual basis without having to reapply periodically. FNUC also received about $5.2 million annually from Saskatchewan. As this book was in final editing, the federal government cancelled its funding of FNUC. Saskatchewan has also cancelled its funding for the institution. In announcing that the federal government would not reconsider its decision to cancel its funding to FNUC, Minister of Indian Affairs Chuck Strahl cited 'serious problems at the university [that] have dragged on for years with no resolution in sight' (CBC News 2010).

Ethical Governance and Leadership

Unfortunately, the ethics role model provided by the institution at the centre of colonizing Canadian Aboriginal people, namely, the residential school, was the antithesis of an open organization in an open culture and society operating for the benefit of those it was created to serve. Arguably, the most devastatingly dysfunctional lesson it taught to its inmates was that of unquestioning service to absolute power, which was enforced by whatever means were necessary to impose that power. This was power imposed by fear and mistrust and expressed with direct disrespect by the individual in charge. Imagine being a young First Nations child and being told that you don't matter by the person now in charge of you: 'Do what I say, accept what I do, or I will hurt you. My point of departure for everything that I will do to you, moreover, is based upon the inherent superiority of mainstream Canadian culture and hence the inferiority of your language and culture. Underpinning my assumption of this absolute power over you is the indisputable fact that nothing Aboriginal has ever been part of an "educated person" or ever will be, so my mission is to eradicate every trace of indigeneity in you. I will use whatever tools are available to accomplish this mission and your duty is only to accept and obey.'

Given this sense of mission among those who were the administrators of and who worked in residential schools, it may be surprising that First Nations education, and particularly its administration, is not more dysfunctional than it is, especially when the debilitating conditions under which it generally labours are taken into consideration. Not only did this sense of mission catastrophically divorce everything 'Indian' from anything associated with the image of an educated person endorsed by schools and schooling, it modelled the exercise of absolute power with impunity as the 'norm' in educational leadership. It is hardly surprising that, despite a great deal of lip service to the contrary, a disturbing amount and degree of self-serve leadership has continued to manifest itself in First Nations education since the beginning of the formal 'devolution of control' a generation ago.

One might almost be tempted to conclude that a great many leaders in First Nations education have adopted an ethos of 'it's our turn now.' Even though some leaders have thankfully worked with great altruism in the interest of the students they serve, many have not. The attitude of these leaders reflects an ethos of self-serve leadership: 'Prior to devolution, it was the turn of residential school masters; they were unquestioned masters of the Indian-education rice bowl, however pitifully under-resourced it was at the time; *now* it is our turn to control the rice bowl – our turn to exercise absolute and arbitrary power with impunity and frequently under a veil of deep secrecy, and *our* turn to get what we can for ourselves and for those entwined in our own network of partisans. That is our agenda. Students are useful if they further that agenda and excess baggage to the extent that they do not.'

INAC has nothing to gain and much to lose if it were to impose anything that looked like true financial accountability for First Nations schools and aggregate organizations. Were INAC to ensure accountable and responsible use of its educational funding, it would be disavowed by First Nations themselves and by the Government of Canada. The uneasy truce between the federal interest in ridding itself of INAC as the official interlocutor with First Nations and the sheer momentum of the status quo, of continuing to deal with First Nations through the 'devil we know' (see our discussion of the Penner report in chapter 3, 'Devolution Debacle,' and chapter 6, 'Regional and National First Nations Aggregate Organizations') would end – and with it would disappear the power of INAC to turn a complacent or even blind eye to self-serve leadership in First Nations education.

At the very heart of a relational pluralistic view of a meaningful renewal of relationships between First Nations and settler governments is the concept of mutual trust. Mutual trust, after all, is the only durable alternative to mutual exploitation, and it is incompatible with the self-serve ethos of the rice bowl, a dilemma to which Paquette (1986) drew attention many years ago. Members of the federal Parliament could not, in good conscience, knowingly abandon control over the funding they assign to another government or agency. The principle of responsibility for the funds that Parliament appropriates would not allow it – at least not knowingly and willingly. The principle or parliamentary responsibility for funds that Parliament appropriates would not allow it – at least not knowingly and wittingly. That is in large measure what the 'sponsorship scandal' was all about, visible loss of control by Parliament as an institution in a politically sensitive context over monies that it had appropriated. This scandal involved payments to various Quebec communication firms for no or highly dubious services beginning in 1995. These payments that originated from Public Works Canada and totalled $100 million had little or no 'paper trail.' The scandal led to the highly publicized Gomery Inquiry and a number of serious criminal convictions.

In our view, it would be very difficult to sustain an argument that, under the current arrangements, Parliament has not lost control in just about every meaningful way over the money that it provides to First Nations education. If that were not the case, the Auditor General would not continue to single out that education as failing its students in one report after another. In the context of a parliamentary democracy, the option of block funding for First Nations education, or government for that matter, in the absence of a transparent audit trail, and probably a solid base of evidence regarding program efficiency and effectiveness, is simply not open. In the parlance of relational pluralism, that is not and can never be 'a reasonable boundary' around First Nations education agencies and governments. Nothing, moreover, in the history of self-government agreements bearing on First Nations education would lead us to believe anything else. 'Kymlicka's constraint' is here to stay. Even if current arrangements between First Nations and INAC seem mired in a time warp that suggests the contrary.

Finally, despite the Trudeau-Chrétien commitment to devolution after rejection of the White Paper, the federal government issued a mandate to INAC to turn over 'control' (in the sense of local administration) to First Nations, but to do so 'on the cheap,' that is, to turn over the existing network of Indian day schools to Indian communities with no supplemental funding to build infrastructure or to encourage intelligent aggregation (Yuzdepski 1983). Essentially, the federal government handed over the existing cash flow to INAC for First Nations education and bailed on its responsibilities. Worst of all, no attention was given to systematic capacity-building in the devolution process. First Nations were, in a very real way, 'set up for failure' from the beginning of the devolution process. Each community was left to its own devices, and abandoned to the administrative mirage that local control is the one and only path to meaningful Indian control.

Ethics and 'Kymlicka's Constraint' in the Canadian *Sittlich* Context

In the course of laying out strategic criteria for a First Nation in pursuing – or abstaining from – litigation under section 35 of the *Canadian Charter of Rights and Freedoms*, Wilkins explains at length from a legal perspective much the same sort of considerations that Turner sets forth with regard to 'Kymlicka's constraint.' In his concluding comments, he summarizes both the context and nature of a prudent approach on the part of First Nations to section 35 litigation. Even as he acknowledges that circumstances may make departures from the 'desiderata' that he offers in any given case desirable, he summarizes his sense of prudent strategy and its context in the following terms:

> My purpose has not been to criticize Aboriginal groups – who often proceed from within conditions more difficult than anything I have ever had to face – for conducting their section 35 litigation as best they can. My only

purpose has been to invite such groups to take realistic and deliberate account, when and as they are able to do so in preparing their litigation, of the evident concerns and propensities of their non-Aboriginal judges. Doing so, in my judgment will improve materially their chances of long-term success.

A more profound and related question is why Aboriginal peoples should feel reduced, in their efforts to obtain enforcement of the rights that have been theirs all along, to keep paying such solicitous attention to the sensitivities of the intruders that have displaced them and colonized their lands. The history of Canada, after all is not replete with occasions in which the settlers and their descendents paid respectful, or really any, attention to the constitutive rhythms and understandings of their Aboriginal hosts. Quite the contrary. And the notion that Aboriginal peoples' best hope for justice today may live in some exemplary attentiveness to their colonizers' fears is one that they may legitimately find galling. How convenient it must seem for someone in my position to be suggesting it.

I accept and respect the objection. There probably are irreducible tensions between the rhythms and currents that characterize litigation and those that constitute the various Aboriginal cultures and world views. (Wilkins 2004, 305)

Nonetheless, the central realpolitik conclusion at the heart of Wilkins' advice is to go slowly, carefully, and in measured steps along a path that is precisely parallel to Turner's insistence on the imperative of being able to speak convincingly to non-Aboriginal power brokers, especially legislators and judges, in ways they understand and trust – and on the critical importance of 'word warriors' who are up to the task. In their own ways, Wilkins and Turner recognize the crucial importance of alignment between Aboriginal intellectuals who are up to the task of speaking convincingly with non-Aboriginal power brokers from within the key philosophical, political, and legal assumptions of both mainstream and Aboriginal thought and Aboriginal political leadership with credibility. That alignment is needed to assuage the fears of colonizer power brokers of unacceptable political, economic, and legal consequences flowing from Aboriginal self-determination, particularly consequences that threaten the existing political, economic, and legal orders.[23]

That such a challenge is fundamental and daunting is hardly doubtful, as Turner (2006) astutely notes:

I believe part of the answer lies in how well indigenous peoples can rec-
oncile an indigenous academic culture with the existing forms of leadership found in indigenous nations. Thinking about indigenous problems,
engaging other people's ideas, publishing one's thoughts, and holding
dialogues with those who disagree with us means little if these ideas do
not lead to transformations in indigenous nations. Those nations require
intellectual leaders and political leaders to work together. (106)

Even if such reconciliation were possible, it strikes us as singularly
improbable that a generation of intellectually well-equipped and morally credible word warriors would have much chance of success in negotiating reasonable boundaries around Aboriginal self-determination,
*unless both Aboriginal political leadership and the exercise of power by Ab-
original leaders inspires confidence and assuages fears on the part of mainstream power brokers – however galling that may be to Aboriginal peoples
and their leaders.* In the end, no way exists to short circuit 'Kymlicka's
constraint' and its implications for renewed relationships between
settler governments and Aboriginal peoples.

Parliamentarians and judges can be expected to continue being more
than hesitant about 'turning over the keys to the treasury' to First
Nations governments or institutions, that is, relinquishing in principle
or practice accountability for funds appropriated by Parliament. It is
unthinkable, for instance, that the federal government would institute
transfers to First Nations under the rubric of 'unaccountable contributions.' Indeed, across experimentation with different forms of block
funding, the rubric of accountability has been front and centre throughout the entire history of transfer payments to First Nations and First
Nation entities. It was the accountability touchstone, moreover, that
was at the centre of the recent confrontation between former minister
of Indian affairs Robert Nault and the Assembly of First Nations in regard to his suite of accountability legislation intended, once and for all,
to ensure First Nations compliance with accepted standards of financial
and administrative accountability (Bill C-6, Specific Claims Resolution
Act, Bill C-7, First Nations Governance Act, and Bill C-19 First Nations
Fiscal and Statistical Management Act) and electoral accountability, at
least as these were conceived at the time from the federal perspective.

Twenty-five years ago, Shkilnyk (1985) recounted movingly the
social, political, economic, health, and moral decimation of Grassy
Narrows reserve in northwestern Ontario. Her description of the rapid
growth of social inequality and a spoilage-system ethic is a sombre re-

minder of the profound ethical dangers surrounding local First Nations governance:

> Furthermore, according to the best intentions of government officials, DIAND economic development programs were to upgrade the community as a whole. But in little over a decade, these programs resulted in an unprecedented level of inequality in earning opportunity. As people became dependent on government programs, in a very real way they also became dependent on the people at the band office. Indian bureaucrats decided who should get work, for how long, and at what rate of pay; they determined who should get welfare and who needed a new house. Decisions on these most basic human needs became subject to political manoeuvring. Those families not represented in the band administration by a close relative found themselves at a disadvantage in this competitive environment. At the same time, other pressures and constraints made it difficult for them to continue to live off the land in the traditional way. Caught between the old and the new ways of life, such families became almost totally dependent upon the statutory provision of social assistance. They came to constitute the underclass of Grassy Narrows society. (151–2)

Of course, the ethical pitfalls associated with 'small-town politics,' particularly in a context of very limited resources and governance capacity, are hardly limited to First Nations. Our point is that education is far too sacred a trust to be turned over to the vagaries of small-community internecine struggles over the political and economic crumbs in a trickle-down system. Even moving these struggles one rung up an aggregation ladder, particularly if participation in the aggregate unit is voluntary and selective, offers little in the way of guaranteed relief from the pathologies of small-town politics. That is precisely why provincial governments have, without exception, imposed massive amalgamation of township school boards into larger regional units.

It is no coincidence that some of the most widely read authors in educational administration in North America have insisted in recent years on the importance of an ethos of stewardship, of servant leadership. As Sergiovanni (1992) noted some time ago, trust is at the very core of leader stewardship and the 'moral authority' it both requires and fosters:

> Stewardship represents primarily an act of trust, whereby people and institutions entrust a leader with certain obligations and duties to fulfill and perform on their behalf. For example, the public entrusts the schools to

the school board. The school board entrusts each school to its principal. Parents entrust their children to teachers. Stewardship also involves the leader's personal responsibility to manage her or his life and affairs with proper regard for the rights of other people and for the common welfare. Finally, stewardship involves placing oneself in service to ideas and ideals and to others who are committed to their fulfillment. (139)

Nor is it coincidental that this line of reasoning and argumentation has such strong resonances with our own repeated insistence on the particular importance of servant leadership in Aboriginal education as a fiduciary, indeed, a sacred trust, and with our corresponding abhorrence of self-serve leadership, especially within that context. Servant leaders keep their 'eyes on the ball,' and the ball is not their personal welfare and career advancement or that of those closest to them. The 'ball' is student learning, social adjustment and integration, intellectual and spiritual growth. Towards these ends, servant leaders not only 'share the limelight,' they share their leadership whenever and however such sharing seems likely to 'move the ball.' They nurture the trust required by servant leadership through equity of treatment, respect for others, honesty in dealing with others, openness, promise-keeping, and competence (Robin 2005, 203–4), and by insisting that all other members of the organization honour these principles in word and deed.

Of course, no one, however altruistic and talented, can be a good steward of what he/she does not have. If good stewardship implies getting the job done, then resources adequate to the task, and adequate enough to facilitate accomplishing the task in a reasonably efficient manner, need to be provided. Before one can decide what would constitute adequate resources for a given educational sector or enterprise, however, one must have some clarity about his/her vision for it. Clear vision, after all, shapes the purposes, mandates, and expectations that one can legitimately ask of an organization and of those who work in it, as well as determining the scope of reasonable resource needs and limitations. It is for that reason that we return to the questions of mission and purpose in the next and final chapter.

As a former principal of the Peguis school noted with regard to grounding trust within what amounts to a moral context of servant leadership: 'If we care about others, our community and the future, then we will make a difference when we join together to practice respect, truth, honesty, wisdom, humility and bravery. Making education meaningful for everyone is our goal; we need the help of everyone to make this a success' (Bell 2004, 207–8). Servant leadership is about caring for students and then *doing something about it*, about putting student welfare first, not just in word but in deed. It inverts the political economy agenda and insists that leaders ask not what the organization can do for them, but what they can do for the children who are the raison d'être of the organization.

Before closing on a slightly more upbeat note, we want to acknowledge what has to be the darkest of all motives for which educational and political leaders might use their power to subvert and work against efficient, effective, and appropriate educational opportunities for the rising generation. It is a motive that surfaced in a First Nations context during the Hawthorne Committee exercise in the 1960s, although it is not a phenomenon or concept limited to that context. According to social utility theory, there can be a distinct social utility value to ignorance. By maintaining very low educational attainment among their progeny, the present-day officeholders and incumbents who themselves have minimal education can assure that better-educated youngsters will not be clamouring for *their* roles and jobs any time soon. Tragically, it is the surest way of ensuring that hierarchical encapsulation is maintained for the benefit of the dominant group while excluding all others from true and significant political participation in the governance of Aboriginal education. The Hawthorne Committee summarized the matter in these terms:

> The concept that youth will become educated is a difficult one for some elders to adjust to, also. Reserve leadership is tending to shift into the hands of the younger and partially educated men. Many councils have a secretary who has eighth grade and maybe some secretarial or commercial training. To the adult generation who are partially educated and whose only opportunity for status remains in their own community, better education of the young is a threat. There is some pressure exerted on adolescents to attend school for so many years but no more. The process reveals a social utility of ignorance whereby the current generation maintains its power by keeping the knowledge and educational levels of the youth at par with or not much beyond their own. This process does not work effectively in all areas and there are several reserves where social control is poor and where youth have little or no respect for Indian authorities and where chaos reigns. In such areas, adults tend to blame too much schooling for the lack of respect. (Hawthorn, Tremblay, and Bownick 1967, 119)

To be sure, this observation needs to be set within the context of its time and

should not, even if suitably adapted to contemporary reality, be applied reck-
lessly and stereotypically to all First Nations communities and organizations.
Some communities and some organizations, as we have seen, have
worked diligently and aggressively to further their educational agendas. They do so with what we would call caring, engaged servant leadership, and often in the face of major structural and resource challenges.

Yet the ghost of the corrosive 'apple' stereotype has by no means disappeared from the landscape of Aboriginal education and politics. A
generation ago it was common for older Aboriginal people to question
the worth of, or even denigrate the value of, formal education, which is
hardly surprising given the residential school legacy of excluding everything
Aboriginal from the 'official' vision of the educated person. Specifically, bilingualism and biculturalism in First Nations language and culture were
seen as inherently suspect, a sure sign of being 'red on the outside but
white on the inside,' hence, 'an apple,' a cultural and linguistic Kisling.

Of course, outside of Nunavut and certain very remote First Nations
communities, anything approaching unilingualism in an Aboriginal
language among children is probably non-existent in Canada today.
Given the ubiquitous accessibility of satellite television, most Aboriginal children grow up with a strong presence of Canada's official
languages in their lives. Being bilingual in an Aboriginal language no
longer automatically burdens an Aboriginal youth with the apple label. Unfortunately, the 'social utility of ignorance' problematic has not
disappeared. It is still the case, for instance, that in many areas of the
country, young Aboriginal people with minimal education, and especially young Aboriginal people who are what some linguists refer to
as semilingual, that is, unable to function well in any of two or more
languages (a much-disputed concept, however, it should be added),
constitute a distinctly less threatening potential competitor to incumbents of influential and lucrative Aboriginal leadership positions both
inside and outside education than do newly minted graduates of well-
respected post-secondary programs.

We wish to end this chapter by saluting those who have worked and
continue to work in Aboriginal education within a spirit of stewardship and servant leadership. Their altruism, caring, and diligence serve
as reassurance and inspiration and especially as a much-needed foil
and antidote to examples of venal opportunism, which continues to
silence and hamstring many committed players in Aboriginal education in their efforts to raise a generation of word warriors in the best
sense of Turner's meaning.

8 Vision and Purpose:
A Second *sine qua non*[1]

> The poet 'carries the fire,' making things and flesh grow warm, extends
> the reach of language (and hence of concept and rationality), steals fire
> from the gods, even – in the limit – seems to reconcile for that instant God
> and Man. House puts it more soberly: 'Such leaders are people who have
> a vision of the future, of society or an organization, and usually state that
> vision in ideological values ... They motivate people by appealing to uni-
> versal end values and call on people to go beyond the call of duty, to put
> their self interests aside.'
>
> C. Hodgkinson,
> *Administrative Philosophy* (1996), 216

Bjarne Stroustrup, inventor of the C++ programming language which
ushered in the era of object oriented programming, once remarked that
no technology can help if one lacks a clear idea of what it is one is
trying to do.[2] We wish to extend Stroustrup's dictum: no amount of
resources, planning, collaboration, consultation, effort, energy, time,
good intentions, caring, or anything else can help much in the absence
of a clear vision of what one is trying to do. Vision in an organization is
an amalgam of poetic fire burning towards a better future,[3] and practical sense of how things ought to occur as members of an organization
work together. It enables members to achieve the most important purposes of what the organization ought to be and do. Vision shapes and
drives a culture that binds organizational members together in pursuit
of a 'cause greater than oneself' (Glickman, Gordon, and Ross-Gordon
2004).

Of course, vision can be evil as well as good. As Margolis (2004) rightly warns, principles and the visions that frame them with moral authority can be dangerous.

> ... in general, a greater danger of producing deep, widespread suffering and destruction through social changes confidently pressed into service on grounds said to be Independent of our *Sitten* [social and historical context] than there is from conformity with whatever is historically entrenched in the *prima facie* way, almost without regard to its specific content. I am thinking of the crusades and recent uses of the *jihad*, the policies of Pol Pot and the Bosnian Serbs, and, supremely, Hitler's vision of greater Germany. I say, quite frankly: beware of men of principle! (16)

Still, without vision and the principles that flow from it, even if we only believe they are good enough for now, we have nothing to shape and give direction to human organizations. Vision, a coherent view of how things should and might be, is all that stands between us and purposelessness, between the moral agency of our humanity, and its abandonment. Vision alone makes it possible to pursue a cause greater than oneself.

However, given that Aboriginal societies include a large number of individuals who are distributed over territories of various sizes and divided into a plurality of groups that differ in ways that are highly significant for education, constructing a common vision and purpose for Aboriginal education will be particularly challenging. Vision and purpose will have to capture whatever relationships are possible under these conditions. They should lead to forms of political and educational association that enable Aboriginal communities to cultivate the rich diversity of their divergent social, cultural, and political forms of life. A common vision and purpose for Aboriginal education must articulate a concept of Indigeneity that is both sufficiently general to embrace a rich plurality of Aboriginal communities and sufficiently determinate to provide principles that most stakeholders can accept as defining a just, ethical, and broadly shared basis for cooperation among Aboriginal communities.

In constructing a vision and overarching purposes for a self-governed Aboriginal education system, and using these to generate political and governance principles, Aboriginal and non-Aboriginal policy-makers will inevitably invoke some conception of the person on the one hand and of Indigeneity on the other. These would be plausible shared images of the Aboriginal and non-Aboriginal selves who are going to be parties to the agreement. Such a vision should consist of a set of assumptions regarding human nature about desirable capacities, the nature and roles of communities, and appropriate ways of being, interacting, and making decisions. Using these assumptions, Aboriginal and non-Aboriginal parties signing the agreement must commit to principles of justice and ethics (especially the acceptance of certain moral constraints on the pursuit of their own interests). These principles must govern their interactions and decision-making processes. Central to any attempt to articulate a vision and purposes for Aboriginal education is a conception of human beings as agents, actors capable of shaping their own lives and directing their actions according to their own purposes. A common vision and purpose for Aboriginal education begins with a concept of human agency that encompasses a system of rights, responsibilities, and principles of justice. In turn, this system should define and pursue educational activities subject to decision-making mandated by Aboriginal communities. Nevertheless, the authority to make such decisions will necessarily be delegated upward to functional aggregate organizations in order to be effective. A clear vision and purpose for Aboriginal education can provide a powerful basis for defining the ways in which public power within Aboriginal communities and aggregate organizations should be organized, and the ends to which it should be directed.

Myopia: The Self-Serve Vision – Aboriginal/First Nations Education as Local Fiefdom and Cash Cow

In our discussion of ethics in the last chapter we spoke about the dangers of Aboriginal and First Nations education being viewed as a local source of income presided over by a local elite for the benefit of its members. We called this self-serve leadership, which is often a symptom of hierarchical encapsulation.

The kind of leadership with this peculiar myopia prefers to cling to the crumbs which have trickled down from a balkanized non-system that is rarely efficient, effective, or appropriate. It rejects the reality of diseconomies of scale, preferring instead to pursue the ICIE chimera of community-level control as a unique and unquestionable synonym for Indian control of Indian education.

This myopic leadership disregards the reality of local politics that has everything to do with dividing spoils and little to do with trying to work collectively towards developing educational, administrative, and

governance capacity that would help move Turner's vision of a generation of 'word warriors' closer to reality. The First Nations University of
Canada takeover offers a telling lesson in how a local spoils system can
attack, absorb, and destroy so much that is good and promising in vi-
sionary action just when it is about to take wing – and precisely because
it is on the verge of doing so. Without recognizing the overwhelming
evidence that First Nations education is (with a few happy exceptions
to the rule), a colossal failure, this self-serving leadership prefers to di-
vert whatever resources it can to local power elites. It turns a blind eye
to the fate of another generation of students caught in the grip of a
balkanized non-system devoid of systemic capacity to do the things
that are most needed. After all, the Auditor General can only attend to
this debacle occasionally – and the political economy of INAC lies in
preserving some version of its unaccountable neocolonial relationship
with First Nations organizations. One cannot avoid wondering to what
degree the 'social utility of ignorance' (see the discussion in the section
titled 'Ethical Governance and Leadership' in chapter 7) preserves this
sad chemistry of delusion, pretence, and self-interest.

An array of impressive health problems, some of which are already
nearing pandemic proportions, stand in the way of any quantum leap
forward in Aboriginal education. They range from social breakdown,
fetal alcohol syndrome, and drug abuse, to serious speech development problems resulting from Otitis media and other unknown causes.
High-quality, culturally appropriate education can't eliminate these
problems – although a sophisticated educational service infrastructure
in the hands of administrators committed to servant leadership might
help substantially with many of them. Consider, for example, the plight
of students with significant speech development problems in communities where a speech therapist has never been available. A small
community will never be able to justify employing a full-time speech
therapist; yet, in the current state of First Nations education, that is the
only way they are ever likely to see one.

A great many of these problems which interfere with education, particularly those grounded in fundamental social dysfunction, are related
to issues only Aboriginal people can address. As Steele (2006) insists
unrelentingly, to be human is to exercise moral agency – and no one else
can do that *for* any other person or group (120–1). Unless we are mentally incapable of doing so, we exercise that agency without fail. And
whether we wish to do so or not, that was the folly of value free education. Even abdicating moral agency is a quintessentially (im)moral

act. We exercise moral agency regardless of our historical and cultural context, although these may greatly influence how we do so.

The challenges in Aboriginal education are far too grave to be solved by each community or a haphazard amalgam of aggregate organizations whose client communities are free to not participate in anything the organization does that does not serve its particular interests. For all but the largest of First Nations communities, *dysfunction is inherent in the individual community focus of jurisdiction*. Indeed, even the largest of First Nations communities are substantially below optimally efficient school jurisdiction size (Baker 2005). Such inherently dysfunctional governance would not be tolerated in any other domain involving the public interest and trust, and historic 'white guilt' is not a good reason for allowing it to persist in Aboriginal education. It is also not a good reason for the Canadian government to allow it to persist through the negotiations of new relationships with First Nations, and it certainly is not a good reason for First Nations to continue allowing disconnected governance layers at the heart of current INAC policy to survive such negotiations.

It seems clear that four starting points are essential to any workable vision for effective, efficient, and appropriate Aboriginal education. First, Aboriginal education must be grounded deeply in Aboriginal culture, and in many circumstances that will also mean being solidly grounded in Aboriginal language. Second, meaningful Indian control of Indian education can only occur within layered, functional integration. Third, real acceptance of responsibility by First Nations aggregate educational organizations must occur – and these organizations must accept full responsibility. If Indian control of high-quality education is the overarching purpose, they will have no alternative. If they wish to emerge from the cocoon of colonial tutelage, they must shed the protective shell of fiduciary obligation. This can only be done if they are prepared to accept responsibility for governance and the decisions that flow from it in a spirit of servant-leadership, contributing within the limits of their means to support of *their* education, and adopting transparent, ethical, and accountable policy and financial frameworks along with reporting mechanisms. These mechanisms should ensure access to accountability information of all relevant kinds on the part of both First Nations members and the broader Canadian public.[4] Fourth, the vision must be firmly committed to rigorous standards – not to making excuses or assigning blame for their absence. Together, these four starting points constitute the basic foundation of the necessary boundaries around First Nations education. With them, a vision that will make it possible to raise a generation of word warriors becomes possible. Without them, such vision will never come into focus in any coherent way.

Le beau risque: Functional National Integration

On the heels of the 1980 Quebec sovereignty referendum failure, René Lévesque proposed a new strategy oriented towards trying to find some way of living with the rest of Canada, a policy which he called *le beau risque* – the beautiful risk. Since then, the term has been applied to other risky but promising steps outside of an existing policy box.

What we propose as an essential component of any plausible vision of efficient, effective, and appropriate education for First Nations students is a *beau risque*. We propose a high-risk policy wager to provide a resolution to seemingly irresolvable gridlock; a layered (local, area, regional, and national) *functional* national integration of First Nations education – articulated to take account of significant differences in the situation of Quebec First Nations – but nonetheless an authentically pan-Canadian functional integration.

We are under no illusion that such an organization can be constructed overnight, especially given the long history of neglect of institutional and personal capacity development that has characterized First Nations education in Canada. Nonetheless, given the diseconomies of scale associated with all aspects of Aboriginal education, and the likelihood that resource gatekeepers in government and the judiciary are unlikely to continue 'sending good money after bad' into First Nations education in the absence of significant improvement in the results, we cannot see any potentially viable alternative.

Of course, grand-scale aggregation can lead to grand-scale goal displacement, and political economy forces running wild. Still, it is hard to imagine goal displacement more pervasive and destructive than that which has characterized most of Aboriginal education since its inception. This includes the time that has elapsed since the mid-1980s efforts to define what section 35 of the patriated Constitution actually entrenches, efforts which prompted one of us to undertake his first critical examination of Aboriginal education policy in Canada over two decades ago.

Functional integration of First Nations education is simply the last best chance of replacing a dysfunctional radically balkanized non-system with something at last resembling authentic Indian control of Indian education. We readily acknowledge, however, that only four things stand between this vision of functionally integrated Indian education and chaos:

1. unflinching commitment to and enforcement of a strong code of ethics and high standards of transparency;
2. commitment to the kind of excellence captured in Turner's 'word warrior' image;
3. major investment in both institutional and personal capacity development; and
4. some version of institutional accountability along the lines of 'management by results.'

Taken together, these requirements constitute a substantial but also distinctly beautiful risk. They also offer an opportunity, one last chance to make things significantly better for Aboriginal learners and, in the process, break the stranglehold that local mini-cartels have on large parts of First Nations education. The vision we propose here provides a desperately needed opportunity to separate once and for all from the current regime of neocolonial dependency and tutelage incarnated by INAC and its policies. This vision offers First Nations an opportunity to accept responsibility, reject permanent fiduciary-victim status and the impotent recriminations that go with it, in order to lay the foundation of a genuinely new relationship with settler governments in education. In the process, it offers an opportunity to lay the foundation of mutual respect and trust for authentically renewed relationships in other areas of governance. Of course such relationship renewal will be impossible without just, reasonable, and expeditious resolution of outstanding land claims. No other solution, however, provides a plausible path out of the entrenched gridlock – along with the penury and local determinism that cements it in place and marginalizes wide portions of Aboriginal communities. Within the current power structure, these segments of Aboriginal communities find themselves unable to articulate their needs, much less respond effectively to them. Such a political process geared towards transformation of the current power structure in Aboriginal education needs to avoid 'false consensus' around any vision by ensuring that individual Aboriginal people develop and exercise capacities for agency. These capacities are essential if someone is to consent meaningfully to educational purpose, vision, and arrangements. Finally, to the degree that this vision becomes reality, the resulting authentic First Nations education system would provide a powerful nucleus, resource, and point of reference for other forms of Aboriginal education as well.

A Plausible Vision

What are the essential elements of a plausible vision of efficient, effective, and appropriate Aboriginal and First Nations education? We have already listed the essential ingredients:

1. deep, organic grounding in Aboriginal culture and language
2. layered, functional integration
3. real acceptance of responsibility, and
4. strong commitment to rigorous standards of excellence

Long-standing resignation and dismay in the face of the parity paradox must give way to a sense of intellectual and spiritual excitement at what this new hybrid educational form can become, and what it can do for Aboriginal students – *as well as for all of Canadian society*. Aboriginal education could be so vital, excellent, and intellectually exciting that some non-Aboriginal parents and students would seek it out.

For this to happen, adequate and appropriate resources must be available, and ownership and responsibility must rest authentically in the hands of Aboriginal peoples – which will never occur so long as the present non-system persists. The central INAC policy dictating (an official myth of) exact equivalence with provincial schools must end. No longer should the lynchpin of First Nations education policy be a hypocritical requirement that students must be able to transfer to provincial schools 'at any time without penalty.' This policy explicitly prevents education imbued with Aboriginal cultures and languages.

None of this should be taken to suggest that the ability to read, write, and speak at least one official language as well as peers in provincial public systems, along with performing as well in math, science, and other subjects that form the canon of provincial school curricula is somehow less important for Aboriginal learners. Ever conscious of 'Kymlicka's constraint,' Turner's word warriors are able to meet the power-brokers of mainstream Canadian society on their own intellectual and philosophical turf. They can hardly do that unless they come from an educational experience that equips them accordingly.

The shallow exact equivalency rationale behind the central INAC policy on education is predicated on nothing less than what one of us long

ago labelled the remediation policy response to poor school performance by minorities (Paquette 1989b). It is an assimilationist policy with
a starting point completely at odds with the image that Turner assigns
to his word warriors. Exact equivalency policy begins with the assumption that Aboriginal culture and language have no place in the image
of an educated person in Canada. All that really counts in this system
is what provincial and territorial governments (and *their* constituents)
decide counts. Aboriginal culture and language is little more than an
ornament graciously tolerated on the mantle of 'real education.'

Cardinal and his colleagues, as we have noted earlier, called for a
view of Aboriginal peoples as 'citizens plus' (Indian Chiefs of Alberta
1970). We call for a vision of Aboriginal education as 'education plus,'
not, as it is currently viewed, as 'education minus.' To fashion a generation of word warriors, Aboriginal education cannot be satisfied with
mere equality. The only way to rise above the parity paradox is to do
more than provincial schools do. That is the inescapable challenge of
moving beyond the parity paradox. There is no magic alchemy to provide an easy way to meet this challenge successfully. To paraphrase
Churchill's words, all we have to offer is the 'blood, sweat, and tears' to
develop the leadership, governance, and pedagogical capacity to rein-
vent First Nations education as 'education plus.'

Resources, especially financial ones are vital to this process, but they
alone are not enough. Without commitment, high ethical standards,
and functional integration, more resources will simply translate into
more waste, recriminations, and disillusionment. Furthermore, one
cannot escape from the question of *whose* resources are at stake. The
status quo crosses lines of accountability in a way that assures complete
lack of responsibility. Questions of historical injustice and appropriate
reparations for them matter, and we do not mean to diminish their
importance. Nonetheless, no amount of policy fiction can substitute a
surrogate sense of ownership for indisputable knowledge that outside
revenues support a school almost entirely. So long as Aboriginal peoples
have a justified sense that financial resources for their education comes
almost entirely from settlers and settler governments, it will not be *their*
education. To cling to fiduciary obligation means eternal dependency
and irresponsibility, along with a willing abdication of agency.

That is why twenty years ago, one of us insisted upon own-source
revenues as an important part of educational resources (Paquette 1986).
It is also why some of the most successful Aboriginal schools are those
whose communities have embraced the principle of using own-source

revenues.[5] All First Nations communities should, *within the limits of their capacity to pay*, tax themselves to support their education. Obviously, equalization mechanisms need to be in place to ensure that those who cannot provide much in the way of local support still have high-quality schools and education. Aggregation is one important equalization strategy, as provinces have recognized historically and in recent years. The bottom line, however, is that without self-taxation, a sense of ownership is almost impossible to fabricate and as a result, no meaningful accountability to First Nations constituents is possible.

Education within Relational Pluralist Assumptions

Our vision of what First Nations education ought to be flows from our conceptual framework. We would characterize this as distinctively Aboriginal education to encourage prosperous coexistence and respectful, mutual interdependence with mainstream Canadian society. This interdependence must develop within an evolving Aboriginal identity protected by appropriate boundaries.

To succeed, such education must engage students. It must convince them that an interesting and inviting intellectual future is possible for them, because of, not in spite of, their Aboriginal heritage and culture. Such a perspective rejects all stereotypes of Aboriginal intellectual inferiority, including those Aboriginal leaders and peoples have adopted to excuse Aboriginal learners from responsibility for their own learning. In short, such Aboriginal 'education plus' starts with the proposition that being intellectually deep *is* a legitimate and culturally faithful way of being Aboriginal.

Word warrior education (from this point forward, we will adopt Turner's epigram as shorthand for our overall vision, although we obviously intend a rich and balanced program of studies not limited to language development, politics, and philosophy) must engage students with the excitement and promise of redefining Aboriginal relationships with settler governments within a context of mutual interdependence, trust, and respect. The possibility of truly rich and engaging programs of study melding Aboriginal history and mainstream Canadian history and exploring evolving relationships with settler governments exists – but only in the context of functional integration, which would allow adequate resources to be focused on developing and implementing such programs.

Figure 2.2 shows that, within the Bertrand and Valois analytic framework, the social paradigm base of our vision of an effective, efficient, appropriate and engaging education is an amalgam of symbiosynergy, some aspects of an existential person-centred context, and sufficient grounding in an industrial context to allow students to be fully functional within the assumptions and lived realities of mainstream Canada. What might this amalgam represent when taken with the corresponding educational paradigm amalgam and applied to Aboriginal education?

First, the predominance of an inventive paradigm educational program reflects the presence and pervasiveness of Aboriginal culture in overall curriculum and pedagogy. As a preponderantly Aboriginal education, word warrior education would nurture a commitment to symbiosynergy and hence oneness with others, the world, and the universe. It would foster and valorize precisely the kind of respectful relations with mainstream Canadian society that offer the best way forward in a creative interdependence. By emphasizing mutual interest, along with the complementary differences between Aboriginal peoples and mainstream Canadians – and among Aboriginal peoples themselves – it will engender lifelong commitment to cohesive diversity. In terms of direct resonances with historic Aboriginal culture, it would invite students to seek meaning in relationships with nature, the Creator, and others, to embark on an intellectual and spiritual journey not unlike a traditional dream quest.

Second, some judicious and limited borrowing from the existential, person-centred paradigm and its corresponding child-centred educational paradigm would probably help accommodate learning styles congruent with the three-L learning style (looking, learning, and listening, widely attributed to Aboriginal children; see Miller 1996, 16). While considerable individualization, particularly in pedagogy, may be appropriate in response to this pervasive approach to learning in traditional Aboriginal cultures, neither the sense of oneness with others and with the universe characteristics of the symbiosynergetic paradigm nor the ability to participate and work competently and creatively in late-industrial post-industrial Canada should be sacrificed to it. Finally, we cannot avoid cautioning against stereotyping Aboriginal learning styles. While many Aboriginal students may be more comfortable with relatively lengthy observation and explanation prior to trying a new capacity or skill, *assuming that there is a unique Aboriginal way of learning would be as disastrous as assuming that there is a unique black way of learning* (see, for example, Steele 2006, 119).

One of us recalls an experience during the early 1980s in which a young Aboriginal education consultant declared knowingly that Aboriginal people were right-brain people and furthermore, that schools were all about language, which encompasses left-brain activities. Therefore, he concluded, Aboriginal students could never be expected to do well in schools since there was a basic mismatch between their brains and the central focus of schooling. With one sweep of this broad stereotyping brush, he absolved Aboriginal students, parents, and educational leaders from any responsibility for academic failure of Aboriginal students.

To put this in context, one needs to remember that the young consultant involved came from a community in which his ancestral language was all but dead. Through no fault of his own, he had had no direct, substantive experience with that language. This stereotype struck the author as paradoxically odd. He had spent a decade immersed in the same culture and language, spoke the language fluently, and had had the privilege of listening to the delight with which older, traditional people used and played with all the riches of their language. They were people whose identity was deeply wrapped up in their language and its use. They were human, and language was at the centre of their beings. Stereotypes such as this one absolve Aboriginal learners from responsibility for their learning and ultimately refuse them the humanity we all share as languaging beings. That is why borrowing from radical individualism and child-centred assumptions and practices must be limited and judicious.

Finally – and crucially as Turner recognizes – word warrior education requires functional competence within the assumptions, knowledge, and skills characteristic of late-industrial or post-industrial Canadian society. To be taken seriously as brokers of new relationships with non-Aboriginal Canadians, word warriors must ultimately be able to meet them on their own terms and do so with confidence, justified by deep knowledge of their culture, politics, philosophy, and science as well as those of non-Aboriginals. That is the inexorable consequence of 'Kymlicka's constraint.'

What this means in practical terms is that the distribution of mainstream knowledge and skills within the Aboriginal population should resemble that of mainstream Canadians. This is *not* the same thing as saying that Aboriginal education should be a clone of mainstream provincial education, essentially the position of current INAC policy on First Nations education in Canada. Rather it means that, at the end of the day, word warrior education should produce roughly the same proportional distribution of knowledge and skills as provincial education – the same number of graduates in the sciences, humanities, and trades – with about the same distribution of programs, courses, marks, and achievement. More formally, the relative representation of Aboriginal students in relation to non-Aboriginal students in the whole range of academic and trade-oriented programs of learning should approach unity. Aboriginal students should not be significantly underrepresented among students scoring at the grade A level in any course or program, due allowance being made for those of particular interest to Aboriginal students. There is no room in word warrior education for ghettos of Aboriginal failure in either the academic or trade world, and certainly no room for complacent acceptance of them either by Aboriginal educational leaders or by mainstream society.

Aboriginal education needs to be grounded in balanced pluralism – but especially in the tenets and processes of relational pluralism, and most particularly in respectful mutual interdependence. It also means Aboriginal education should *not* be grounded in a pluralism managed through hierarchical encapsulation in which one group excludes all others from genuine political participation (Moon 1993). Schouls insists that all three dimensions of pluralism are important for establishing a foundation for the mutually attractive renewal of relationships between Aboriginal peoples and settler governments. At the same time, he insists that the dominant view of pluralism in such renewal must be relational rather than either individual identity-based or cultural difference-based views. We agree that all three versions of pluralism have legitimate and necessary places in Aboriginal education but relational pluralism must be its socio-political theory centrepiece.

Aboriginal education needs to balance the reality that students and their families draw important elements of their personal identity from their group history and culture, with their right to fashion identities that are not mere products of a monolithic and immutable historic culture. They need to be able to incorporate significant elements of divergent, personally chosen culture and identity. The need for such a balance has enormous implications for how Aboriginal and non-Aboriginal culture and history at all levels are constructed in the classroom. Above all, such balance recognizes the importance of culture and history but defies stereotypes and essentialisms of all sorts, avoiding anything that suggests that some Indians are 'more Indian' than others.

Of equal significance to establishing a shared culture of respectful interdependence is what both the formal and the hidden curriculum in Aboriginal schools (and those with significant Aboriginal enrolment that may not be under Aboriginal jurisdiction) teach about the meaning of culture in evolving relationships with significant others – especially settler governments and other Aboriginal groups. Figure 2.3 is a representation of Schouls' overall relational pluralist gestalt. Having already discussed this social theory in chapter 2, we turn here to its implications for education. We believe the Schouls framework leads to three key implications for education.

First, shared group history and cultural roots lead to one personal identity component that is shaped from historic cultural differences. While it is important that education recognize and honour such cultural differences, it is equally important that they are not transformed into a dysfunctional myth of absolute difference (i.e., 'we are so different that compromise and fruitful cooperation with "others" is impossible'). Difference must not become an obsession or an end in itself. Although the rationale of current jurisprudence seems to be moving towards historic difference as the only thing that matters legally, Aboriginal education must not fall into the trap of deification of cultural difference. If for no other reason (and there are several other good reasons), it should avoid that trap because, pushed too far, the logic of historic cultural difference strips Aboriginal groups more heavily acculturated than others into the majority culture of any potential rights claims associated with their Aboriginal identity.

Culture cannot be an insular difference – hermetically sealed off in time. As Schouls insists self-determination only has meaning if there is something to determine, so schools need to approach culture as inherently malleable and welcome that flexibility intelligently. This inevitable result from sharing the country and the world with cultural others has two important consequences for education, in addition to the requirement that schools approach culture as something inherently malleable over time. First, an important component of group cultural identity is free adhesion by individuals to the group along with acceptance of elements of the group identity as integral components of their personal identity. Educational programs and Aboriginal schools need to avoid treating local Aboriginal identity as if it were something to which all students are bound to an equal degree and in an identical way by some sort of irresistible, deterministic fate. While survival of the group requires that many students ultimately *choose* to identify in significant ways with the evolving group identity, education should never present the personal identification choice as binary – that either you are fully a member of the group and membership constitutes the essence of your personal identity, or else you are not really a member. On the contrary, education needs to recognize that different students will choose to draw into their personal identities different components and degrees of the evolving group identity and, furthermore, that their adoption of components of the group identity will likely change over time.

Ultimately, we are calling for maximum feasible control over social and cultural reproduction – and evolution – by Aboriginal communities, community members, and collectives, and for education that serves this quintessential expression of human agency. Paradoxically, such control can only be meaningful when it is shared across Aboriginal communities and groups that differ significantly in their social and cultural form and commitments. Diseconomies of scale render this paradox inescapable.

Historically, interpretation of and communication about Aboriginal cultures has been dominated by non-Aboriginals. To a disturbing degree, that is still the case. Indeed, even in our own time discourses about Aboriginal culture tend to marginalize Aboriginal voices and perspectives, and are largely dominated by non-Aboriginals, although the situation is not as dire as it was two decades ago. To pass control of such discourses definitively to Aboriginal word warriors requires broad cooperation, functional aggregation, and integration of authentically Aboriginal education systems. Reclaiming control over interpretation, understanding, and communication of Aboriginal cultures necessitates such broad cooperation and integration across lines of social and cultural differences. That is the inescapable governance challenge in First Nations education.

In a similar vein, Aboriginal education needs to reinforce the importance of balance between reasonable boundaries necessary to protect reasonable types and degrees of Aboriginal self-determination on the one hand, and nurturing fruitful interdependence with the rest of mainstream Canadian society on the other (the construction is deliberate – we take Aboriginal groups to be an important part of, not hopelessly different and separate from mainstream Canadian society). Highlighting the importance of interdependence does not mean distorting historical fact. Aboriginal students have a right to their history told from their perspective. Nevertheless, they also need to understand what that history looks like when viewed from a contemporary non-Aboriginal perspective. Only in this way can they develop the capacity to become word warriors, boundary persons capable on the one hand of meeting the power brokers of the rest of mainstream Canadian society 'on their own conceptual and intellectual turf,' while on the other hand bringing to the process what is distinctive and important in Aboriginal history, culture, philosophy, and politics.

The kinds of boundaries that Aboriginal education should encourage over the long term are more like membranes than walls. Suitably porous to allow creative and fruitful interaction of all types with mainstream society, these membranes must also provide sufficient protection for evolving Aboriginal group identities – but never at the cost of imposing these identities entirely on individuals. That is precisely the image of a proper relationship between Aboriginal Canadians and other Canadians that education should instill in the minds and hearts of young students from both cultures. Figure 2.3 indicates with its large arrows substantial interaction with mainstream society on the one hand, and reciprocal interaction between evolving individual identities and group identities on the other hand, but with a palpable (membrane-like) boundary around evolving Aboriginal personal and group identities. Education should encourage such a view of the place of Aboriginal persons in the evolving matrix of cultural and political relationships within Canada. In no way should this be taken to suggest that we view Aboriginal peoples as 'a minority like all the others.' It simply indicates that any possible future for Aboriginal peoples and other Canadians must be founded on interdependence, not on conflict, recriminations, and separatism. It is for that better future that Aboriginal and non-Aboriginal education must prepare the students of today and tomorrow.

Figure 2.4 distils the essence of what we understand as Turner's overarching political rights theory base, at least the concentrated essence of what matters for education. Like Schouls, Turner concludes that a balance between individual and Aboriginal group rights is needed, some adjustment between the individual rights paradigm of conventional liberalism, and recognition that Aboriginal *peoples* have rights by virtue of their first occupancy of this continent, and that those rights are group rights. At the same time, Turner recognizes the compelling force for the foreseeable future of 'Kymlicka's constraint.' The power brokers (legislators, judges, financiers, leaders of business and commerce, among others) with whom Aboriginal peoples must *relate* in order to realize a reasonable degree of self-determination are and will remain for the foreseeable future products of mainstream Euro-Canadian culture.

The central importance of Turner's insight for education is this: only word warriors capable of meeting mainstream power brokers on their own turf, who can make Aboriginal cultural values, historical perspectives, philosophy, and politics comprehensible to them, will have any chance of succeeding in redesigning relationships between Aboriginal peoples and settler governments. Aboriginal education must produce such word warriors – and to do so, only an education-plus view of its mission will suffice.

Parity – Not Exact Equivalence

An affirmative action approach that substitutes excuses for excellence will not suffice here. By definition, word warriors are strong in two cultural and intellectual heritages, not strong in one and weak in the other, and certainly not weak in both. The starting point of such education has to be intellectual excitement at an early age about the possibilities that new relationships between Aboriginal peoples and settler governments offer all Canadians. This necessarily implies a strong and vibrant social studies program that engages most students at an early age in critical contemplation of differences and similarities among Aboriginal and non-Aboriginal traditions, and of future possibilities for balancing reasonable Aboriginal self-determination with creative interdependence. Of course, such social studies programs will never be created with resources currently available to individual community-level schools.

We reject the principle of exact program equivalency with provincial school systems. The way to parity is decidedly *not* through exact equivalency. In fact, there is probably no better way to ensure the status quo of sub-mediocre education for most First Nations students than to perpetuate the INAC goal of exact program equivalence at all levels. That being said, we do not believe that Aboriginal education can simply go its own way. Provincial curricula will continue – and ought to continue – to have persuasive force in shaping Aboriginal curricula.

An education-plus view of Aboriginal education cannot accept that Aboriginal students ought to be less competent in math, science, language arts, and in all else that matters in the larger world of Canadian education. Or, worse yet, that they have no choice in the matter due to genetic deficiencies – an inherently racist perspective – or because 'real Indian' students just don't engage with mainstream curricula. These views effectively sell Aboriginal students 'down the river' of disconnectedness, irrelevance, and alienation from everything that constitutes mainstream Canadian society – whether through collective indifference, or the intergenerational malevolence of the 'social utility of ignorance' (see discussion in chapter 7, 'Ethical Governance and Leadership'). Worse than useless, it breeds despair just where it ought to build bridges, confidence, and mutual understanding. Of course, weaving a fabric of creative interdependence also requires that mainstream education do a much better job than it currently does of connecting with Aboriginal culture, history, philosophy, and politics.

Nonetheless, our main reason for rejecting the INAC lynchpin policy of exact equivalence is that any education-plus program in Aboriginal education can only be constructed by Aboriginal people. Although such a program will inevitably have huge overlap and resonances with mainstream education – in fact, have parity with it – it will also be distinctively different. If it is not so in ways potentially creative and fruitful in raising a generation of word warriors, it is difficult to justify its existence outside the purview of conventional provincial education (not that we are under any illusion that provinces are eager to assimilate First Nations schools into their systems).

Such programs, of course, will never be created so long as Aboriginal education remains balkanized into tiny community-level units and aggregates in which communities participate only on a voluntary basis and only on the terms and conditions that they choose. Such fragmented governance is a recipe for ongoing educational disaster. More efficient, effective, and appropriate Aboriginal education will not be identical to provincial education in the way dictated by current INAC policy, but it will provide parity in core subject matter.

One More Time – How Important Is Language and How Important Are Schools to Its Survival?

No language can survive as a living language only in schools. But in the contemporary world, no language can long survive without them or in spite of them either. It is for this reason that language of instruction has been such a touchstone issue in Canadian education, particularly since section 23 of the *Charter of Rights and Freedoms* entrenched certain rights of official language minorities in the Canadian Constitution.

Perhaps the most difficult decision confronting Aboriginal educational leaders revolves around language, and the place Aboriginal languages should occupy in an educational program. Obviously, the place that they 'should' occupy has been shaped by INAC insistence on exact equivalency, by a chronic shortage of resources to develop and implement meaningful Aboriginal-language programs, and by the limiting effect of diseconomies of scale across highly fragmented school non-systems.

It would be wishful thinking for us to provide a single rule of thumb for the place of Aboriginal languages in the varied circumstances in which Aboriginal communities, areas, and regions find themselves. The one relevant characteristic which we believe is shared across First Nations generally, is a profound under-development of capacity in the area of ancestral language teaching, be it in the context of language preservation or language restoration. Again, this is hardly surprising; it could scarcely be otherwise given the extremely fragmented nature of First Nations education across Canada.

Although we are not in a position to provide broad recommendations with regard to ancestral language programs, we do believe that Aboriginal education entities that neglect them or provide only nominal programs in them run a grave risk of never being able to fulfil their primary purpose of nurturing future generations of word warriors. We take this position for two reasons. First, it is well known that culture is deeply embedded in language. There is something dangerously artificial about trying to preserve the 'distilled essence' of a culture, however minimalist and rapidly evolving it may be, in the absence of the language that once framed it. In a similar vein, an essential part of the word warrior formula is deep knowledge of one's most important cultural values and traditions. It is hard to imagine such deep knowledge in the absence of functional fluency in one's ancestral language. Second, we believe that it may be very difficult to generate vibrant intellectual excitement on the part of Aboriginal students in the absence of strong competency in their ancestral language. A large part of what must be repaired in Aboriginal education is precisely that Aboriginal cultures – and hence languages – can be a legitimate and integral part of an educated, indeed erudite person.

These considerations lead us back to the three policy propositions for language that we offered in chapter 6 (in the section 'Enduring Problems'). These propositions are not a silver bullet that can easily transform weak ancestral language programs into vibrant ones. The disappearance of the INAC exact equivalency requirement and creation of functionally integrated aggregates at multiple levels in First Nations education will not make difficult problems such as language, dialect, and orthographic diversity along with the scarcity of both human and material resources for such programs vanish overnight. What they can do is to concentrate program development resources into viable critical masses, favour ongoing relevant capacity development and institutional learning, and provide a base for authentic Aboriginal strategic planning in the area of language and culture education.

Results-Based Management for Aboriginal Education: 'By Their Fruits You Shall Know Them'

> The Government direction and policy is to provide members of Parliament and the public with relevant, accurate, consolidated, and timely information on how tax dollars are being spent and what Canadians receive as a result. The Government of Canada is committed not only to measuring and reporting on results, but also to establishing clear standards against which actual performance will be reported.
>
> Treasury Board Secretariat, *Guide for the Development of Results-Based Management and Accountability Framework* (2001), 2

Vision is not enough. Careful, strategic planning is not enough. Not even meticulous attention to implementation and change will suffice. In the end, results are what matter, for only in their light can one assess efficiency, effectiveness, and appropriateness. Of course, evaluation is anything but an exact science in human institutions. Given the notoriously inexact technology of teaching and learning, moreover, evaluation in education is fraught with difficulty and controversy. Nonetheless, electors of provincial governments, like their counterparts throughout the Western world, have become more and more impatient over the last two decades with school systems that are unable to demonstrate efficiency and effectiveness in terms of measurable *results*. It also seems clear enough that in this era of an increasingly pervasive results-based management ethos in government, First Nations education cannot long survive in the absence of results-based accountability. Unless we are very much mistaken, the status quo in First Nations education and governance will not be sustainable in the face of many more Auditor General reports decrying complete lack of accountability in this sensitive policy domain.

Implicit in servant-based leadership is a requirement that results in the sense of outcomes in the lives of students and impacts on their communities and society in general should be at the centre of governance and administration. This is hardly a new idea. It has been around in the policy literature since at least the 1960s. In its most rudimentary form, it appears as what is now called the classical-rational model of policy-making. All such models have been subjected to sharp and damaging criticism over the last fifteen years. The most extreme criticism holds that all public policy is, at best, a chaos theory game in which the rules change as one plays and the very best one can hope for from policy is some degree of influence on an evolving problem set (Geller and Johnston 1990). Despite such extreme pessimism about the possibility of rational policy-making in general, and of linking results to policy inputs and outputs in particular, and despite broad recognition of the validity of many of these criticisms (see, for instance Pal 2001, 21), we haven't much choice as reasoning persons who wish to use public policy to change things we regard as unacceptable in society. We must try to find ways of making such connections, however tenuous, evolving, and context-specific they may prove to be. Abandonment of rationality – of the possibility of linking policy and resources that support it to outputs and impacts – empties both policy analysis and evaluation of just about everything of interest to policy-makers, leaving them with little more to offer than 'deconstruction of language and arguments' (Pal 1997, 22). From a policy perspective, such abandonment would be tantamount to hanging an 'abandon hope all ye who enter here' sign over public policy in general. It is one thing to be very cautious and sceptical about large-scale social engineering policy projects, or to insist that there is much that is not rational in policy-making; it is quite another to abandon policy completely as an instrument of intervention in public problem sets about which there is broad agreement within society. Surely the lamentable state of Aboriginal education qualifies as one such widely agreed-upon problem set.

We believe that a strategic, iterative, results-based management (RBM) approach offers the most promising method to connect resource inputs to achieving Aboriginal education plus and the desirable impact of a creative, fruitful interdependence between Aboriginal and the rest of mainstream Canadian society. This interdependence would be bound up in renewed relationships that offer appropriate, but by the same token, appropriately permeable boundaries for Aboriginal self-determination. At the same time, we are acutely aware of the imposing capacity development implications of what we are recommending, and of the inevitable time implications of that capacity development need. What we propose must ultimately be a process rather than a prefabri-

Figure 8.1 Basic results chain

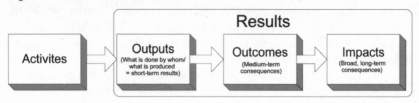

cated solution – however strongly we believe that movement towards responsibility, accountability, and transparency within an education plus vision of the policy endgame is desperately needed in First Nations education.

The central concept in any RBM model is the results chain. Figure 8.1 illustrates such a chain in simplest terms. The key point is that one begins at the end of the chain with the ultimate long-term impact one hopes to achieve. These desired impacts will need to be re-evaluated repeatedly and may change significantly over the course of any policy lifespan. Such broad, long-term results provide a working target; they are the raison d'être for everything else in the results chain. One starts at the end and maps back to what might plausibly contribute to desired impacts, just as a traveller first decides where she is going and then how she might get there.

Outputs are what happen in the short term as a result of policy activities associated with a results chain. They are short-term results, if you will. Outputs consist mainly of the actions of various policy and organizational actors and any products they produce. Essentially, outputs consist of what is done by whom – and to or with whom – and what is produced by activities directly associated with the results chain. Outcomes are medium-term consequences of the activities and outputs associated with the results chain. Impacts are long-term global results associated with the vision that motivated and shaped the policy in the first place. Impacts are intended to solve or ameliorate problem sets that give birth to a vision of a state of affairs better than the status quo. These problem sets represent a gap between what is and what ought to be in the view of the policy-makers who craft a tentative, working results chain.

Activities associated with obtaining results inevitably require resources first to mount them and then to sustain them. Resources generally come in four forms, as illustrated in figure 8.2: human – particularly knowledge and skills – financial, material, and political. Any proposed

Figure 8.2 Basic results chain with resources

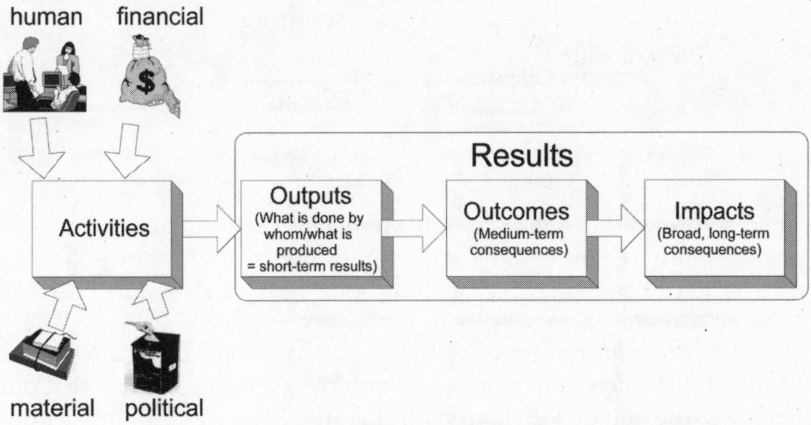

policy resource chain will absorb resources that might have been used for other purposes, either public or private. Every public policy has an opportunity cost associated with it – other activities, investments, or expenditures that must be foregone to support the activities associated with that policy's results chain. Political resources are therefore every bit as important as the other three types. Indeed, in public policy they are the ultimate source of the other three. Thus, Hall, Land, Parker, and Webb (1975) rightly insist that no policy can succeed unless it can

- be seen as feasible (i.e., implementable in a reasonable time and at a reasonable cost) by all those whose cooperation and support is essential to its realization;
- be broadly perceived as legitimate; and
- be seen as politically supportable by key constituencies of decision-makers involved. (475–86)

That insight seems pertinent in the context of Aboriginal education with its disconnected layers of governance. It also resonates strongly with Turner's idea of the unavoidability of 'Kymlicka's constraint.'

Any real-world results chain involves multiple activities with numerous outputs, an array of outcomes, some unplanned and unforeseen, and impacts which may not be those intended in the first place. Figure 8.3 hints at some of the complexity and uncertainty involved in pursuing a results chain. Some activities contribute to more than one

Figure 8.3 Complexity and risk in real-world results chains

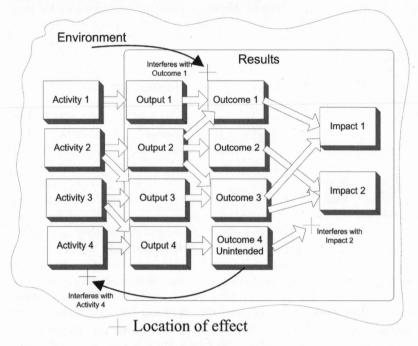

output. Activity 3 contributes to both output 3 and output 4. Output 4, however, is leading to an unintended outcome (outcome 4), which is actually interfering with desired impact 2. Outcome 4 is also changing the way activity 4 is being carried out. Finally, events are occurring in the environment that are actively interfering with outcome 1. This is a very limited portrayal of the real complexity involved in trying to apply the results chain logic to policy implementation. Reality is infinitely more complicated than any model, and the game does change during play.

Beyond sheer complexity, such a model raises questions that should drive policy-making firmly in the direction of an RBM model of accountability. What basic conditions and opportunities do RBM-model reforms require if they are to arrive at real accountability in Aboriginal education? To what extent do Aboriginal students currently have access to these resources and conditions? How does the distribution of these basic educational tools interweave with students' current educational needs to nurture the qualities of word warriors – or not? To what extent do aggregated self-governed Aboriginal educational institutions' policies ensure that all Aboriginal students have adequate and equitable opportunities to learn what an RBM educational system demands of them? What kinds of data are available to answer these questions; to whom are data available, and what data are lacking? In short, movement towards authentic Indian control of Indian education through an RBM model requires that the model not be denatured into yet another limited (hierarchically encapsulated) approach to educational accountability that leaves aggregated forms of Aboriginal governance of education unable to prevent, discover, and correct inadequacies in and inequalities among their schools.

Ultimately, the ability of a results chain to achieve planned outcomes and desired impacts depends on three things: the degree to which assumptions behind the result chain model prove useful over the short, medium, and long term, the degree to which appropriate and useful data are collected and used for 'in-course corrections' during the lifetime of the results chain policy, and unforeseen changes outside and inside policy activities and their multiple results chains. That's a lot of uncertainty and risk. Figure 8.4 shows that the risk is cumulative, in the sense that the further one moves along the results chain from starting assumptions towards eventual impacts, the greater the risk of encountering faulty assumptions – or assumptions that once were valid but no longer are. That is why it is vital to collect, collate, analyse, and use interim data to adjust all aspects of the results chain repeatedly over time. Figure 8.5 captures the general sense of this continuous, multilayered, data-informed course correction dynamic. Data relevant to outputs, outcomes, and impacts need to feed back on a regular basis into overall program or policy management strategic planning. Adjustments are made accordingly in outputs provided, with a view towards modifying outcomes appropriately and, to the extent necessary, even targeted impacts themselves.

None of this should be taken to condone vagueness and uncertainty in any aspect of the initial planning of the results chain. It is simply to acknowledge that there are serious risks in a policy results chain, and that the only way to exercise some control over them is to take careful account of them repeatedly over time. The less clear one is about the desired impacts that justify a results chain and provide direction to it through backward mapping, the greater the chance of confusion, conflict, and failure.

Figure 8.4 Risk in results chain logic

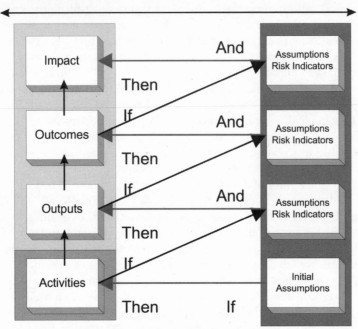

Source: Canadian International Development Agency (2006), fig. 6.

Most stage theories of policy implementation or change began with awareness and initial buy-in by key stakeholders. Figure 8.6 translates this difficult but necessary initial step into RBM language and imagery. Figure 8.6 admittedly conceals far more than it reveals. First, it fails to address the fundamental question of what might move First Nations educational leaders who are reasonably satisfied with the political economy payoffs of the status quo to participate in such a process, much less buy into the existence of a pressing need for change in First Nations education – especially change that would permanently alter responsibility and accountability in it. The response is nothing, at least in the current context. It is far easier and more comfortable simply to blame the federal government and inadequate funding for shortcomings in First Nations education.

Barring an unlikely collective crisis of conscience on the part of such leaders, only robust insistence by the federal government on account-

Figure 8.5 Iterative use of performance information

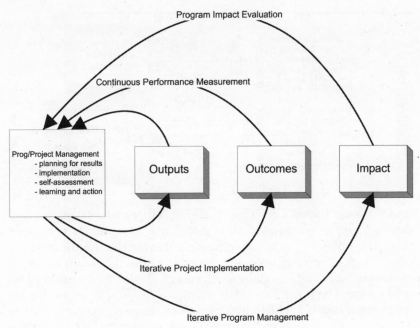

Source: Canadian International Development Agency (2006), fig. 9.

ability in the sense intended by the Auditor General in her critical reports on First Nations education (see discussion in chapter 3, 'Devolution Debacle'), that is, in the sense of program value added for dollars spent in student learning would provoke a shared sense of crisis sufficient to trigger this type of fundamental rethinking of the basic parameters within which First Nations education currently occurs. We see little else that could make such a national round table possible and productive except firm resolution on the part of the federal government to break the cycle of widespread irresponsibility and unaccountability in First Nations education by refusing to continue to support it.

Several policy wild cards are currently in play that might make the federal government take a firm stance on the accountability issue. First, the zeitgeist of our time is against waste and in favour of responsibility and accountability. Second, the current prime minister is reputedly closely linked to Tom Flanagan, whose radical 'White Paper liberal

Figure 8.6 Awareness and buy-in, difficult but necessary first steps

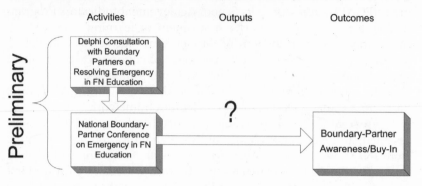

stance' (to use Turner's descriptor) on First Nations issues we discussed earlier. It seems quite conceivable that Prime Minister Harper might succeed in obtaining a majority government in the near future, in which case all bets are off about the sustainability of the status quo in Indian affairs generally, but especially in education. Finally, there is always the unexpected. The possibility exists that some unforeseen event that attracts major media attention may provoke outrage on the part of either mainstream Canadians or Aboriginal leaders, or even both, about the status quo in Aboriginal education.

Assuming Aboriginal education should arrive at some 'critical juncture' (Koenig 1986), who are the 'boundary partners,' 'individuals, groups, and organizations with whom the program interacts directly and with whom the program anticipates opportunities for influence' (Patton 2001) that should be at the table in such consultations, and why? Also, how should such consultations occur, and why? Without a doubt, key First Nations organizations would have to be central players – but not the only players – in such consultations. Furthermore, these consultations could only be fruitful if it was understood from the beginning by all participants that the status quo is untenable and would no longer be supported by the federal government. It seems clear to us that the Chiefs Committee on Education (CCOE), the National Indian Education Council (NIEC), the Assembly of First Nations (AFN), and the Assembly of First Nations of Quebec would have to be central players at this consultation table. It is equally clear to us that the Council of Ministers of Education of Canada (CMEC) would need to be at the table as well – and for a very good reason, although it may not be immediately obvious. The CMEC produces the Pan-Canadian Assessment Program (PCAP), successor to its School Achievement Indicators Program (SAIP), a national comparative assessment of learning and reading, math, and science on the part of thirteen year-olds across Canada. To produce PCAP and SAIP, CMEC has been and continues to be involved in a substantial distillation of elementary and primary curricula across Canada, a major component of what needs to occur in establishing a basic cross-Canada First Nations curriculum framework.

The federal government would also need to be appropriately represented, and we do not mean simply by an education representative from INAC. On the contrary, since what is at stake here is ultimately the institutionalization of real responsibility and accountability for First Nations education on the part of First Nations entities – once and for all connecting disconnected layers of accountability – at the very least, all residual education functions of INAC should be terminated in the shortest reasonable timeframe. While it is certainly appropriate and necessary that the minister of Indian Affairs be at the table, it is equally essential that the minister of Finance and chair of the Treasury Board also have senior representation, since substantial resource issues will arise if the changes we propose go forward.

With regard to how such consultations should occur, however, they should be reasonably thorough but not extend over more than eight months, given the urgent need for timely change. We believe that some sort of working committee structure would facilitate the work of the group of the whole, and that firm timelines should be set and adhered to throughout the process, with a clear understanding that the process cannot be bogged down by committees that don't do their homework on time. It seems to us that standard 'post presentational' procedures would be most appropriate (a clear description of problems and issues that arise from an initial Delphi exercise, followed by delegation to appropriate working committees that would report back to the entire 'table' for discussion, followed by a two-week period for discussion and notice of motions, and then a final meeting for a vote on the motions). The purpose of the preliminary consultation is one of awareness and buy-in, and hence, necessarily, of finding common grounds for that buy-in. Although matters of substance will undoubtedly arise, focus needs to be kept on the endgame – ultimate transfer of real control and responsibility for First Nations education to First Nations entities. Ideally, the prime minister himself should chair at least the first meeting, and should make it clear that the status quo is not an option.

Figure 8.7 (part 1) An RMB starting point for transfer of responsibility and accountability

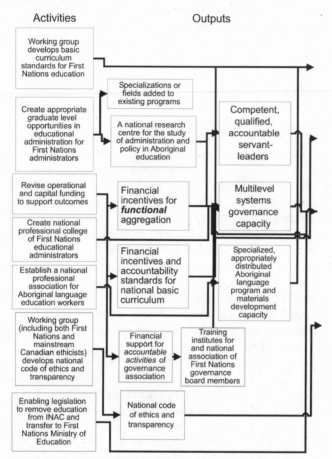

Figure 8.7 offers an RBM starting point for institutionalization of meaningful responsibility for First Nations education on the part of First Nations entities, and for taking major steps away from the current disconnected layers of accountability and towards 'education plus' that will be a source of pride and satisfaction to all the boundary partners in the process. A real-world RBM would be significantly more comprehensive and complex. It would, for instance, need to deal explicitly with post-secondary issues. These are present only implicitly in figure

Figure 8.7 (part 2) An RMB starting point for transfer of responsibility and accountability

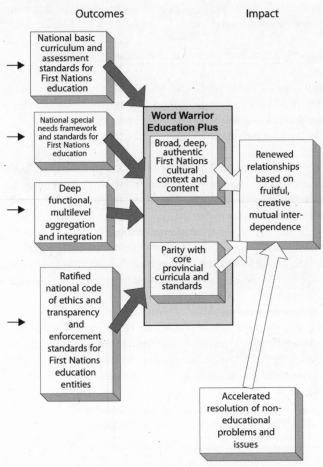

8.7. Still, we believe that figure 8.7 provides a reasonably clear idea of what kinds of activities, outputs, and outcomes are needed to move towards a First Nations education that combines deep, authentic First Nations cultural context and content on the one hand and parity with core provincial curricula and standards on the other. To be sure, any RBM map towards those impacts will need in-course adjustments on a regular basis. Notwithstanding, the model portrayed in figure 8.7 offers at least a plausible beginning point for a promising alternative to a status quo that pleases no one except those who profit from it.

Given our treatment of these issues in previous chapters, the key outcome building blocks in this vision are:

- national basic curriculum and assessment standards for First Nations education
- a national special needs framework and standards
- deep functional, multilevel aggregation and integration
- a ratified and enforced national code of ethics and transparency, with clear and effective enforcement standards

To arrive at such outcomes, an adequate pool of competent, qualified, accountable servant-leaders are needed, leaders with the capacity to operate a complex multilevel education 'system' worthy of the name. To 'do' First Nations cultural context and content well, specialized, appropriately distributed Aboriginal-language program and materials development capacity must be established and nurtured over time. As we discussed earlier, while Cultural Centres may have a role to play in this, direction and priority-setting needs to come from First Nations aggregate education entities.

To develop a sufficient pool of suitable servant-leaders, appropriate graduate-level programs are urgently needed. Resources need major redirection and, almost certainly, significant new money will be necessary to realize this vision although we do not believe that all of this money should come from the federal government, especially over the medium and long term. Of particular importance are financial incentives to promote and encourage accountable use of a national basic curriculum and related assessment standards. Appropriate support and training for those involved in the governance of First Nations education are urgently needed.

Professionalization of First Nations educational administration should be encouraged in all potentially useful ways, including establishment of a professional college with the ability both to certify and decertify First Nations administrators and perhaps to provide differential certification. At long last, the perennial and quasi-universal complaint of Aboriginal language teachers about professional isolation needs to be addressed, by creation of a national professional association of Aboriginal language teachers. Finally, as soon as reasonable First Nations educational governance capacity is in place, INAC needs to get out of the business of meddling in First Nations education and of confusing and obscuring layers of accountability associated with it.

Whose Education, Whose Resources?

An ineluctable link binds resources to control in education. Own-source revenues do not automatically ensure meaningful control over education. Without results-based management – or something very much like it – own-source revenues can be squandered as easily as 'external source' revenues on inefficient, ineffective, and inappropriate programs, to say nothing of being absorbed in self-serving leadership. People are much more likely, however, to take action to stop such squandering of resources when they perceive resources for education as their own rather than those of some external 'third party' beyond the citizen-educator relationship – especially when accountability for results is a shadowy link to some fourth party! Own-source revenues are a necessary but not a sufficient condition for meaningful control over education, including its governance and administration.

So long as the majority of First Nations remain opposed in principle to any form of self-taxation for education, they cannot legitimately expect, individually or collectively, to exercise meaningful control and autonomy in educational matters. Such rejection can only perpetuate the rentier nature of Aboriginal dependence on external 'rents,' and would remove from the accountability equation any legitimate basis for Aboriginal communities to demand accountability from those who manage the provision of education to their children. Furthermore, it would maintain the numerous organizational defensive routines that have emerged in a balkanized local control structure, while preventing much-needed learning and capacity development within. It would prevent Aboriginal organizations from ameliorating or eliminating the underlying problem of dysfunctional governance in education. Rejection in principle of reliance to some degree, and to a degree that will increase over time as tax capacity and governance and administrative capacity increase, is nothing less than abandonment of the quest for meaningful control in education, a de facto preference to continue jousting at windmills of illusory control.

This observation is valid, regardless of issues of historical wrongs and oppression. Historical wrongs need to be dealt with – but not by insisting that First Nations people should be forever exempt from providing the resources, especially financial resources, for the education of their young – a sure recipe for carrying forward the disconnected layers of accountability we have described, as well as their invidious effects. Prior to contact, First Nations peoples exercised complete control over the education of their young. They were able to do so because they provided all of the human and physical resources (which is what most of the money is spent on in contemporary education), as well as moral, spiritual, and intellectual resources for that education. If authentic control is the real objective, they will need to reassume, over time as their fiscal, governance, and leadership capacity grows, responsibility for providing the majority of *all* resources for the education of their young. In twenty-first century Canada, First Nations peoples cannot reassume responsibility and control unless they are also willing to assume the costs. No room exists in any authentic Indian control agenda for a permanent exemption from self-taxation for education.

The answer to 'whose education' is usually 'whoever pays the bill.' Of course, political economy issues up to and including complete 'provider capture' can mute – or even nullify – citizen-taxpayer control over education. Still, no credible educational policy analyst has ever suggested that one can hive off control from financial responsibility in the radical way that the two are nominally separated in most (not all, of course, because some First Nations under SGAs or in exceptional circumstances do fund education to a considerable extent) First Nations education programs at the moment.

Time to Think Outside the Box and to Begin Getting Out of It

The time has come to do more than think 'outside the box' of the current generalized gridlock in Aboriginal and First Nations education; the time has arrived to begin taking major steps to *move* outside of that box. The patience of Canadian taxpayers with waste and inefficiency in government is exceptionally thin these days and acquiescence in the status quo can only lead to yet another generation of undereducated young Aboriginals. A very large proportion of these youth will find themselves intellectually impoverished, as well as alienated from both their ancestral culture and mainstream Canadian culture and resigned to the impossibility of being able to choose a meaningful future and identity. This is indeed a recipe for confrontation rather than creative and fruitful interdependence.

We therefore offer in a spirit of determination tempered by humility on the one hand and a sense of urgency on the other a set of fourteen propositions, each of which we will discuss briefly in this section. These propositions have been shaped by our extensive research, our long and arduous reflection, our personal experience with Aboriginal education and the issues surrounding it, and a sense of having an opportunity that is not likely to come again anytime soon, if ever. We also share a sense of foreboding about what could follow if this opportunity were missed. Here, then, is what we propose.

1. *Consensus and commitment*

> Consensus is urgently needed on the overarching goal of renewing relationships that are based on fruitful and creative interdependence. A commitment by key stakeholders who must do what it takes to get education to the next level is absolutely necessary.

Hope for a better and mutually enriching future appears at best ill-founded and at worst an exercise in self-delusion if there is no consensus among all key stakeholders on the overarching policy goal of renewing relationships based on fruitful and creative interdependence. There must also be a commitment to do what it takes to immediately take education to the next level. Tinkering around the edges of the status quo rather than opting collectively for fundamental change that is based on mutual respect and relational pluralist principles can only make action on the next thirteen propositions impossible.

It is admittedly a tall order to expect consensus and commitment from all key stakeholders. Over a generation ago Hall and her colleagues (1975) enunciated three principles necessary for the success of implementing policy. They never claimed that these principles could *ensure* successful implementation of a policy. What they did claim, however, was that policy could not succeed unless all stakeholders whose cooperation is necessary for implementation success are likely to perceive it as legitimate, feasible, and politically supportable (475–86). It is hard to imagine stakeholders who are invested in solving the problems the policy addresses embarking upon the implementation of such policy unless these three conditions can be applied from their respective points of view. One could easily view 'Kymlicka's constraint' as a specialized subset of this principle. Given that the assent and cooperation of mainstream power brokers is necessary to achieve progress on all Aboriginal claims and issues, they in particular must see proposed policy changes, and especially major policy framework changes, as potentially 'legitimate, feasible, and politically supportable.' The bottom line is that consensus and commitment among both Aboriginal parties to a fundamentally new arrangement in education (and, of course, in governance generally) *and* mainstream power brokers is a *sine qua non* for breaking out of the current gridlock.

2. *Education Plus!*

> This renewed relationship requires a strong dose of 'education plus' and an influx of word warriors as a way to offset the pervasive sense of failure and complacency, which come from the preservation of existing interests.

Pervasive failure and complacent mediocrity are no longer tolerable in Aboriginal education. The standard of 'education plus' is required, and nothing less. To be sure, there will not be an instant turnaround, even with the most ardent servant leadership, strong ethics, and commitment to achieving an 'education plus' vision and results. This is not justification, however, for maintaining the current gridlock. Only those who profit from the political economy of the status quo would want to remain within the waste and tragedy of that situation.

Aboriginal education can be unique, intellectually rigorous, and mentally, morally, and spiritually engaging for a great many Aboriginal students. The reason that this is not experienced by most students has complex and painful roots, particularly those that extend back to the residential school legacy. It is also related to personal and group interests that are deeply vested in the current order of things. However, these interests can no longer be allowed to trump the education of Aboriginal students on a grand scale. Those who take too much from the 'rice bowl' of Aboriginal education and contribute little or nothing in return must step aside or be pushed aside – one way or another. That they are not shamed by the diligence and altruism of those who work in Aboriginal education with commitment and perseverance despite a largely hopeless and self-defeating governance and leadership arrangement is a sad and great mystery.

3. *Building the necessary conditions for renewed relationships*

> Education alone cannot guarantee these types of renewed relationships but such relationships will prove impossible without efficient, effective, appropriate First Nations education – 'Kymlicka's constraint'!

Education on its own cannot assure that relationships are renewed in the way we advocate. Nonetheless, education is a moral and political touchstone in democratic societies because of its visibility, symbolic importance, and because it engages the welfare and future of society's most vulnerable members, which is true for Aboriginal students to an even greater extent than it is for mainstream students. It is inconceivable, as 'Kymlicka's constraint' reminds us, that the power brokers in mainstream Canadian society could enthusiastically pursue fundamentally renewed relationships with Aboriginal communities in the absence of solid and convincing evidence that Aboriginal peoples and especially First Nations people are putting their educational house in order in some convincing way.

Thus, taking the first steps towards fundamentally changing the structure and operation of Aboriginal and especially First Nations education is going to be the necessary precondition to fundamental and generalized renewal of relationships along the lines suggested by relational pluralist principles. Until and unless the power brokers are convinced that Aboriginal peoples have solidly – and irrevocably – embarked upon a convincing path towards effective, efficient, and appropriate education, they are unlikely to respond favourably to visions of Aboriginal self-determination. In short, failure to move beyond the current disorganization in education would preserve the gridlock in the larger self-determination exercise.

4. Responsibility, not dependency!

> Progress is not possible without a First Nations commitment to assuming responsibility.

Fiduciary responsibility is a dangerous two-edged sword. When applied in a mindless white-guilt campaign to evade responsibility for one's own destiny and fate, it results in a tragic narcotic effect. In its worst incarnation, it embodies the claim that since mainstream Canadians wronged Aboriginal peoples, *they* should be forever responsible for the welfare and well-being, including the education, of Aboriginal peoples. This is worse than a parody of self-determination. It is a complete inversion of the logic of self-determination!

At best, the principle of fiduciary responsibility is useful insofar as it suggests that mainstream Canadians have an obligation to do what they reasonably can do to facilitate assumption of responsibility for self-determination, and with it responsibility for education. This view of fiduciary responsibility suggests that mainstream Canadians and their governments have an obligation to resist and certainly to refuse sanctioning and financing enduring arrangements that reduce Aboriginal peoples to agents of non-Aboriginal policy and programs. That is especially true in the culturally and intellectually central exercise constituted by education. Yet that is precisely what the *Indian Act* does, as everyone familiar with it will recognize. What is less obvious but equally true is that INAC policy governing what is and is not acceptable, and fundable, in regard to First Nations education, *even in the case of so-called comprehensive self-government agreements*, just as surely reduces First Nations education entities to agents of INAC and provincial policy. It does so in a very direct and inescapable way.

Responsibility is the endgame here. Responsibility is the antithesis of dependency in matters of politics and policy.

5. Responsibility implies financial responsibility in the here and now

Assuming responsibility ultimately implies assuming financial responsibility. Without this, not much more than a relationship of agency for the funder is likely.

This seemed like a harsh statement to many Aboriginal leaders when Paquette (1986) enunciated it, although in somewhat different terms, two decades ago. No doubt it will still seem very harsh to many Aboriginal leaders today. We are encouraged, however, by the number of Aboriginal communities that believe this principle is a sound one, especially those communities that have negotiated self-government agreements with self-taxation provisions. We also note with satisfaction (although without the temerity to claim any kind of direct cause-and-effect relationship) that these communities count among them some of the most prosperous and promising First Nations schools in Canada.

Responsibility is the endgame. At least it is the only endgame that makes any sense for people who believe in the dignity and importance of human agency. In the realities of twenty-first-century Canada, responsibility is incontestably 'a package deal.' No political or policy philosophers' stone can work the alchemy of changing financial dependency into authentic control. To insist that settler governments should pay all the costs of Aboriginal education indefinitely is to insist on forever sacrificing the right to self-determination both culturally and intellectually to those governments. Whatever the past history, there is no substitute or surrogate for a sense of direct day-in and day-out, year-in and year-out contribution to education from one's *own* resources. As long as the resources of 'the other' support education, education will remain the property of 'the other' and will pursue 'the other's' agenda. All the arguments in the world about historical injustice, however valid they may be, will not change this dynamic.

Control implies responsibility. In the realities of our time, responsibility implies the willingness to assume financial responsibility to the degree that one's capacity to do so permits. It implies as well a willingness to develop the educational, governance, and leadership capacities necessary for wealth- and tax-generating activity – but not at the cost of betraying ecological principles fundamental to Aboriginal relationships with our much beleaguered Mother Earth.

6. *Responsibility is accepting blame when warranted and working diligently and transparently to correct mistakes*

Assuming responsibility implies accepting blame for mistakes and working to correct them transparently, honestly, and in light of the best information available. If one cannot be accountable in this way, one should leave his/her position of authority.

Responsibility involves accepting blame for one's mistakes and oversights and not blaming others, individually or collectively. It means working diligently, honestly, and transparently to correct them, and doing so by taking into account all relevant knowledge available at the time. Leadership is about working hard and working smart, not about exercising privilege and evading blame. Competent, responsible leaders practise accountability, not evasion and excuses. They do not try to implement new ideas with the same old skills while learning to cover up their mistakes ever more skilfully. Accepting blame means it is legitimate for outsiders to require insiders to discuss the undiscussable. Responsible leaders work within the principle that 'the buck stops with me,' at least within my 'span of control.' They work long hard hours to search for and apply the best available knowledge to remedy past mistakes and oversights. Except when breach of privacy would harm others for whom they are responsible, they work openly and transparently – even if that proves a very difficult thing for them to do in a particular case. Responsibility requires courage and integrity.

Finally, where leaders lack the appropriate education and credentials, or simply the work ethic to be accountable in the positions they occupy, it is imperative that a process be in place to assure that they step aside or are removed if they do not. Although the rules of natural justice and due process need to be respected in cases of incompetence, incompetence cannot be tolerated. That is part of the reason we strongly recommend the creation of a professional college for Aboriginal school administrators (see point 10 below). Responsibility plays a prominent role in one form or the other in most of the definitions of professionalism, and for good reason. Without responsibility, any claim to professionalism is void and empty.

7. Control through functional integration

There can be no progress without functional integration. Indian control of Indian education is a good idea, but so far it has been very ineptly packaged. The notion of Indian control as exclusively local control is a bankrupt idea, and it always has been.

As long as First Nations education is broken up into over 500 independent school non-systems bound together only by volunteer and frequently ad hoc participation in second-level service organizations, little real functionally integrated capacity development can take place along the lines we have proposed. Whether by design or default (i.e., by deliberate strategy or as a result of instinctive unwillingness to think outside the box of federal–band agency relationships), INAC has pursued with relentless consistency over the years a strategy of divide and conquer with regard to First Nations education. Coupled with divestment by DIAND of what little educational capacity it had in the 1980s (in all fairness, we note that INAC has, largely in response to the recent recurrent criticism of the Auditor General that First Nations education is completely bereft of accountability, acquired some minimal educational capacity at its most senior administrative levels), this divide-and-conquer strategy has not surprisingly led to the current fragmented non-system. This non-system is largely paralyzed by a lack of capacity, vision, and commitment either to suitable educational standards or to appropriate standards of ethics and transparency. Not surprisingly, this legacy of more than a generation of divide-and-conquer in the name of devolution has, for the most part, led to a dysfunctional rice bowl mentality that is focused more on delivering benefits to local people involved in education than on providing high-quality education plus that is efficient, effective, and appropriate.

The question of whether schools exist for students or for all the other people involved in the political economy of schooling is an old and thorny one. Consistent with our position on servant leadership, of course, we believe that schools ought to exist for students and that everything and everyone involved with schooling ought to serve the educational and general development needs of students. Consistent with our position on the centrality of the political economy of schooling, we are not blind to the fact that schooling and schools serve many other purposes and agendas beyond the education and socialization of students. Still, it is difficult to find a parallel, at least within Canada, to the degree and nature of 'goal displacement' that seems to be associated with Aboriginal and particularly First Nations education in Canada. Indeed, the impact of decades of DIAND/INAC divide-and-conquer policy has, it seems to us, produced a generalized despair about the possibility of ever moving outside the current box of outrageous fragmentation and dysfunction.

8. Ethics and transparency

Functional integration is not possible without strong codes of ethics and a level of transparency that is framed within an ethos of servant leadership. Without these, only dysfunction on an even grander scale than what we have at the moment is possible.

Functional integration requires, among other things, strong codes of ethics and transparency crafted within an ethos of servant leadership. Only with generalized commitment to a 'cause greater than oneself' (Glickman, Gordon, and Ross-Gordon 2004) can one legitimately aspire to move beyond self-interest and towards functional integration. Strong codes of ethics and transparency accompanied by effective sanctions for violations of those codes can help all those involved in a functionally integrated educational organization keep their eye on the vision and shared purpose, as formally enunciated by organizational leaders and as embedded in the policy that frames and delimits organizational action and, in particular, the actions of administrators and teachers in furthering the educational and socialization mission of the organization. Cliques, misappropriation of resources, secrecy, or any other form of collusion simply has no place in a functionally integrated organization with strong commitments to ethics and transparency.

9. Stepping outside the Aboriginal education box now!

> Shared common interest in a creative, fruitful interdependence means that the prudential interests of both First Nations and non-Aboriginal Canadians require fundamental change to First Nations education *now!* Although education is essential to self-determination, fundamental change to education cannot wait for self-determination. Otherwise self-determination will prove to be an empty promise.

Educational reforms are not a prerequisite for self-government; the two go hand in hand (Royal Commission on Aboriginal Peoples 1996c, 2–3). Following a relational pluralist conceptual analysis, we have argued that the policy endgame, is to renew the existing relationships so as to build a deep and creative interdependence between Aboriginal and non-Aboriginal peoples; relationships that are sustained with mutual respect and trust.

The question of timing here is a delicate one. On the one hand, Aboriginal peoples are legitimately concerned about framing education within agreements that provide appropriate space and boundaries as part of their comprehensive self-determination. On the other hand, development of the capacities required to exercise meaningful self-determination requires high-quality education as a prerequisite. Without it, most Aboriginal and especially First Nations communities and aggregates are doomed to repeat the past. No way exists to short-circuit this fundamental human resource requirement. Either one has a pool of qualified and competent people who can develop and nurture self-determination or one does not. Without effective, efficient, and appropriate education, an adequate pool of appropriately educated people will simply not be available for the self-determination exercise.

In this sense, it seems self-evident to us that stepping outside of the current and largely dysfunctional box of Aboriginal education cannot wait for comprehensive self-government arrangements. One telling indicator of the dangers in insisting that major reforms to First Nations education await comprehensive self-government is precisely the relative paucity and poverty of provisions with regard to education within existing self-government agreements and agreements in principle. In general, these provisions seem to us barely more promising than the threadbare provisions that currently exist within the *Indian Act*.

Furthermore, education is fundamentally different in kind from other aspects of and domains within potential self-determination frameworks. To a far greater extent than other aspects of self-government, education requires, as we have insisted repeatedly, strong, distinctively Aboriginal capacities that absolutely require functional integration to achieve reasonable economies of scale. One cannot 'contract out' the core educational business of planning, developing, delivering, and evaluating programs of study to an outside consulting or service firm, or even to an Aboriginal cultural centre, for that matter. In fact, experiments in United States with such contracting out of educational administration in cities such as Minneapolis and St Louis (see, for example, Hardy 2003) have generally failed to sustain their promise of more efficient and effective education.

If Aboriginal affairs should be reshaped in pursuit of renewed relationships that resonate with and support the prudential interests of both Aboriginal and non-Aboriginal partners, then fundamental restructuring and reform of Aboriginal education cannot continue waiting for a comprehensive self-government to emerge from some nebulous human resource alchemy.

Educational steps towards renewing relationships between Aboriginal and non-Aboriginal peoples in Canada cannot, of course, be limited only to reforms in Aboriginal education. Substantial reform of provincial and territorial curricula are also needed to ensure that non-Aboriginal students obtain a clearer and deeper understanding than they currently do of Aboriginal peoples, their histories, their aspirations for self-determination, and the challenges they face. Such education must also teach that creative and fruitful interdependence requires substantial self-determination for Aboriginal peoples and that self-determination can only occur within a context of assumption of responsibility for self-governance and education.

10. RBM or similar outcomes/results-based policy mechanisms

Responsibility and accountability mean making a commitment to a common vision and to achieving specific learning and other outcomes – to results-based management – or some other way of linking policy and resources to results.

A common vision, as we have noted, is essential to coherent reform; however necessary a condition it is, nonetheless, it is not sufficient to achieve the goal. The days have long since passed in public education when reform, and funding, could be based solely on concerns about inputs, programs, and processes. Not one educational jurisdiction in Canada today allows school boards or districts the luxury of not bothering to measure learning outcomes in some way and of failing to use data on learning outcomes to shape evolving policy and practice. Serious concerns, of course, exist about many of the measures that are currently in use both in terms of their conceptual validity and in terms of the scope of knowledge and skills that they tap into. Nonetheless, it is unthinkable that any credible interlocutor in provincial education should propose that provinces abandon either their efforts to measure schooling outcomes, however partial and questionable these may be, or their attempts to insist that school boards and districts use these data to improve instruction in their jurisdictions. In a word, engage in some form of results-based management (RBM).

First Nations education is unique in Canada in that it is not subject to any meaningful RBM expectations or processes. Little wonder, given the broader context of Canadian education, that Auditor General Sheila Fraser has found the state of First Nations education to be devoid of accountability (2004a, 2004b, 2006). The paradox of her repeated declamations on the subject, is that she has no choice but to address her criticism to INAC, which has neither the capacity nor the mandate to impose any kind of an RBM system on First Nations. Thus the cat-and-mouse game of deploring the lack of accountability and of INAC being unable to do much to change this fact continues.

RBM or some other way of linking policy and resources to results are crucial to if we are to escape this situation. Even if the federal government were disposed to revise the educational provisions of the *Indian Act* so that they resembled in scope and depth the provisions of a provincial education or school act (and nothing suggests that the federal government has any interest in doing so), INAC as an instrument of settler-government policy could simply never have any credibility imposing an RBM system on First Nations education across Canada. In a very real way, given contemporary understandings of what constitutes accountability in education, INAC *can never do* what the Auditor General continues to insist that it *must* do, that is, bring order and account-ability to First Nations education.

11. *We cannot build it in a day*

Building these relationships cannot be done quickly, but they aren't likely to be built if we don't take the first steps towards reaching that goal.

This declaration comes close to the trivial when viewed in light of the strong consensus in the organizational-change literature on the impossibility of imposing instant deep change. A new order in Aboriginal and particularly First Nations education will clearly not be built in a day, or a week, or even a single decade. Capacity-building takes time. It does so, moreover, even in the best of times and with the best of people involved!

That said, in our view it is imperative that the first steps towards meaningful Indian control of Indian education be taken sooner rather than later. We believe this to be the case for at least two critically important reasons. One, failure to move ahead with Aboriginal self-determination over the course of the next generation will probably result in it falling off the radar of public policy in Canada and staying off for a very long time to come. In fact, it might permanently disappear with all of the undesirable consequences for both Aboriginal and non-Aboriginal peoples across Canada. No substantial progress will occur without major improvements to Aboriginal education. As we have noted, improved Aboriginal education is a *prerequisite* to capacity development for general self-determination and therefore must *precede* the main thrust of comprehensive self-determination. Second, if fiduciary responsibility has any meaning at all in terms of moral responsibility, it surely implies that non-Aboriginal Canadians should do all that is reasonably within their power to provide an opportunity for Aboriginal people to assume control and responsibility for the education of their children. If this is achieved, another generation of Aboriginal children will not be abandoned by a non-system whose major agenda is delivering benefits to key stakeholders.

12. *A federal 'nudge' for change or federal complicity in the status quo*

Progress is unlikely without firm insistence from the federal level that there be fundamental change in the organization, structure, goals, and governance of First Nations education. The government must also make it clear that it will not tolerate anyone who acts complicitly in preserving the current gridlock.

However important, however essential to the future of Aboriginal children assuming responsibility for the shape, content, and process of education for and by Aboriginal peoples, it is not likely to occur without a very strong nudge for change from the federal government. The federal government has a choice, undoubtedly not a very enviable one from a political perspective, but a choice nonetheless. The government can choose to acquiesce to the status quo and, perhaps in the name of fiduciary responsibility, continue to bankroll and underwrite a non-system that fails its students in just about every way that matters.

Or, alternatively, the government might serve notice that it will *not* continue to sanction and bankroll the status quo in First Nations education. Possible fallout from such an announcement would undoubtedly be unwelcome even to the most ardently small-c conservative government imaginable in Canada. Still, doing nothing will have its political costs as well. How many more Auditors General reports decrying complete lack of accountability in First Nations education will it take before Canadian taxpayers conclude that sending good money after bad in increasing quantities is not a very promising strategy and order their parliamentarians to pull the rug on the whole enterprise? If the status quo is viewed in Ottawa as the only politically viable option, one might plausibly argue that fiduciary responsibility might best be served by opting for a White Paper liberal solution in Aboriginal education – that is, turning it all over to provincial and territorial school boards (not that anyone involved would be very keen on that solution).

The status quo is simply untenable. In fact, in our view, it is ready to implode. Nonetheless, only Ottawa can force change and there are a great many local rice bowl (political economy) interests that are opposed to any meaningful change to the current order of things. The choice for Parliament comes down to the following: either Parliament can take the initiative by refusing to continue to fund the status quo, or parliamentarians can wait until almost inevitable future catastrophic events provide the critical junctures for fundamental and irresistible change. Of course, the aborted Nault accountability reforms will no doubt continue to serve as a cautionary tale for parliamentarians for quite some time to come about what can happen when Parliament takes the initiative in trying to impose accountability on First Nations.

The solution we offer is precisely the opposite of that solution. What we offer, taken as a whole, is an opportunity for First Nations to develop the capacity to assume responsibility for the education of their young and, progressively over time, to do so in a meaningful and convincing way – not in the context of the local-control-equals-Indian-control hoax. The choice is ultimately one of trying to brace up the non-system and provide bits and shreds of window dressing for an untenable status quo gridlock or of taking the steps necessary to trigger deep change. Only Ottawa can do that. Doing so will require considerable political courage, but not doing so will require even more political fortitude because at some point soon the current non-system is going to implode, and then there will be even greater chaos and a higher political price to pay.

13. Coping with diseconomies of scale

Because of acute and pervasive diseconomies of scale, Indian control requires a national curriculum, national standards, and national assessment criteria. In addition, there must be suitable distribution of the capacity to develop curriculum and Aboriginal-language programs and materials.

Diseconomies of scale are endemic in Aboriginal and First Nations education. Ironically, in this context, the only plausible way forward on the Indian-control agenda is precisely in the opposite direction from that of the ICIE hoax. Carried to its logical conclusion, functional integration should ultimately lead to a Canada-wide First Nations Ministry of Education. Clearly, and for several reasons including, but not limited to, the prevalence of French-language instruction in many Quebec First Nations schools, the Quebec First Nations will require a special place in any such meta-organization. Nonetheless, we have come away from the research and writing of this book convinced that such a ministry is needed in order to provide the spectrum of highly specialized educational and program-development and support services that are needed in First Nations education. As we have acknowledged in several places, such deep functional integration will not occur magically or easily or without a great deal of commitment and effort. Nor will it occur as long as local rice bowl agendas dominate resource-allocation questions in First Nations education.

Obviously work towards such a ministry will need to conform with the evolving capacity within First Nations governance and educational administrations. Such capacity development will take time, but it needs to begin now.

14. Sharing good practices effectively

> Good practices (not 'best' because there are no 'best practices' for all contexts and all students) must be shared intelligently and broadly and in a focused way.

Much has been written over the last two decades about the importance in education and elsewhere of sharing best practices and about organizational learning, or, in its most recent incarnation, the creation of professional learning communities. In general, we believe that these literatures contribute some important insights, especially when taken collectively; however, many of these insights are not nearly as novel as some writers contributing to these literatures have claimed. First, we insist that the 'uncertain technology' of teaching and learning as well as its highly context-bound nature, preclude the existence of generalizable *best* practices. Education is not, for instance, orthopaedic surgery – and even there, after all, a standard canon of procedures does not exist for any and all situations an orthopaedic surgeon might face. Education, however, is radically different in that, while there may be broadly acceptable procedures associated with doing a hip replacement, there is no one best procedure for developing in all students in all situations the ability to read with comprehension or write with precision.

These cautionary observations about the folly of overblown claims with regard to excellent teaching practices aside, we believe that the ability of teachers to learn from one another and to contribute to each other's professional growth in powerful and positive ways is a sadly underdeveloped resource for positive change in Aboriginal education. Here again diseconomies of scale coupled with the ICIE local-control mythology take a distressing toll. Beleaguered and overburdened local First Nations education organizations, for instance, hardly have the time and resources to develop broad and intelligently targeted online resources to nurture virtual professional learning communities of teachers and administrators, and furthermore to link such online resources to professional development opportunities of a more traditional nature, or to link such self-help communities to relevant academic input and support. The possibilities here, it seems to us, are quite stunning given the recent quantum leap in the availability of broadband Internet access and proliferation of video-conferencing equipment in even the most remote Canadian Aboriginal communities. Teachers and administrators in First Nations schools should no longer have to compound the angst of professional isolation with all of the other challenges they face. No compelling technological reasons exist for them to do so. Yet without the technological resource concentration that only functional integration can bring, they will almost certainly continue to work in much the same kind of professional isolation that was common when one of us worked in First Nations schools well over a generation ago.

Taken together, implemented with patience and determination, these principles can go far towards shaping a better future for Aboriginal and First Nations students across Canada. They can lead to a better working environment for teachers, paraprofessionals, and servant leaders. Most importantly, they can lead to 'education plus,' 'word warrior' education that will command the respect and support of Aboriginal as well as non-Aboriginal Canadians.

Notes

Preface

1 R.S.C., 1985, c. I-5.

1 Prologue: Historic Context

1 We say almost completely, since the family of the spouse of one author was, and continues to be, deeply affected by the residential school legacy.
2 Some missionaries considered them to be intellectually capable enough and believed they were only handicapped by their childlike simplicity (see, for example, Miller 1996,154).
3 *Hoffman v. Board of Education of City of New York*, 410 NYS 2d 99 (1978).
4 *Gould v. Regina (East) School Division No. 77*, [1996] SJ no. 843 (QB).
5 The agreement also establishes a 'Truth and Reconciliation Commission' with a budget of $60 million over five years to engage in various public education activities to inform the population of Canada at large about what happened in Indian residential schools.

2 Framing First Nations Education

1 This and all subsequent quotations from Bertrand and Valois (1980) are the authors' translations.
2 By virtue of this focus, the inventive paradigm as Bertrand and Valois (1980) characterize it, has strong conceptual affiliation with Schouls' idea of self-determination being grounded in relational pluralism.
3 Of course, sobering warnings of how 'market fundamentalism' will affect not only society but also the market system itself have not been wanting

– sometimes coming from startling sources (see, for example, Soros 1997, 1998).

4 One is immediately reminded of various reform projects in educational policy over the last fifteen years that have ranged from various versions of total quality management to the idea of 'acceptable yearly progress' built into the No Child Left Behind legislation in the U.S.

5 The use of the word 'organism' in this context strikes us as peculiar. Surely a paradigm that centres on the *whole* person and even on his/her teleological relationship to nature and the cosmos must regard persons as more than 'organisms.' Indeed, it ought to regard other organisms as more than an aggregate of cells, parts, and organs!

6 Hardly far from Aboriginal ideas of essential unity of humankind with the universe.

7 We are reminded of Roszak's (1986) powerful arguments in this respect.

8 Here we are reminded not only of the rich literature on phenomenology but also of the insistence of some phenomenological theorists on a 'transcendental' reality beyond concepts derived directly from 'percepts' (Schutz 1966; Thevenaz 1962).

9 We find this to be an odd choice of words given the semantic 'baggage' associated with 'function' (mechanism, mechanical, structural functionalism as a body of social theory fashioned from positivism and its assumptions). We would have thought that the word 'live' would have been much more consistent with the authors' point here.

10 Bertrand and Valois (1980) use the terms 'new democratic society communities,' 'biosynergetic,' and 'symbiosynergetic' interchangeably (263).

11 To appreciate the significance of the claim, one needs to recall the classic distinction between inquiry as pursuit of (scientific, causal) explanation as opposed to understanding in the sense of Weber (MacIntyre 1981, see especially 88–108; Schutz 1966).

12 The expression, we realize, has since been picked up and applied in a variety of contexts, including one that is, by most standards, less than edifying.

13 We acknowledge, of course, the point that Holmes (1992) made that, for historic and related reasons, sometimes the paradigmatic orientations of teachers and school administrators can be profoundly 'out of sync.'

14 We find the use of the word 'function' here more than a bit troubling because of its intimate association with structural functionalism and its positivist assumptions. We adopt it here because it is the word Bertrand and Valois (1980) use but we would be much more comfortable with 'purpose' because it reveals rather than conceals human will, intent, and choice in these matters.

15 We see no particular direct relevance of the dialectic ('workers') paradigm to the situation of Aboriginal education.

16 Schouls (2003, 54) regards First Nations communities, far more so than national political groups such as the Assembly of First Nations, as central to his analysis. At the same time he is acutely aware of the limitations imposed on individual communities by self-determining political structures, however flexible they might be, because of the problem of diseconomies of scale. In the end he concludes that small individual bands will choose 'to delegate authority to political entities such as tribal councils in functional areas such as education and human resource training' (54).

17 The notion of goods refers to money, membership, services, commodities, and politics produced and/or distributed within the boundaries of each sphere of life (Moon 1993, 952).

18 For a summary tabulation of key aspects of the Schouls typology of pluralism and what we see as its most important implications, see http://www.utppublishing.com/product.php?productid=2733.

19 See discussion above at pages 42–3.

20 A sense he distinguishes from Tully's (1995) vision of 'mediators' as those who facilitate crafting of a new, global, and permanent constitutional *settlement* (surely a term that, in itself, signifies entrenching permanent and unchanging relationships) (211).

21 Essentially Flanagan's (2000) solution as described above in our discussion of Schouls' work.

22 Recently, Widdowson and Howard (2008) published an even more virulent attack on the worth and validity of Aboriginal cultures and Aboriginal claims to civilization and nationhood.

23 Section 35(1) of the *Constitution Act, 1982*, states, 'The existing aboriginal and treaty rights of the aboriginal peoples of Canada are hereby recognized and affirmed.'

24 See Turner (2006, 93).

3 Policy Context

1 The *Constitution Act, 1867*.

2 Discussed above as part of the rise of self-governance discourses in First Nations affairs.

3 See, for instance, Hawthorn, Tremblay, and Bownick (1967, 22–3).

4 This document was commonly referred to as the White Paper. There are no page numbers on the original printed copy. Pages indicated in all citations of this text are the result of a manual page count using an image scanned

into Adobe format and available at http://www.ainc-inac.gc.ca/pr/lib/phi/histlws/cp1969_e.pdf.

5 *Official Languages Act*, S.C. 1968–9, c. 54.

6 We adopt the term here, even though it did not emerge until the 'Constitution Express' chapter in the First Nations–Federal Government conflict over Aboriginal rights that surrounded the patriation of the Constitution in 1982.

7 The reference here is to *Indian Control of Indian Education* (National Indian Brotherhood, 1972/1984). See discussion above.

8 *Calder v. Attorney-General of B.C.*, [1973] S.C.R. 313, 1973 CanLII 4 (S.C.C.).

9 See chapter 3, 'Social Theory Base.'

10 These issues of lack of legitimacy may be caused by a mismatch between the formal institutions of governance and Aboriginal conceptions of how authority should be organized and exercised. The perceived legitimacy among Aboriginal peoples of any form of Aboriginal self-governance in education will depend on the relationship between those forms of self-governance and Aboriginal political culture (Cornell, Jorgensen, and Kalt 2002).

11 Unhelpful because of its connotation of 'extra' or 'ancillary,' hence not essential or integral!

12 We resist the temptation here to embark on the important question of *who* determines what constitutes 'remediation.' For the purposes of the argument we wish to make in this paragraph, it is sufficient to think of remediation as supplementary instruction intended to help students who are 'behind' in terms of widely used measures of educational achievement in a particular jurisdiction 'catch up' with their age-peers on such measures.

13 The first such model was the hugely detailed and elegant model that Parrish and Chambers developed for the State of Illinois. That model proved far too cumbersome to be workable. Since then, a number of Canadian provinces have opted for variations on resource-cost modelling with varying degrees of acceptance by key policy constituencies.

14 Most constitutions of individual American states contain some sort of wording obligating the state to provide education.

15 The authors obtained this report (no final report was produced, owing to the withdrawal of the AFN from the project) and all related documentation through an Access to Information request to INAC.

16 The authors obtained a copy of the draft report and all supporting papers through an Access to Information request to the federal government.

17 Matthew (2000) puts the time of initial development of this formula at 1987 (13).

18 In cases where local property taxation was still significantly under local board control, imputing revenues from such sources to First Nations communities for simulation purposes requires particularly 'brave' assumptions. Such brave assumptions are not required, however, in the case of a province like Ontario, which has a completely separate funding regime for small, isolated school boards.

19 For a more detailed description of the Hull draft report (BOFF Work Study Group) findings, go to http://www.utppublishing.com/product.php?productid=2733.

20 And provincial governments in the case of non-First Nations Aboriginal education.

21 INAC reported in 2004 that about $248 million dollars would be invested in on-reserve special education between 2002 and 2005 under the new special education program (SEP) national guidelines (Indian and Northern Affairs Canada/Affaires indiennes et du Nord Canada 2004b).

22 For instance, funding 'portability' has recently captured considerable interest in the United States.

23 One doesn't have to look far in the broader world of public education in Canada for evidence of the accountability 'disconnect' that occurs when local boards cease to have any local discretionary revenues, that is, cease to be able to make meaningful decisions about tax rates for education. The result in Nova Scotia and New Brunswick, and more recently in Ontario, is disinterest in school board elections, in many cases to the point that a substantial proportion of trustees are elected by acclamation.

4 Post-Secondary Education

1 With very rare exceptions (e.g., the Gabriel Dumont Institute in Saskatchewan), such Aboriginal post-secondary institutions are First Nations based.

2 Obviously, wealthy and powerful minorities can use many means to manipulate and control majority views on matters of great import for PSE policy, in fact, for just about any policy area that attracts broad public interest. Nonetheless, in the end, it is individuals who go to the polls and elect governments. In a democracy, minority interests must attract majority support to be taken seriously in the broader public policy agenda.

3 For information on such provincial programs, see 'Provincial PSE Support Program Funding for Aboriginal Students' at http://www.utppublishing.com/product.php?productid=2733.

4 For detailed information on such institutional programs, see 'Institutional

PSE Support Program Funding for Aboriginal Students' at http://www
.utppublishing.com/product.php?productid=2733.

5 The demise of 'manpower forecasting' is a direct result of this impossibility of predicting changes in the labour market of free, dynamic, and
interlocking national economies (Psacharopoulos 1990, 377).

6 We do not believe that such a claim can simply be ruled out of order by
claiming, as Flanagan (2000) does, that all inherent-right claims are false
because of an inherent inferiority on the part of Aboriginal cultures. To
arrive at such a conclusion we would need to subscribe to Flanagan's 'civilization gap' theory, which we do not (Turner 2006, 35). Beyond endorsing
a 'civilization gap' in Flanagan's (2000) terms, we would need to take the
position that the existence of such a gap abrogated any moral obligation of
settler governments to respect both inherent and treaty rights, a position
we find not just untenable but odious. That said, we take very seriously
Flanagan's caution that blindly carrying forward in policy a regime of
special status for Aboriginal people can easily leave them in a worse state
than at present vis-à-vis the rest of the Canadian population. It is for that
reason that we believe adopting a relational-pluralist approach to renewing relationships between settler governments and Aboriginal peoples
within a context of strong commitment to high ethical standards on both
sides is so critically important.

7 For eligibility rules, see Indian and Northern Affairs Canada/Affaires indiennes et du Nord Canada (2005, 10)

8 Statistics Canada, Table 326-0002, Consumer price index (CPI), 2001 basket
content, annual (index, 1992=100).

9 For a summary of the salient points of this compelling study see 'INAC
Post-Secondary Study' at http://www.utppublishing.com/product
.php?productid=2733.

10 In general, income earned 'on-reserve' or working for First Nations organizations with headquarters on a reserve and providing mainly services to
status Indians living on reserve is untaxable.

11 The authors of the INAC post-secondary evaluation study found that only
5 of the 441 First Nations students and recent graduates interviewed for
that exercise had obtained a Millennium Scholarship (Indian and Northern
Affairs Canada/Affaires indiennes et du Nord Canada 2005, 31).

12 Finnie (2002, 158) estimated an average debt load for 1995 graduates at
$9,500 (all values in 1997 dollars) for college students who had borrowed
from the CSLP (41 per cent of male and 44 per cent of female college
graduates had borrowed from CSLP), $13,390 for 1995 male bachelor's
graduates (47 per cent of whom had loaned from CSLP), and $13,840 for

female graduates (45 per cent of whom had loaned from CSLP). Finnie provides comparable data for the master's and doctoral levels. Human Resources and Development Canada (2004) reports $12,436 per university student, which corresponds to $13,892 in 1997 dollars when corrected with the Statistics Canada Annual Consumer Price Index. This result confirms that student indebtedness has levelled off in recent years.

13 Treaty 1 between Her Majesty the Queen and the Chippewa and Swampy Cree tribes at The Stone Fort, otherwise known as the Lower Fort Garry, 3 August 1871; Treaty 2 between Her Majesty the Queen and the Chippewa tribe of Indians at Manitoba Post, 21 August 1871; Treaty 3 between Her Majesty the Queen Saulteaux tribe of Ojibbbeway [sic] Indians at the north-west of the Lake Of The Woods, 3 October 1871; Treaty 5 between Her Majesty the Queen and the Saulteaux and Swampy Cree Tribes of Indians at Berens River, 20 September 1875 and at Norway House, 24 September 1875; and Treaty 9 between Her Majesty the Queen and the Ojibeway, Cree and other chiefs and headmen at Osnaburg, 12 July 1905, at Fort Hope 19 July 1905, at Marten Falls 25 July 1905, at Fort Albany 3 August 1905, at Moose Factory 9 August 1905, at New Post 21 August 1095, at Matachewan 20 June 1906, at Mattagami 17 July 1906, at Flying Post 16 July 1906, at New Brunswick House 25 July 1906, at Lo Long Lake, 9 August 1906.

14 See, for example, MacPherson (1991, 33).

15 *Delgamuukw v. The Queen in Right of B.C.*, [1997] 3 S.C.R. 1010.

16 *Van der Peet v. The Queen*, [1996] 2 S.C.R. 507.

17 'Before' is admittedly problematic here. If taken purely in the temporal sense of 'occurring prior in time to,' this requirement would foreclose any claim by current Aboriginal education to inherent right status since education occurring in the present cannot also occur prior to contact. However, we believe that 'before' can and should be interpreted as reinforcing the idea of being 'apart from,' in the sense of 'not directly derived in any way from' contemporary mainstream provincial education.

18 See, for instance, our discussion of earliest post-Confederation funding in the opening of chapter 1, 'Prologue: Historic Context.'

19 If inflated by values reported in Statistics Canada, Table 326-0002, Consumer price index (CPI), 2001 basket content, annual (index, 1992=100).

20 We are aware of, and quite frankly perplexed by, MacPherson's (1991) repeated laudatory remarks regarding *Tradition and Education*.

21 We acknowledge that Stonechild (2004) ascribes a broader impact to *Tradition and Education* (see, for instance, 156). The subsequent developments he ascribes in part to *Tradition and Education* occurred more despite it than

because of it, in our view. In fact, events such as the Oka uprising that gave birth to the Royal Commission and its broad mandate had nothing to do with *Tradition and Education,* the only tangible legacy of which, beyond introducing the discourse of jurisdiction to First Nations education (hardly an original contribution), was to demonstrate how so little could cost so much.

22 John Dudley, personal communication to author, 10 October 2006.

23 *Lovelace v. Canada* (1981) 2 *Human Rights Law Journal* 158 (U.N. Human Rights Committee).

24 Bill C-31, *An Act to Amend the Indian Act,* S.C. 1985, c. 27.

25 *Nowegijick v. The Queen,* [1983] 1 S.C.R. 29, 36.

26 Corrected to coincide with wording in original text, 'impossible' rather than 'possible' as in the Stonechild (2004) quotation.

27 *R. v. Marshall; R. v. Bernard,* [2005] 2 S.C.R. 220, 8.

28 Ibid., 6.

29 It is one thing, after all, for funds appropriated by Parliament to be misused or squandered. That such things will happen is part of the reason for the Auditor General's mandate to inquire into them. It would be quite another for Parliament to transfer resource revenues (say tax revenues or tax 'points') directly to Aboriginal groups.

30 Taking due account of family responsibilities for parents and couples.

31 For detailed discussion, see 'INAC Post-Secondary Study' at http://www .utppublishing.com/product.php?productid=2733.

5 Up the Down Staircase

1 Perhaps the most obvious simplification is that this diagram presents a false image of the lines of voice, authority, and accountability from citizen-resident to local school as a closed system when it is very much an open one – insofar as it is a 'system' in any meaningful sense. All voters who are not in a local school zone have a voice at each governance level above the school zone in decisions that ultimately impact on funding and programs in that school. Voter behaviour impacting educational funding and programs interacts in complex ways with voter behaviour in response to all other policy issues particular to each level of governance. Stakeholders of various sorts interact with policy actors at all levels to try to influence policy, resource flows, accountability mechanisms, and expectations in ways favourable to their interests and priorities. In a globalized economy, neither the Government of Canada nor Canadian provinces can make decisions about tax effort and resource allocations in isolation from similar decisions being made by other governments around the world. Our purpose

in this discussion and in the accompanying figures is to focus analytically on voice, authority, and accountability links between citizen-residents and their local schools.

2 This definition neatly sidesteps the issue of whether the 'results' in question are process results (e.g., classes provided in certain content areas taught to certain standards) or outcome results such as average test performance or acceptable gains in test or multiple-assessment results. The issue is an important one but, for purposes of a simplified model of governance, better left to the side.

3 We are well aware of the rich literature on policy implementation as an integral part of the policy process. This is, however, a simplified model.

4 The simplifications here are much the same as those in figure 5.1 (see note 1 in this chapter). Again, what is shown is not a closed system. All manner of issues and contextual realities, national and international, impinge on government policy towards First Nations, including funding levels and allocation for education. As in figure 5.1, however, our purpose is to focus on voice, authority, and accountability links between citizen-residents (band/community members) and their local schools.

5 The SGAs included the Federal Framework for Transferring Programs and Services to Self-Governing Yukon First Nations, 1998 (YFN); Mi'kmaq Education in Nova Scotia, 1997 (ME); the Manitoba Framework Agreement, 1994 (MFA); Nisga'a Treaty Negotiation: Agreement in Principle, 1996 (NTM); the James Bay and Northern Quebec Agreement (JBNQA); the United Anishaabeg Councils Government Agreement-in-Principle, 1998 (UAC). Some of the Yukon agreements approach it from a slightly different direction, but the coupling to territorial education is nonetheless clear in them.

6 For a more detailed critique of this 'second-level' and 'third-level' service discourse, see 'Just-In-Time Services' at http://www.utppublishing.com/product.php?productid=2733.

7 We define 'jurisdiction' here in the usual sense of 'lawful right to exercise official and binding authority.'

8 The Working Group summarizes its 'vision' for First Nations education in these terms: 'Our vision is a holistic, quality First Nations education system that begins in early childhood and includes adult education and training and post-secondary education, where the weight of education decision-making rests with First Nations in an appropriately funded infrastructure where parents, elders, professionals and leaders at the community, regional and national level come together to plan their learners' education' (Minister's National Working Group on Education 2002, 9). While helpful in its emphasis on quality and adequate funding for appro-

priate 'infrastructure,' this vision is, in our view, dangerously vague on the key governance issues of voice and authority.

9 The Auditor General's (2000a) report couched this criticism in these terms:

> To obtain assurance and effectively discharge its responsibilities, the Department needs to resolve several major issues. These include the need to articulate its role in education, to develop and use appropriate performance measures and to improve operational performance. In addressing these issues, the Department will need to further take into account the cultural and special needs of Indian students as well as socio-economic factors that can affect success in education. (section 4.2)

The 2004 report made essentially the same point with regard to elementary and secondary education, adding that INAC had failed to make any real progress in educational accountability:

> Despite more studies and several new initiatives, Indian and Northern Affairs Canada made limited progress in addressing most of the issues and recommendations raised in our April 2000 Report, as well as those raised in the June 2000 Report of the Public Accounts Committee. The Department does not know whether funding levels provided to First Nations are sufficient to meet the education standards it has set and whether the results achieved are in line with the resources provided. (Auditor General of Canada 2004a, section 5.95)

In short, the Auditor General has repeatedly castigated INAC for lack of accountability in education (among other social policy domains).

10 *An Act Respecting Education on Mi'kmaq Reserves in Nova Scotia*, S.N.S. 1998, c. 17.

11 *Mi'kmaq Education Act*, SC. 1998, c. 24.

12 Detailed analysis of the salient terms and conditions with respect to education of self-government agreements, agreements in principle, and related documents can be found at 'Self-Government Agreements' at http://www.utppublishing.com/product.php?productid=2733.

13 *Access to Information Act* (R.S., 1985, c. A-1).

14 *Privacy Act* (R.S., 1985, c. P-21).

6 Breaking the Gridlock

1 *Indian Act*, R.S.C. 1985, c. I-5.

2 Hart, Lapkin, and Swain (1988) found parents with children in a French

immersion program in Toronto had considerable doubt about whether their children would be able to transfer into regular English-language programs at any time without penalty.

3 Cummins (1981) makes a similar sociolinguistic argument regarding minority second-language students in general in his 'think tank' theory, according to which language input and output in first and second languages is controlled by motivational control 'valves': 'It seems likely that the poor performance of, for example, Navajo Indian and Finnish immigrant children in L2 [the second language in which schooling is conducted], is due to a partial closure of the L2 valve caused by negative attitudes toward the L2 community. If the L2 valve is partially closed, and there is little stimulation coming in through the L1 [first-language] valve, then growth in the Think Tank will be relatively sluggish' (31).

4 Nikkel's (2006) thesis stands quite alone in this area and may perhaps serve as a cautionary tale about what bilingual programs can accomplish in certain contexts in Canada. Still, this single case study can hardly be generalized to Canadian Aboriginal education.

5 Although widely criticized as too little, too late, the *Native American Languages Act* (NALA) provided both resources and 'an expression of Indigenous linguistic and education rights' (McCarty, in press, 10). Nothing remotely resembling this exists in Canada.

6 For details on Hawaiian medium schooling, see McCarty (in press, 11).

7 All things considered, 'devolution' seems to be the best word to use here, despite its general connotation of downward delegation.

8 In fact, a habitual concern of provincial and state governments is to keep the local taxation playing field 'level' so that some municipalities don't use unfair tax advantages to undercut unduly the ability of other municipalities to attract business and industry.

9 An earlier version of this work included an extensive school-by-school summary of the SAEE study focused on elements of particular interest to our analysis. A reviewer persuaded us that this lengthy summary and critique was not a good use of available space. Subsequently one of us prepared a detailed table comparing the SAEE schools along several key dimensions. In the end, we have concluded that all that is really needed here from the SAEE study is a short discussion focused on aspects of the study of particular relevance to our analysis. That, plus some observations of Amiskwaciy Academy in Edmonton, provides the substance of the following section. Anyone interested in reading our synthesis and full critical analysis of the SAEE study can find it at http://www.utppublishing.com/product.php?productid=2733 ('Bell').

10 This principle should not prevent collaboration, consultation, and appropriate integration with other aspects of First Nations self-determination/self-government any more than insisting that employees of provincial ministries of education focus mainly on education prevents them from working with counterparts in other ministries as the need arises.

11 We resist any temptation to adopt the misleading language of 'best' practice with all of its positivist connotations. What works depends on context; there is no single best practice that is guaranteed to work in all contexts. That is the gaping blind spot of the effective schools movement and its research-theory grounding.

7 Values, Principles, and Ethics

1 We are deeply grateful for the assistance of Dr Frederick Ellett with a number of the conceptual lynchpins of this chapter.

2 See discussion in this chapter under 'Ethics and Moral Objectivity.'

3 Parliamentary committee evidence can be found at http://cmte.parl.gc.ca/cmte/PublicationSearch.aspx?retAdvancedSearch=1&retKeyword=INAC+education&retDateFrom=2000%2f01%2f01&retDateTo=2007%2f03%2f20&retParliament=Parl39%7eSes0&retSortBy=Publication&retMaxResults=10&retSourceDebates=False&retSourceCommitteeEvidence=True&retBooleanSearch=False&retCommitteeAcronymList=&Lang=1&Mode=1&Parl=39&Ses=1&SelId=e99_&COM=0. Parliamentary committee reports and responses can be found at http://cmte.parl.gc.ca/cmte/CommitteeList.aspx?Lang=1&PARLSES=391&JNT=0&SELID=e8_&COM=0.

4 Indeed, we hardly have the expertise to do so.

5 In both *After Virtue* (1984) and *Whose Justice? Which Rationality?* (1988), for instance, McIntyre struggles with and largely concedes the historical and cultural contextedness of morality claims. Still, careful reading indicates that he remains deeply attached to the Aristotelian tradition and would like to recover some version of the Aristotelian virtues. Consider, for instance, the following quotation from *After Virtue*:

> My own conclusion is very clear. It is that on the one hand we still, in spite of the efforts of three centuries of moral philosophy and one of sociology, lack any coherent rationally defensible statement of a liberal individualist point of view; and that, on the other hand, the Aristotelian tradition can be restated in a way that restores intelligibility and rationality to our moral and social attitudes and commitments. (289)

6 'Universal' in the sense of not being fundamentally grounded in or at-

tached to any particular culture at any particular time in history and being, in principle at least, ultimately 'discoverable' through rational inquiry.

7 For example, he says at one point, 'The very difference between the legal and the moral is more a matter of a stable and honored division of labor than a matter of principle, for the legal is, everywhere, the respected deputy (when it *is* so respected) *of* the moral and the political. If so, then moral positivism makes no sense at all' (53). Legal positivists, of course, would argue otherwise, but Margolis is no legal positivist.

8 Very small unit scale and organizational units tightly linked to individual small communities, for example, provide fertile ground for overlooking incompetence in the name of providing jobs for local people. This is not, by any means, to suggest that all local people in First Nations communities are incompetent – far from it, but the temptation is greater in just such small 'parochial' situations, especially in the absence of a meaningful local financial–accountability link, to succumb to the worst sort of cronyism and nepotism.

9 See discussion in chapter 6, 'Accountability, Ethics, and Adequate Resourcing.'

10 On 26 January 2007 we extended an invitation to Vice-Chief Watson to participate in an interview about the events surrounding the 2005 takeover. Unfortunately, he never replied to our invitation.

11 One of us discovered this particular anomaly to his surprise in investigating some very atypical appointment and tenure practices and standards that came to his attention by accident.

12 Former senior FNUC administrator, interview with Jerry Paquette, 15 December 2006.

13 Ibid.

14 Ibid.

15 Ibid.

16 Ibid.

17 Ibid.

18 Ibid.

19 Ibid.

20 Ibid.

21 Ibid.

22 Ibid.

23 One of us is indebted to Kerry Wilkins for this insight (personal communication, 20 December 2006), at least in so far as it pertains to the legal order, although he has taken it further here and applied it to the political and economic order within which the legal order is framed and sustained.

8 Vision and Purpose

1 We are indebted to Dr William J. Smith for feedback on an earlier version of this chapter.

2 We have searched in vain for the exact reference, but one of us is absolutely certain of the attribution.

3 We do not believe that all organizations at all times are in need of transformation, and hence of transformational or charismatic leadership. That said, an organization that has *no* Type I (in Hodgkinson's sense) value foundation or claims is at best uninspiring and unlikely to command much diligence or self-sacrifice in pursuit of its goals from its members. At worst it is a boring, irrelevant fifth wheel to the environment within which it exists. Of course, there are dangers in strong organizational cultures too, but that is another matter.

4 As in the case of freedom of information and privacy legislation at both the federal and provincial levels, some exclusions from access to information rights are necessary and legitimate. These exclusions, however, need to be carefully defined as they are in federal and provincial legislation. Responsible First Nations governance cannot engage in Star Chamber secrecy any more than responsible settler governments can.

5 See our discussion of the Nisga'a Agreement in 'Self Government Agreements' and in 'Chalo School,' under 'Bell' at http://www.utppublishing .com/product.php?productid=2733.

References

Aboriginal Healing Foundation (2005). Mission, vision, values. Aboriginal Healing Foundation statement. Retrieved 4 July 2006 from http://www.ahf.ca/e_Values.aspx.

Aboriginal Institutes Consortium (2005). *A struggle for the education of Aboriginal students, control of Indigenous knowledge, and recognition of Aboriginal institutions: An examination of government policy.* Toronto: Canadian Race Relations Foundation.

Anderson, D.W. (2004). Report on second level services for First Nations education: Current and future need. In Chiefs-In-Assembly (Ed.), *The new agenda: A manifesto for First Nations education in Ontario.* Toronto: Chiefs of Ontario.

Appleby, J., Fougère, M., & Rouleau, M. (2002). *Is post-secondary education in Canada a cost-effective proposition?* Hull, QC: Applied Research Branch Strategic Policy, Human Resources Development Canada.

Assembly of First Nations (2005). First Nations education action plan. Retrieved 12 March 2007 from http://www.afn.ca/cmslib/general/Education-Action%20Plan.pdf.

Assembly of Manitoba Chiefs Youth Secretariat (2006). First Nations Code of Ethics. Retrieved 12 March 2008 from http://www.umanitoba.ca/student/asc/media/Pamphlet_02a.pdf.

Association of Canadian Community Colleges (2005). *Canadian colleges and institutes: Meeting the needs of Aboriginal learners, an overview of current programs and services, challenges, opportunities and lessons learned, final report.* Ottawa: Author.

Auditor General of Canada (2000a). Indian and Northern Affairs Canada. Chapter 4, elementary and secondary education. In *Report of the Auditor General of Canada to the House of Commons.* Ottawa: Office of the Auditor General of Canada.

- (2000b). Indian and Northern Affairs Canada. Elementary and secondary education. In *Report of the Auditor General of Canada to the House of Commons*. Ottawa: Office of the Auditor General of Canada.
- (2004a). Indian and Northern Affairs Canada. Chapter 5, education program and post-secondary student support. In *Report of the Auditor General of Canada to the House of Commons*. Ottawa: Office of the Auditor General of Canada.
- (2004b). Indian and Northern Affairs Canada. Education program and post-secondary student support. In *Report of the Auditor General of Canada to the House of Commons*. Ottawa: Office of the Auditor General of Canada.
- (2006). Indian and Northern Affairs Canada. Management of programs for First Nations. In *Report of the Auditor General of Canada to the House of Commons*. Ottawa: Office of the Auditor General of Canada.

Baker, B.D. (2005). The emerging shape of educational adequacy: From theoretical assumptions to empirical evidence. *Journal of Education Finance, 30*(3), 259–87.
- (2006). Evaluating the reliability, validity, and usefulness of education costs studies. *Journal of Education Finance, 32*(2), 170–201.

Battiste, M. (1998). Enabling the autumn seed: Toward a decolonized approach toward Aboriginal knowledge, language and education. *Canadian Journal of Native Education, 22*(1), 16–27.
- (2002). *Indigenous knowledge and pedagogy in First Nations education: A literature review with recomendations*. Ottawa: Apamuwek Institute.

Battiste, M., & Barman, J. (1995). *First Nations education in Canada: The circle unfolds*. Vancouver: UBC Press.

Battiste, M., Bell, L., & Findlay, L.M. (2002). Decolonizing education in Canadian universities: An interdisciplinary, international, Indigenous research project. *Canadian Journal of Native Education, 26*(2), 82–95.

Beaulieu, A. (1990). *Convertir les fils de Caïn*. Montreal: Les Presses de l'Université de Montréal.

Bell, D. (Ed.). (2004). *Sharing our success: Ten cases in Aboriginal schooling*. Kelowna, BC: Society for the Advancement of Excellence in Education.

Bertrand, Y., & Valois, P. (1980). *Les options en éducation*. Quebec: Ministère de l'Éducation.

Blaug, M. (1968). The rate of return on investment in education. In M. Blaug (Ed.), *Economics of Education* (Vol. 1, 215–59). Middlesex, UK: Penguin Books.

Booth, T. (2001, February). The evolution of university governance. Retrieved 20 September 2006 from http://www.caut.ca/en/bulletin/issues/2001_feb/presmessage.asp.

Borrows, J. (2002). *Recovering Canada: The resurgence of Indigenous law*. Toronto: University of Toronto Press.

Bowers, C.A. (2006). *Revitalizing the commons: Cultural and educational sites of resistance and affirmation*. Lanham, MD: Lexington Books.

Boyd, W.L. (1982). The political economy of public schools. *Educational Administration Quarterly, 18*(3), 11–130.

Breaker, R., & Kawaguchi, B. (2002). *Infrastructure and funding in First Nations education*. Calgary: Buffalo Signal Associates.

Burnaby, B. (1980). *Languages and their roles in educating Native children*. Toronto: OISE Press.

Cairns, A. (2000). *Citizens plus: Aboriginal peoples and the Canadian state*. Vancouver: UBC Press.

Canada. Indian Affairs Branch, & Hawthorn, H.B. (1967). *A survey of the contemporary Indians of Canada; a report on economic, political, educational needs and policies, Part 2*. Ottawa: Queen's Printer.

Canada. Parliament. House of Commons. Special Committee on Indian Self-Government, & Penner, K. (1983). *Indian self-government in Canada: Report of the Special Committee*. Ottawa: Queen's Printer for Canada.

Canadian House Of Commons. Standing Committee on Aboriginal Affairs (1989). *A review of the post-secondary student assistance program of the Department of Indian Affairs and Northern Development. First Report of the Standing Committee on Aboriginal Affairs*. Ottawa: Canadian House Of Commons Standing Committee on Aboriginal Affairs.

Canadian International Development Agency (2006, May 16). Results-based management in CIDA: An introductory guide to the concepts and principles. Retrieved 16 May 2007 from http://www.acdi-cida.gc.ca/CIDAWEB/acdicida.nsf/prnEn/EMA-218132656-PPK.

Cardinal, H. (1969). *The unjust society: The tragedy of Canada's Indians*. Edmonton: M.G. Hurtig.

Cardinal, P. (1999). *Aboriginal perspective on education: A vision of cultural context within the framework of Social Studies*. Edmonton: Alberta Learning-Curriculum Standards.

CBC News (2010). FNUC funding hopes dashed. *CBC News Canada*. Retrieved 16 March 2010 from http://www.cbc.ca/canada/saskatchewan/story/2010/03/16/sk-norris-strahl-1003.html.

Chrétien, J., & Canada, Department of Indian Affairs and Northern Development (1969). *Statement of the Government of Canada on Indian policy, 1969; presented to the First session of Twenty-eighth Parliament by the Hon. Jean Chrétien*. Ottawa: Department of Indian Affairs and Northern Development.

Chrisjohn, R.D., Young, S.L., & Maraun, M. (1997). *The circle game: Shadows and substance in the Indian residential school experience in Canada*. Penticton, BC: Theytus Books.

Churchill, S. (1986). *The education of linguistic and cultural minorities in the OECD countries*. Clevedon, Avon,UK: Multilingual Matters.

Coleman, J.S., Campbell, E.Q., Hobson, C.J., McPartland, J., Mood, A.M., Weinfeld, F.D., et al. (1966). *Equality of educational opportunity*. Washington, DC: U.S. Government Printing Office.

Comprehensive Claims Branch, Claims and Indian Government Sector, Indian Affairs and Northern Development (2006). *General briefing note on the comprehensive and claims policy of Canada and the status of claims*. Ottawa: Author.

Cornell, S. (2002). *The Harvard project findings on good governance: Speaking truth to power III Self-government options and opportunities*. Vancouver: BC Treaty Commission.

Cornell, S., Jorgensen, M., & Kalt, J.P. (2002). *The First Nations Governance Act: Implications of research findings from the United States and Canada*. Tucson, AZ: Udall Center for Studies in Public Policy, The University of Arizona.

Crombie, D. (1996, December 2). Letter from Who Does What Panel to the Honourable Al Leach and the Honourable John Snobelen. Retrieved 29 January 2007 from http://www.mah.gov.on.ca/userfiles/HTML/nts_1_1793_1.html.

CTV.ca News (2007, June 13). Prentice wants land claims tribunal ready by 2008. Retrieved 28 June 2007 from http://www.ctv.ca/servlet/ArticleNews/story/CTVNews/20070612/land_claims_070612/20070612?hub=TopStories.

Cummins, J. (1981). *Bilingualism and minority-language children*. Toronto: OISE Press.

Cuthand, D. (2006a, July 17). McLeod couple's legacy lives on. *Leader Post*, B1.

– (2006b, June 2). Save FNUC with task force recommendations. *Star-Phoenix*, A11.

Dantley, M.E. (1990). The ineffectiveness of effective schools leadership: An analysis of the effective schools movement from a critical perspective. *The Journal of Negro Education, 59*(4), 585–98.

Denis, C. (1997). *We are not you: First Nations and Canadian modernity*. Peterborough, ON: Broadview Press.

Dinham, S., & Scott, C. (1998). A three domain model teacher and school executive career satisfaction. *Journal of Educational Administration, 36*(3–4), 362–78.

Dror, Y. (1983). *Public policy making reexamined*. New Brunswick, NJ: Chandler Publishing.

Duncombe, W. (2006). Responding to the charge of alchemy: Strategies for evaluating the reliability and validity of costing-out research. *Journal of Education Finance, 32*(2), 137–69.

Emirbayer, M., & Mische, A. (1998). What is agency? *The American Journal of Sociology, 103*(4), 962–1023.

Finnie, R. (2002). Student loans, student financial aid and post-secondary education in Canada. *Journal of Higher Education Policy and Management, 24*(2), 155–70.

First Nations University of Canada (2006a). First Nations University of Canada: Departments and schools. Retrieved 20 September 2006 from http://www.firstnationsuniversity.ca/default.aspx?page=4.

– (2006b). First Nations University of Canada: Our vision. Retrieved 20 September 2006 from http://www.firstnationsuniversity.ca/default.aspx?page=52.

Fiscal Realities (1999). *First nation taxation and new fiscal relationships*. Kamloops, BC: The Indian Taxation Advisory Board and the Research and Analysis Directorate Policy and Strategic Direction Branch of the Department of Indian Affairs and Northern Development. Retrieved 20 April 2008 from http://dsp-psd.pwgsc.gc.ca/Collection/R32-228-1997E.pdf.

Fishman, Joshua A. (1991). *Reversing language shift: Theoretical and empirical foundations of assistance to threatened languages*. Clevedon, UK : Multilingual Matters.

Flanagan, T. (2000). *First Nations? Second thoughts*. Montreal: McGill-Queen's University Press.

FNEC/DIAND Tuition Fees Committee (2005). *An analysis of educational costs and tuition fees: Pre-school, elementary school and high school levels, final report*. Quebec: Author.

Foster, W.F. (1985). Educational malpractice: A tort for the untaught. *University of British Columbia Law Review, 19*(161), 161–244.

Friesen, J.W., & Friesen, V.L. (2002). *Aborignal education in Canada: A plea for integration*. Calgary: Detselig Enterprises.

Furi, M., & Wherrett, J. (2003). Indian status and band membership issues. Retrieved 20 January 2007 from http://www.parl.gc.ca/information/library/PRBpubs/bp410-e.htm#11.

Galbraith, J.K. (1992). *The culture of contentment*. Boston: Houghton Mifflin.

Galloway, G. (2010). Status debate mounts as bill offers benefits to another 45,000 Natives. *The Globe and Mail – National Edition*. Retrieved 11 March 2010 from http://www.theglobeandmail.com/news/national/bill-would-create-up-to-45000-new-status-indians/article1497899/.

Geller, H., & Johnston, A. (1990). Policy as linear and nonlinear science. *Journal of Education Policy, 5*(1), 49–65.

Glickman, C.D., Gordon, S.P., & Ross-Gordon, J.M. (2004). *Supervision and instructional leadership: A developmental approach* (6th. ed.). New York: Pearson.

Government of Canada (2006). Highlights: Indian residential schools settlement agreement. Retrieved 12 June 2007 from http://www.irsrrqpi.gc.ca/english/pdf/IRS_SA_Highlights.pdf.

Governor General of Canada (2002). *The Canada we want: Speech from the throne to open the Second session of the Thirty-seventh Parliament of Canada*. Ottawa: Government of Canada.

Greenfield, T.B. (1993). Science and service: The making of the profession of educational administration. In T.B. Greenfield & P. Ribbins (Eds.), *Greenfield on educational administration: Towards a humane science* (199–228). London: Routledge.

Haig-Brown, C. (1988). *Resistance and renewal: Surviving the Indian residential school*. Vancouver: Tillacum Library.

– (1997). *Making the spirit dance within: Joe Duquette High School and an Aboriginal community*. Toronto: J. Lorimer.

Hall, P., Land, H., Parker, R., & Webb, A. (1975). *Change, choice, and conflict in social policy*. London: Heinemann.

Hampton, E. (1995). Towards a redifinition of Indian education. In M. Batiste & J. Barman (Eds.), *First Nations education in Canada: The circle unfolds* (5–46). Vancouver: UBC Press.

Hanushek, E. (2005). *The alchemy of 'costing out' an adequate education*. Paper presented at the conference on Adequacy lawsuits: Their growing impact on American education. Cambridge, MA.

Hardy, L. (2003). The governance challenge. *American School Board Journal, 190*(12), 40–42, 44, 46.

Hart, D., Lapkin, S., & Swain, M. (1988). *Report on this study of attrition in early and middle immersion programs to grade 8: An addendum to the park one report on early and middle French immersion programs: Linguistic outcomes and social character*. Toronto: Modern Language Centre, OISE.

Hawkins, R.E. (2006). President's report to the board of governors. Retrieved 21 September 2006 from http://www.uregina.ca/presoff/board/minutes/2006/04-18%20Board%20Agenda%20&%20Reports.pdf.

Hawthorn, H.B., Tremblay, M.-A., & Bownick, A.M. (1967). *A survey of the contemporary Indians of Canada: A report on economic, political, educational needs and policies: Part 2*. Ottawa: Queen's Printers.

Hedges, L., Laine, R., & Greenwald, R. (1994). Does money matter? A meta-analysis of studies of the effects of differential school inputs on student outcomes. *Educational Researcher, 23*(3), 5–14.

Her Majesty the Queen in Right of Canada, & Mi'kmaq Bands in Nova Scotia (1997). An agreement with respect to Mi'kmaq education in Nova Scotia *Mi'kmaw Kina'matnewey: Return of education jurisdiction to the Mi'kmaq*. Sydney, NS: Author.

Hertzberg, F. (1966). *Work and the nature of man*. Cleveland, OH: World Publishing.

Hirschland, M.J., & Steinmo, S. (2003). Correcting the record: Understanding the history of federal intervention and failure in securing U.S. educational reform. *Educational Policy, 17*(3), 343–64.

Hirst, P.H. (1974). *Knowledge and the curriculum: A collection of philosophical papers*. London: Routledge and Kegan Paul.

Hirst, P.H., & Peters, R.S. (1970). *The logic of education*. London: Routledge and Kegan Paul.

Hodgkinson, C. (1978). *Towards a philosophy of administration*. Oxford: Blackwell.

– (1983). *The philosophy of leadership*. Oxford: Basil Blackwell.

– (1996). *Administrative philosophy: Values and motivations in administrative life*. New York: Pergamon.

Holdaway, E.A. (1978). *Satisfaction of teachers in Alberta with their work and working conditions*. Edmonton: University of Alberta.

Holmes, D. (2006). *Redressing the balance: Programs in support of Aboriginal students*. Ottawa: Association of Universities and Colleges of Canada.

Holmes, M. (1992). The revival of school administration: Alasdair MacIntyre in the aftermath of the common school. *Canadian Journal of Education, 17*(4), 422–36.

Hull, J. (2005). *Comparison of federal and provincial funding for elementary-secondary education in First Nations schools in Canada, 2003/04: Summary of regional findings* (Draft: For discussion only). Winnipeg: Prologica Research.

Human Resources and Social Development Canada (2004). Canada Student Loan Program statistics: Average CSLP indebtedness. Retrieved 10 October 2006 from http://www.hrsdc.gc.ca/asp/gateway.asp?hr=/en/hip/cslp/statistics/07_st_CSLPIndebtedness.shtml&hs=cxp.

Hurton, G. (2002). *A review of First Nations special education policies and funding directions within the Canadian context*. Ottawa: INAC Minister's National Working Group on Education.

Indian and Northern Affairs Canada (1982). *Indian education paper: Phase 1*. Ottawa: Indian and Inuit Affairs Program: Education and Social Development Branch.

– (1986). *Alternative Funding Arrangements/Modes optionnels de financement*. Ottawa: Author.

– (2003). *Elementary/secondary education: National program guidelines*. Ottawa: Author.

– (2004, November). Fact sheet – education. Retrieved 16 February 2007 from http://www.ainc-inac.gc.ca/nr/prs/s-d2004/02539bbk_e.html.

– (2006). Indian residential schools resolution Canada/Résolution des questions des pensionnats indiens Canada. Retrieved 4 July 2006 from http://www.irsr-rqpi.gc.ca/english/index.html.

Indian and Northern Affairs Canada/Affaires indiennes et du Nord Canada (2002). *Special education: National program guidelines.* Ottawa: Author.

– (2004a, April 23). Cultural/Educational Centres Program. Retrieved 13 March 2007 from http://www.ainc-inac.gc.ca/ps/edu/cecp_e.html.

– (2004b, April 23). Education programming: Elementary/secondary education. Retrieved 13 September 2006 from http://www.ainc-inac.gc.ca/ps/edu/rep03/educ_e.html.

– (2005). *Evaluation of the post-secondary education program.* Ottawa: Author, Deparmental Audit and Evaluation Branch.

Indian Chiefs of Alberta (1970). *Citizens plus.* Edmonton: Indian Association of Alberta.

Johnston, B. (1988). *Indian school days.* Toronto: Key Porter Books.

Junor, S., & Usher, A. (2004). *The price of knowledge 2004: Access and student finance in Canada.* Montreal: The Canada Millennium Scholarship Foundation.

Kahnawake Survival School (1995). Goals of the Survival School. Retrieved 18 March 2007 from http://www.schoolnet.ca/aboriginal/survive/goals-e.html.

Kanter, R.M. (2004). How leaders restore confidence. In R. Gandossy & J. Sonnenfeld (Eds.), *Leadership and governance from the inside out* (39–49). Hoboken, NJ: John Wiley.

Kēpa, M., & Manu'atu, L. (2006). Indigenous Māori and Tongan perspectives on the role of Tongan language and culture in the community and in the University of Aotearoa, New Zealand. *American Indian Quarterly, 30*(1 & 2), 11–26.

Knockwood, C.A. (1994). Urban first peoples and self-determination. In E. Peters (Ed.), *Aboriginal self-government in urban areas* (163–5). Kingston, ON: Institute of Intergovernmental Relations.

Knockwood, I., & Thomas, G. (1992). *Out of the depths: The experiences of Mi'kmaw children at the Indian Residential School at Shubenacadie, Nova Scotia.* Lockeport, NS: Roseway.

Koenig, L.W. (1986). Who makes public policy? *An introduction to public policy* (1–28). Englewood, NJ: Prentice-Hall.

Kymlicka, W. (1989). *Liberalism, community, and culture.* Toronto: Clarendon Press, Oxford.

Lawton, S.B., Freedman, J., Robertson, H.-J., & Institute for Research on Public Policy (1995). *Busting bureaucracy to reclaim our schools.* Montreal: Institute for Research on Public Policy.

Leap, W.L. (1982). Semilingualism as a form of linguistic proficiency. In R. St

Clair & W. Leap (Eds.), *Language renewal among American Indian tribes: Issues, problems, and prospects* (149–59). Rosslyn, VA: National Clearinghouse for Bilingual Education.

Lemelin, C. (1998). *L'économiste et l'éducation*. Sainte-Foy: Presses de l'Université du Québec.

Les, J. (1994). Approaches to Aboriginal self-government in urban areas: What could self-government look like? In E. Peters (Ed.), *Aboriginal self-government in urban areas* (173–8). Kingston, ON: Institute of Intergovernmental Relations.

Leslie, P.M. (1985). Financing techniques, good and bad. In D. Conklin & T. Courchene (Eds.), *Ontario universities: Access, operations, and funding* (303–35). Toronto: Ontario Economic Council.

Levin, H. (1994). The necessary and sufficient conditions for achieving educational equity. In R. Berne & L. Picus (Eds.), *Outcome equity in education* (167–90). Thousand Oaks, CA: Corwin Press.

MacIntyre, A.C. (1981). *After virtue: A study in moral theory*. Notre Dame, IN: University of Notre Dame Press.

– (1984). *After virtue: A study in moral theory* (2nd ed.). Notre Dame, IN: University of Notre Dame Press.

– (1988). *Whose justice? Which rationality?* Notre Dame, IN: University of Notre Dame Press.

MacKay, A.W., & Dickinson, G.M. (1998). *Beyond the 'careful parent': Tort liability in education*. Toronto: Emond Montgomery.

MacKinnon, D. (1998). *Review of literature on fiscal relationships*. Ottawa: Indian and Northern Affairs Canada.

MacPherson, J.C., & Canada. Department of Indian Affairs and Northern Development (1991). *MacPherson report on tradition and education: Towards a vision of our future*. Ottawa: Department of Indian Affairs and Northern Development.

Malone, M., & Queen's University Institute of Intergovernmental Relations (1986). *Financing Aboriginal self-government in Canada*. Kingston, ON: Institute of Intergovernmental Relations Queen's University.

Manzer, R. (1994). *Canadian public educational policy: Schools and political ideas in historical perspective*. Toronto: University of Toronto Press.

Margolis, J. (1995). *Historied thought, constructed world: A conceptual primer for the turn of the millennium*. Berkeley: University of California Press.

– (2004). *Moral philosophy after 9/11*. University Park: Pennsylvania State University Press.

Matthew, M. (2000). *The cost of quality: First Nations education*. Vancouver: First Nations Education Steering Committee.

McCarty, T. (In Press). Bilingual education by and for American Indians, Alaska Natives, and Native Hawaiians. In J. Cummins & N.H. Hornberger (Eds.), *Encyclopedia of language and education* (2nd ed.) (Vol. 5). Norwell, MA: Springer.

McCue, H. (2004). An overview of federal and provincial policy trends in First Nations education. In Chiefs-In-Assembly (Ed.), *The new agenda: A manifesto for First Nations education in Ontario*. Toronto: Chiefs of Ontario.

Mendelson, M. (2006). *Aboriginal peoples and postsecondary education in Canada*. Ottawa: Caledon Institute of Social Policy.

Merton, R.K., & Nisbet, R.A. (1976). *Contemporary social problems* (4th ed.). New York: Harcourt Brace Jovanovich.

Meyer, J.W. (1986). Organizations as ideological systems. In T. Sergiovanni & J.E. Corbally (Eds.), *Leadership and organizational culture: New perspectives on administrative theory and practice* (186–205). Urbana, IL: University of Illinois Press.

Michaelsen, J.B. (1977). Revision, bureaucracy, and school reform: A critique of Katz. *School Review, 85*(2), 229–46.

Miller, J.R. (1996). *Shingauk's vision*. Toronto: University of Toronto Press.

Milloy, J.S. (1999). *A national crime: The Canadian government and the residential school system, 1879–1986*. Winnipeg: University of Manitoba Press.

Minister's National Working Group on Education (2002). *Our children: Keepers of the sacred knowledge*. Ottawa: Indian Affairs and Northern Development Canada.

Minnis, J.R. (2006). First Nations education and rentier economics: Parallels with the Gulf states. *Canadian Journal of Education, 29*(4), 975–97.

Monk, J. (2000). The returns to individual and college characteristics: Evidence from the National Longitudinal Survey of Youth. *Economics of Education Review, 19*(3), 279–89.

Moon, J.D. (1993). *Constructing community: Moral pluralism and tragic conflicts*. Princeton, NJ: Princeton University Press.

Moynihan, D.P. (1965). *The negro family: The case for national action*. Washington, DC: U.S. Department of Labor.

– (1969). *Maximum feasible misunderstanding: Community action in the war on poverty*. New York: Free Press.

National Indian Brotherhood (1972/1984). Indian control of Indian education. In J.R. Mallea & J.C. Young (Eds.), *Cultural diversity and Canadian education*. Ottawa: Carleton University Press.

National Indian Brotherhood, & Assembly of First Nations (1988). *Tradition and education: Towards a vision of our future*. Territory of Akwesasne, Hamilton's Island, Summerstown, ON: National Indian Brotherhood Assembly of First Nations.

Nias, J. (1981). Teacher satisfaction and dissatisfaction: Herzberg's 'two-factor' hypothesis revisited. *British Journal of Sociology of Education, 2*(3), 235–46.

Nikkel, W. (2006). *Language revitalization in northern Manitoba: A study of an elementary school Cree bilingual program.* Unpublished MEd, University of Manitoba.

Nisga'a Nation (2001). *113: Nishga'a final agreement, 2001 annual report.* Ottawa–New Aiyansh, BC: Minister of Indian Affairs and Northern Development–Nisga'a Nation.

Noël, L. (1994). *Intolerance: A general survey.* (A. Bennett Trans.). Montreal, QC: McGill-Queen's University Press.

Norman, P. (1989). Letter addressed to Dr. Jerry Paquette (2). Brantford, ON: Indian and Northern Affairs.

Norris, D., & Siggner, A. (2003). What census and the Aboriginal peoples survey tell us about aboriginal conditions in Canada. *2003 Aboriginal Strategies Conference.* Retrieved 6 May 2008 from http://209.123.49.177/~statcan/presentations/dougnorris01.pdf.

Odden, A., & Clune, W.H. (1998). School finance systems: Aging structures in need of renovation. *Educational Evaluation and Policy Analysis, 20*(3), 157–77.

Pal, L.A. (1997). *Beyond policy analysis: Public issue management in turbulent times.* Scarborough, ON: ITP Nelson.

– (2006). *Beyond policy analysis: public issue management in turbulent times* (3rd ed.). Toronto: Nelson.

Paquette, J. (1986). *Aboriginal self-government and education in Canada* (Vol. 10). Kingston, ON: Institute of Intergovernmental Relations, Queen's University.

– (1989a). From propositions to prescriptions: Belief, power, and the problem of minority education. *Curriculum Inquiry, 19*(4), 437–51.

– (1989b). Minority education policy: Assumptions and propositions. *Curriculum Inquiry, 19*(4), 405–20.

– (1991). *Social purpose and schooling: Alternatives, agendas, and issues.* London: Falmer Press.

– (1992). Assessing the educational fates of minority students in Canada: Piloting a fine-grained descriptive approach. *Equity and Excellence, 25*(2–4), 57–66.

Paquette, J., & Smith, W.J. (2000). *Final Report on FNEC analysis of spending on special and regular education.* Wendake: First Nations Education Council of Quebec.

Participating members of Nishnawbe-Aski Nation, & Her Majesty the Queen in Right of Canada (2006). *Nishnawbe-Aski Nation education agreement in principle with respect to the recognition of certain law-making authority in the area of education and the establishment of education governance structures under Canada's 1995 Aboriginal self-government policy.* Thunder Bay, ON: Nishnawbe-Aski Nation.

Patton, M.Q. (2001). Outcome mapping: Building learning and reflection into development programs. Retrieved 17 May 2007 from http://www.idrc.ca/openebooks/959-3/.

Perrow, C. (1978). Demystifying organizations. In R.C. Sarri & Y. Hasenfeld (Eds.), *The management of human services* (104–20). New York: Columbia University Press.

Phelps, E.S. (1985). *Political economy: An introductory text*. New York: W.W. Norton.

Psacharopoulos, G. (1981). Returns to education: An updated international comparison. *Comparative Education, 17*(3), 321–41.

– (1990). Comparative education: From theory to practice, or are you A: .* or B:*. ist? *Comparative Education Review, 34*(3), 369–80.

Rawls, J. (1971). *A theory of justice*. Cambridge, MA: Belknap Press of Harvard University Press.

Reyhner, J. (1999). Some basics of Indigenous language revitalization. In J. Reyhner, G. Cantoni, R.N. St Clair & E.P. Yazzie (Eds.), *Revitalizing Indigenous languages* (v–xx). Flagstaff, AZ: Northern Arizona University.

Reyhner, J., Cantoni, G., St Clair, R.N., & Yazzie, E.P. (Eds.) (1999). *Revitalizing Indigenous languages*. Flagstaff: Northern Arizona University.

Robin, D.P. (2005). Why ethics and profits can and must work together in business. In R.A. Peterson & O.C. Ferrel (Eds.), *Business ethics: New challenges for business schools and corporate leaders* (196–221). New York: M.E. Sharpe.

Roszak, T. (1986). *The cult of information: The folklore of computers and the true art of thinking* (1st ed.). New York: Pantheon.

Royal Commission on Aboriginal Peoples (1996a). *Report of the Royal Commission on Aboriginal peoples* (Vols. 1–5). Ottawa: Canada Communication Group Publishing.

– (1996b). *Report of the Royal Commission on Aboriginal peoples: Gathering strength* (Vol. 3). Ottawa: Canada Communication Group Publishing.

– (1996c). *Report of the Royal Commission on Aboriginal peoples: Renewal, a twenty-year commitment* (Vol. 5). Ottawa: Canada Communication Group Publishing.

Schaefer, T.E. (1990). One more time: How do you get both equality and excellence in education? *Journal of Educational Thought, 24*, 39–51.

Schein, E. (1986). *Organizational culture and leadership*. San Francisco: Jossey-Bass.

Schouls, T.A. (2003). *Shifting boundaries: Aboriginal identity, pluralist theory, and the politics of self-government*. Vancouver: UBC Press.

Schutz, A. (1966). Some leading concepts of phenomenology. In M. Natanson (Ed.), *Essays in Phenomenology* (23–39). The Hague, Netherlands: Martinus Nijhoff.

Sergiovanni, T.J. (1992). Leadership as stewardship: 'Who's serving who?' In T.J. Sergiovanni (Ed.), *Moral leadership: Getting to the heart of school improvement* (119–44). San Francisco: Jossey-Bass Publishers.

Shanahan, D., & Canadian Institute of Jesuit Studies (2004). *The Jesuit residential school at Spanish: 'More than mere talent.'* Toronto: Canadian Institute of Jesuit Studies.

Shkilnyk, A. (1985). *A poison stronger than love: The destruction of an Ojibwa community.* New Haven: Yale University Press.

Slavin, R.E., Karweit, N.L., & Wasik, B.A. (1993). Preventing early school failure: What works? *Educational Leadership, 50*(4), 10–18.

Smith, W.J., Paquette, J.E., & Bordonaro, T. (1995). *Educational governance in Canada: A model for comparative analysis* (Policy Research Paper No. 95-01). Montreal: McGill University, Office of Research on Educational Policy.

Smyth, J. (1999). Schooling and the enterprise culture: Pause for a critical policy analysis. *Journal of Education Policy, 14*(4), 435–44.

St Clair, R., & Leap, W. (Eds.) (1982). *Language renewal among American Indian tribes: Issues, problems, and prospects.* Rosslyn, VA: National Clearinghouse for Bilingual Education.

Standing Committee on Public Accounts: 38th Parliament–1st Session (2005). EVIDENCE, CONTENTS Monday, 31 January 2005. Retrieved 25 May 2005 from http://www.parl.gc.ca/committee/CommitteePublication. aspx?SourceId=99223.

Statistics Canada (1998, February 18). Prison population and costs, 1996/97. Retrieved 12 March 2007 from http://www.statcan.ca/Daily/English/ 980218/d980218.htm#ART2.

– (2002). *Profile of the Canadian population by age and sex: Canada ages.* Ottawa: Author.

– (2003a, January). Aboriginal peoples of Canada. *2001 Census.* Retrieved 18 January 2007 from http://www12.statcan.ca/english/census01/products/ analytic/companion/abor/canada.cfm.

– (2003b). Youth custody and community services: Disposition of offenders (4) by Aboriginal origin (4) and sex (4), 1997/1998 to 2002/2003, for Canada, provinces and territories (17). Retrieved 12 March 2007 from http://janus .scc.uwo.ca (file YCCSETHN.IVT).

– (2005a, December 21). Projected population by age group and sex according to a medium growth scenario for 2006, 2011, 2016, 2021, 2026 and 2031, at July 1 (2016, 2021). Retrieved 20 January 2007 from http://www40.statcan .ca/l01/cst01/demo23b.htm.

– (2005b). *Projections of Aboriginal populations, Canada, provinces and territories: 2001 to 2017.* Ottawa: Author.

Steele, S. (2006). *White guilt: How blacks and whites together destroyed the promise of the civil rights era*. New York: HarperCollins.

Stephens, C.V. (2004). *The semiotics of community experience: The residential school legacy at Walpole Island First Nation*. London, ON: Faculty of Graduate Studies, University of Western Ontario.

Stonechild, B. (2004). *Pursuing the new buffalo: First Nations higher education policy in Canada*. Unpublished PhD thesis, University of Regina.

Task Force on Aboriginal Languages and Cultures (2005). *Towards a new beginning: A foundational report for a strategy to revitalize First Nation, Inuit, and Métis languages and cultures*. Ottawa: Department of Canadian Heritage, Aboriginal Affairs Branch.

Thevenaz, P. (1962). What is phenomenology? (J.M. Edie, Trans.). In J.M. Edie (Ed.), *What is Phenomenology? and other essays* (37–112). Chicago: Quadrangle Books.

Treasury Board Secretariat (2001). *Guide for the development of results-based management and accountability frameworks*. Ottawa: Author.

Tschanz, L. (1980). *Native languages and government policy: An historical examination*. London, ON: Centre for Research and Teaching of Canadian Native Languages, University of Western Ontario.

Tully, J. (1995). *Strange multiplicity:Constitutionalism in an age of diversity*. Cambridge: Cambridge University Press.

Turk, J.L. (2006). Protecting the First Nations University of Canada: The importance of academic freedom and collegial governance. Retrieved 21 September 2006 from http://www.urfa.uregina.ca/documents/2005.04.13%20 FNUC.final.pdf.

Turner, D. (2006). *This is not a peace pipe: Towards a critical Indigenous philosophy*. Toronto: University of Toronto Press.

Union of BC Indian Chiefs (2000). *Union of BC Indian Chiefs' initial response re: Canada's civil society consultations for the world conference against racial discrimination, xenophobia and related intolerance 2001*. Vancouver: Author.

University of Regina Faculty Association (2006). First Nations University violates academic freedom. Retrieved 21 September from http://www.aptn .ca/forums/index.php?showtopic=434&st=300.

Verstegen, D.A. (2002). Financing the new adequacy: Towards new methods of state education finance systems that support standards based reform. *Journal of Education Finance, 27*(3), 749–82.

Walzer, M. (1983). *Spheres of justice: A defense of pluralism and equality*. New York: Basic Books.

Ward, B. (1970). The first international nation. In W. Kilbourn (Ed.), *Canada: A guide to the peaceable kingdom* (45–48). Toronto: MacMillan.

Wheeler, W., & Henning, D. (2006). What's up at FNUC? *Canadian Dimension*. Retrieved 20 September 2006 from http://canadiandimension.com/articles/2006/01/01/286/.

White, J.P., Maxim, P., & Spence, N. (2004a). *Permission to develop: Aboriginal treaties, case law and regulations*. Toronto: Thompson Educational.

White, J.P., Maxim, P., & Spence, N. (2004b). An examination of educational success. In J.P. White, P. Maxim & D. Beavon (Eds.), *Aboriginal policy research: Setting the agenda for change* (Vol. 1, 129–45). Toronto: Thompson Educational.

—— Wilkins, K. (1999a). But we need the eggs: The Royal Commission, the Charter of Rights and the inherent right of Aboriginal self-government. *University of Toronto Law Journal, 49*(53), 1–58.

– (1999b). But we need the eggs: The Royal Commission, the Charter of Rights and the inherent rights of Aboriginal self-government. *University of Toronto Law Journal* Retrieved 21 November 2004 from http://ql.quicklaw.com/qltemp/C2KocgMdFklfToDJ/00003utlj-00000062.htm.

– (2004). Conclusion: Judicial aesthetics and Aboriginal claims. In K. Wilkins (Ed.), *Advancing Aboriginal claims: Visions, strategies, directions* (288–312). Saskatoon: Purich Publishing.

Wolfe, T. (1941). *You can't go home again*. New York: Harper.

Wotherspoon, T., & Schissel, B. (1988). *Marginalization, decolonization and voice: Prospects for Aboriginal education in Canada*. Pan-Canadian Education Research Agenda: Council of Ministers of Education, Canada.

Young, D. (1994). Some approaches to urban Aboriginal governance. In E. Peters (Ed.), *Aboriginal self-government in urban areas* (153–62). Kingston, ON: Institute of Intergovernmental Relations.

Yuzdepski, I. (1983). Indian control of Indian education. *Canadian Journal of Native Education, 11*(1), 37–43.

Index